Debating Democracy

A Reader in American Politics

Fifth Edition

Bruce Miroff
STATE UNIVERSITY OF NEW YORK–ALBANY

Raymond Seidelman
SARAH LAWRENCE COLLEGE

Todd Swanstrom
SAINT LOUIS UNIVERSITY

Houghton Mifflin Company   Boston   New York

*To our parents: Martin and Sophie Miroff, Herb and Thelma Seidelman,
and Beatrice and Glenn Swanstrom*

Publisher: Charles Hartford
Sponsoring Editor: Katherine Meisenheimer
Senior Development Editor: Frances Gay
Senior Project Editor: Tracy Patruno
Manufacturing Manager: Karen Banks
Executive Marketing Manager: Nicola Poser
Marketing Assistant: Kathleen Mellon
Cover image: #10 Six Flags Coverlet/ Julie Silber; Courtesy of The Quilt
    Complex/Albion, CA

Printed in the U.S.A.

Library of Congress Control Number: 2003110188

ISBN: 0-618-43766-5

123456789-FFG-08 07 06 05 04

However unwillingly a person who has strong opinion may admit the possibility that his opinion may be false, he ought to be moved by the consideration that, however true it may be, if it is not fully, frequently, and fearlessly discussed, it will be held as a dead dogma, not as a living truth.

John Stuart Mill, *On Liberty* (1859)

C O N T E N T S

P R E F A C E   ix

I N T R O D U C T I O N   **How to Read This Book**   **1**

C H A P T E R   1
The Founding: Debating the Constitution   **14**

James Madison, *Federalist No. 10*   17
Brutus, *Anti-federalist Paper, 18 October 1787*   23

C H A P T E R   2
Democracy: Overrated or Undervalued?   **31**

John Mueller, *Democracy's Romantic Myths*   34
Paul Rogat Loeb, *The Active Citizen*   41

C H A P T E R   3
**The New Federalism: Does It Create Laboratories
of Democracy or a Race to the Bottom?**   **52**

William D. Eggers and John O'Leary, *Beyond the Beltway*   55
John D. Donahue, *The Devil in Devolution*   60

CHAPTER **4**
**Civil Society: Does America Face a Crisis
in Civic Engagement?**   68

Robert D. Putnam, *Bowling Alone: The Collapse and Revival
   of American Community*   72
William A. Galston and Peter Levine, *America's Civic Condition:
   A Glance at the Evidence*   83

CHAPTER **5**
**Political Economy: How Democratic
Is the Free Market Economy?**   90

Milton Friedman, *Capitalism and Freedom*   93
Samuel Bowles, Frank Roosevelt, and Richard Edwards,
   Corporate Capitalism Hurts American Democracy   103

CHAPTER **6**
Civil Liberties and War: Debating the USA Patriot Act   118

Viet Dinh, *Defending Liberty Against the Tyranny of Terror*   121
Stephen J. Schulhofer, *No Checks, No Balances: Discarding
   Bedrock Constitutional Principles*   129

CHAPTER **7**
Civil Rights: How Far Have We Progressed?   142

Stephan Thernstrom and Abigail Thernstrom,
   One Nation, Indivisible   144
David K. Shipler, *A Country of Strangers*   153

CHAPTER **8**
Public Opinion: The American People and War   164

Greg Shafer, *Lessons from the U.S. War on Iraq*   166
David Brooks, *The Collapse of the Dream Palaces*   174

CHAPTER **9**
**The New Media and the Internet:
Corporate Wasteland or Democratic Frontier?**   182

Cass R. Sunstein, *The Daily We*   184
Robert McChesney, *The Power of the Producers*   196

CHAPTER **10**
Political Parties and Elections:
Are Voters United or Divided?   203

David Brooks, *One Nation, Slightly Divisible*   205
Michael Tomasky, *The Clinton Formula*   217

CHAPTER **11**
Campaigns and Elections: Organized Money Versus
(Dis)Organized People?   226

Bradley A. Smith, *Free Speech Requires Campaign Money*   229
Dan Clawson, Alan Neustadtl, and Mark Weller,
    Dollars and Votes   235

CHAPTER **12**
Debating the Deficit and the Size of Government   248

Stephen Moore, *Tax Policy: The Theory Behind the Supply-Side Model*   251
Jonathan Chait, *Race to the Bottom*   258

CHAPTER **13**
Congress: Can It Serve the Public Good?   269

Morris P. Fiorina, *The Rise of the Washington Establishment*   272
William F. Connelly Jr. and John J. Pitney Jr., *The House
    Republicans: Lessons for Political Science*   280

CHAPTER **14**
The Presidency: How Much Difference Does
the Individual Make?   291

Fred I. Greenstein, *Lessons from the Modern Presidency*   294
Stephen Skowronek, *The Changing Political Structures
    of Presidential Leadership*   301

CHAPTER **15**
The Judiciary: What Should Its Role Be in a Democracy?   316

Edwin Meese III, *A Jurisprudence of Original Intention*   318
William J. Brennan Jr., *Reading the Constitution
    as Twentieth-Century Americans*   324

CHAPTER **16**
Economic Inequality: A Threat to Democracy?   **334**

W. Michael Cox and Richard Alm, *Myths of Rich and Poor*   338
Paul Krugman, *For Richer*   344

CHAPTER **17**
The United States and the Global Economy:
Serving Citizens or Corporate Elites?   **355**

Thomas Friedman, *Revolution Is U.S.*   358
David C. Korten, *When Corporations Rule the World*   365

CHAPTER **18**
U.S. Foreign Policy After September 11:
American Hegemony or International Cooperation?   **375**

George W. Bush, *The Bush Doctrine and the War in Iraq*   378
Benjamin R. Barber, *Fear's Empire*   386

P R E F A C E

We have been very pleased by readers' and reviewers' enthusiastic reactions to the previous editions of *Debating Democracy*. They warmly endorsed our belief in the need for a reader for courses in American politics that makes democracy its unifying theme. Of course, Americans agree in the abstract about democracy, but in practice we often disagree about democracy's meaning and implications. To explore these crucial disagreements, the fifth edition is constructed around a series of debates about democracy in America. Three recent events that have critical implications for American democracy—the disputed presidential contest of 2000, the terrorist strikes of September 11, 2001, and the war in Iraq—provide a special focus for this edition.

Special Features of *Debating Democracy*

Debating Democracy is different from other readers in American politics. The selections in our reader are organized around a common theme. All the chapters address the meaning and improvement of American democracy. Thus, reading through the selections has a cumulative effect, helping students to think more clearly and deeply about democracy.

Our experience as teachers of introductory courses in American politics suggests that debate-type readers can leave students confused, wondering how to respond to a bewildering array of different arguments. Many students conclude that political debates are just a matter of opinion, that there is no cumulative knowledge generated by debating the issues. To prevent such confusion, we provide an Introduction, highly praised by reviewers of the first four editions, that gives students a framework for evaluating democratic debates. This framework is designed to help students develop their own political philosophies and critical abilities for analyzing political issues. In the end, we believe, engaging students in these democratic debates will help them to understand that democracy is a complex and contested idea and that although there is no One Truth, the search for democratic truths is well worth the effort.

In order to engage students in the search for democratic truths, we have included lively and clearly written selections from political leaders, journalists, and scholars. In each case we have chosen two contrasting views on a controversial topic. To help students in evaluating the selections, we introduce each debate with a short essay that places the issue in a meaningful context and alerts the reader to be on the lookout for contrasting values and hidden assumptions.

Debating Democracy seeks to generate further debate. After each set of selections we include questions that can be used by readers to analyze the issues or by teachers to spark class discussions. We end with suggested readings and websites that students can use to pursue the topic further.

Each chapter in the book can be used as the basis for a structured in-class debate. Our own introductory lecture courses have discussion sections of ten to twenty students led by teaching assistants. The TA divides the class in two and assigns each group one side in the debate. The students are asked to meet outside of class and prepare their arguments based on the readings. A session of the discussion section is then devoted to a formal debate. We do two or three of these structured debates in the course of a semester. Students enjoy these debates and often report that this is the high point of the course for them.

Following the formal debates, each student is required to write a short paper setting out the arguments of her or his side and rebutting the arguments of the other side. We are convinced that this exercise helps students to achieve what is often an important goal in introductory American politics courses: improving writing skills. Requiring students to take a stand on a political issue and develop a coherent argument for their position in a thematic essay is an effective way, we believe, to teach writing.

Structure of *Debating Democracy*

Debating Democracy has been structured to fit with almost all introductory texts in American politics. We cover topics usually covered in an introductory text, but we have also included debates on civil society and political economy because we believe these are important subjects for understanding American democracy.

The editors of this book make no claim to being impartial observers of democratic debates. We support the extension of democratic decision making into broader spheres of the economy and society with greater emphasis on equality and community. Our participatory democratic inclinations are evident in our textbook, *The Democratic Debate: An Introduction to American Politics,* Third Edition (Houghton Mifflin, 2002).

Although we make no claim to impartiality, we have made every effort in the chapters that follow to select the strongest arguments on both sides of the issues. The reader can be used with any textbook in American government, no matter what the political inclinations of the professor. The reader can also stand by itself as an introduction to the critical issues facing American democracy at the beginning of the twenty-first century.

New to the Fifth Edition

The fifth edition contains thirteen new selections, comprising over one-third of the book. Several of the new chapters concern profound issues for American democracy raised by three recent events: the 2000 presidential election, the terrorist attacks of September 11, 2001, and their aftermath, and the war in Iraq.

There are four new chapters:

Chapter 6   Civil Liberties and War: Debating the USA Patriot Act

Chapter 8   Public Opinion: The American People and War

Chapter 12   Debating the Deficit and the Size of Government

Chapter 18   U.S. Foreign Policy After September 11: American Hegemony or International Cooperation?

In addition, we have new essays in five chapters continued from the previous edition:

Chapter 5   Political Economy: How Democratic Is the Free Market Economy?

Chapter 10   Political Parties and Elections: Are Voters United or Divided?

Chapter 13   Congress: Can It Serve the Public Good?

Chapter 14   The Presidency: How Much Difference Does the Individual Make?

Chapter 16   Economic Inequality: A Threat to Democracy?

Many of the essays in the book have been written by leading figures in political science, law, journalism, and politics. Former President Bill Clinton defends the prospects of the Democratic Party in Chapter 10. President George W. Bush promotes his foreign policy and the war in Iraq in Chapter 18. We are especially pleased that three prominent individuals have prepared original essays for the book: Law professor Viet Dinh, formerly assistant attorney general and principal drafter of the USA Patriot Act (Chapter 6); Stephen Moore, president of the Club for Growth (Chapter

12); and Professor Stephen Skowronek, a leading scholar of the presidency (Chapter 14).

Acknowledgments

We are grateful to all of those who helped us to carry forward our original hopes for *Debating Democracy*. At SUNY, Albany, skillful research assistance was supplied by Molly Flynn, Paul Goggi, Timothy Gordinier, Christopher Latimer, Liu Runyu, Jordan Wishy, Christopher Witko, and Fred Wood. Allan Lamberg of Saint Louis University helped with the fifth edition. The folks at Houghton Mifflin—especially Frances Gay, Tracy Patruno, Katherine Meisenheimer, and Jean Woy—brought just the right blend of professional expertise and good cheer to the project.

The outside reviewers selected by Houghton Mifflin, whose names are listed in the following paragraphs, were of more than usual help. Their incisive suggestions led us to change some selections, add new subjects, and improve our pedagogical framework.

Six scholars provided helpful criticisms of the draft manuscript for the first edition: John L. Anderson, University of Nebraska at Kearney; Edmond Costantini, University of California at Davis; William R. Lund, University of Idaho; David J. Olson, University of Washington; Marvin L. Overby, University of Mississippi; and Gregory G. Rocha, University of Texas at El Paso.

The following individuals gave us valuable feedback in response to the first and second editions: Stephen C. Baker, Jacksonville University; Jennifer Disney, John Jay College of Criminal Justice; Dana K. Glencross, Oklahoma City Community College; Thomas Hensley, Kent State University; William J. Hughes, Southern Oregon University; Fredrick Paul Lee, Winona State University; Suzanne Marilley, Capital University; Noelle Norton, University of San Diego; Paula L. O'Loughlin, University of Minnesota at Morris; Larry Schwab, John Carroll University; Dennis Shea, State University of New York College at Oneonta; Kevin Smith, University of Nebraska, Lincoln; Linda O. Valenty, San Jose State University; Kenneth F. Warren, St. Louis University; and Stephen Wiener, University of California at Santa Barbara.

We are grateful to the following reviewers of the third edition who gave us valuable suggestions for the fourth revision: Scott Adler, University of Colorado at Boulder; Matthew H. Bosworth, Winona State University; Thomas P. Dolan, Columbus State University; Keith Rollin Eakins, University of Central Oklahoma; Philip Meeks, Creighton University; Stuart W. Schulman, Drake University; James R. Simmons, University of Wisconsin–Oshkosh; Donna J. Swarthout, Montana State University; Robert C. Turner, Skidmore College; and Bruce Wallin, Northeastern University.

And we would like to thank the following reviewers of the fourth edition who gave us very helpful suggestions for this revision: Jerry Calvert, Montana State University; Joseph P. Heim, University of Wisconsin–

LaCrosse; Ronald King, San Diego State University; and Delbert J. Ringquist, Central Michigan University.

Finally, we continue to depend on the love, the support, and especially the patience of our families: Melinda, Nick, and Anna; Fay, Eva, and Rosa; Katie, Jessica, Madeleine, and Eleanore.

B. M.

R. S.

T. S.

How to Read
This Book

Wen we think of democratic debates, we often think of the debates that take place every four years between or among the leading candidates for president. Beginning with the 1960 Kennedy-Nixon debate, these nationally televised events have often been a crucial part of presidential campaigns. Presidential debates, however, are very different from the debates about the key issues facing American democracy that we have gathered together in this volume. A good way to understand this difference is to examine the first debate between Al Gore and George W. Bush in the 2000 presidential campaign.

A skilled debater with many decades of experience in the federal government, Gore was widely expected to outshine the relatively inexperienced Bush, a man known for his lack of foreign policy experience and his many verbal gaffes. Indeed, immediately after the debate most commentators declared that Gore had won. Bush did do better than many people expected, showing, for example, that he could talk knowledgeably about foreign policy. But Gore frequently scored debater's points by using his knowledge of complex issues such as taxes and prescription drug plans. Gore came across as clearly more informed.

Within a few days, however, public opinion polls showed that Bush had in fact won with the voters. Most pundits had mistakenly judged the outcome as if it had been a college debate, deciding who had been most persuasive using facts and logic. But the average voter was primarily interested not in who was the better debater but in who had the best character, temperament, and leadership qualities to be president.

Gore came across as a know-it-all who, instead of explaining his positions, lectured to the audience in a condescending manner. He appeared eager to show off his knowledge and frequently broke the rules by interrupting both Bush and the moderator, Jim Lehrer. By contrast, Bush was more folksy and relaxed. Instead of focusing on complex issues, Bush spent more time stressing his principles, criticizing those who "rely upon polls and focus groups." This meant that Bush often spoke in generalities, such as "End the bickering in Washington" and "Empower people in their own lives," but nevertheless he came across as more authentic than Gore. Bush's performance was reminiscent of Ronald Reagan's in his 1980 debates with Jimmy Carter. In those, too, commentators thought that Carter had prevailed, but Reagan's folksy charm won over voters.

In presidential debates, the candidates frequently attack their opponents. In an issues debate, this is considered a logical fallacy (called the *ad hominem* fallacy, literally, addressing the man instead of the issue). Because the issue in presidential debates is choosing a president, attacking your opponent's judgment or character is relevant. On this dimension, Bush clearly outshone Gore. In probably the most memorable exchange of the debate, Bush responded to Gore's attack on his tax cut as biased toward the rich by going on the offensive. "Look, this is a man, he's got great numbers. He talks about numbers. I'm beginning to think not only did he invent the Internet, but he invented the calculator. It's fuzzy math. It's scaring—trying to scare people in the voting booth."

Instead of trying to persuade voters to change their positions on the issues, presidential candidates generally try to convince the voters that they are closest to the positions most voters already hold. Thoroughly briefed by pollsters about what the voters want to hear, each candidate, without appearing unprincipled, tries to mold his views to please the undecided voters—especially the undecided voters in key states where the electoral votes are still up for grabs. Thus, Bush downplayed his views on abortion and Gore kept repeating his support for the middle class.

The debates we have gathered together in *Debating Democracy* are far different from presidential debates. In this book, each chapter addresses a central issue in American democracy and the debaters focus exclusively on the issue. The personality or background of the debaters is irrelevant. In the real world no debate is perfectly free and fair, if only because one side has more resources to make itself heard. Nevertheless, we can approximate the conditions of a free and fair debate, as we have attempted to do in the pages that follow. We present arguments by authors who are experts on the issues. They concentrate on the issue at hand, not on their image. Each gets equal time. For the most part, they avoid begging (ignoring) the question, mudslinging, or manipulating stereotypes. The contest is decided not by who has the most money or who projects the best image but by who has the best arguments using logical reasoning and facts.

Political debates are not just methods for acquiring information in elections; they are the heart of a democratic system. In a true democracy, debates do not just concern who will be elected to office every few years; they address the issues of everyday life, and they occur every day, extending from television studios to dinner tables, from shop floors to classrooms. Even though political debates can become heated because they involve our most deeply held beliefs, democracies do not deny anyone the right to disagree. In a democracy we recognize that no one has a monopoly on the truth. Debates are not tangential to democracy; they are central to its meaning. "Agreeing to disagree" is the essence of democracy.

Debate as the Lifeblood of Democracy

Debate as dialogue, not demagoguery, is the lifeblood of democracy. Democracy is the one form of government that requires leaders to give reasons for their decisions and defend them in public. Some theorists argue that free and fair deliberation, or debate, is not only a good method for arriving at democratic decisions but is also the essence of democracy itself.[1]

Debate is crucial to a democracy not just because it leads to better decisions but also because it helps to create better citizens. Democratic debate requires that we be open-minded, that we listen to both sides. This process of listening attentively to different sides and examining their assumptions helps us to clarify and critically examine our own political values. As the nineteenth-century British political philosopher John Stuart Mill wrote:

> So essential is this discipline [attending equally and impartially to both sides] to a real understanding of moral and human subjects that, if opponents of all-important truths do not exist, it is indispensable to imagine them and supply them with the strongest arguments which the most skillful devil's advocate can conjure up.[2]

According to Mill, if we are not challenged in our beliefs, they become dead dogmas instead of living truths. (Consider what happened to communist ideologies in Eastern Europe, where they were never tested in public debate.) Once we have honed our skills analyzing political debates, we are less vulnerable to being manipulated by demagogues. By hearing the rhetoric and manipulation in others' speech, we are better able to purge it from our own.[3] Instead of basing our beliefs on unconscious prejudices or ethnocentric values, we consciously and freely choose our political beliefs.

In order for a debate to be truly democratic, it must be free and fair. In a free and fair debate, the only power exerted is the power of reason. We are moved to adopt a position not by force but by the persuasiveness of the argument. In a democratic debate, proponents argue for their positions not by appealing to this or that private interest but by appealing to the public interest, the values and aspirations we share as a democratic people. Democracy is not simply a process for adding up the individual preferences that citizens bring with them to the issues to see which side wins. In a democratic debate people are required to frame their arguments in terms of the public interest.[4] And as citizens deliberate about the public interest through debates, they are changed.[5]

In this book we have gathered two contrasting arguments on a range of the most pressing issues facing American democracy. The reader's task is to compare the two arguments and decide which is more persuasive. After reading the selections, readers may feel frustrated seeing that opponents can adopt diametrically opposed stands on the same issue depending on their point of view. It may seem as if political positions on the issues are based only on personal values, as if political judgments are simply a matter of opinion. Being able to understand viewpoints divergent from our own, however, is the beginning of political toleration and insight. There is no One Truth on political issues that can be handed to us on a platter by experts. Nevertheless, making public choices is *not* simply a matter of opinion. There are fundamental political values that Americans subscribe to and that we struggle to achieve in our political decisions. Political stands are not just a matter of opinion, because some decisions will promote the democratic public interest better than others.

The purpose of this introduction is to give you, the reader, tools for evaluating democratic debates. The agreements and disagreements in American politics are not random; they exhibit patterns, and understanding these patterns can help orient you in the debates. In the pages that follow we draw a preliminary map of the territory of democratic debates in the United States to guide you in negotiating this difficult terrain. Your goal should not be just to take a stand on this or that issue but to clarify your own values and chart your own path in pursuit of the public interest of American democracy.

Democratic Debates: Conflict Within Consensus

In order for a true debate to occur, there must be both consensus and conflict. If there were no consensus, or agreement, on basic values or standards of evaluation, the debaters would talk past each other, like two people speaking in foreign tongues. Without some common standard of evaluation, there would be no way to settle the debate. But, if there were no fundamental disagreements, no conflict, the debate would be trivial and boring. Factual disagreements are not enough. Consider a debate between two political scientists about this question: How many people voted in the last election? The debate might be informative, but few people would care about the outcome because it does not engage deeply held values or beliefs. Factual disputes are important, but they rarely decide important political debates. Democratic debates are interesting and important when they engage us in struggles over the meaning and application of our basic values.

Judging a political debate is tricky. Political reasoning is different from economic reasoning or individual rational decision making. Political debates are rarely settled by toting up the costs and benefits of alternative courses of action and choosing the one that maximizes benefits over costs. It is not that costs and benefits do not matter; rather, what we see as benefits or costs depends on how we frame the issue. In political debates each side tries to get the audience to see the issue its way, to frame the issue in language that reinforces its position. On the issue of abortion, for example, is your position best described as pro-choice or pro-life? Should programs to help minorities be characterized as affirmative action or reverse discrimination? Clearly, the terms we use to describe a political position make a difference. Each term casts light on the issue in a different way, highlighting different values that are at stake in the controversy. The terms used to describe the abortion issue, for example, emphasize either the right of an unborn fetus or the right of a woman to control her body.

As these examples illustrate, in political debates the outcome frequently hinges on the standard of evaluation itself, on what values and principles will be applied to the decision at hand. In political debates the issue is always what is good for the community as a whole, the public interest, not just some segment of the community. The selections that follow are all examples of debates over the meaning of the public interest in American democracy. In the United States, political debates, with the notable exception of debates over slavery, have been characterized by consensus on basic democratic principles *combined with* conflicts over how best to realize those principles in practice.

As conflicts within a consensus, democratic debates in this country go back more than two hundred years ago to the nation's founding and the original debate over the U.S. Constitution. Americans worship the Constitution as an almost divinely inspired document that embodies the highest ideals of democracy. Yet throughout history Americans have disagreed vehemently on what the Constitution means. This is not surprising. The Constitution was born as much in conflict and compromise as in consensus. In the words of former Supreme Court Justice William J. Brennan Jr., the framers "hid their differences in cloaks of generality."[6] The general language of the Constitution left many conflicts over specifics to later generations. The Constitution, for example, gave the federal government the power to provide for the "general welfare," but we have been debating ever since about what this should include. Thus, the Constitution is both a source of consensus, by embodying our ideals, and a source of conflict, by failing to specify exactly how those ideals should be applied in practice.[7]

Three Sources of Conflict

Behind the words of the Constitution lie three ideals that supposedly animate our system of government: *democracy, freedom,* and *equality.* Americans agree that we should have a government of, by, and for the people (as President Lincoln so eloquently put it), a government that treats everybody equally, and a government that achieves the maximum level of freedom consistent with an ordered society. These ideals seem simple, but they are not. While Americans are united in their aspirations, they are divided in their visions of how to achieve those aspirations.[8] Democracy, freedom, and equality are what political theorists call "essentially contested concepts."[9]

I. Democracy

Democracy comes from the Greek words *demos,* meaning "the people," and *kratein,* meaning "to rule." Hence, democracy means, simply, "rule by the people." Americans agree that democracy is the best form of government. They disagree, however, on what this means.

Elite (Limited) Democracy   For some, democracy is basically a method for making decisions. According to this minimalist definition of democracy, a decision is democratic if it is made according to the criterion of majority rule. Of course, there are other requirements of democratic decision making, such as open nominations for office and free speech, but once the basic conditions have been met, the resulting decision is by definition democratic.

Following this limited definition, the most important characteristic of a democracy is free and fair elections for choosing government officials. Democracy basically means the ability of citizens to choose their leaders.[10] Elites compete for the votes to win office, but once in office, they have substantial autonomy to rule as they see fit. According to this view, ultimate power rests in the hands of the people at election time, but between elections they cede decision-making authority to elites who have the expertise and experience to make the right decisions in a technologically complex and dangerous world. We call this school of democracy *elite democracy.*[11]

Elite democrats favor a minimal definition of democracy not because it is ideal but because it is the only type of democracy that is achievable in large modern nation-states. Thus, as you will see in the selection by John Mueller in Chapter 2, elite democrats question the validity of many of the precepts of participatory democracy. In contrast, Paul Rogat Loeb maintains that active citizens who sacrifice for the common good are possible, even in our flawed democratic system.

Popular (Expansive) Democracy   Opponents of elite democrats adopt a more demanding definition of democracy. They argue that we cannot call a decision democratic just because it came out of a democratic process. Democratic decisions must also respect certain values such as tolerance, a respect for individual freedom, and the attainment of a basic level of social and economic equality. If the majority rules in a way that violates people's rights or enacts policies that result in extreme inequalities of wealth, the system cannot be called democratic. For this group, democracy means more than a political system with free and fair elections; it means an economy and society that reflect a democratic desire for equality and respect for differences.

For adherents of an expansive definition of democracy, democracy means more than going to the polls every few years; it means citizens participating in the institutions of civil society, including corporations, unions, and neighborhood associations. In Chapter 5, Samuel Bowles, Frank Roosevelt, and Richard Edwards represent this position, calling for expanding democratic decision making into the economy. Countering the view of elite democrats that people are not interested in or capable of governing effectively, those who advocate a more participatory system argue that in an atmosphere of toleration, respect, and rough equality, citizens are capable of governing themselves fairly and effectively. We call those who advocate a more participatory conception of democracy *popular democrats*.[12]

II. Freedom

Most of us have a basic intuitive idea of freedom: to be free means being able to do what we want, without someone telling us what to do. Any time we are forced to do something against our will by somebody else, our freedom is reduced. Freedom seems like an exceedingly simple idea. Once again, however, we find that there is plenty of room for disagreement.

Negative (Freedom From)   The central issue for freedom is deciding where to draw the line between the power of the group and the freedom of the individual. In other words, how far should government power extend? Any time the government imposes a tax or passes a law, it limits someone's freedom. In a justly famous essay, *On Liberty*, John Stuart Mill argues that the only justification for government power over individuals is self-protection: "[T]he only purpose for which power can be rightfully exercised over any member of a civilized community, against his will, is to prevent harm to others."[13] In other words, your freedom to swing your arm ends where my nose begins.

Under Mill's view, the purpose of government is to maximize individual freedom. Freedom is understood negatively, as freedom from external constraints. Since government actions always reduce individual freedom, their only justification is to counter other restrictions on our freedom, as when the government passes laws against robbery or assault. Clearly, this view places severe limits on what democracies can legitimately do, even under the principle of majority rule. If the majority passes laws that restrict someone's freedom, without those laws being justified by the principle of self-protection, then it is no longer a true democracy because the laws violate a basic democratic value.

Positive (Freedom To)   In contrast to the negative conception of freedom—freedom *from*—there is an equally compelling positive definition of freedom—freedom *to*.[14] The positive idea of freedom recognizes that in order to be free, to exercise meaningful choice, we need to possess certain resources and have certain capacities. Education, for example, increases our freedom because it increases our ability to imagine alternatives and find solutions to problems. Freedom, therefore, is not simply the absence of external coercion but freedom to get an education, travel to foreign countries, or receive expert medical care.

A positive conception of freedom justifies an expanded role for government and for citizens acting together in other ways. When government taxes us, it reduces negative freedom, but when it uses the money to build a highway or a public library, it gives us a greater freedom to do things we previously were unable to do. Under the positive conception of freedom, the scope of freedom is increased when the capacity of individuals to act is enhanced by government action, such as protecting the right of workers to join a union (thus giving workers the ability to bargain collectively over wages and working conditions) or requiring buildings to be handicapped accessible (thus giving the handicapped access to places they were previously excluded from).[15]

Whether one subscribes to a positive or a negative conception of freedom will make a big difference in one's political philosophy. The negative conception of freedom is conducive to limited government and highlights the more acquisitive and competitive side of human nature. Under this view, the expansion of power in one part of society necessarily leads to a reduction of freedom in some other part of society. The selection by Milton Friedman on political economy in Chapter 5 is based on a negative conception of freedom. Friedman warns that too much government leads to coercion and a reduction in individual freedom, which is maximized by free competition in the marketplace. The positive conception of freedom emphasizes the more cooperative side of human beings. According to this conception, government as a form of social cooperation can actually expand the realm of freedom by bringing more and more matters of social importance under human control.

III. Equality

Like democracy and freedom, equality seems an exceedingly simple idea. Equality marches forward under banners that read "Treat everybody equally" or "Treat like cases alike." These are not working definitions, however, but political rhetoric that hides serious ambiguities in the concept of equality. In truth, how we apply the idea of equality depends on how we envision it in a broader context.

Process Orientation   For some people, equality is basically generated by a fair process. So long as the competition is fair—everybody has an equal opportunity to succeed—then the results are fair, even if the resulting distribution is highly unequal. Inequalities that reflect differences among people in intelligence, talent, ambition, or strength are viewed as legitimate. Inequalities that result from biases in the rules of competition are unjustified and should be eliminated.

The process orientation toward equality is best reflected in free market theory. According to market theory, the distribution of income and wealth is fair if it is the result of a process of voluntary contracting among responsible adults. As long as the requirements for a free market are met (perfect competition, free flow of information, the absence of coercion or manipulation, and so on), no one exerts power over the market and market outcomes are just and fair. Market theorists, like Milton Friedman, stress equal opportunity, not equal results. The role of government, in this view, is to serve as a neutral umpire, enforcing the rules and treating everyone alike.[16]

Results Orientation   Opponents argue that if the government treats everybody equally, the results will still be highly unequal because people start the race from very different positions. Some have a head start in the race, while others enter with serious handicaps. To ignore these differences is to perpetuate inequalities. Treating unequals equally is, in effect, unequal. The French writer Anatole France mocked what he called "the majestic egalitarianism of the law, which forbids rich and poor alike to sleep under bridges, to beg in the streets, and to steal bread."[17] Even though the law formally treats everyone alike, it is clear that only certain people will suffer the consequences.

Those who take a results orientation toward equality don't deny the importance of equal opportunity but argue that equal opportunity means the ability of everyone to participate equally in the decisions that affect their lives. These democrats charge that their opponents elevate the individual over the community and privileged elites over ordinary citizens, as if the wagon train could make it to the promised land only if some of the weak and frail were left behind alongside the trail. Those who support a results orientation argue that it is possible for everyone to make it together.

Those who support a results orientation do not believe in a strict leveling of society but argue that certain resources are necessary for people to participate fully in society and realize their potential. In other words, government cannot just stand aside and watch people compete; it must establish the conditions for equal participation. At a minimum, many would argue, adequate nutrition, good education, safety, and decent health care are necessary for a fulfilling life.

American Ideologies: Patterns in Political Stands

With two contrasting positions on each of the three issues just discussed—democracy, equality, and freedom—there are eight possible combinations of issue positions. Stands on the three issues are not random, however; they correlate in ways that generate distinct patterns characteristic of American political ideologies.

One of the clearest ideological distinctions in American politics is between those who favor markets and those who favor government. As Charles Lindblom has noted, "Aside from the difference between despotic and libertarian governments, the greatest distinction between one government and another is in the degree to which market replaces government or government replaces market."[18] A central issue in American politics is where to draw the line between the public and private sectors. If you believe that the market is basically free and fair, then you will support only a limited role for government. Generally, those who favor the market subscribe to a negative conception of freedom and a process orientation toward equality. This position corresponds to what we call *free market conservatism.* If, however, you believe that markets are penetrated by relations of power and are prone to discrimination, then you will support an expanded role for political participation and democratic government. Those who advocate an increased role for government generally subscribe to a positive conception of freedom and favor a results orientation toward equality. These views correspond to what is commonly called *liberalism.*

Usually, we think of social conservatives as adhering to a more elite view of democracy and social liberals as being more inclined toward popular democracy. In the 1960s, for example, *left-wing populists* supported maximum feasible participation by poor people to solve poverty and advocated democratic control of corporations. In recent years, however, because they support a large role for the federal government in Washington, D.C., liberals have been accused by conservatives of being, in effect, elitist. A *right-wing populist* movement has arisen that combines popular democratic appeals with a negative conception of individual freedom and a process approach to equality, opposing the redistribution of wealth through government. To add to the complexity, however, right-wing populists do not always favor limiting the role of government. The *religious right* generally wants the government to interfere less in the economy but more in society—exerting more democratic control over moral issues, such as abortion and pornography.

Although distinct patterns appear in American politics on the issues of democracy, freedom, and equality, they are not set in stone. It is possible to mix and match different positions in putting together your own political philosophy. In developing your own political philosophy, you will need to address a fundamental question: What are human beings capable of; that is, what is your conception of human nature?

Human Nature: The Big Debate

Throughout history, political philosophers have debated different conceptions of human nature. Human nature is the clay out of which all political systems must be molded. The nature of this clay, its elasticity or hardness, its ability to assume different shapes and hold them, largely determines what we can and cannot do in politics. Since the original debate over the U.S. Constitution, Americans have disagreed about human nature and therefore about politics.

The Private View   Many argue that Americans are quintessentially individualistic, well suited to the marketplace and private pursuits but not well suited to democratic citizenship. The framers of the Constitution, the Federalists, argued that the common people were self-interested and passionate creatures who should not be entrusted with all of the reins of government. Thus, as you will see in Chapter 1, James Madison argues in "Federalist No. 10" that the greatest danger in a democracy is the tyranny of the majority, especially the majority of common people taking away the property of wealthy elites. Madison recommended various checks on majority rule that would guarantee the rights of minorities and give elites substantial autonomy to rule in the public interest.

This view of human nature is reflected in contemporary debates. In the United States the debate shifts from human nature to the nature of Americans as a people and whether we are different from other people. According to the theory of exceptionalism, Americans are more individualistic and self-interested than other people.[19] As a nation of immigrants, we fled feudal systems and traditional cultures in search of greater freedom and assimilated into an American value system that stressed upward mobility through individual effort. The pursuit of fortune in the marketplace is the special genius of Americans. Whether this is good or bad depends on your view of markets and governments.

The Social View   During the debate over the Constitution in the 1780s, a group of dissenters, the Anti-federalists, argued that the Constitution placed too many limits on citizen participation. (We have included a selection by the Anti-federalist Brutus in Chapter 1.) The Anti-federalists argued that the common people could overcome or check their selfish inclinations through democratic participation and education in civic virtue. As much power as possible, therefore, should be placed in the hands of the people at the grassroots level. The main threat to democracy, Anti-federalists believed, came not from the tyranny of the majority but from power-hungry elites. The best way to protect against elite tyranny was to have the people participate directly in deciding important issues. The Anti-federalists founded the tradition of popular (expansive) democracy that is still alive in the United States.

Even today, when Americans seem caught up in acquisitive pursuits and politics seems so mean-spirited, some observers argue that there are important sources of social commitment in American culture. An influential book by Robert Bellah and colleagues, *Habits of the Heart,* argues that Americans are attached to powerful civic traditions that pull us out of our individualistic orientations. These civic traditions are rooted in religion and republicanism, both of which emphasize commitments to public service. Indeed, Americans exhibit lively commitments to grassroots participation and public service.

Conclusion: A Guide to Critical Thinking

Everyone has a political philosophy. Whether we recognize it or not, we bring certain assumptions about democracy, freedom, equality, and human nature to political debates. The goal is not to give up these assumptions but to convert them from unconscious prejudices into carefully chosen elements of a political philosophy. A good way to develop a thoughtful political philosophy is to analyze political debates like those included here. Clever debaters, for example, will appear as if they are supporting equality in general, but in order to make their argument work, they must adopt one conception of equality over another. Readers must delve beneath the rhetoric and evaluate these assumptions, as well as the logic and evidence of the argument itself.

As a guide to critical thinking, we suggest that readers keep in mind these five questions and evaluate the evidence that supports their answers. (Some questions may not apply to some selections.)

1. What is the author's concept of democracy—elite (limited) or popular (expansive)?
2. What is the author's concept of freedom—negative (freedom from) or positive (freedom to)?
3. What is the author's concept of equality—process or results?
4. How would you classify the author's ideology?
5. What concept of human nature, individualist or social, lies behind the author's argument?

This book is going to press during the run-up to the 2004 presidential election, a time when the democratic debate is rancorous and deeply divided along partisan lines. Bitter conflicts over the war on terrorism, Iraq, and cultural issues such as abortion and gay marriage threaten to tear the political fabric of our democracy. Especially during times like these, we need to keep in mind that there is one thing that finally does unite us: the belief that open and public debate is the best, in fact the only, democratic way to settle our differences.

NOTES

1. See Jon Elster, ed., *Deliberative Democracy* (New York: Cambridge University Press, 1998). The German political theorist Jürgen Habermas has spent many years developing a theory of the ideal speech situation as the foundation of democracy. See especially his *The Theory of Communicative Action,* 2 vols. (Boston: Beacon Press, 1984–1987).

2. John Stuart Mill, *On Liberty,* ed. and with an introduction by Currin V. Shields (Indianapolis, Ind.: Bobbs-Merrill, 1956), p. 46.

3. See Stephen L. Esquith, *Intimacy and Spectacle: Liberal Theory as Political Education* (Ithaca, N.Y.: Cornell University Press, 1994).

4. Amy Gutmann and Dennis Thompson call this the principle of reciprocity—that in a democratic debate citizens appeal to reasons that can be mutually acceptable to other citizens. See *Democracy and Disagreement* (Cambridge, Mass.: Harvard University Press, 1996).

5. Joshua Cohen, "Deliberation and Democratic Legitimacy," in *The Good Polity: Normative Analysis of the State* (Oxford: Basil Blackwell, 1989), p. 29.

6. Justice William J. Brennan Jr., "Federal Judges Properly and Inevitably Make Law Through 'Loose' Constitutional Construction," in *Debating American Government,* ed. Peter Woll (2d ed.; Glenview, Ill.: Scott, Foresman, 1988), p. 338.

7. It is neither possible nor desirable for a constitution to specify every application. If it did, it would be a rigid constitution that would be incapable of adapting to changing conditions.

8. The following discussion of the sources of democratic disagreements in the United States draws heavily on Deborah A. Stone, *Political Paradox: The Art of Political Decision Making* (New York: Norton, 1997), and Frances Moore Lappé, *Rediscovering America's Values* (New York: Ballantine Books, 1989).

9. For an insightful discussion of essentially contested concepts, see William E. Connolly, *The Terms of Political Discourse* (2d ed.; Princeton, N.J.: Princeton University Press, 1983).

10. For the most famous definition of democracy along these lines, see Joseph A. Schumpeter, *Capitalism, Socialism, and Democracy* (3d ed.; New York: Harper, 1950), p. 269.

11. For elaboration on the concepts of elite and popular democracy, see Bruce Miroff, Raymond Seidelman, and Todd Swanstrom, *The Democratic Debate: An Introduction to American Politics* (3d ed.; Boston: Houghton Mifflin, 2002).

12. Robert A. Dahl is the most influential contemporary political scientist who has written on the ideas of elite and popular democracy. Dahl began his career by defending a version of elite democratic theory in *A Preface to Democratic Theory* (Chicago: University of Chicago Press, 1956), and *Who Governs? Democracy and Power in an American City* (New Haven, Conn.: Yale University Press, 1961). In later works, Dahl shifted dramatically to a more popular democratic position. See *A Preface to Economic Democracy* (Berkeley and Los Angeles: University of California Press, 1985); *Democracy and Its Critics* (New Haven, Conn.: Yale University Press, 1989); and *How Democratic Is the American Constitution?* (New Haven, Conn.: Yale University Press, 2001).

13. Mill, *On Liberty*, p. 13.

14. The classic statement on positive and negative freedom is Isaiah Berlin's "Two Concepts of Liberty," in *Four Essays on Liberty* (New York: Oxford University Press, 1969), pp. 118–172.

15. For an eloquent defense of a positive conception of freedom, see President Franklin D. Roosevelt's speech to Congress on "An Economic Bill of Rights," in *Documents of American History,* ed. Henry Steele Commager (New York: Appleton-Century-Crofts, 1963), Vol. 2, pp. 483–485.

16. One of the best statements of a process orientation toward equality is Robert Nozick, *Anarchy, State, and Utopia* (New York: Basic Books, 1974).

17. *The Oxford Dictionary of Quotations* (3d ed.; Oxford: Oxford University Press, 1979), p. 217.

18. Charles Lindblom, *Politics and Markets: The World's Political-Economic Systems* (New York: Basic Books, 1977), p. ix.

19. For an influential statement on American exceptionalism, see Louis Hartz, *The Liberal Tradition in American Thought* (New York: Harcourt, Brace, 1955).

1

The Founding: Debating the Constitution

Although Americans relish political controversy in the present, we project onto the distant past of our nation's origins a more dignified political consensus. The founders of our republic—Washington, Adams, Jefferson, Hamilton, Madison—are cast in stone monuments and treated as political saints. Their ideas are invoked as hallowed truths that should inspire us. Seldom are these ideas treated as arguments that we should ponder and debate.

In fact, consensus was hardly the hallmark of the era in which the American republic was founded. Passionate political controversies raged during the American Revolution and its aftermath. These controversies ranged over the most basic issues of political life. The most profound was the debate over the ratification of the Constitution. The supporters of the Constitution, known as Federalists, and its opponents, known as Anti-federalists, disagreed over what kind of a republic Americans should have. Although the debate took place over two hundred years ago, it still illuminates the core dilemmas of our democratic society.

The readings that follow highlight some of the fundamental issues debated by Federalists and Anti-federalists. They pit the greatest thinker among the Federalists, James Madison, against a New York Anti-federalist, who used the pseudonym Brutus, in an argument over the appropriate scale of democratic political life. (Scholars are not absolutely certain who Brutus was; the most likely candidate is Robert Yates, a New York judge. The pseudonym, by recalling the Roman republican who killed the tyrant Julius Caesar, evokes the threat allegedly posed by the Constitution to republican liberty.)

In his classic essay "Federalist No. 10," Madison favors the large, national republic established by the Constitution over small republics (state governments). In small republics, Madison warns, selfish factions can attain majority status and will use their power over the government to oppress minorities (such as the wealthy or those who hold unorthodox religious beliefs). Small republics thus allow the worst qualities in human nature to prevail: they allow irrational passion to overwhelm reasoned deliberation and injustice to supplant the public good.

The large republic created by the new Constitution, Madison prophesies, will be more rational and more just. Elected in large districts, representatives will likely be the most distinguished and patriotic citizens, and they will "refine and enlarge the public views" by filtering out the most selfish and shortsighted popular impulses. There will also be a greater diversity of factions in the large republic, making it unlikely that a majority can come together except on the basis of the common good. In Madison's essay, the chief threat to republican liberty comes, ironically, from the people themselves. His solution is to create a large republic in which the people will be divided into so many different interest groups that they can do little harm, while a small number of decision makers at the top take care of the common needs.

Brutus's essay (the first in a series that he wrote) takes issue with Madison on every count. He predicts that the large republic established by the Constitution will be run by aristocratic rulers who will eagerly expand their powers and oppress the common people. The greater distance from voters that Madison thinks will promote deliberation and public spirit in representatives will instead, Brutus argues, foster corruption and self-seeking in them. The diversity of the large republic is also, for Brutus, an unwelcome development since it will increase selfish factionalism, conflict, and stalemate.

Whereas Madison sees small republics as scenes of turbulence and misery, Brutus portrays them in a favorable light. In the smaller political scale of a state, the people will share common economic and social characteristics. Electoral districts will be smaller, so voters will personally know and trust their representatives and these representatives in turn will mirror their constituents' values and sentiments. Rather than breeding tyrannical majorities, small republics, as Brutus depicts them, educate law-abiding and virtuous citizens. In sum, Brutus rests his political hopes on the mass of ordinary people in the small republic, whose political impulses Madison fears, while directing his criticisms against a national elite, to whom Madison looks for wise political rule.

Anti-federalist fears that the Constitution would create an oppressive government, fatal to republican liberty, strike us today as grossly exaggerated. Yet in at least one respect these fears were fortunate—they helped produce the Bill of Rights. Initially, Federalists such as Madison and his collaborator on *The Federalist Papers,* Alexander Hamilton, claimed that a national bill of rights was both unnecessary and undesirable. By establishing a national government that possessed only enumerated, limited powers, they insisted, the Constitution had not granted any authority to invade the liberties and rights of the people; but if a list of particular rights was nonetheless appended to the Constitution, it might imply that the government *could* invade rights that had not been listed. These arguments were brushed aside by the Anti-federalists, who continued to argue that without specific guarantees the liberties for which Americans had fought in the Revolution might be usurped by a government of their own creation. To conciliate the Anti-federalists and win greater public support for the new Constitution, Madison dropped his objections and took the lead in pushing for the Bill of Rights in the first Congress.

Although Federalists and Anti-federalists could ultimately find common ground in the Bill of Rights, the philosophical and political differences between them remained profound. Their disagreements began the American debate between elite democracy and popular democracy. Nowhere is this more evident than in the contrast between Madison's reliance on a deliberative elite and Brutus's regard for the capacities of ordinary citizens. But it can also be seen in the difference between Madison's belief that liberty will inevitably produce inequality of property and Brutus's belief that in a small republic large-scale inequalities can be avoided.

The Federalists and Anti-federalists debated basic questions about democracy, and their disagreements still echo in our politics today. Thinking about the issues in their debate can help to clarify your own perspective toward democracy in the United States. Do you believe, with Madison, that it is only at the national level that selfish majorities can be blocked and government policies can be framed by deliberative and public-spirited representatives? Do you believe, with Brutus, that we should prefer state and local governments in order to promote greater civic participation and to enhance the trust between representatives and their constituents? Even more fundamentally, do you agree with Madison that ordinary citizens are too uninformed and self-seeking to be trusted with great political influence and that decisions are best left to elected representatives who can "refine and enlarge" what the people think? Or do you agree with Brutus that elites pose the greater danger to democracy and that democracy flourishes only when conditions are established that encourage ordinary citizens to involve themselves in the search for the public good?

Federalist No. 10

JAMES MADISON

Among the numerous advantages promised by a well-constructed Union, none deserves to be more accurately developed than its tendency to break and control the violence of faction.[1] The friend of popular governments never finds himself so much alarmed for their character and fate as when he contemplates their propensity to this dangerous vice. He will not fail, therefore, to set a due value on any plan which, without violating the principles to which he is attached, provides a proper cure for it. The instability, injustice, and confusion introduced into the public councils have, in truth, been the mortal diseases under which popular governments have everywhere perished, as they continue to be the favorite and fruitful topics from which the adversaries to liberty derive their most specious declamations. The valuable improvements made by the American constitutions on the popular models, both ancient and modern, cannot certainly be too much admired; but it would be an unwarrantable partiality to contend that they have as effectually obviated the danger on this side, as was wished and expected. Complaints are everywhere heard from our most considerate and virtuous citizens, equally the friends of public and private faith and of public and personal liberty, that our governments are too unstable, that the public good is disregarded in the conflicts of rival parties, and that measures are too often decided, not according to the rules of justice and the rights of the minor party, but by the superior force of an interested and overbearing majority. However anxiously we may wish that these complaints had no foundation, the evidence of known facts will not permit us to deny that they are in some degree true. It will be found, indeed, on a candid review of our situation, that some of the distresses under which we labor have been erroneously charged on the operation of our governments; but it will be found, at the same time, that other causes will not alone account for many of our heaviest misfortunes; and, particularly, for that prevailing and increasing distrust of public engagements and alarm for private rights which are echoed from one end of the continent to the other. These must be chiefly, if not wholly, effects of the unsteadiness and injustice with which a factious spirit has tainted our public administration.

By a faction I understand a number of citizens, whether amounting to a majority or minority of the whole, who are united and actuated by some

---

1. In modern terms, both interest groups and political parties are examples of Madison's factions. Note that by the definition Madison offers later, no faction can legitimately claim to represent the public interest.

common impulse of passion, or of interest, adverse to the rights of other citizens, or to the permanent and aggregate interests of the community.

There are two methods of curing the mischiefs of faction: the one, by removing its causes; the other, by controlling its effects.

There are again two methods of removing the causes of faction: the one, by destroying the liberty which is essential to its existence; the other, by giving to every citizen the same opinions, the same passions, and the same interests.

It could never be more truly said than of the first remedy that it was worse than the disease. Liberty is to faction what air is to fire, an aliment without which it instantly expires. But it could not be a less folly to abolish liberty, which is essential to political life, because it nourishes faction than it would be to wish the annihilation of air, which is essential to animal life, because it imparts to fire its destructive agency.

The second expedient is as impracticable as the first would be unwise. As long as the reason of man continues fallible, and he is at liberty to exercise it, different opinions will be formed. As long as the connection subsists between his reason and his self-love, his opinions and his passions will have a reciprocal influence on each other; and the former will be objects to which the latter will attach themselves. The diversity in the faculties of men, from which the rights of property originate, is not less an insuperable obstacle to a uniformity of interests. The protection of these faculties is the first object of government. From the protection of different and unequal faculties of acquiring property, the possession of different degrees and kinds of property immediately results; and from the influence of these on the sentiments and views of the respective proprietors ensues a division of the society into different interests and parties.

The latent causes of faction are thus sown in the nature of man; and we see them everywhere brought into different degrees of activity, according to the different circumstances of civil society. A zeal for different opinions concerning religion, concerning government, and many other points, as well of speculation as of practice; an attachment to different leaders ambitiously contending for pre-eminence and power; or to persons of other descriptions whose fortunes have been interesting to the human passions, have, in turn, divided mankind into parties, inflamed them with mutual animosity, and rendered them much more disposed to vex and oppress each other than to co-operate for their common good. So strong is this propensity of mankind to fall into mutual animosities that where no substantial occasion presents itself the most frivolous and fanciful distinctions have been sufficient to kindle their unfriendly passions and excite their most violent conflicts. But the most common and durable source of factions has been the various and unequal distribution of property. Those who hold and those who are without property have ever formed distinct interests in society. Those who are creditors, and those who are debtors, fall under a like discrimination. A landed interest, a manufacturing interest, a mercantile interest, a moneyed interest, with many lesser interests, grow up of necessity in civilized nations, and divide them into different classes, actuated by different sentiments and views. The regulation of these various and interfering interests forms the principal task of modern legislation and involves the spirit of party and faction in the necessary and ordinary operations of government.

No man is allowed to be a judge in his own cause, because his interest would certainly bias his judgment, and, not improbably, corrupt his integrity. With equal, nay with greater reason, a body of men are unfit to be both judges and parties at the same time; yet what are many of the most important acts of legislation but so many judicial determinations, not indeed concerning the rights of single persons, but concerning the rights of large bodies of citizens? And what are the different classes of legislators but advocates and parties to the causes which they determine? Is a law proposed concerning private debts? It is a question to which the creditors are parties on one side and the debtors on the other. Justice ought to hold the balance between them. Yet the parties are, and must be, themselves the judges; and the most numerous party, or in other words, the most powerful faction must be expected to prevail. Shall domestic manufacturers be encouraged, and in what degree, by restrictions on foreign manufacturers? are questions which would be differently decided by the landed and the manufacturing classes, and probably by neither with a sole regard to justice and the public good. The apportionment of taxes on the various descriptions of property is an act which seems to require the most exact impartiality; yet there is, perhaps, no legislative act in which greater opportunity and temptation are given to a predominant party to trample on the rules of justice. Every shilling with which they overburden the inferior number is a shilling saved to their own pockets.

It is in vain to say that enlightened statesmen will be able to adjust these clashing interests and render them all subservient to the public good. Enlightened statesmen will not always be at the helm. Nor, in many cases, can such an adjustment be made at all without taking into view indirect and remote considerations, which will rarely prevail over the immediate interest which one party may find in disregarding the rights of another or the good of the whole.

The inference to which we are brought is that the *causes* of faction cannot be removed and that relief is only to be sought in the means of controlling its *effects*.

If a faction consists of less than a majority, relief is supplied by the republican principle, which enables the majority to defeat its sinister views by regular vote. It may clog the administration, it may convulse the society; but it will be unable to execute and mask its violence under the forms of the Constitution. When a majority is included in a faction, the form of popular government, on the other hand, enables it to sacrifice to its ruling passion or interest both the public good and the rights of other citizens. To secure the public good and private rights against the danger of such a faction, and at the same time to preserve the spirit and the form of popular government, is then the great object to which our inquiries are directed. Let me add that it is the great desideratum by which alone this form of government can be rescued from the opprobrium under which it has so long labored and be recommended to the esteem and adoption of mankind.

By what means is this object attainable? Evidently by one of two only. Either the existence of the same passion or interest in a majority at the same time must be prevented, or the majority, having such coexistent passion of interest, must be rendered, by their number and local situation, unable to concert and carry into effect schemes of oppression. If the impulse and the opportunity be suffered to coincide, we well know that neither moral nor religious motives can be relied on as an adequate control. They are not found to be such on the injustice and violence of individuals, and lose their efficacy in proportion to the number combined together, that is, in proportion as their efficacy becomes needful.

From this view of the subject it may be concluded that a pure democracy, by which I mean a society consisting of a small number of citizens, who assemble and administer the government in person, can admit of no cure for the mischiefs of faction. A common passion or interest will, in almost every case, be felt by a majority of the whole; a communication and concert results from the form of government itself; and there is nothing to check the inducements to sacrifice the weaker party or an obnoxious individual. Hence it is that such democracies have ever been spectacles of turbulence and contention; have ever been found incompatible with personal security or the rights of property; and have in general been as short in their lives as they have been violent in their deaths. Theoretic politicians, who have patronized this species of government, have erroneously supposed that by reducing mankind to a perfect equality in their political rights, they would at the same time be perfectly equalized and assimilated in their possessions, their opinions, and their passions.

A republic, by which I mean a government in which the scheme of representation takes place, opens a different prospect and promises the cure for which we are seeking. Let us examine the points in which it varies from pure democracy, and we shall comprehend both the nature of the cure and the efficacy which it must derive from the Union.

The two great points of difference between a democracy and a republic are: first, the delegation of the government, in the latter, to a small number of citizens elected by the rest; secondly, the greater number of citizens and greater sphere of country over which the latter may be extended.

The effect of the first difference is, on the one hand, to refine and enlarge the public views by passing them through the medium of a chosen body of citizens, whose wisdom may best discern the true interest of their country and whose patriotism and love of justice will be least likely to sacrifice it to temporary or partial considerations. Under such a regulation it may well happen that the public voice, pronounced by the representatives of the people, will be more consonant to the public good than if pronounced by the people themselves, convened for the purpose. On the other

hand, the effect may be inverted. Men of factious tempers, of local prejudices, or of sinister designs, may, by intrigue, by corruption, or by other
means, first obtain the suffrages, and then betray the interests of the people. The question resulting is, whether small or extensive republics are most
favorable to the election of proper guardians of the public weal; and it is
clearly decided in favor of the latter by two obvious considerations.

In the first place it is to be remarked that however small the republic
may be the representatives must be raised to a certain number in order to
guard against the cabals of a few; and that however large it may be they
must be limited to a certain number in order to guard against the confusion
of a multitude. Hence, the number of representatives in the two cases not
being in proportion to that of the constituents, and being proportionally
greatest in the small republic, it follows that if the proportion of fit characters be not less in the large than in the small republic, the former will present a greater option, and consequently a greater probability of a fit choice.

In the next place, as each representative will be chosen by a greater
number of citizens in the large than in the small republic, it will be more
difficult for unworthy candidates to practise with success the vicious arts by
which elections are too often carried; and the suffrages of the people being
more free, will be more likely to center on men who possess the most attractive merit and the most diffusive and established characters.

It must be confessed that in this, as in most other cases, there is a mean,
on both sides of which inconveniencies will be found to lie. By enlarging
too much the number of electors, you render the representative too little
acquainted with all their local circumstances and lesser interests; as by reducing it too much, you render him unduly attached to these, and too little
fit to comprehend and pursue great and national objects. The federal Constitution forms a happy combination in this respect; the great and aggregate
interests being referred to the national, the local and particular to the State
legislatures.

The other point of difference is the greater number of citizens and extent of territory which may be brought within the compass of republican
than of democratic government; and it is this circumstance principally
which renders factious combinations less to be dreaded in the former than
in the latter. The smaller the society, the fewer probably will be the distinct
parties and interests composing it; the fewer the distinct parties and interests, the more frequently will a majority be found of the same party; and
the smaller the number of individuals composing a majority, and the
smaller the compass within which they are placed, the more easily will they
concert and execute their plans of oppression. Extend the sphere and you
take in a greater variety of parties and interests; you make it less probable
that a majority of the whole will have a common motive to invade the
rights of other citizens; or if such a common motive exists, it will be more
difficult for all who feel it to discover their own strength and to act in
unison with each other. Besides other impediments, it may be remarked
that, where there is a consciousness of unjust or dishonorable purposes,

communication is always checked by distrust in proportion to the number whose concurrence is necessary.

Hence, it clearly appears that the same advantage which a republic has over a democracy in controlling the effects of faction is enjoyed by a large over a small republic—is enjoyed by the Union over the States composing it. Does this advantage consist in the substitution of representatives whose enlightened views and virtuous sentiments render them superior to local prejudices and to schemes of injustice? It will not be denied that the representation of the Union will be most likely to possess these requisite endowments. Does it consist in the greater security afforded by a greater variety of parties, against the event of any one party being able to outnumber and oppress the rest? In an equal degree does the increased variety of parties comprised within the Union increase this security. Does it, in fine, consist in the greater obstacles opposed to the concert and accomplishment of the secret wishes of an unjust and interested majority? Here again the extent of the Union gives it the most palpable advantage.

The influence of factious leaders may kindle a flame within their particular States but will be unable to spread a general conflagration through the other States. A religious sect may degenerate into a political faction in a part of the Confederacy; but the variety of sects dispersed over the entire face of it must secure the national councils against any danger from that source. A rage for paper money, for an abolition of debts, for an equal division of property, or for any other improper or wicked project, will be less apt to pervade the whole body of the Union than a particular member of it, in the same proportion as such a malady is more likely to taint a particular county or district than an entire State.[2]

In the extent and proper structure of the Union, therefore, we behold a republican remedy for the diseases most incident to republican government. And according to the degree of pleasure and pride we feel in being republicans ought to be our zeal in cherishing the spirit and supporting the character of federalists.   PUBLIUS

---

2. The examples of factional objectives (for example, paper money's benefiting debtors at the expense of creditors) that Madison cites are drawn from the economic conflicts that pervaded the states in the 1780s. The movement for a new national constitution aimed to put an end to the possibility that radical factional goals might be achieved in the states.

Anti-federalist Paper 18 October 1787

BRUTUS

To the Citizens of the State of New-York.

Perhaps this country never saw so critical a period in their political concerns. We have felt the feebleness of the ties by which these United-States are held together, and the want of sufficient energy in our present confederation, to manage, in some instances, our general concerns. Various expedients have been proposed to remedy these evils, but none have succeeded. At length a Convention of the states has been assembled, they have formed a constitution which will now, probably, be submitted to the people to ratify or reject, who are the fountain of all power, to whom alone it of right belongs to make or unmake constitutions, or forms of government, at their pleasure. The most important question that was ever proposed to your decision, or to the decision of any people under heaven, is before you, and you are to decide upon it by men of your own election, chosen specially for this purpose. If the constitution, offered to your acceptance, be a wise one, calculated to preserve the invaluable blessings of liberty, to secure the inestimable rights of mankind, and promote human happiness, then, if you accept it, you will lay a lasting foundation of happiness for millions yet unborn; generations to come will rise up and call you blessed. . . . But if, on the other hand, this form of government contains principles that will lead to the subversion of liberty—if it tends to establish a despotism, or, what is worse, a tyrannic aristocracy; then, if you adopt it, this only remaining asylum for liberty will be shut up, and posterity will execrate your memory. . . .

With these few introductory remarks, I shall proceed to a consideration of this constitution:

The first question that presents itself on the subject is, whether a confederated government be the best for the United States or not. Or in other words, whether the thirteen United States should be reduced to one great republic, governed by one legislature, and under the direction of one executive and judicial; or whether they should continue thirteen confederated republics, under the direction and control of a supreme federal head for certain defined national purposes only?

This enquiry is important, because, although the government reported by the convention does not go to a perfect and entire consolidation,[1] yet it

---

1. The Anti-federalists charged that the proposed Constitution aimed not at federalism (a division of powers between the national government and the state governments) but at consolidation (the centralization of all powers in the national government).

approaches so near to it, that it must, if executed, certainly and infallibly terminate in it.

This government is to possess absolute and uncontrolable power, legislative, executive and judicial, with respect to every object to which it extends, for by the last clause of section 8th, article 1st, it is declared "that the Congress shall have power to make all laws which shall be necessary and proper for carrying into execution the foregoing powers, and all other powers vested by this constitution, in the government of the United States; or in any department or office thereof." And by the 6th article, it is declared "that this constitution, and the laws of the United States, which shall be made in pursuance thereof, and the treaties made, or which shall be made, under the authority of the United States, shall be the supreme law of the land; and the judges in every state shall be bound thereby, any thing in the constitution, or law of any state to the contrary notwithstanding." It appears from these articles that there is no need of any intervention of the state governments, between the Congress and the people, to execute any one power vested in the general government, and that the constitution and laws of every state are nullified and declared void, so far as they are or shall be inconsistent with this constitution, or the laws made in pursuance of it, or with treaties made under the authority of the United States.—The government then, so far as it extends, is a complete one, and not a confederation. It is as much one complete government as that of New-York or Massachusetts, has as absolute and perfect powers to make and execute all laws, to appoint officers, institute courts, declare offences, and annex penalties, with respect to every object to which it extends, as any other in the world. So far therefore as its powers reach, all ideas of confederation are given up and lost. It is true this government is limited to certain objects, or to speak more properly, some small degree of power is still left to the states, but a little attention to the powers vested in the general government, will convince every candid man, that if it is capable of being executed, all that is reserved for the individual states must very soon be annihilated, except so far as they are barely necessary to the organization of the general government. The powers of the general legislature extend to every case that is of the least importance—there is nothing valuable to human nature, nothing dear to freemen, but what is within its power. It has authority to make laws which will affect the lives, the liberty, and property of every man in the United States; nor can the constitution or laws of any state, in any way prevent or impede the full and complete execution of every power given. The legislative power is competent to lay taxes, duties, imposts, and excises—there is no limitation to this power, unless it be said that the clause which directs the use to which those taxes, and duties shall be applied, may be said to be a limitation: but this is no restriction of the power at all, for by this clause they are to be applied to pay the debts and provide for the common defence and general welfare of the United States; but the legislature have authority to contract debts at their discretion; they are the sole judges of what is necessary to provide for the common defence, and they only are to determine what is for the general welfare; this power therefore is neither more nor less, than a power to lay and collect taxes, imposts, and excises, at their pleasure; not only [is] the power to lay taxes unlimited, as to the amount they may require, but it is perfect and absolute to raise them in any mode they please. No state legislature, or any power in the state governments, have any more to do in carrying this into effect, than the authority of one state has to do with that of another. In the business therefore of laying and collecting taxes, the idea of confederation is totally lost, and that of one entire republic is embraced. . . .

Let us now proceed to enquire, as I at first proposed, whether it be best the thirteen United States should be reduced to one great republic, or not? It is here taken for granted, that all agree in this, that whatever government we adopt, it ought to be a free one; that it should be so framed as to secure the liberty of the citizens of America, and such an one as to admit of a full, fair, and equal representation of the people. The question then will be, whether a government thus constituted, and founded on such principles, is practicable, and can be exercised over the whole United States, reduced into one state?

If respect is to be paid to the opinion of the greatest and wisest men who have ever thought or wrote on the science of government, we shall be constrained to conclude, that a free republic cannot succeed over a country of such immense extent, containing such a number of inhabitants, and these encreasing in such rapid progression as that of the whole United States. Among the many illustrious authorities which might be produced to this point, I shall content myself with quoting only two. The one is the baron de Montesquieu, spirit of laws, chap. xvi. vol. I [book VIII].[2] "It is natural to a republic to have only a small territory, otherwise it cannot long subsist. In a large republic there are men of large fortunes, and consequently of less moderation; there are trusts too great to be placed in any single subject; he has interest of his own; he soon begins to think that he may be happy, great and glorious, by oppressing his fellow citizens; and that he may raise himself to grandeur on the ruins of his country. In a large republic, the public good is sacrificed to a thousand views; it is subordinate to exceptions, and depends on accidents. In a small one, the interest of the public is easier perceived, better understood, and more within the reach of every citizen; abuses are of less extent, and of course are less protected." Of the same opinion is the marquis Beccaria.[3]

History furnishes no example of a free republic, any thing like the extent of the United States. The Grecian republics were of small extent; so also was that of the Romans. Both of these, it is true, in process of time, extended their conquests over large territories of country; and the con-

2. Baron Charles de Montesquieu was an eighteenth-century French political theorist whose ideas were highly influential in the era of the American Revolution and the Constitution.
3. Cesare Beccaria was an eighteenth-century Italian legal philosopher.

sequence was, that their governments were changed from that of free governments to those of the most tyrannical that ever existed in the world.

Not only the opinion of the greatest men, and the experience of mankind, are against the idea of an extensive republic, but a variety of reasons may be drawn from the reason and nature of things, against it. In every government, the will of the sovereign is the law. In despotic governments, the supreme authority being lodged in one, his will is law, and can be as easily expressed to a large extensive territory as to a small one. In a pure democracy the people are the sovereign, and their will is declared by themselves; for this purpose they must all come together to deliberate, and decide. This kind of government cannot be exercised, therefore, over a country of any considerable extent; it must be confined to a single city, or at least limited to such bounds as that the people can conveniently assemble, be able to debate, understand the subject submitted to them, and declare their opinion concerning it.

In a free republic, although all laws are derived from the consent of the people, yet the people do not declare their consent by themselves in person, but by representatives, chosen by them, who are supposed to know the minds of their constituents, and to be possessed of integrity to declare this mind.

In every free government, the people must give their assent to the laws by which they are governed. This is the true criterion between a free government and an arbitrary one. The former are ruled by the will of the whole, expressed in any manner they may agree upon; the latter by the will of one, or a few. If the people are to give their assent to the laws, by persons chosen and appointed by them, the manner of the choice and the number chosen, must be such, as to possess, be disposed, and consequently qualified to declare the sentiments of the people; for if they do not know, or are not disposed to speak the sentiments of the people, the people do not govern, but the sovereignty is in a few. Now, in a large extended country, it is impossible to have a representation, possessing the sentiments, and of integrity, to declare the minds of the people, without having it so numerous and unwieldy, as to be subject in great measure to the inconveniency of a democratic government.

The territory of the United States is of vast extent; it now contains near three millions of souls, and is capable of containing much more than ten times that number. Is it practicable for a country, so large and so numerous as they will soon become, to elect a representation, that will speak their sentiments, without their becoming so numerous as to be incapable of transacting public business? It certainly is not.

In a republic, the manners, sentiments, and interests of the people should be similar. If this be not the case, there will be a constant clashing of opinions; and the representatives of one part will be continually striving against those of the other. This will retard the operations of government, and prevent such conclusions as will promote the public good. If we apply this remark to the condition of the United States, we shall be convinced that it forbids that we should be one government. The United States includes a variety of climates. The productions of the different parts of the union are very variant, and their interests, of consequence, diverse. Their manners and habits differ as much as their climates and productions; and their sentiments are by no means coincident. The laws and customs of the several states are, in many respects, very diverse, and in some opposite; each would be in favor of its own interests and customs, and, of consequence, a legislature, formed of representatives from the respective parts, would not only be too numerous to act with any care or decision, but would be composed of such heterogenous and discordant principles, as would constantly be contending with each other.

The laws cannot be executed in a republic, of an extent equal to that of the United States, with promptitude.

The magistrates in every government must be supported in the execution of the laws, either by an armed force, maintained at the public expence for that purpose; or by the people turning out to aid the magistrate upon his command, in case of resistance.

In despotic governments, as well as in all the monarchies of Europe, standing armies are kept up to execute the commands of the prince or the magistrate, and are employed for this purpose when occasion requires: But they have always proved the destruction of liberty, and [are] abhorrent to the spirit of a free republic. In England, where they depend upon the parliament for their annual support, they have always been complained of as oppressive and unconstitutional, and are seldom employed in executing of the laws; never except on extraordinary occasions, and then under the direction of a civil magistrate.

A free republic will never keep a standing army to execute its laws. It must depend upon the support of its citizens. But when a government is to receive its support from the aid of the citizens, it must be so constructed as to have the confidence, respect, and affection of the people. Men who, upon the call of the magistrate, offer themselves to execute the laws, are influenced to do it either by affection to the government, or from fear; where a standing army is at hand to punish offenders, every man is actuated by the latter principle, and therefore, when the magistrate calls, will obey: but, where this is not the case, the government must rest for its support upon the confidence and respect which the people have for their government and laws. The body of the people being attached, the government will always be sufficient to support and execute its laws, and to operate upon the fears of any faction which may be opposed to it, not only to prevent an opposition to the execution of the laws themselves, but also to compel the most of them to aid the magistrate; but the people will not be likely to have such confidence in their rulers, in a republic so extensive as the United States, as necessary for these purposes. The confidence which the people have in their rulers, in a free republic, arises from their knowing them, from their being responsible to them for their conduct, and from the power they have of displacing them when they misbehave: but in a republic of the extent of this continent, the people in general would be acquainted with very few of their rulers: the people at large would know little of their proceedings, and it would be extremely difficult to change them. . . . The consequence will be, they will have no confidence in their legislature, suspect them of ambitious views, be jealous of every measure they adopt, and will not support the laws they pass. Hence the government will be nerveless and inefficient, and no way will be left to render it otherwise, but by establishing an armed force to execute the laws at the point of the bayonet—a government of all others the most to be dreaded.

In a republic of such vast extent as the United-States, the legislature cannot attend to the various concerns and wants of its different parts. It cannot be sufficiently numerous to be acquainted with the local condition and wants of the different districts, and if it could, it is impossible it should have sufficient time to attend to and provide for all the variety of cases of this nature, that would be continually arising.

In so extensive a republic, the great officers of government would soon become above the control of the people, and abuse their power to the purpose of aggrandizing themselves, and oppressing them. The trust committed to the executive offices, in a country of the extent of the United-States, must be various and of magnitude. The command of all the troops and navy of the republic, the appointment of officers, the power of pardoning offences, the collecting of all the public revenues, and the power of expending them, with a number of other powers, must be lodged and exercised in every state, in the hands of a few. When these are attended with great honor and emolument, as they always will be in large states, so as greatly to interest men to pursue them, and to be proper objects for ambitious and designing men, such men will be ever restless in their pursuit after them. They will use the power, when they have acquired it, to the purposes of gratifying their own interest and ambition, and it is scarcely possible, in a very large republic, to call them to account for their misconduct, or to prevent their abuse of power.

These are some of the reasons by which it appears, that a free republic cannot long subsist over a country of the great extent of these states. If then this new constitution is calculated to consolidate the thirteen states into one, as it evidently is, it ought not to be adopted. . . .

DISCUSSION QUESTIONS

1. How do the Federalists and the Anti-federalists view human nature? Why does Madison think individuals are "much more disposed to vex and oppress each other than to co-operate for their common good"? Why is

Brutus more hopeful that, under the proper political circumstances, citizens will cooperate for their common good? Whose perspective on human nature do you find more persuasive?

2. How do the Federalists and the Anti-federalists view participation by ordinary citizens at the local level? Why does Madison feel that "pure democracy" leads to disaster? Why does Brutus have a more positive view of politics within local communities? Do you think a "face-to-face" politics of ordinary citizens fosters individual growth and public spirit or produces ignorant decisions and unfairness to minorities?

3. How do the Federalists and the Anti-federalists view the role of elected representatives? Why does Madison want representatives to deliberate at a distance from the demands of their constituents? Why does Brutus want representatives to be closely tied to their constituents' ideas and interests? Do you think, like Madison, that representatives should be trustees who do what they think is best for the country, or do you believe, like Brutus, that representatives should be delegates who follow the expressed wishes of their constituents?

4. In what ways is the debate between Madison and Brutus reflected in today's political debates? In what ways have the arguments changed? Do contemporary defenders of a large policy role for the federal government share Madison's fundamental assumptions? Do contemporary critics of the federal government share Brutus's fundamental assumptions?

SUGGESTED READINGS AND INTERNET RESOURCES

The best source on the debate between the Federalists and the Anti-federalists is the original texts themselves. For inexpensive editions, see Clinton Rossiter, ed., *The Federalist Papers* (New York: Mentor Books, 1999), and Ralph Ketcham, ed., *The Anti-Federalist Papers* (New York: Mentor Books, 1996). On the political ideas of the founding era, see Gordon S. Wood, *The Creation of the American Republic, 1776–1787* (Chapel Hill: University of North Carolina Press, 1998), and Jack N. Rakove, *Original Meanings: Politics and Ideas in the Making of the Constitution* (New York: Knopf, 1996). In *If Men Were Angels: James Madison and the Heartless Empire of Reason* (Lawrence: University Press of Kansas, 1995), Richard K. Matthews provides a provocative interpretation of the great Federalist's political theory. Instructive commentaries on the political philosophy of the Anti-federalists are Herbert J. Storing, *What the Anti-Federalists Were For* (Chicago: University of Chicago Press, 1981), and Saul Cornell, *The Other Founders: Anti-Federalism and the Dissenting Tradition in America, 1788–1828* (Chapel Hill: University of North Carolina Press, 1999).

Emory Law School
www.law.emory.edu/FEDERAL
This searchable index of information on the Constitution and *The Federalist Papers* requires a forms-capable browser.

The Founders' Constitution
www.press-pubs.uchicago.edu/founders/
This site presents over 3,200 pages of documents containing the founders' ideas and arguments about the U.S. Constitution.

Democracy: Overrated or Undervalued?

Almost everybody in America believes in democracy. When Americans are asked by interviewers about basic questions of majority rule, equality of opportunity, or individual freedom, more than 95 percent profess a belief in democratic values. As our introduction to this book suggests, however, once we probe a bit deeper into what Americans think democracy means, we find that they are not at all of one mind about how far democracy should extend into political, social, and economic life. Elite democrats believe that democracy is a valuable method for selecting those who will govern us, but they are skeptical about the political capacities and interests of ordinary citizens and want important decisions left to those with experience and expertise. Popular democrats distrust elites as potentially self-serving and believe that under the right circumstances ordinary citizens are both capable of and entitled to a significant share in deciding public matters.

The debate over democracy began at the time of the nation's founding and has continued to this day. In the previous chapter, we saw Federalists and Anti-federalists arguing about whether the American experiment in self-government should rest on elite democracy or popular democracy. To James Madison, only a national republic manned by a deliberative elite, who could filter out the irrational passions of the public, could sustain the American experiment. In the eyes of Brutus, this national republic would breed an oppressive aristocracy, who would crush popular democracy, which must be rooted in law-abiding and virtuous citizens and flourish at the local and state levels.

Although the Federalists prevailed in the original American debate over democracy, securing the ratification of the Constitution, nineteenth-century

America looked more like the Anti-federalists' (and Thomas Jefferson's) vision of democracy than the Federalists'. For most of the century, political and economic life was small scale and decentralized, with the federal government in Washington, D.C., exercising only limited powers. Nineteenth-century America witnessed the establishment of the most democratic society the world had contained since the Golden Era of democracy in ancient Athens. Levels of political involvement and rates of voting among ordinary citizens were remarkably high—much higher, in fact, than they would be a century later. To be sure, this was a white man's democracy; Native Americans, African Americans, and women paid a high price for white men's freedoms, and the latter two groups had to launch long and painful struggles for democratic inclusion that would not achieve much success until the twentieth century.

The transformation of the United States between the Civil War and World War I from a largely agrarian and decentralized society into an urbanized and industrialized nation called into question the popular democratic assumptions held by the heirs of the Anti-federalists and Jefferson. Could ordinary citizens obtain, understand, and act on the increasingly complex information that characterized modern American society? America's premier journalist, Walter Lippmann, argued in the 1920s that ordinary citizens viewed the world through stereotypes, simplistic pictures that distorted reality, and that effective government for the industrial age required a greater emphasis on trained, dispassionate experts. Agreeing with Lippmann that the American public had been eclipsed by forces that seemed beyond its control, America's premier philosopher, John Dewey, warned of the elitist tendencies of Lippmann's experts. Dewey sought to revive popular democracy in face-to-face communities where ordinary citizens, informed by the latest findings of social science, would participate in public affairs.

In the 1950s (like the 1920s, a decade of apparent public apathy), Lippmann's argument received reinforcement from the empirical surveys conducted by political scientists. Most Americans, these surveys suggested, were not very interested in political life, did not know much about public affairs, and did not participate at very high levels in politics. Prevailing American conceptions about democracy would have to be modified, many political scientists now argued, to reflect what Robert Dahl called "citizenship without politics." But a minority of political scientists began in the 1960s to object, on both theoretical and empirical grounds, to this redefinition of democracy, claiming that the new perspective was less democratic realism than it was democratic elitism. These critics found support among the emerging political movements that would mark the 1960s as a decade of popular democratic upsurge. Students for a Democratic Society (SDS), the most important organization of the '60s New Left, gave the period its political watchword: *participatory democracy.*

Our selections in this chapter, excerpted from books published in 1999, are two of the latest versions of America's enduring debate over democracy. John Mueller attacks what he considers to be the romantic and unrealistic conception of democracy put forward by popular democrats. All that is required for democracy, Mueller contends, is a political system that eschews violence and that allows citizens to criticize, pressure, and remove those in power. Democracy, he suggests, will always consist of a messy, unequal conflict for advantage among special interests. What it will never achieve, he argues, are the misty ideals of popular democrats: political equality, participation, and an enlightened citizenry. Holding democracy to these standards only fosters cynicism. Mueller's analysis updates the classic elite democratic perspective of Madison, Lippmann, and Dahl.

Paul Rogat Loeb represents the popular democratic perspective of the Anti-federalists, Jefferson, Dewey, and the SDS. He ascribes the widespread cynicism about politics in the 1990s not to the romantic ideals of popular democrats but to the skeptical views of public involvement broadcast by the dominant forces in American society. "We've all but forgotten," he writes, "that public participation is the very soul of democratic citizenship, and how much it can enrich our lives." In our selection, Loeb tells the story of Pete Knutson (one of many stories in his book), a commercial fisherman who organized his fellow fishermen, environmentalists, and Native Americans to defeat an initiative by large industries that would have destroyed salmon spawning grounds. Loeb argues that active citizenship is required both to fulfill our responsibility to take care of the common good and to grow as individuals in psychological and spiritual depth.

Evaluating the debate between Mueller and Loeb should help to clarify your own conception of democracy. Do you believe, with Mueller, that Americans have many more interesting things to do than spend their time on political pursuits? Or do you believe, with Loeb, that political involvement is necessary for a sense of freedom and personal dignity? Do you believe, with Mueller, that self-interest and inequality will always characterize democracy and that attempts to reduce their influence through political and economic reforms will inevitably fail? Or do you believe, with Loeb, that politics can also reflect our more social impulses and can redress political and economic injustices? Above all, do you agree with Mueller that acceptance of elite democracy is the only realistic perspective, or do you agree with Loeb that the abandonment of popular democracy is a surrender to cynicism?

Democracy's Romantic Myths

JOHN MUELLER

T here is a famous Norman Rockwell painting that purports to portray democracy in action. It depicts a New England town meeting in which a workingman has risen in a contentious situation to present his point of view. His rustic commonsense, it appears, has cut through the indecisiveness and bickering to provide a consensual solution to the problem at hand, and the others in the picture are looking up at him admiringly.

As it happens, that misty-eyed, idealized snapshot has almost nothing to do with democracy in actual practice. Democracy is not a process in which one shining idea conquers all as erstwhile contenders fall into blissful consensus. Rather, it is an extremely disorderly muddle in which clashing ideas and interests (all of them "special") do unkempt and unequal, if peaceful, battle and in which ideas are often reduced to slogans, data to distorted fragments, evidence to gestures, and arguments to poses. Speculation is rampant, caricature is routine, and posturing is de rigueur. If one idea wins out, it is likely to be severely compromised in the process, and no one goes away entirely reconciled or happy. And there is rarely a sense of completion or finality or permanence: in a democracy, as Tod Lindberg points out, "the fat lady never sings." It's a mess, and the only saving grace is that other methods for reaching decisions are even worse.

. . . I develop an approach to democracy that contrasts substantially with the romantic Rockwell ideal. It stresses petition and lobbying—the chaotic and distinctly nonconsensual combat of "special interests"—as the dominant and central characteristic of democracy and it suggests that while elections are useful and often valuable in a democracy, they may not be absolutely necessary. I also argue that democracy in practice is not about equality, but rather about the freedom to become politically unequal, and that it functions not so much by rule by the majority as by minority rule with majority acquiescence. . . .

. . . I also contrast democracy with other governmental forms. Although the advantage is only comparative, democracy seems to do better at generating effective governments, choosing leaders, addressing minority concerns, creating a livable society, and functioning effectively with real, flawed human beings. . . .

In defining democracy, it is particularly important, I think, to separate the essential institution itself from the operating devices that are commonly associated with it—mechanisms like written constitutions, the separation of powers or "checks and balances" (including an independent judiciary), and even elections. Any definition of democracy is inadequate, I think, if it can logically be taken to suggest that Britain (which has neither a written constitution nor separation of powers) is not a democracy or that Switzerland did not become one until 1971 (when women were finally given the vote). . . .

In my view, democracy is characterized by government that is necessarily and routinely responsive—although this responsiveness is not always even, fair, or equal. It comes into effect when the people effectively agree not to use violence to replace the leadership, and the leadership effectively leaves them free to criticize, to pressure, to organize, and to try to dislodge it by any other means. This approach can be used to set up a sort of sliding scale of governmental forms. An *authoritarian* government may effectively and sometimes intentionally allow a degree of opposition—a limited amount of press disagreement, for example, or the freedom to complain privately, something sometimes known as the freedom of conversation. But it will not tolerate organized attempts to replace it, even if they are peaceful. A *totalitarian* government does not allow even those limited freedoms. On the other end of the scale is *anarchy:* a condition which holds when a government "allows" the use of violence to try to overthrow it—presumably mainly out of weakness or ineffectiveness.

Authoritarian and even totalitarian governments can sometimes be responsive as well, of course. But their responsiveness depends on the will and the mindset of the leadership. By contrast, democracy is *routinely, necessarily* responsive: because people are free to develop and use peaceful methods to criticize, pressure, and replace the leadership, the leaders must pay attention to their critics and petitioners.

It seems to me that the formal and informal institutional mechanisms variously applied in democracies to facilitate this core consideration are secondary—though this does not mean that all institutions are equally fair or efficient. One can embellish this central democratic relationship with concerns about ethos, way of life, social culture, shared goals, economic correlates, common purposes, customs, preferred policy outcomes, norms, patriotism, shared traditions, and the like. These issues are interesting, but . . . they don't seem to be essential or necessary to the functioning of democracy. . . .

Apathy

. . . One of the great, neglected aspects of free speech is the freedom not to listen. As Hubert Humphrey reportedly put it, "The right to be heard doesn't automatically include the right to be taken seriously."[1] It is no easy task to

---

1. Hubert Humphrey was a Democratic senator from Minnesota and served as vice president under President Lyndon B. Johnson.

persuade free people to agree with one's point of view, but as any experienced demagogue is likely to point out with some exasperation, what is most difficult of all is to get them to pay attention at all. People, particularly those in a free, open society, are regularly barraged by shysters and schemers, by people with new angles and neglected remedies, with purveyors of panaceas and palliatives. Very few are successful—and even those who do succeed, including Adolf Hitler, owe their success as much to luck as to skill.

. . . [Such] apathy helps importantly with the problem that is usually called the tyranny of the majority. It is not difficult to find a place where the majority harbors a considerable hatred for a minority—indeed, it may be difficult to find one where this is not the case. Polls in the United States regularly have found plenty of people who would cheerfully restrict not only the undeserving rich, but also homosexuals, atheists, accused Communists, Nazi paraders, flag burners, and people who like to shout unpleasant words and perpetrate unconventional messages. But it is not easy to get this majority to do anything about it—after all, that would require a certain amount of work.

Because of apathy, therefore, people, sometimes despite their political predispositions, are effectively tolerant. For democracies the danger is not so much that agile demagogues will play on hatreds and weaknesses to fabricate a vindictive mob-like tyranny of the majority: the perversions of the French Revolution have proved unusual. More to be feared, it seems, is the tyranny of a few who obtain bland acquiescence from the uninterested, and essentially unaffected, many. . . .

The Quest for Political Equality

. . . The notion that all men are created equal suggests that people are *born* equal—that is, that none should necessarily be denied political opportunity merely because of their hereditary entrance into the wrong social or economic class or because they do not adhere to the visions or dictates of a particular ideological group. The notion does not, however, suggest that people must necessarily be equal in their impact on the political system, but this damaging extrapolation is often made by reformers, at least as a goal to be quested after.

An extensive study on the issue of equality by a team of political scientists finds, none too surprisingly, that people in a real democracy like the United States differ in the degree to which they affect the political system. Political effectiveness, the study concludes, depends on three varying factors: resources, especially time, money, and skills; psychological engagement with politics; and "access to networks through which individuals can be recruited to political life." The variance of effectiveness, the authors then conclude, poses a "threat to the democratic principle of equal protection of interests." Another analyst, reviewing their findings, makes a similar observation: "liberal democracies fail to live up to the norm of equal responsiveness to the interests of each citizen."

But instead of seeking to reform the system or the people who make it up, we may want instead to abandon, or at least substantially to modify, the principle and the norm. They clearly express a romantic perspective about democracy, a perspective which has now been fully and repeatedly disconfirmed in practice. Democracies are responsive and attentive to the interests of the citizenry—at least when compared to other forms of government—but they are nowhere near equally responsive to the interests of each citizen.

Related is the perennial clamor against "special interests." As the futile struggle for campaign finance reform in the United States suggests, people who want or need to influence public policy are very likely to find ways to do so no matter how clever the laws that seek to restrict them. As Gil Troy observes, "for all the pious hopes, the goal of the Watergate-era reforms—to remove the influence of money from presidential elections—was, in hard and inescapable fact, ridiculous." (He also notes that the entire cost of the 1996 election campaigns was about 25 percent of what Procter & Gamble routinely spends every year to market its products.) A rare voice of realism amid all the sanctimonious, politically correct bluster from politicians about campaign finance reform in the United States in the 1990s was that of Senator Robert Bennett of Utah: "rich people will always have influence in politics, and the solution is not to create barriers that cause the rich people to spend even more money to hire lawyers and consultants to find ways around the law to get the same results."

In the end, "special interests" can be effectively reined in only by abandoning democracy itself, because their activities are absolutely vital to the form. Indeed, it is quite incredible that two prominent Washington reporters merely deem it "simplistic" to argue that "people with common interests should not attempt to sway government policy." In a democracy the free, competitive play of "special interests" is fundamental. To reform this out of existence would be uncomprehending and profoundly anti-democratic.

Most of the agitation against political inequality is focused on the special privileges business is presumed to enjoy. For example, concern is voiced that the attention of public officials can be differently arrested: "a phone call from the CEO of a major employer in the district may carry considerably more weight than one from an unknown constituent." It is possible, of course, that the unweighty and unknown constituent has just come up with a plan which will achieve permanent worldwide bliss in the course of the next six months, but, since there are only twenty-four hours in a day, public officials (like the rest of us) are forced to ration their time, and they are probably correct to assume, as a first approximation at least, that the concerns of a major employer are likely to be of wider relevance to more people than are those of the hapless lone constituent.

But if the CEO's access advantage to a time-pressured politician is somehow reprehensible and must be reformed, what about other inequalities—that is, why focus only on economic ones? A telephone call from a big-time political columnist like David Broder of the *Washington Post* is likely to get the politician's attention even faster than that of the CEO. Should the influential David Broder hold off on his next column until the rest of us deserving unknowns have had a chance to put in our two cents in the same forum? Inequalities like these are simply and unavoidably endemic to the whole political system as, indeed, they are to life itself. It may be possible to reduce this inequality, but it is difficult to imagine a reform that could possibly raise the political impact of the average factory worker—or even of the average business executive—remotely to equal that enjoyed by Broder. . . .

The Quest for Participation

Democratic theorists, idealists, and image-makers maintain that "democratic states require . . . participation in order to flourish," or that "a politically active citizenry is a requisite of any theory of democracy," or that "democracy was built on the principle that political participation was not only the privilege of every man, but a necessity in ensuring the efficiency and prosperity of the democratic system," or that "high levels of electoral participation are essential for guaranteeing that government represents the public as a whole," or that "to make a democracy that works, we need citizens who are engaged."

But we now have over two hundred years of experience with living, breathing, messy democracy, and truly significant participation has almost never been achieved anywhere. Since democracy exists, *it simply can't be true* that wide participation is a notable requirement, requisite, guarantee, need, or necessity for it to prosper or work. Routinely, huge numbers of citizens even—in fact, especially—in "mature" democracies simply decline to participate, and the trend in participation seems to be, if anything, mostly downward. In the United States, nearly half of those eligible fail to vote even in high-visibility elections and only a few percent ever actively participate in politics. The final winner of a recent election for the mayor of Rochester, N.Y., received only about 6 percent of the vote of the total electorate. (However, he is a very popular choice: if everybody had voted, he would almost certainly have achieved the same victory.) Switzerland is Europe's oldest democracy, and it also boasts the continent's lowest voter turnout.

Statistics like these frequently inspire a great deal of concern—after all, it is argued, "political participation" is one of the "basic democratic ideals." But it may be more useful to reshape democratic theories and ideals to take notice of the elemental fact that democracy works even though it often fails to inspire very much in the way of participation from its citizenry.

And it might also be asked, why, exactly, is it so important for citizens to participate? Most analyses suggest that nonvoters do not differ all that much from voters in their policy concerns, though there are some (controversial) suggestions that leftist parties might do a bit better in some countries if everyone were forced to vote. However, once in office, responsible leftist and rightist parties both face the same constraining conditions and, despite their ideologies and campaign promises, often do not differ all that much from each other in their policies—frequently to the disillusionment and disgust of their supporters who may come to feel they have been conned.

Some hold voting to be important because "of the problem of legitimacy." The idea is that "as fewer and fewer citizens participate in elections, the extent to which government truly rests on the consent of the governed may be called into question"; moreover the "quality of the link between elites and citizens" will erode. Actually, such callings into question seem to happen mostly when a candidate, like Bill Clinton in 1992, gets less than half of the recorded *vote*—and these are principally inspired by partisan maneuvering by the losers to undercut any claim that the winner has a mandate. And in local elections, the often exceedingly low turnout and participation levels rarely even cause much notice: I have yet to hear anyone suggest that the mayor of Rochester is illegitimate or "unlinked" because hardly anybody managed to make it to the polls when he was elected.

Moreover, it really seems to strain credulity to suggest that "if people feel distant from the electoral process, they can take no pride in the successes of the government." *No* pride? It seems that even nonvoters celebrated victory in the Gulf War. Or that nonvoters "avoid responsibility for the problems facing the nation." But nonvoters seem to have no more difficulty than voters in routinely (and sometimes even correctly) blaming the politicians for whatever is wrong. And it is simply too glib to conclude that "if you don't vote, you don't count." If that were true, women would never have gotten the vote, slavery would still exist, and there would never have been prison reform or legislation aiding the homeless.

There are also claims that low turnout levels "contribute to the problem of an unrepresentative policy agenda." But it is difficult to understand what this could possibly mean—or, better, what a "representative policy agenda" would look like. Agendas are set by people actively trying to pursue their interests; they are not out there somewhere in the miasma waiting for us objectively to snap them up. As Steven Rosenstone and John Mark Hansen argue, "political participation is the product of strategic interactions of citizens and leaders." People "participate when politicians, political parties, interest groups, and activists persuade them to get involved." Thus, there will not be an "ideal" or even "normal" degree of participation. Rather, participation will increase when "salient issues reach the public agenda . . . when governments approach crucial decisions . . . when competitive election campaigns stimulate, when social movements inspire."

Hundreds of years of experience, then, suggest that the pursuit of participation for the sake of participation is rather quixotic. Instead, applying a philosophical observation attributed to impresario Sol Hurok, perhaps we should accept the fact that "if people don't want to come, nothing will stop them." Moreover, discontent and cynicism about the system itself (and consequently perhaps nonvoting) are increased when alarmists passionately lament that many people, as they have throughout democratic eternity, freely decide to pursue interests they find more pressing than politics, or manage to come up with more interesting things to do on election day than to go through the often inconsequential ritual of voting. (Sometimes, actually, nonvoters, by the very act of not voting, may be indicating their concerns and preferences more eloquently than those who actually do vote.)

The Quest for an Enlightened Citizenry

"If a nation expects to be ignorant and free," Thomas Jefferson once said, "it expects what never was and never will be." Pretty much ever since those memorable words were issued, the United States has managed to be both, and with considerable alacrity.

Fortunately for America, eternal vigilance has not proven to be the price of democracy—it can come quite a bit cheaper. In ideal democracies, James Bryce once suggested, "the average citizen will give close and constant attention to public affairs, recognizing that this is his interest as well as his duty"—but not in real ones.[2] And Horace Mann's ringing prediction that "with universal suffrage, there must be universal elevation of character, intellectual and moral, or there will be universal mismanagement and calamity" has proven untrue.[3]

Nonetheless, democratic idealists continue to insist that "democracies require responsibility." Or they contend that democracy "relies on informed popular judgment and political vigilance." Or they persist in defining democracy "as a political system in which people actively attend to what is significant." One would think it would be obvious by now that democracy works despite the fact that it often fails to inspire or require very much in the way of responsibility and knowledge from its citizenry. Democracy does feed on the bandying about of information, but that is going to happen pretty much automatically when people are free to ferret it out and to exchange it. Democracy clearly does not require that people generally be well informed, responsible, or actively attentive.

Recent surveys find that around half the American people haven't the foggiest idea which party controls the Senate or what the first ten amendments of the Constitution are called or what the Fifth Amendment does or who their congressional representative or senators are. Moreover, this lack of knowledge has generally increased (particularly when education is controlled for) since the 1940s. A month after the Republican victory in the 1994 election that propelled the vocal and energetic Newt Gingrich into the speakership of the House of Representatives and into the media stratosphere, a national poll found that 50 percent hadn't heard enough about

2. James Bryce was a British writer who published a classic study, *The American Commonwealth,* in the late nineteenth century.
3. Horace Mann was a nineteenth-century educational reformer.

Gingrich even to have an opinion about him. Four months later, after endless publicity over Gingrich's varying fortunes and after *Time* magazine had designated him its "Man of the Year," that number had not changed (so much for the power of the press). In a poll conducted two years later, half were still unable to indicate who the speaker was. Meanwhile, less than 20 percent guessed correctly that over the preceding twenty years air pollution and the number of the elderly living in poverty had declined, and most people were of the wildly distorted impression that foreign aid comprised a larger share of the federal budget than Medicare.

One recent analysis observes that "for the last 200 years the United States has survived as a stable democracy, despite continued evidence of an uninformed public." It also notes that "in theory, a democracy requires knowledgeable citizens." Although it then labels the contradictory condition "the paradox of modern democracy," it seems, rather, that it is the theory that should be called into question, not the reality.

Moreover, it may not be entirely clear why one should expect people to spend a lot of time worrying about politics when democratic capitalism not only leaves them free to choose other ways to get their kicks, but in its seemingly infinite quest for variety is constantly developing seductive distractions. Democratic theorists and idealists may be intensely interested in government and its processes, but it verges on the arrogant, even the self-righteous, to suggest that other people are somehow inadequate or derelict unless they share the same curious passion. Many studies have determined that it is the politically interested who are the most politically active. It is also doubtless true that those most interested in unidentified flying objects are the ones most likely to join UFO clubs. UFO enthusiasts, however, get no special credit by political theorists for servicing their particular obsession, while politics junkies are lauded because they seem to be fulfilling a higher, theory-sanctified function.

In the end, the insistence that terrible things will happen unless the citizenry becomes addicted to C-SPAN can inspire cynicism about the process when it is observed that the Beverly Hillbillies (or whatever) enjoy vastly higher ratings.

The Active Citizen

PAUL ROGAT LOEB

I n the personal realm, most Americans are thoughtful, caring, generous. We try to do our best by family and friends. At times we'll even stop to help another driver stranded with a roadside breakdown, or give some spare change to a stranger. But increasingly, a wall now separates each of us from the world outside, and from others who've likewise taken refuge in their own private sanctuaries. We've all but forgotten that public participation is the very soul of democratic citizenship, and how much it can enrich our lives.

However, the reason for our wholesale retreat from social involvement is not, I believe, that most of us feel all is well with the world. I live in Seattle, a city with a seemingly unstoppable economy. Yet every time I go downtown I see men and women with signs saying "I'll work for food," or "Homeless vet. Please help." Their suffering diminishes me as a human being. I also travel extensively, doing research and giving lectures throughout the country. Except in the wealthiest of enclaves, people everywhere say, "Things are hard here." America's economic boom has passed many of us by. We struggle to live on meager paychecks. We worry about layoffs, random violence, the rising cost of health care, and the miseducation of our kids. Too stretched to save, uncertain about Social Security, many of us wonder just how we'll survive when we get old. We feel overwhelmed, we say, and helpless to change things.

Even those of us who are economically comfortable seem stressed. We spend hours commuting on crowded freeways, and hours more at jobs whose demands never end. We complain that we don't have enough time left for families and friends. We worry about the kind of world we'll pass on to our grandchildren. Then we also shrug and say there's nothing we can do.

To be sure, the issues we now face are complex—perhaps more so than in the past. How can we comprehend the moral implications of a world in which Nike pays Michael Jordan more to appear in its ads than it pays all the workers at its Indonesian shoe factories combined? Today the five hundred richest people on the planet control more wealth than the bottom three billion, half of the human population. Is it possible even to grasp the process that led to this most extraordinary imbalance? More important, how do we even begin to redress it?

Yet what leaves too many of us sitting on the sidelines is not only a lack of understanding of the complexities of our world. It's not only an absence of readily apparent ways to begin or resume public involvement. Certainly we need to decide for ourselves whether particular causes are wise or foolish—be they the politics of campaign finance reform, attempts to address the growing gap between rich and poor, or efforts to safeguard water, air, and wilderness. We need to identify and connect with worthy groups that take on these issues, whether locally or globally. But first we need to believe that our individual involvement is worthwhile, that what we might do in the public sphere will not be in vain.

This means we face a challenge that is as much psychological as political. As the Ethiopian proverb says, "He who conceals his disease cannot be cured." We need to understand our cultural diseases of callousness, short-sightedness, and denial, and learn what it will take to heal our society and heal our souls. How did so many of us become convinced that we can do nothing to affect our common future? And how have some other Americans managed to remove the cataracts from their vision and work power-fully for change?

When we do take a stand, we grow psychologically and spiritually. Pete Knutson is one of my oldest friends. During his twenty-five years as a com-mercial fisherman in Washington and Alaska, he's been forced, time and again, to respond to the steady degradation of salmon spawning grounds. "You'd have a hard time spawning, too, if you had a bulldozer in your bed-room," he says, explaining the destruction of once-rich salmon habitat by commercial development and timber industry clear-cutting. Pete could have simply accepted this degradation as fate, focusing on getting a maxi-mum share of the dwindling fish populations. Instead, he's gradually built an alliance between Washington State fishermen, environmentalists, and Native American tribes, persuading them to work collectively to demand that the habitat be preserved and restored.

The cooperation Pete created didn't come easy: Washington's fisher-men were historically individualistic and politically mistrustful, more in-clined, in Pete's judgment, "to grumble or blame the Indians than to act." Now, with their new allies, they began to push for cleaner spawning streams, preservation of the Endangered Species Act, and an increased flow of water over major regional dams to help boost salmon runs. But large in-dustrial interests, such as the aluminum companies, feared that these mea-sures would raise their electricity costs or restrict their opportunities for development. So a few years ago they bankrolled a statewide initiative to regulate fishing nets in a way that would eliminate small family fishing operations.

"I think we may be toast," said Pete, when Initiative 640 first surfaced. In an Orwellian twist, its backers even presented the initiative as environ-mentally friendly, to mislead casual voters. It was called "Save Our Sealife," although fishermen soon rechristened it "Save Our Smelters." At first, those opposing 640 thought they had no chance of success: They were outspent, outstaffed, outgunned. Similar initiatives had already passed in Florida, Louisiana, and Texas, backed by similar industrial interests. I remember Pete sitting in a Seattle tavern with two fisherman friends, laughing bitterly and saying, "The three of us are going to take on the aluminum companies? We're going to beat Reynolds and Kaiser?"

But they refused to give up. Instead, Pete and his coworkers systemati-cally enlisted the region's major environmental groups to campaign against the initiative. They worked with the media to explain the larger issues at stake. And they focused public attention on the measure's powerful finan-cial backers, and their interest in its outcome. On election night, November 1995, Initiative 640 was defeated throughout the state. White fishermen, Native American activists, and Friends of the Earth staffers threw their arms around each other in victory. "I'm really proud of you, Dad," Pete's twelve-year-old son kept repeating. Pete was stunned.

"Everyone felt it was hopeless," Pete said, looking back. "But if we were going to lose, I wanted at least to put up a good fight. And we won because of all the earlier work we'd done, year after year, to build up our environmental relationships, get some credibility, and show that we weren't just in it for ourselves."

We often think of social involvement as noble but impractical. Yet as Pete's story attests, it can serve enlightened self-interest and the interests of others simultaneously, while giving us a sense of connection and purpose nearly impossible to find in purely private life. "It takes energy to act," said Pete. "But it's more draining to bury your anger, convince yourself you're powerless, and swallow whatever's handed to you. The times I've compromised my integrity and accepted something I shouldn't, the ghosts of my choices have haunted me. When you get involved in something meaningful, you make your life count. What you do makes a difference. It blows my mind that we beat 640 starting out with just a small group of people who felt it was wrong to tell lies."

In fighting to save the environment and his economic livelihood, Pete strengthened his own soul. How the rest of us might achieve something similar is not always clear. We often don't know where to start. Most of us would like to see people treated more justly, to have the earth accorded the respect it deserves, and to feel less pressure in our lives. But we find it hard to imagine having much of a role in this process. We mistrust our own ability to make a difference. The magnitude of the issues at hand, coupled with this sense of powerlessness, has led far too many of us to conclude that social involvement isn't worth the cost.

Such resignation isn't an innate response, or the creation of some inevitable fate. Rather, it's what psychologists call learned helplessness. Society has systematically taught us to ignore the ills we see, and leave them to others to handle. Understandably, we find it unsettling even to think about crises as huge and profound in their implications as the extinction of species, depletion of the ozone layer, and destruction of the rainforests. Or the desperate poverty that blights entire neighborhoods in our nation's largest cities. We're led to believe that if we can't solve every one of these kinds of problems, we shouldn't bother to become socially active at all. We're also taught to doubt our voice—to feel we lack either the time to properly learn and articulate the issues we care about, or the standing to speak out and be heard. To get socially involved, we believe, requires almost saintlike judgment, confidence, and character—a standard we can never meet. Whatever impulses toward involvement we might have, they're dampened by a culture that demeans idealism, enshrines cynicism, and makes us feel naive for caring about our fellow human beings or the planet we inhabit. . . .

Learned Helplessness

America's prevailing culture of cynicism insists that nothing we do can matter. It teaches us not to get involved in shaping the world we'll pass on to our children. It encourages us to leave such important decisions to others—whether they be corporate and government leaders, or social activists whose lifestyles seem impossibly selfless or foreign. Sadly, and ironically, in a country born of a democratic political revolution, to be American today is to be apolitical. Civic withdrawal has become our norm. To challenge this requires courage. It also requires creating a renewed definition of ourselves as citizens—something closer to the nation of active stakeholders that leaders like Thomas Jefferson had in mind.

The importance of citizens' direct participation in a democracy was expressed thousands of years ago, by the ancient Greeks. In fact, they used the word "idiot" for people incapable of involving themselves in civic life. Now, the very word "political" has become so debased in our culture that we use it to describe either trivial office power plays or the inherently corrupt world of elected leaders. We've lost sight of its original roots in the Greek notion of the polis: the democratic sphere in which citizens, acting in concert, determine the character and direction of their society. "All persons alike," wrote Aristotle, should share "in the government to the utmost." . . .

Bowling Alone

Creating any kind of activist community is harder when the civic associations and institutions that might once have offered a foundation have themselves eroded. In a much-discussed article, "Bowling Alone" [see Chapter 4 of this book], the Harvard political theorist Robert Putnam observes that during the past thirty years Americans have steadily reduced their participation not only in voting, but also in traditional forms of community involvement, such as the PTA, the League of Women Voters, unions, mainstream churches, the Boy Scouts and Campfire Girls, and service clubs like the Lions and Kiwanis. We've squandered the "social capital" that allows people to work together effectively to pursue shared objectives. As a strangely poignant example of this trend, Putnam notes that local bowling leagues have seen a 40 percent decline in membership since 1980. During the same period, however, the number of individuals who actually bowl has risen until it now exceeds the number who vote in congressional elections. These trends bode ill for American democracy, Putnam argues, because the more socially isolated our citizens become, the fewer chances they have for the kinds of civic conversations that fuel involvement in crucial public concerns.

Putnam's critics, like *Atlantic Monthly* writer Nicholas Lemann, have argued that citizens are still just as likely to get involved in community social networks, but that as America's population shifts toward the suburbs, the networks have changed form. Youth soccer leagues, in which parents participate on the weekends, are booming, he says. So are Internet discussion groups and self-help associations like Alcoholics Anonymous. Organizations from NOW and the Sierra Club to the NRA and the Christian Coalition have taken the place of the old political machines.[1]

1. NOW is an acronym for the National Organization for Women; NRA is an acronym for the National Rifle Association.

Such examples notwithstanding, I remain convinced by Putnam's basic proposition, that civic involvement has dropped off significantly. In a follow-up article, Putnam examines a number of possible causes for the decline, including suburbanization, the increased numbers of women in the workforce, and the general demands of modern life. While most of these factors seem to play some role, they don't account for the fact that the decline cuts across cities and suburbs, the married and the single, working men, working women, and stay-at-home moms. The key change during the past fifty years, Putnam concludes, is the steadily increasing influence of television. Regardless of background or current circumstances, the more people watch TV, he finds, the less they involve themselves in civic activities of any kind, and the more mistrusting and pessimistic they become about human nature. As their sense of connectedness and common purpose erodes, they find it easy to scapegoat others, to view the world in prejudicial and unforgiving terms, and to believe that ordinary citizens can do nothing to shape the history of our time. This is all the more troubling given that extensive TV watching now begins in early childhood, taking up as much time among average kids aged nine to fourteen as all other discretionary activities combined. For many adults, TV has gradually replaced nearly every social activity outside the home.

It worries me that so many of us now sit alone for hours on end, passive spectators, paying more attention to the strangers on the screen than to the real people next door. What are the consequences for ourselves and our society? The greatest misfortune, in my view, is that by focusing so much on stories scripted by others, we forfeit the opportunity to create our own.

Fishing Together

Whatever the reasons for our declining civic involvement, we need to rebuild local communities even as we work to expand their vision. Pete Knutson took this approach in working with his fellow fishermen: First he helped create a cohesive community; then he involved its members in larger public issues. Pete, the son of a plainspoken Lutheran minister, grew up in the hardscrabble mill town of Everett, Washington. He had a Barry Goldwater poster on his wall, "because Goldwater spoke his mind."[2] At first Pete supported the Vietnam War, and even got a jingoistic letter published on the *Everett Herald*'s youth page. His views changed as friends who'd enlisted came back, feeling betrayed, and told him, "Don't believe anything the military tells you. They always lie." Before long, Pete was organizing an antiwar moratorium at his high school; then he went off to Stanford, and became the only draft-age man to testify before Congress. He even got his

---

2. Barry Goldwater, a founder of modern American conservatism and a senator from Arizona, was the Republican candidate for president in 1964.

fifteen minutes of fame on the national news, after Strom Thurmond stormed out when Pete had the audacity to ask a Senate committee, "If you're so eager to fight this war, why don't you pick up an M16 and lead the first wave?"

Pete began fishing to work his way through school. Soon, fishing became a way of life, as he bought his own boat, with borrowed money, to support his wife and two young sons. Because he knew his fellow fishermen were powerless in isolation, he helped build the Puget Sound Gillnetters' Association, which enabled members to market fish jointly, lobby on laws that affected them, and gain leverage against the giant canneries. "I felt we had to trust each other," he says. "If we didn't, we had no chance." The association became a base through which fishermen gradually became conversant with large ecological issues, such as the destruction of salmon habitat, upon whose outcome their livelihoods depended.

Pete worked steadily to bridge the gap between fishermen and the generally more middle-class environmentalists. That was no easy task, given long-standing mutual mistrust fed by class divides and stereotypes. Yet a coalition did in fact emerge, and the fishermen brought a powerful blue-collar presence to issues like the Endangered Species Act and habitat protection. When President Clinton visited Seattle for a Pacific Rim trade conference, a parade of fishing boats joined with Greenpeace activists to challenge his environmental timidity. Both Pete's ethical stand and pride in craft were evoked by the bumper sticker on his truck: "Jesus Was a Gillnetter."

This hard-won and unexpected alliance proved critical when Initiative 640 threatened to shut down the gillnetters' operations by banning the nets they used. The fishermen held joint press conferences with the now-supportive environmental groups, picketed a pleasure-boat company that was a prime initial backer of the initiative, and generally refused to succumb quietly to their opponents' well-financed campaign. They survived because Pete, along with a few others, had helped change their vision from one of enlightened self-interest to a more complex and sustainable ethic, best summed up when he spoke of nurturing the salmon habitat "so my kids can fish, too, and everyone's children can inherit a healthy planet." First the fishermen learned to work together, then to reach beyond their own ranks. Building their association's internal cohesion made it easier for them to tackle difficult issues later on. . . .

The Fullness of Time

However we promote social change, we do so in time: We link past, present, and future in our attempts to create a better world. Some historical eras, however, seem more pregnant with possibility than others. . . .

The 1960s were marked by a . . . sense of urgency and creative ferment. Ordinary people worldwide challenged entrenched institutions and policies. They talked of realizing a more humane and generous future. These

movements then collapsed because of powerful opposition, their participants' exhaustion, and some dangerous moments of arrogance. But for a
time, people unleashed powerful dreams.

Our lives today are hardly stagnant. We have access to a world of food,
music, sights, sounds, and healing traditions. We can log onto Websites
from Bangkok and Reykjavik to Nairobi and Calcutta. As technology
changes by leaps and bounds, it alters our lives and the earth at an almost
incomprehensible pace. So does the relentless global economy. Change
happens so fast we can barely keep up.

But politically, we often feel powerless, incapable of moving forward.
We may have witnessed citizens fighting for democracy in the streets of
Prague, Berlin, and Moscow, Tiananmen Square and Soweto, Manila, and
Jakarta. But we saw them from a distance on TV. People risked their lives to
have a say in their common future, but the lessons seemed remote from our
world. They didn't apply to us. Not here, and certainly not now.

It's tempting to gaze back longingly toward the most dramatic periods
of history, while disdaining our own era as unheroic and meaningless.
"People seem so stuck these days," says Ginny Nicarthy. "But things looked
pretty grim in the late 1950s too, when I first got involved. A dozen of us
would picket the bomb shelters or stores that were racist in their hiring, and
people would yell at us, tell us to 'Go back to Russia,' 'Go back to your
kitchen, where you belong.' There were no clear reasons to believe that we
could change things, but somehow we did. We leaped forward, started the
ball rolling, and built enough political mass that it kept going. Maybe we
need to do that again."

Seeding the ground for the next round of highly visible social progress
will take work. Yet major gains for human dignity are possible, even in
seemingly resistant times. Indeed, our efforts may be even more critical
now than in periods when the whole world seems to be watching.

The Turnings of History

Historical contexts can change shape suddenly and dramatically. As Václav
Havel wrote before the epochal Eastern European revolutions, "Hope is not
prognostication."[3] Richard Flacks remembers visiting Berkeley in September
1964 and hearing members of the activist student group SDS complain that
their fellow students were almost terminally apathetic, uncaring, and passive. They said that nothing they could try would work. A few weeks later,
the free speech movement erupted.

We can never predict when a historical mood will suddenly shift and
new hopes and possibilities emerge. But we do know that this shift won't

---

3. Václav Havel, a prominent playwright and a dissident during communist rule in
Czechoslovakia, became president of the Czech Republic.

occur unless someone takes action. Recall the struggle of Susan B. Anthony. She labored her entire life for women's suffrage, then died fourteen years before it was achieved. Thirty years ago, few would have thought that the Soviet bloc would crumble, thanks in part to the persistence of individuals from Havel to Lech Walesa and Andrei Sakharov, who voiced prophetic truths despite all costs. Few would have thought that South Africa would become a democracy, with Nelson Mandela its president. Few would have imagined that women throughout the world would begin to insist on shaping their own destiny. Major victories for human dignity rarely come easily or quickly. But they do come.

"When nothing seems to help," said the early twentieth-century reformer Jacob Riis, "I go and look at a stonecutter hammering away at his rock perhaps a hundred times without as much as a crack showing in it. Yet at the hundred and first blow it will split in two, and I know it was not that blow that did it—but all that had gone before." . . .

Faith and Hope

Even if the past holds no guarantees for the future, we can still take heart from previous examples of courage and vision. We can draw hope from those who came before us, to whom we owe so much. We can remember that history unfolds in ways we can never predict, but that again and again bring astounding transformations, often against the longest of odds. Our strength can come, as I've suggested, from a radical stubbornness, from savoring the richness of our journey, and from the victories we win and the lives that we change. We can draw on the community we build.

More than anything, activists religious and secular keep going because participation is essential to their dignity, to their very identity, to the person they see in the mirror. To stay silent, they say, would be self-betrayal, a violation of their soul. Plainly stated, it would feel cheap and tacky. "That's why we were put here on this earth," they stress again and again. "What better thing can you do with your life?" "There'll be nobody like you ever again," says veteran environmentalist David Brower. "Make the most of every molecule you've got, as long as you've got a second to go. That's your charge."

This means responding to the ills of our time with what Rabbi Abraham Heschel once called "a persistent effort to be worthy of the name human." A technical editor who chaired her local Amnesty International chapter felt demeaned just by knowing about incidents of torture. To do something about it helped her recover her spirit. "When you stand in front of the Creator," says Carol McNulty, "you want to say, 'I tried to make a difference.' It isn't going to be what kind of car I had or how big a house. I'd like to think I tried."

Being true to oneself in this fashion doesn't eradicate human destructiveness. We need to live, as Albert Camus suggests, with a "double memory—a memory of the best and the worst."[4] We can't deny the cynicism and callousness of which humans are capable. We also can't deny the courage and compassion that offer us hope. It's our choice which characteristics we'll steer our lives by. . . .

DISCUSSION QUESTIONS

1. What are the most important differences between the elite democratic perspective and the popular democratic perspective? In your view, which side has the stronger case?

2. Mueller argues that "'special interests' can be effectively reined in only by abandoning democracy itself." Do you agree?

3. Mueller believes that there is no greater intrinsic value in being a "politics junky" than in pursuing any other interest or hobby, while Loeb sees public involvement as essential for personal growth. Is there anything distinctive about political participation that makes it especially worthy of our time and commitments?

4. Are most Americans too preoccupied with their private affairs to pay much attention to public ones, or can they be taught to see critical links between their own needs and interests and the shared pursuit of public goods?

SUGGESTED READINGS AND INTERNET RESOURCES

The classic work on the meaning, practices, and dilemmas of American democracy remains Alexis de Tocqueville, *Democracy in America,* Vols. 1 and 2 (New York: Vintage Books, 1990). Two provocative histories of American democracy are Robert H. Wiebe, *Self-Rule: A Cultural History of American Democracy* (Chicago: University of Chicago Press, 1995), and Michael Schudson, *The Good Citizen: A History of American Civic Life* (Cambridge, Mass.: Harvard University Press, 1999). Perhaps the greatest work of modern political science in the elite democratic vein is Robert A. Dahl, *Who Governs? Democracy and Power in an American City* (New Haven, Conn.: Yale University Press, 1961). For a fascinating study of the 1960s experiment with participatory democracy, see James Miller, *"Democracy Is in the Streets": From Port Huron to the Siege of Chicago* (Cambridge, Mass.: Harvard University Press, 1994). A prominent attempt to develop the theory of participatory democracy is Benjamin Barber, *Strong Democracy: Participatory Politics for a New Age* (Berkeley and Los Angeles: University of California Press, 1984).

4. Albert Camus was a French philosopher and novelist who won the Nobel Prize for Literature in 1957.

Center for Democracy and Citizenship
www.publicwork.org
The Center for Democracy and Citizenship, located at the University of
Minnesota's Hubert H. Humphrey Institute of Public Affairs, offers information
about various citizenship projects as well as information about the center's own
publications; it provides links to other sites on citizenship.

Institute for the Study of Civic Values
www.iscv.org
A nonprofit organization in Philadelphia, its website provides classic articles and
lectures on American democratic values as well as information on civic values
projects.

The Democracy Collaborative
www.democracycollaborative.org
The Democracy Collaborative's website provides scholarly materials "in support
of democratic renewal, civic participation, and community building."

3

The New Federalism: Does It Create Laboratories of Democracy or a Race to the Bottom?

A merican politics often takes a peculiar form: instead of debating *what* policy should be enacted, people argue about *where* the policy decision should be made—at the federal, state, or local level. One side will proclaim its adherence to "states' rights" or "community control," while the other side touts the need for the federal government to guarantee fairness and equal protection of the laws. Usually the two sides are sincere in their defense of different levels of democracy. As you might suspect, however, the debate is not just about ideals but about who will win and who will lose. This is because where decisions are made strongly affects who wins and who loses. This peculiar quality of the "game" of politics in the United States is determined by a system we call *federalism.*

Federalism is a system of government that divides power between a central government and state and local governments. As a concept of government, federalism was born in compromise during the struggle over the U.S. Constitution. Some of the framers of the Constitution favored a unitary system in which all significant powers would be placed in the hands of a central government. Realizing that such a system would never be approved by the

---

Note: Both phrases in the chapter title, "laboratories of democracy" and "race to the bottom," were coined by Louis Brandeis, U.S. Supreme Court justice from 1916 to 1939.

voters, the framers compromised on a system that divided power between the two levels of government. As we saw in Chapter 1, the opponents of the Constitution, the Anti-federalists, still feared that too much power had been given to the federal government at the expense of the states.

The ratification of the Constitution in 1789 did not settle the federalism issue, primarily because the language in the Constitution is exceedingly vague. The framers were themselves divided, so they left it up to future generations to settle the issue. The biggest crisis of federalism occurred over slavery. In 1861, the southern states decided they had the right to secede from the United States if they did not agree with the policies of the federal government. The issue was settled in a bloody civil war: states do *not* have the right to secede unilaterally from the union; they have to work out their differences within the federal system.

Until Franklin Roosevelt's New Deal of the 1930s, the federal government was remarkably uninvolved in a wide range of domestic policy functions that we now take for granted. The halting response of states and localities to the Great Depression changed all that. Roosevelt swiftly moved the federal government into a whole range of functions, including social security, welfare, and regulation of the economy, that had previously been considered off limits. For the most part, however, Washington did not take over these functions but instead funded new programs with grants that were administered by state and local governments under varied federal rules. In the 1960s, under President Lyndon Johnson's leadership, the system of intergovernmental grants expanded tremendously.

Richard Nixon's election in 1968 began a period of reaction against the expanded powers of the federal government that has continued to this day. For the most part, Nixon did not try to roll back the functions of the federal government but instead deregulated the federal grant system and gave more power over grants to states and localities. The election of Ronald Reagan inaugurated a more radical phase of this new federalism in which efforts were made to return to the system that had existed before the New Deal when the federal government left many domestic policy functions to the states. Although confidence in all levels of government has fallen since the 1960s, the drop in confidence has been most severe for the federal government. A 1995 CBS/*New York Times* poll found that 48 percent of the respondents felt that the federal government had "too much power," whereas only 6 percent felt that the states had too much.

The 1994 Republican takeover of Congress accelerated the trend toward devolution of federal powers to the states. In 1996, Congress passed, and President Bill Clinton signed, the Personal Responsibility and Work Opportunity Act, which converted welfare from a federal entitlement for individuals to a block grant to states, leaving them significant freedom to set their own eligibility criteria and conditions for aid.

The Supreme Court is also moving in the direction of restricting federal power. In 1995, the Court ruled for the first time in sixty years that Congress had exceeded its authority under the Interstate Commerce Clause of the Constitution and declared the federal Gun-Free School Zone Act of 1990 unconstitutional

(*U.S.* v. *Lopez*). In a series of cases decided in 1999, 2000, and 2001, the Supreme Court made it more difficult for the federal government to enforce uniform national standards by giving states immunity against lawsuits alleging violation of federal laws in areas such as labor rights, violence against women, and discrimination on the basis of age or disability. As a former governor, President George W. Bush has promised to nominate justices who will support states' rights.

Those who favor devolution, however, have not completely carried the day. President Clinton pushed modest but popular extensions of federal responsibility in areas such as day care and education and appointed justices more supportive of federal power. In *Bush* v. *Gore* (2000), the conservative majority on the Supreme Court abandoned states' rights and overturned the order of the Florida Supreme Court to proceed with a statewide hand recount of the votes. The Court's decision effectively handed the presidency to Bush. The September 11 terrorist attacks greatly strengthened the case for expanded federal responsibilities, especially in law enforcement, public health, and airline safety. Finally, the 2002 Enron bankruptcy and scandal renewed calls for the federal government to more closely regulate corporations and ensure that accurate information about the financial condition of companies is available to stockholders.

In their essay "Beyond the Beltway," William Eggers and John O'Leary identify themselves with the "devolution revolution" sweeping the country at the grassroots. They stress that the purpose of devolution is not just to make the existing government programs work more efficiently but to raise the question of whether certain functions should be the responsibility of government at all. Such decisions, they maintain, are better left with those governments that are closest to the grassroots, where citizens can see immediately the costs as well as the benefits of government programs. Shrink the federal government, Eggers and O'Leary say, and grassroots organizations will flourish, becoming "laboratories of democracy." In place of the "one-size-fits-all" approach of the federal government, local organizations can fine-tune their policies to suit local conditions. Moreover, argue Eggers and O'Leary in a section of their book not reprinted here, the expanded powers of the federal government violate the U.S. Constitution, which in the Tenth Amendment reserves all powers not specifically given to the federal government "to the States respectively, or to the people."

John Donahue, the author of "The Devil in Devolution," argues that the words of the Constitution are much more ambiguous about the division of power between the federal government and the states than Eggers and O'Leary admit. Moreover, Donahue argues, it is up to each generation to adapt the federal system to the needs of the time. Donahue is critical of the recent trend toward devolution. Whereas Eggers and O'Leary base their argument primarily on what we call in the Introduction negative freedom—getting the government out of individuals' lives—Donahue stresses positive freedom, or the idea that by acting together, we can accomplish things we cannot accomplish separately. Donahue argues that when each state acts separately, those things that we all share, what he calls the "commons," can be damaged. For example, states may pursue economic development knowing that much of the pollution produced by it will drift to neighboring states. Donahue admits that federal bureaucracy may be wasteful, but he says the gains from decentralization have been greatly exaggerated. Moreover, the "courtship of capital" by individual states results in greater inequality. Instead of devolution resulting in "laboratories of democracy," Donahue suggests, the more likely result will be a "race to the bottom."

The contemporary debate on federalism reverberates with the same issues and arguments that have been made since the country's founding. It is unlikely that this debate will ever be completely settled. It seems as though each generation is doomed to decide anew the proper balance between Washington, D.C., and the states and localities. Even though there is no one neat answer, this does not mean there is not a better answer for our time. It is up to the reader to decide which position will best serve the core values of American democracy.

An intriguing aspect of this debate is that both sides argue that their position is reinforced by modern technology. The reader will have to sort this out. Do you think that new technologies make it easier for decision making to be decentralized, or do they increase the interdependencies in society, thus requiring more central coordination? Note that the two sides in the debate stress different values. Eggers and O'Leary emphasize individual freedom and local democracy, whereas Donahue puts more stress on national values and equality. In this debate, are we forced to choose among competing values, or is there some way to slip between the horns of the dilemmas of devolution and serve all values?

Beyond the Beltway

WILLIAM D. EGGERS
AND JOHN O'LEARY

Our swollen federal government is in large measure incompatible with the demands of a modern society. In today's Information Age, there is little rationale for the federal government to control as much as it does. Large, centralized bureaucracies—whether that be IBM headquarters, the Kremlin, or Washington, D.C.—aren't well suited to an age of rapid technological change. In business, companies are decentralizing, empowering workers, and establishing autonomous business units. (It's not just trendy, it's an economic necessity.) In politics, economic reality is relegating central planning to the dustbin of history.

Washington, D.C., is becoming increasingly irrelevant. Explain authors Alvin and Heidi Toffler:

> It is not possible for a society to de-massify economic activity,
> communications and many other crucial processes without also, sooner

or later, being compelled to decentralize government decision-making as well. There is no possibility of restoring sense, order, and management "efficiency" to many governments without a substantial devolution of central power.

In today's rapidly changing world, the performance of the federal government looks worse and worse. There is a reason for this. As technology advances, decentralized decision making becomes more efficient in more and more cases. The problems of centralized decision making are inherent to *any* central authority, whether corporate or governmental, and are based on the relationship between knowledge, decision-making power, and technology.

As technology advances, productivity increasingly depends on knowledge. And, as communications technology advances, *general* knowledge—the kind that can be written down—becomes widely accessible. But *specific* knowledge—the kind that requires firsthand experience and that is difficult to communicate—is as difficult to obtain today as it has ever been. Other things being equal, *specific* knowledge—the kind that is dispersed throughout society—is growing in importance relative to *general* knowledge. Thus, as technology advances, it makes less and less sense to bottle up decision-making authority in a distant, centralized bureaucracy. Dictating the "one best way" from Washington, whether in education, welfare, or crime fighting, makes less and less sense. In particular cases, there may be a compelling reason for maintaining centralized control, such as the need for a coordinated national defense. But as a general principle, for efficiency's sake we should be increasingly devolving power *away* from centralized bureaucracies.

More than simply efficiency is at stake, however. We need to return to our roots as a self-governing people. Democracy is not a spectator sport. In a healthy democracy, citizens are actively involved in their own governance—and not simply on election day. Americans need to reconnect with the political process. Numerous functions now handled (and mishandled) by the federal government should be transferred back to the states and, wherever possible, to communities and individuals. Radical devolution brings government closer to home.

The Revolt Against Washington

In 1992, a highly respected economist wrote, "The federal government should eliminate most of its programs in education, housing, highways, social services, economic development, and job training."

These radical sentiments come from Alice Rivlin, then a Brookings Institution scholar and currently President Clinton's director of the Office of Management and Budget. Writing as an independent scholar, Rivlin called for a massive, radical devolution of federal programs to states.

Devolution is not a partisan issue. It is a recognition that centralized control and centralized decision making carries unacceptably high costs, both in terms of efficiency and democratic accountability. It is not a question of Democratic dictates from Washington versus Republican dictates. Following the election of 1994, Republican governors seem ready to oppose federal usurpation even when orchestrated by their fellow party members. "My priority is for Texans to be running Texas," says Texas Governor George W. Bush. "We're pretty good at what we do in Texas, and we like to be left alone by the federal government as much as possible." It's time to end the unequal partnership and the whole idea of one-size-fits-all national prescriptions. The American people have said it's time to move power *and responsibility* out of Washington—for good.

Devolution would restore clearer lines of responsibility between state and federal tasks. By bringing government closer to home, citizens could once again understand what each level of government does and hold the appropriate officials accountable at election time. Radical devolution will make much of what goes on inside the Beltway redundant or unnecessary. "You have to get rid of a lot of those vested interests in Washington," says Mayor [Stephen] Goldsmith [of Indianapolis]. "There are tens of thousands of people there whose only job in life is to control what I do."

The Department of Education, for example, spends about $15 billion a year on 150 different elementary and secondary programs. Since the department was created in 1979, Washington has become fond of imposing top-down solutions on local schools. Ohio Governor George Voinovich says his state's school superintendents spend nearly half their time filling out federal forms to get money that makes up only 5 to 6 percent of their school budgets.

. . . Joann Wysocki, [a] first-grade teacher from the Los Angeles Unified School District, . . . told us that the federal government was providing money for school days lost due to the 1994 earthquake. The rules required a special form, so every teacher had to copy *by hand* the attendance register. Photocopies were not acceptable. That's the rule. Wysocki doesn't like to jump through hoops for money from Washington, "That 'federal money' is our money to begin with, on the local level," she says. "Please don't insult anyone's intelligence saying anything else. The money comes back to us with strings attached. Why should the money go in the first place? Let it stay!"

Former Education Secretary William J. Bennett concurs: "We really do not need a Department of Education. We were educating our kids better before we had a Department of Education. Why do we have to pass the dollars from the states and locales to Washington and back out again?"

Sending housing, welfare, and social service programs to the states, as Rivlin proposes, would mean that Health and Human Services (HHS) and the Department of Housing and Urban Development (HUD) can also be dramatically downsized or eliminated. Even [former] Housing Secretary Henry Cisneros has admitted that much of what HUD does is expendable. "Many aspects of this department are simply indefensible," said Cisneros. "Change is necessary."

As for the Environmental Protection Agency (EPA), state environmental agencies are better positioned to know the problems of their states. "We don't need an EPA in Washington, D.C.," says [Arizona] Governor [Fife] Symington. "We have a Department of Environmental Quality in Arizona that is better at dealing with environmental problems in our state. You don't need an EPA in Washington with a command-and-control structure dictating environmental policies to the states." Though we believe the EPA's powers should be greatly curtailed, we're not as radical as Governor Symington in this regard. There are certain cross-border pollution issues that may require some form of federal involvement.

No More Federal Santa Claus

For radical devolution to become a reality will require a fundamental change in mind-set not only in Washington, but also among state and local politicians. Since the beginning of the Great Society, state and local officials have come to see the federal government as a kind of Santa Claus, doling out money for all sorts of programs. Many mayors and governors became professional beggars at the Capitol's steps. Programs that would never be funded with local tax dollars become "vital" so long as they are paid for with "federal" dollars.

Even more than states, big cities turned to Washington for help. Today, most cities are addicted to federal funds. Local politicians fear the loss of federal funds, but where do they imagine this money comes from in the first place? France, perhaps? Jersey City Mayor Bret Schundler, one of the few big-city mayors to oppose the crime bill, did so because he recognized that all "federal money" comes from people living in one of the 50 states to begin with. Says Schundler:

> Clinton wants to shift the burden of policing to the federal gov-
> ernment and increase taxes. After he takes his big cut, he'll give us a
> portion of the money back for local policing. What a bonehead idea.
> The solution is not to shift taxes and make us pay more. The solution is
> reducing the cost of local policing.

Washington doesn't add any value to the tax dollars it receives and then sends back down to cities and states; in fact, the federal bureaucracy subtracts value as it takes its cut before sending money back to local governments.

Less federal money flowing out of Washington should mean less money flowing into Washington from the residents of cities and states. Keeping the money closer to home will also mean more flexibility, control, and accountability. "We understand this is going to mean less dollars from Washington," says New Jersey Governor Christine Todd Whitman, "but if you relieve us of some of the most onerous mandates, we will live with that." State and local officials need to stop judging the worth of joint federal/state programs merely in terms of whether they are funded by "federal dollars." "We as Governors need to begin to ask a new question about programs,"

says Utah Governor Mike Leavitt. "Instead of asking is this a funded program, we should ask, should there be a federal role?"

In the transportation arena, for example, the federal government could
get out of highway and airport funding by forgoing the gasoline tax and letting states raise construction money themselves—whether through a state
gasoline tax, by raising landing fees or highway tolls, or by securing private
debt. This approach would allow states to avoid a host of federal mandates—including the 55-mile-per-hour speed limit, the Davis Bacon Act,
and the minimum drinking age—that accompany acceptance of federal
highway funds.

Local Money for Local Problems

In many areas the ultimate goal of policy must be to transfer as much
power, authority, and responsibility as possible from government to individuals and local communities. Once citizens see the true cost of local programs now being financed from Washington, they may not think they're
worth the tax dollars spent on them.

Consider, for example, the uproar that ensued in Manhattan Beach,
California, (where one of us lives) after the city council voted to spend
money expanding a parking garage that residents felt would benefit only
merchants. A front-page story in *The Beach Reporter* noted that "three dozen
residents . . . bombarded the Manhattan Beach City Council on Tuesday. . . ."
Another story noted:

> [M]any residents complained that they were continually having to
> come down to City Hall to protect their interests. District 4 Council-
> member Bob Pinzler told the residents that they should continue
> voicing their opinions and concerns. "You have to keep coming down
> here to protect your interests," Pinzler said, "because the special
> interest groups are here all the time."

This is democracy at its local, messy best, with vigilant residents watching over elected officials spending their tax dollars. Chances are no one in
Manhattan Beach even knew that the federal government spent $2.5 mil-
lion of tax money to build a parking garage in Burlington, Iowa. That little
item didn't make the front page of *The Beach Reporter,* and no Manhattan
Beach residents drove the 3,000-odd miles to Washington, D.C., to testify
before a congressional committee. At the federal level, organized interests
have an enormous advantage. Former Education Secretary William Bennett
estimates that 285 education lobbying groups have offices within walking
distance of the Department of Education headquarters. The average Manhattan Beach parent doesn't have a prayer.

The parking garage story illustrates the phenomenon known as "bill av-
eraging." Imagine going out to dinner by yourself. When ordering, you'll
closely watch the cost of each menu selection because you'll be paying the

entire bill. Even if you were going out to dinner with one or two friends, you still wouldn't spend outrageously because you'd still be footing a good portion of the bill.

Now imagine that you are going out to dinner with 75 strangers, and that the bill is to be divided evenly. If you are like most people, you are going to order liberally, enjoy an extra drink, maybe even dessert and coffee. And why not? Your order will only affect your bill a minuscule amount; besides, you can bet that everyone else will be ordering big. The only way to get your "fair share" is to order lobster and Lowenbrau.

The federal government is like going to dinner with 250 million strangers. Rather than everyone paying his own way, a complex tangle of cross-subsidies obscures everyone's actual bill.

It's time to ask for separate checks. The good folks of Burlington, Iowa, got a new parking garage because Uncle Sam took about one penny from every Manhattan Beach resident—and every other American. Because local taxpayers don't feel the bite, local officials love to spend "federal dollars." Would Altoonans have approved Altoona, Pennsylvania's multimillion dollar moving sidewalk if Altoonan taxes were going to pay for it? Unlikely. But since the folks in Burlington, Iowa, and Manhattan Beach, California, are footing the bill, the Altoonans are happy to be carried along.

The Devil in Devolution

JOHN D. DONAHUE

The shift in government's center of gravity away from Washington and toward the states—a transition propelled by both popular sentiment and budget imperatives, and blessed by leaders in both major parties—reflects an uncommon pause in an endless American argument over the balance between nation and state.

This moment of consensus in favor of letting Washington fade while the states take the lead is badly timed. The public sector's current trajectory—the devolution of welfare and other programs, legislative and judicial action circumscribing Washington's authority, and the federal government's retreat to a domestic role largely defined by writing checks to entitlement claimants, creditors, and state and local governments—would make sense if economic and cultural ties reaching across state lines were *weakening* over time. But state borders are becoming more, not less, permeable.

From a vantage point three-fifths of the way between James Madison's day and our own, Woodrow Wilson wrote that the "common interests of a nation brought together in thought and interest and action by the telegraph and the telephone, as well as by the rushing mails which every express train carries, have a scope and variety, an infinite multiplication and intricate interlacing, of which a simpler day can have had no conception." Issues in which other states' citizens have no stakes, and hence no valid claim to a voice, are becoming rarer still in an age of air freight, interlinked computers, nonstop currency trading, and site-shopping global corporations. Our current enchantment with devolution will be seen one day as oddly discordant with our era's challenges.

The concept of "the commons" can help to cast in a sharper light the perils of fragmented decision-making on issues of national consequence. In a much-noted 1968 article in *Science,* biologist Garrett Hardin invoked the parable of a herdsman pondering how many cattle to graze on the village commons. Self-interest will lead the herdsman to increase the size of his herd even if the commons is already overburdened, since he alone benefits from raising an extra animal, but shares the consequent damage to the common pasture. As each farmer follows the same logic, overgrazing wrecks the commons.

Where the nation as a whole is a commons, whether as an economic reality or as a political ideal, and states take action that ignores or narrowly exploits that fact, the frequent result is the kind of "tragedy" that Hardin's metaphor predicts: Collective value is squandered in the name of a constricted definition of gain. States win advantages that seem worthwhile only because other states bear much of the costs. America's most urgent public challenges—shoring up the economic underpinnings of an imperiled middle-class culture; developing and deploying productive workplace skills; orchestrating Americans' engagement with increasingly global capital—involve the stewardship of common interests. The fragmentation of authority makes success less likely. The phenomenon is by no means limited to contemporary economic issues, and a smattering of examples from other times and other policy agendas illustrate the theme.

Environmental Regulation

Antipollution law is perhaps the most obvious application of the "commons" metaphor to policy-making in a federal system. If a state maintains a lax regime of environmental laws it spares its own citizens, businesses, and government agencies from economic burdens. The "benefits" of environmental recklessness, in other words, are collected instate. Part of the pollution consequently dumped into the air or water, however, drifts away to do its damage elsewhere in the nation. If states held all authority over environmental rule-making, the predictable result would be feeble regulations against any kinds of pollution where in-state costs and benefits of control are seriously out of balance. Even in states whose citizens valued the environment—even if the citizens of *all* states were willing to accept substantial economic costs in the name of cleaner air and water—constituents and representatives would calculate that their sacrifice could not on its own stem the tide and reluctantly settle for weaker rules than they would otherwise prefer.

A state contemplating tough antipollution rules might calculate that its citizens will pay for environmental improvements that will be enjoyed, in part, by others. Even worse, by imposing higher costs on business than do other states, it risks repelling investment, and thus losing jobs and tax revenues to states with weak environmental laws. Congress explicitly invoked the specter of a "race for the bottom"—competitive loosening of environmental laws in order to lure business—to justify federal standards that would "preclude efforts on the part of states to compete with each other in trying to attract new plants." In a series of legislative changes starting in the early 1970s, the major choices about how aggressively to act against pollution were moved to the federal government. While aspects of enforcement remained state responsibilities—introducing another level of complications that continues to plague environmental policy—the trade-off between environmental and economic values moved much closer to a single national standard.

National regulation in a diverse economy does have a downside. States differ in their environmental problems, and in the priorities of their citizens. Requiring all states to accept the same balance between environmental and economic values imposes some real costs and generates real political friction. Yet even if the tilt toward national authority is, on balance, the correct approach to environmental regulation, there is reason to doubt we got all the details right. Moreover, logic suggests that the federal role should be stronger for forms of pollution that readily cross state borders, and weaker for pollution that stays put. But federal authority is actually weaker under the Clean Air Act and the Clean Water Act than under the "Superfund" law covering hazardous waste. Toxic-waste sites are undeniably nasty things. But most of them are situated within a single state, and stay there.

Governmental Efficiency

There is an alluring a priori case for predicting that public-sector efficiency will increase as responsibilities flow to lower levels of government. Yet this *potential* advantage largely fails to pan out; there is little evidence of a significant or systematic state efficiency edge. The states share with Washington the basic operational handicaps of the public sector.

The devolution debate, moreover, is almost wholly irrelevant to the debt service and middle-class entitlements causing most of the strain on citizens' tolerance for taxation. It is safe to assert that the ascendancy of the states will have, at best, a limited impact on the cost of American government. This is not an argument based on ideology, or economic theory, or learned predictions about comparative administrative behavior. It is a matter of arithmetic. In 1996 total public spending came to about $2.3 trillion. State and local activities, funded by state and local taxes, *already* accounted for about one-third of this total. Another one-third consisted of check-writing programs like Social Security and Medicare. National defense (12 percent of the total), interest on the national debt (10 percent), and federal grants to state and local governments (another 10 percent) accounted for most of the remaining third of the public sector. All other federal domestic undertakings, taken together, claimed between 4 and 5 percent of total government spending. Suppose every last thing the federal government does, aside from running defense and foreign affairs and writing checks (to entitlement claimants, debt holders, and state and local governments) were transferred to the states—national parks and museums, air-traffic control, the FBI, the border patrol, the Centers for Disease Control, the National Weather Service, student loans, the space program, and all the rest. Suppose, then, that the states proved able to do *everything* that the federal government used to do a full 10 percent more efficiently. The cost of government would fall by a little under one-half of one percent.

Beyond the low ceiling on cost savings—and more pertinent to the hidden issue of the *quality* of government—is the similarity between most federal agencies and most state agencies on the core characteristics of scale, complexity, and administration by legislative statute and formal rules. It is rare that economic or managerial imperatives will call for the reassignment of authority away from central government, but then stop at the states. State boundaries have been drawn by a capricious history, and only occasionally (and then by accident) does a state constitute the most logical economic unit for either making policy or delivering services. The coalition between the state-sovereignty constitutionalists and the efficient-scale decentralizers is based on a misunderstanding, and will break down as soon as it begins to succeed.

More promising strategies for improving the efficiency with which public purposes are pursued usually involve going *beyond* devolution to the states. The array of options includes privatization, to enlist private-sector efficiency advantages in the service of public goals; vouchers, to assign purchasing power while letting individuals choose how to deploy it; and the empowerment (through authority and resources) of levels of government smaller than the state, including cities, towns, and school districts. None of these strategies is without its risks and limits, but together they form a far richer menu of reform possibilities than the simple switch from federal to state bureaucracy.

Devolution is often, though misleadingly, cast as a way station toward such fundamental reforms. Its popularity among those convinced of American government's shortcomings, and committed to repairing them, diverts reformist energy that could be put to better use. State governments are only slightly, if any, less bureaucratic than Washington, and no less jealous of power or resistant to change. Power dislodged from federal bureaus is likely to stick at the state level instead of diffusing further. The characteristic pattern of American intergovernmental relations is rivalry between state and local officials, and Washington more often acts as local government's shield against state hegemony than as the common oppressor of cities and states. The ascendancy of the states is thus unlikely either to liberate local governments or to unleash fundamental reform in how government operates.

Rising Inequality

It is by no means certain that America will prove able to reverse growing economic inequality and the erosion of the middle class, no matter how we structure our politics. Devolution, however, will worsen the odds. Shared prosperity, amid the maelstrom of economic change tearing away at the industrial underpinnings of middle-class culture, is an artifact of policy. Policies to shore up the middle class include work-based antipoverty efforts that become both more important and more expensive as unskilled jobs evaporate; relentless investments in education and job training; measures to strengthen employees' leverage in the workplace; and a more progressive tilt in the overall burden of taxation. The individual states—each scrambling to lure mobile capital, fearful of losing businesses and well-off residents to lower-tax rivals, anxious to minimize their burden of needy citizens—will find such policies nearly impossible to sustain. As Washington sheds responsibilities and interstate rivalry intensifies, only a small-government agenda becomes realistic. But even for principled small-government conservatives, devolution is likely to prove less satisfying than many expect. Since it has been justified in terms of improving, not shrinking, government, the ascendancy of the states represents no conclusion to the debate over the public sector's proper size and scope.

Like the run-up in federal debt in the 1980s and early 1990s, devolution short-circuits (rather than settles) deliberation over government's purpose by making activism impossible—for a time. America's federal system is sufficiently resilient that unless citizens are convinced of small government's merits, the tilt toward the states that suppress public-sector ambition will eventually be reversed, though only after an unpredictable price has been paid. The conservative intellectual Herbert Storing has argued that a strategy of crippling the activist impulse through devolution, instead of discrediting it through reasoned appeal, was "not only contrary to the best conservative tradition but also hopelessly unrealistic." By attempting to enthrone the states as the sole locus of legitimate government, conservatives muffle their own voices in the conversation over the country's future.

By the standards of those who credit any diagnosis of what ails America *other than* "big government," shifting authority to competing states is likely to solve minor problems while causing, or perpetuating, far graver ills. As states gain a greater share of governmental duties but prove reluctant or unable to tax mobile firms or well-off individuals, the burden of funding the public sector will tilt even more heavily toward middle-class taxpayers. Their resentment of government can be expected to intensify. Efforts to use state laws or regulations to strengthen employees' leverage in the workplace will often be rendered unworkable by interstate competition for business. America's largest source of fiscal imbalance—the unsustainability of middle-class entitlement programs as the baby boom generation ages—will be untouched by devolution, feeding cynicism about the imperviousness to solution of America's public problems. And the fragmentation of taxing and spending authority puts in peril the education and training agenda that defines our single most promising tactic for shoring up the middle class.

The global marketplace both gives new fuel to America's culture of opportunity *and* allows the range of economic conditions experienced within this erstwhile middle-class country to reflect, with less and less filtering, the whole planet's disparate array of fates. A middle-class national economy, within a world of economic extremes, is a precious but unnatural thing. The policies that sustain shared prosperity will be difficult, perhaps impossible, to pursue if America's center of gravity in economic policy-making continues its precipitous shift toward the separate states. Federal officials, as a class, are certainly no wiser, more farsighted, or defter at implementation than their state counterparts. But our country as a whole remains much less subject to the flight of wealth and the influx of need than are its constituent states. Policies to shrink the underclass and solidify the middle class are thus far more sustainable at the federal level.

Fixing the federal government is an intimidating proposition in the late 1990s. The trajectory of fiscal and political trends suggests that devolution will remain the focus of politicians' promises and citizens' hopes for some time to come. But the inherent limits of a fragmented approach to national adaptation will eventually inspire America to reappraise the ascendancy of the states. Not too far into the new century we will again collect the resolve to confront together our common fate. And we will once more take up, in the two-century tradition of Americans before us, the echoing challenge of George Washington's 1796 farewell address: "Is there a doubt whether a common government can embrace so large a sphere? Let experience solve it."

DISCUSSION QUESTIONS

1. Think of a policy issue that you are interested in. Which level of government do you think is the most appropriate one to make decisions on this issue? Why?

2. Which level of government do you think is the most democratic—federal, state, or local? Can privileged elites more easily dominate at the local level or at the national level?

3. Many people argue that justice should be the same no matter where you live and that therefore the federal government should establish minimal standards of justice on certain issues. Do you agree or disagree? Do you think the federal government should guarantee every American medical care or a minimum income?

4. One of the problems with decentralizing decision making is that some local governments have much larger tax resources than others. Many inner cities, for example, are very poor. How would Eggers and O'Leary respond to this problem? What can be done about it?

5. Do you think that marriage law (divorce, child custody, and so on) should be decided by the federal government or the states? What about educational policy? Should the federal government establish national standards in education?

SUGGESTED READINGS AND INTERNET RESOURCES

In *From New Federalism to Devolution* (Washington, D.C.: Brookings Institution Press, 1998), Timothy Conlan argues that Nixon and Reagan actually had very different approaches to federalism. Jeffrey M. Berry, Kent E. Portney, and Ken Thomson in *The Rebirth of Urban Democracy* (Washington, D.C.: Brookings Institution Press, 1993) present evidence that decentralizing power all the way to neighborhood governments makes sense. Grant McConnell, in *Private Power and American Democracy* (New York: Vintage Books, 1966) argues, in contrast, that decentralization of power leads to tyranny by elites. Probably the best book on the possibilities and limits of state economic development efforts is Paul Brace, *State Government and Economic Performance* (Baltimore, Md.: Johns Hopkins University Press, 1993). In *Tense Commandments: Federal Prescriptions and City Problems* (Washington, D.C.: Brookings Institution Press, 2002), Pietro S. Nivola argues that federal programs often tie the hands of local administrators, making city renewal even more difficult. For an interesting change of pace, read Ernest Callenbach's *Ecotopia* (New York: Bantam Books, 1975), an entertaining novel about environmentalists who take over part of the Northwest and secede from the United States.

James Madison Institute
www.jamesmadison.org
The James Madison Institute is a public policy research organization dedicated to promoting economic freedom, limited government, federalism, the rule of law, and individual liberty coupled with individual responsibility. The site includes a list of current books and policy studies.

Center for the Study of Federalism
www.temple.edu/federalism
This is the website of a research and educational institute dedicated to the scholarly study of federal principles, institutions, and processes. The center seeks to increase and disseminate knowledge about federal systems around the world. The site includes links to publications, including abstracts of articles in the center's journal, *Publius.*

National Council of State Governments
www.csg.org
The website of the National Council of State Governments has information on state governments and state-level public policies.

U.S. Federalism Site
www.min.net/~kala/fed
In addition to descriptions of the issues and overviews of major contemporary debates, the U.S. Federalism Site links to essential documents, key legal decisions, and sites where debates are currently under way as part of the unfolding debate on federalism.

Close Up Foundation
www.closeup.org/federal.htm
The Close Up Foundation Special Topic Page on federalism in the United States features an overview, a time-line, a teaching activity, and an annotated list of links to additional sources of information.

CHAPTER 4

Civil Society: Does America Face a Crisis in Civic Engagement?

I n his magisterial *Democracy in America,* first published in 1835, the French political theorist Alexis de Tocqueville emphasized how important voluntary associations were to the health of American democracy. "Americans of all ages, all conditions, and dispositions, constantly form associations," wrote Tocqueville. Associations come in a thousand different types, he noted, "religious, moral, serious, futile, extensive or restricted, enormous or diminutive. . . . Wherever at the head of some new undertaking, you see the Government in France, or a man of rank in England, in the United States you will be sure to find an association."

The idea that associations are crucial to democracy is known as the theory of civil society. All voluntary associations that are neither part of government nor part of private, profit-making activities are included in civil society. These associations range all the way from the huge American Association of Retired Persons and the Red Cross to the local neighborhood association or even bridge club. Many of the associations of civil society are incorporated as nonprofits and therefore enjoy certain tax privileges. They can have large payrolls and raise large amounts of money through charitable contributions and government grants. Others are informally organized, have few staff, and struggle to fundraise.

Associations, both political and nonpolitical, are thought to perform important functions for democracy. First, they provide what are called "mediating institutions" between powerful public and private corporations on the one hand and isolated individuals on the other. By joining together, people can protect themselves from being dominated or repressed by large bureaucratic organizations. Voluntary associations also provide important services that the public and private sectors do not perform or perform poorly. Churches, a very important part of civil society in the United States, take care of the homeless and often provide hospice care for the dying. In fact, the government now provides many social services through grants to nonprofits, recognizing that nonprofits may be more sensitive to the needs of particular populations and may be able to leverage volunteers to extend the reach of government funds.

Perhaps the most important function assigned to associations in American democracy is lifting citizens out of extreme individualism and educating them into more public-spirited commitments. Tocqueville called this "self interest rightly understood," meaning that by participating in voluntary associations citizens begin to identify their own individual well-being with the well-being of the group. Eventually, people attach these local public commitments to the nation as a whole. In the body of thought known as *republicanism* (not to be confused with the Republican Party), this is known as educating citizens into "civic virtue."

Periodically, throughout our history, Americans have become anxious about our tendency to become excessively individualistic and materialistic. In 1985 a much-discussed book, *Habits of the Heart,* examined the problem of excessive individualism and explored its antidotes in religion, politics, and work. Many people argued that Americans had become too preoccupied with their rights and were ignoring their responsibilities. Led by the sociologist Amitai Etzioni, they formed themselves, in classically American fashion, into an association, the Communitarian Network. In 1991, they issued the Communitarian Platform, a manifesto that stressed that our democratic rights ultimately depend on strong communities rooted in moral values.

The collapse of communism in 1989 stimulated interest in civil society. As the fledgling democracies in Eastern Europe and the former Soviet Union tried to sink roots, it became clear that the soil of democracy was thin. Under totalitarian communist governments, people were discouraged from forming independent associations that could challenge the authority of the Communist Party. The new democracies lacked a rich association life that could give citizens experience in self-government and pull them out of parochial mindsets. Democracy did better in nations that had formed strong associations. The democratic revolution in Poland was led by Solidarity, which gained its strength from defiant trade unions and the Catholic Church.

In 1995, an article in an obscure academic journal entitled "Bowling Alone" riveted the public's attention on the condition of civil society. Written by Harvard University professor Robert Putnam, the title was based on the fact that Americans were bowling more than ever but increasingly they were doing it alone instead of in bowling leagues. In the article, Putnam documented the decline of civic engagement, including voting, as well as more general membership in associations. To organize his findings, Putnam utilized the concept of social capital. This concept refers to the network, norms, and trust that enable people to accomplish together what they cannot accomplish alone. Like financial or physical capital, social capital enables us to become more productive. Social capital does not just improve the functioning of democracy; it also can produce better schools, faster economic growth, and lower crime rates (for example, community watch programs, where neighbors watch each other's homes, reduce crime). By forcefully raising the question of whether the store of social capital in American society is dangerously depleted, "Bowling Alone" became the subject of innumerable editorials and Putnam was invited more than once to discuss his theory at the Clinton White House.

The selection by Putnam that follows is from the book he published on the subject five years after the article came out. In the book Putnam analyzes an enormous amount of data on the condition of civil society. Nearly all the indicators point in the same direction—civic participation is declining, and Americans are simply not joining groups as much as they did in earlier periods. While older Americans are still quite civic-minded, those born after World War II, the Baby Boomers and Generation Xers, are much less involved. The decline of social capital, Putnam warns, could have dire consequences for American democracy. The political skills of citizens could atrophy, and they could lose trust in politicians and become alienated from politics. The result would be a political system that is less able to represent the various parts of society in decision making and less able to solve problems.

The article by William Galston and Peter Levine of the National Commission on Civic Renewal questions both the factual basis of Putnam's analysis and his interpretation of the facts. Many commentators have argued, as Galston and Levine do, that Putnam exaggerates the decline of social capital in the United States. Compared to other nations, Americans are still joiners. Instead of withdrawing from associations, Galston and Levine suggest, Americans may be simply shifting their activities from national and formal political organizations to more local and voluntary activities. They argue that we cannot simply equate membership in civic associations with a healthier democracy. Instead of voluntary associations being a steppingstone to political involvement, they may serve as a retreat from a political system that is viewed as immoral and untrustworthy.

In these two selections, we focus on the questions of whether there has been a decline in civil society and if there is, what this means. In his book Putnam extensively analyzes the question of the causes of the alleged decline of civil society. He cites a number of culprits, including work pressures and suburban sprawl, but attributes the most explanatory power to the privatization of leisure, particularly increased television viewing. Those who came of age when television became the dominant form of entertainment, his data show, have much less interest and involvement in civic affairs. In contrast, what Putnam calls the "long civic generation," those born between 1910 and 1940, have sustained impressive levels of civic engagement.

The debate over the causes of the decline in civil society has taken many different forms. One wing of the debate has been a dispute between conservatives and liberals. Conservatives argue that big government in the form of the welfare state has taken over many of the functions of voluntary associations, causing them to shrivel up and in many cases die. Welfare laws allegedly treat everyone the same and do not recognize the importance of community self-help and charity that builds on moral relationships. President George W. Bush's faith-based initiative is an effort to transform the relationship between government and churches, the most important voluntary associations in America. Bush wants to contract with churches to deliver social welfare services, such as drug counseling and job training. This is known as "charitable choice." Liberals are concerned that this will violate the separation of church and state, with public funds being used by churches to proselytize. Conservatives are concerned that public funding will force churches to give up their distinctive religious and spiritual commitments.

Instead of focusing on government, liberals frequently argue that the private economy is the main cause of the decline of civil society. Consumption and the accumulation of wealth, stimulated by advertising and economic booms (as occurred in the 1990s), have crowded out civic voluntarism and political activism. Americans are working longer hours than ever and have less free time to devote to civic affairs. Increasingly, Americans have substituted writing a check for being involved in face-to-face associations. Political scientist Theda Skocpol argues that, far from being harmful to voluntary groups, federal social policies have strengthened them. The American Legion played a major role in passing the 1944 GI Bill, which gave returning veterans free college tuition, and this bill, in turn, helped the American Legion to grow. More recently, former President Bill Clinton pushed passage of the AmeriCorps, which rewards young Americans for participating in voluntary activities by giving them a voucher at the end of their tour of duty that can be used to pay for education.

Although most analysts agree that a strong civil society is necessary for a strong democracy, there is much less agreement about how to go about building a stronger civil society. Civic commitments often grow not by deliberate actions but by accidents of history. The terrorist attacks of September 11, 2001, are an excellent case in point. Americans really seemed to unite together in the wake of the attacks. New Yorkers, widely known for their insularity, engaged in widespread acts of heroism and bravery to aid strangers. People volunteered to help out with the dangerous work of cleaning up and carting away the rubble. Voluntary contributions poured in from around the country to help the victims of terror. Roughly a quarter of all Americans reported giving blood immediately following the attacks. People's trust in government soared. Whether the surge in civic commitments following 9/11 will be long lasting or short lived remains to be seen.

Bowling Alone: The Collapse and Revival of American Community

ROBERT D. PUTNAM

n recent years social scientists have framed concerns about the changing character of American society in terms of the concept of "social capital." By analogy with notions of physical capital and human capital—tools and training that enhance individual productivity— the core idea of social capital theory is that social networks have value. Just as a screwdriver (physical capital) or a college education (human capital) can increase productivity (both individual and collective), so too social contacts affect the productivity of individuals and groups.

Whereas physical capital refers to physical objects and human capital refers to properties of individuals, social capital refers to connections among individuals—social networks and the norms of reciprocity and trustworthiness that arise from them. In that sense social capital is closely related to what some have called "civic virtue." The difference is that "social capital" calls attention to the fact that civic virtue is most powerful when embedded in a dense network of reciprocal social relations. A society of many virtuous but isolated individuals is not necessarily rich in social capital. . . .

American society, like the continent on which we live, is massive and polymorphous, and our civic engagement historically has come in many sizes and shapes. A few of us still share plowing chores with neighbors, while many more pitch in to wire classrooms to the Internet. Some of us run for Congress, and others join self-help groups. Some of us hang out at the local bar association and others at the local bar. Some of us attend mass once a day, while others struggle to remember to send holiday greetings once a year. The forms of our social capital—the ways in which we connect with friends and neighbors and strangers—are varied.

So our review of trends in social capital and civic engagement ranges widely across various sectors of this complex society. . . . The dominant theme is simple: For the first two-thirds of the twentieth century a powerful tide bore Americans into ever deeper engagement in the life of their communities, but a few decades ago—silently, without warning—that tide reversed and we were overtaken by a treacherous rip current. Without at first noticing, we have been pulled apart from one another and from our communities over the last third of the century. . . .

Political Participation

. . . We begin with the most common act of democratic citizenship—voting. In 1960, 62.8 percent of voting-age Americans went to the polls to choose between John F. Kennedy and Richard M. Nixon. In 1996, after decades of slippage, 48.9 percent of voting-age Americans chose among Bill Clinton, Bob Dole, and Ross Perot, very nearly the lowest turnout in the twentieth century. Participation in presidential elections has declined by roughly a quarter over the last thirty-six years. Turnout in off-year and local elections is down by roughly this same amount. . . .

Voting is by a substantial margin the most common form of political activity, and it embodies the most fundamental democratic principle of equality. Not to vote is to withdraw from the political community. . . . On the other hand, in some important respects voting is not a typical mode of political participation. Based on their exhaustive assessment of different forms of participation in American politics, political scientists Sidney Verba, Kay Schlozman, and Henry Brady conclude that "it is incomplete and misleading to understand citizen participation solely through the vote. . . . Compared with those who engage in various other political acts, voters report a different mix of gratification and a different bundle of issue concerns as being behind their activity. . . . [V]oting is sui generis." Declining electoral participation is merely the most visible symptom of a broader disengagement from community life.[1] Like a fever, electoral abstention is even more important as a sign of deeper trouble in the body politic than as a malady itself. It is not just from the voting booth that Americans are increasingly AWOL.

Political knowledge and interest in public affairs are critical preconditions for more active forms of involvement. If you don't know the rules of the game and the players and don't care about the outcome, you're unlikely to try playing yourself. Encouragingly, Americans in the aggregate at century's end are about as likely to know, for example, which party controls the House of Representatives or who their senators are as were their grandparents a half century ago. On the other hand, we are much better educated than our grandparents, and since civics knowledge is boosted by formal education, it is surprising that civics knowledge has not improved accordingly. The average college graduate today knows little more about public affairs than did the average high school graduate in the 1940s.[2]

Roughly every other month from 1974 to 1998 Roper pollsters asked Americans, "Have you recently been taking a good deal of interest in current events and what's happening in the world today, some interest, or not very much interest?" Popular interest in current events naturally tends to rise and fall with what's in the news, so this chart of attention to public affairs looks like the sawtooth traces left by an errant seismograph. Beneath these choppy waves, however, the tide of the public's interest in current events gradually ebbed by roughly 20 percent over this quarter century. . . .

Scandals and war can still rouse out attention, but generally speaking, fewer Americans follow public affairs now than did a quarter century ago.

Even more worrying are intergenerational differences in political knowledge and interest. Like the decline in voting turnout, to which it is linked, the slow slump in interest in politics and current events is due to the replacement of an older generation that was relatively interested in public affairs by a younger generation that is relatively uninterested. Among both young and old, of course, curiosity about public affairs continues to fluctuate in response to daily headlines, but the base level of interest is gradually fading, as an older generation of news and politics junkies passes slowly from the scene. The fact that the decline is generation-specific, rather than nationwide, argues against the view that public affairs have simply become boring in some objective sense.

The post-baby boom generations—roughly speaking, men and women who were born after 1964 and thus came of age in the 1980s and 1990s—are substantially less knowledgeable about public affairs, despite the proliferation of sources of information. Even in the midst of national election campaigns in the 1980s and 1990s, for example, these young people were about a third less likely than their elders to know, for instance, which political party controlled the House of Representatives.[3]

Today's generation gap in political knowledge does not reflect some permanent tendency for the young to be less well informed than their elders but is instead a recent development. From the earliest opinion polls in the 1940s to the mid-1970s, younger people were at least as well informed as their elders were, but that is no longer the case. This news and information gap, affecting not just politics, but even things like airline crashes, terrorism, and financial news, first opened up with the boomers in the 1970s and widened considerably with the advent of the X generation. Daily newspaper readership among people under thirty-five dropped from two-thirds in 1965 to one-third in 1990, at the same time that TV news viewership in this same age group fell from 52 percent to 41 percent. Today's under-thirties pay less attention to the news and know less about current events than their elders do today or than people their age did two or three decades ago.[4]

. . . Voting and following politics are relatively undemanding forms of participation. In fact, they are not, strictly speaking, forms of social capital at all, because they can be done utterly alone. As we have seen, these measures show some thinning of the ranks of political spectators, particularly at the end of the stadium where the younger generation sits. But most of the fans are still in their seats, following the action and chatting about the antics of the star players. How about the grassroots gladiators who volunteer to work for political parties, posting signs, attending campaign rallies, and the like? What is the evidence on trends in partisan participation?

On the positive side of the ledger, one might argue, party organizations themselves are as strong as ever at both state and local levels. Over the last thirty to forty years these organizations have become bigger, richer, and more professional. During presidential campaigns from the late 1950s to the late 1970s, more and more voters reported being contacted by one or both of the major political parties. After a slump from 1980 to 1992, this measure of party vitality soared nearly to an all-time high in 1996, as GOTV ("Get out the vote") activities blossomed.[5]

Party finances, too, skyrocketed in the 1970s and 1980s. Between 1976 and 1986, for example, the Democrats' intake rose at more than twice the rate of inflation, while the Republicans' rose at more than four times the rate of inflation. More money meant more staff, more polling, more advertising, better candidate recruitment and training, and more party outreach. The number of political organizations, partisan and nonpartisan, with regular paid staff has exploded over the last two decades. . . .

Yet viewed by the "consumers" in the political marketplace, this picture of vigorous health seems a bizarre parody. The rate of party identification—the voter's sense of commitment to her own team—fell from more than 75 percent around 1960 to less than 65 percent in the late 1990s. Despite a partial recovery in the late 1980s, at century's end party "brand loyalty" remained well below the levels of the 1950s and early 1960s. What is more, this form of political engagement is significantly lower in more recent cohorts, so that as older, more partisan voters depart from the electorate to be replaced by younger independents, the net attachment to the parties may continue to decline.[6] Again, the Grim Reaper is silently at work, lowering political involvement.

Beyond party identification, at the grassroots level attending a campaign meeting or volunteering to work for a political party has become much rarer over the last thirty years. From the 1950s to the 1960s growing numbers of Americans worked for a political party during election campaigns, ringing doorbells, stuffing envelopes, and the like. Since 1968, however, that form of political engagement has plunged, reaching an all-time low for a presidential election year in 1996. Attendance at political meetings and campaign rallies has followed a similar trajectory over the last half century—up from the 1950s to the 1960s, instability in the 1970s, and general decline since the 1980s. . . .[7] In short, while the parties themselves are better financed and more professionally staffed than ever, fewer and fewer Americans participate in partisan political activities.

How can we reconcile these two conflicting pictures—organizational health, as seen from the parties, and organizational decay, as seen from the voters' side? . . . On reflection, . . . the contrast between increasing party organizational vitality and declining voter involvement is perfectly intelligible. Since their "consumers" are tuning out from politics, parties have to work harder and spend much more, competing furiously to woo votes, workers, and donations, and to do that they need a (paid) organizational infrastructure. Party-as-organization and party-in-government have become stronger, even as the public has grown less attached to the parties.[8] If we think of politics as an industry, we might delight in its new "labor-saving efficiency," but if we think of politics as democratic deliberation, to leave people out is to miss the whole point of the exercise. . . .

So far we have been considering political participation from the important but limited perspective of partisan and electoral activities. For most Americans, however, national election campaigns occupy only a small part of their time and attention. What about trends in political participation outside the context of national elections, especially at the local level? . . . The answer is simple: *The frequency of virtually every form of community involvement measured in . . . Roper polls* [from 1973 through 1994] *declined significantly, from the most common—petition signing—to the least common—running for office.* Americans are playing virtually every aspect of the civic game less frequently today than we did two decades ago.

Consider first the new evidence on trends in partisan and campaign activities. . . . In round numbers, Americans were roughly half as likely to work for a political party or attend a political rally or speech in the 1990s as in the 1970s. Barely two decades ago election campaigns were for millions of Americans an occasion for active participation in national deliberation. Campaigning was something we did, not something we merely witnessed. Now for almost all Americans, an election campaign is something that happens around us, a grating element in the background noise of everyday life, a fleeting image on a TV screen. Strikingly, the dropout rate from these campaign activities (about 50 percent) is even greater than the dropout rate in the voting booth itself (25 percent). . . .

That Americans in recent years have deserted party politics is perhaps not astonishing news, for antiparty sentiments had become a commonplace of punditry even before Ross Perot rode the antiparty bandwagon to national prominence in 1992. But how about communal forms of activity, like attending local meetings, serving local organizations, and taking part in "good government" activities? Here the new evidence is startling, for involvement in these everyday forms of community life has dwindled as rapidly as has partisan and electoral participation. The pattern is broadly similar to that for campaign activities—a slump in the late 1970s, a pause in the early 1980s, and then a renewed and intensified decline from the late 1980s into the 1990s. . . .

Like battlefield casualties dryly reported from someone else's distant war, these unadorned numbers scarcely convey the decimation of American community life they represent. In round numbers every single percentage-point drop represents two million fewer Americans involved in some aspect of community life every year. So, the numbers imply, we now have sixteen million fewer participants in public meetings about local affairs, eight million fewer committee members, eight million fewer local organizational leaders, and three million fewer men and women organized to work for better government than we would have had if Americans had stayed as involved in community affairs as we were in the mid-1970s. . . .

Let's sum up what we've learned about trends in political participation. On the positive side of the ledger, Americans today score about as well on a civics test as our parents and grandparents did, though our self-congratulation should be restrained, since we have on average four more years of formal schooling than they had.[9] Moreover, at election time we are no less likely than they were to talk politics or express interest in the campaign. On the other hand, since the mid-1960s, the weight of the evidence suggests, despite the rapid rise in levels of education Americans have become perhaps 10–15 percent less likely to voice our views publicly by running for office or writing Congress or the local newspaper, 15–20 percent less interested in politics and public affairs, roughly 25 percent less likely to vote, roughly 35 percent less likely to attend public meetings, both partisan and nonpartisan, and roughly 40 percent less engaged in party politics and indeed in political and civic organizations of all sorts. We remain, in short, reasonably well-informed spectators of public affairs, but many fewer of us actually partake in the game. . . .

So What?

By virtually every conceivable measure, social capital has eroded steadily and sometimes dramatically over the past two generations. The quantitative evidence is overwhelming, yet most Americans did not need to see charts and graphs to know that something bad has been happening in their communities and in their country. Americans have had a growing sense at some visceral level of disintegrating social bonds. It is perhaps no coincidence that on the eve of the millennium the market for civic nostalgia was hotter than the market for blue-chip stocks. For example, newscaster Tom Brokaw's book profiling the heroic World War II generation got mixed reviews from critics yet was a runaway best-seller. In Los Angeles there was an on-again, off-again movement to rename the LAX airport after the actor Jimmy Stewart, a military hero in real life who brought civic heroes Jefferson Smith and George Bailey to the silver screen. American nostalgia in the late twentieth century is no run-of-the-mill, rosy-red remembrance of things past. It is an attempt to recapture a time when public-spiritedness really did carry more value and when communities really did "work." As we buy books and rename airports, we seem to be saying that at a profound level civic virtue and social capital do matter.

Are we right? Does social capital have salutary effects on individuals, communities, or even entire nations? Yes, an impressive and growing body of research suggests that civic connections help make us healthy, wealthy, and wise. Living without social capital is not easy, whether one is a villager in southern Italy or a poor person in the American inner city or a well-heeled entrepreneur in a high-tech industrial district. . . .

The playwright Oscar Wilde is said to have mused, "The trouble with socialism is that it would take too many evenings."[10] Fair enough, but how many evenings does liberal democracy take? That democratic self-government requires an actively engaged citizenry has been a truism for centuries. (Not until the middle of the twentieth century did some political theorists begin to assert that good citizenship requires simply choosing among competing teams of politicians at the ballot box, as one might choose among competing brands of toothpaste.)[11] [Here] I consider both the conventional claim that the health of American democracy requires citizens to perform our *public* duties and the more expansive and controversial claim that the health of our *public* institutions depends, at least in part, on widespread participation in *private* voluntary groups—those networks of civic engagement that embody social capital.

The ideal of participatory democracy has deep roots in American political philosophy. With our experiment in democracy still in its infancy, Thomas Jefferson proposed amending the Constitution to facilitate grassroots democracy. In an 1816 letter he suggested that "counties be divided into wards of such size that every citizen can attend, when called on, and act in person." The ward governments would have been charged with everything from running schools to caring for the poor to operating police and military forces to maintaining public roads. Jefferson believed that "making every citizen an acting member of the government, and in the offices nearest and most interesting to him, will attach him by his strongest feelings to the independence of his country, and its republican constitution."[12]

Visiting American shores a decade later, Alexis de Tocqueville struck a similar note, suggesting that even in the absence of Jeffersonian ward governments, Americans' local civic activity served as the handmaiden of their national democratic community: "It is difficult to draw a man out of his own circle to interest him in the destiny of the state," Tocqueville observed, "because he does not clearly understand what influence the destiny of the state can have upon his own lot. But if it is proposed to make a road cross the end of his estate, he will see at a glance that there is a connection between the small public affair and his greatest private affairs; and he will discover, without its being shown to him, the close tie that unites private to general interest." . . .[13]

Echoing Tocqueville's observations, many contemporary students of democracy have come to celebrate "mediating" or "intermediary" associations, be they self-consciously or only indirectly political, as fundamental to maintaining a vibrant democracy.[14] Voluntary associations and the social networks of civil society that we have been calling "social capital" contribute to democracy in two different ways: they have "external" effects on the larger polity, and they have "internal" effects on participants themselves.

Externally, voluntary associations, from churches and professional societies to Elks clubs and reading groups, allow individuals to express their interests and demands on government and to protect themselves from abuses of power by their political leaders. Political information flows through social networks, and in these networks public life is discussed. As so often, Tocqueville saw this point clearly: "When some view is represented by an association, it must take clearer and more precise shape. It counts its supporters and involves them in its cause; these supporters get to know one another, and numbers increase zeal. An association unites the energies of divergent minds and vigorously directs them toward a clearly indicated goal." . . .[15]

Internally, associations and less formal networks of civic engagement instill in their members habits of cooperation and public-spiritedness, as well as the practical skills necessary to partake in public life. Tocqueville observed that "feelings and ideas are renewed, the heart enlarged, and the understanding developed only by the reciprocal action of men one upon another."[16] Prophylactically, community bonds keep individuals from falling prey to extremist groups that target isolated and untethered individuals. Studies of political psychology over the last forty years have suggested that "people divorced from community, occupation, and association are first and foremost among the supporters of extremism."[17]

More positively, voluntary associations are places where social and civic skills are learned—"schools for democracy." . . . The most systematic study of civic skills in contemporary America suggests that for working-class Americans voluntary associations and churches offer the best opportunities for civic skill building, and even for professionals such groups are second only to the workplace as sites for civic learning. Two-thirds or more of the members of religious, literary, youth, and fraternal/service organizations exercised such civic skills as giving a presentation or running a meeting.[18] Churches, in particular, are one of the few vital institutions left in which low-income, minority, and disadvantaged citizens of all races can learn politically relevant skills and be recruited into political action.[19] The implication is vitally important to anyone who values egalitarian democracy: without such institutions, the class bias in American politics would be much greater.[20]

Just as associations inculcate democratic habits, they also serve as forums for thoughtful deliberation over vital public issues. Political theorists have lately renewed their attention to the promise and pitfalls of "deliberative democracy."[21] Some argue that voluntary associations best enhance deliberation when they are microcosms of the nation, economically, ethnically, and religiously.[22] Others argue that even homogeneous organizations can enhance deliberative democracy by making our public interactions more inclusive. When minority groups, for example, push for nondiscrimination regulations and mandatory inclusion of ethnic interests in school curricula and on government boards, they are in effect widening the circle of participants.[23]

Voluntary associations may serve not only as forums for deliberation, but also as occasions for learning civic virtues, such as active participation in public life.[24] A follow-up study of high school seniors found that regardless of the students' social class, academic background, and self-esteem, those who took part in voluntary associations in school were far more likely than nonparticipants to vote, take part in political campaigns, and discuss public issues two years after graduating.[25] Another civic virtue is trustworthiness. Much research suggests that when people have repeated interactions, they are far less likely to shirk or cheat.[26] A third civic virtue acquired through social connectedness is reciprocity. . . . The more people are involved in networks of civic engagement (from club meetings to church picnics to informal get-togethers with friends), the more likely they are to display concern for the generalized other—to volunteer, give blood, contribute to charity, and so on. To political theorists, reciprocity has another meaning as well—the willingness of opposing sides in a democratic debate to agree on the ground rules for seeking mutual accommodation after sufficient discussion, even (or especially) when they don't agree on what is to be done.[27] Regular connections with my fellow citizens don't *ensure* that I will be able to put myself in their shoes, but social isolation virtually guarantees that I will not. . . .

Voluntary groups are not a panacea for what ails our democracy. And the absence of social capital—norms, trust, networks of association—does not eliminate politics. But without social capital we are more likely to have politics of a certain type. American democracy evolved historically in an environment unusually rich in social capital, and many of our institutions and practices—such as the unusual degree of decentralization in our governmental processes, compared with that of other industrialized countries—represent adaptations to such a setting. Like a plant overtaken by climatic change, our political practices would have to change if social capital were permanently diminished. How might the American polity function in a setting of much lower social capital and civic engagement?

A politics without face-to-face socializing and organizing might take the form of a Perot-style electronic town hall, a kind of plebiscitary democracy. Many opinions would be heard, but only as a muddle of disembodied voices, neither engaging with one another nor offering much guidance to decision makers. TV-based politics is to political action as watching *ER* is to saving someone in distress. Just as one cannot restart a heart with one's remote control, one cannot jump-start republican citizenship without direct, face-to-face participation. Citizenship is not a spectator sport. . . .

NOTES

1. Sidney Verba, Kay Lehman Schlozman, and Henry E. Brady, *Voice and Equality: Civic Voluntarism in American Politics* (Cambridge, Mass.: Harvard University Press, 1995), 23–24 *et passim*. On the decline in turnout, see Richard A. Brody, "The Puzzle of Political Participation in America," in *The New American Political System,* ed. Anthony King (Washington, D.C.: American Enterprise Institute for Public Policy Research, 1978); Raymond E. Wolfinger and Steven J. Rosenstone, *Who Votes?* (New Haven, Conn.: Yale University Press, 1980); Ruy Teixeira, *The Disappearing American Voter* (Washington, D.C.: Brookings Institution Press, 1992); Steven J. Rosenstone and

John Mark Hansen, *Mobilization, Participation, and Democracy in America* (New York: Macmillan, 1993); and Warren E. Miller and J. Merrill Shanks, *The New American Voter* (Cambridge, Mass.: Harvard University Press, 1996).

2. Verba, Schlozman, Brady, *Voice and Equality,* 362 *et passim,* and Michael X. Delli Carpini and Scott Keeter, *What Americans Know About Politics and Why It Matters* (New Haven, Conn.: Yale University Press, 1996), 116–134, 196–199.

3. When political interest in the DDB Needham Life Style surveys and interest in current events in the Roper surveys are each regressed on year of birth and year of survey, the regression coefficient for year of birth is quite high, while the coefficient for year of survey is virtually insignificant. In other words, the trends are entirely attributable to intercohort, not intracohort, change. On this methodology, see Glenn Firebaugh, "Methods for Estimating Cohort Replacement Effects," in *Sociological Methodology 1989,* ed. C. C. Clogg (Oxford: Basil Blackwell, 1989), 243–262; Stephen Earl Bennett, "Young Americans' Indifference to Media Coverage of Public Affairs," *PS: Political Science & Politics* 31 (September 1998): 540, 539, reports that "individuals between 18 and 29 years of age are less likely than those over 30 to read, listen to, or watch political news stories, and less likely to pay close attention to media coverage of public affairs." See also Delli Carpini and Keeter, *What Americans Know About Politics,* 170.

4. Times Mirror Center for the People and the Press, "The Age of Indifference" (Washington, D.C.: Times Mirror Center, June 28, 1990). Delli Carpini and Keeter, *What Americans Know About Politics,* 172, confirm that "the knowledge gap . . . is driven more by generational than life cycle processes."

5. Joseph A. Schlesinger, "The New American Political Party," *American Political Science Review* 79 (December 1985): 1152–1169; Larry Sabato, *The Party's Just Begun* (Glenview, Ill.: Scott, Foresman, 1988); John H. Aldrich, *Why Parties?* (Chicago: University of Chicago Press, 1995), esp. 15, 260. Author's analysis of National Election Studies, 1952–1996.

6. On declining party identification, see Miller and Shanks, *The New American Voter,* ch. 7; Rosenstone and Hansen, *Mobilization, Participation, and Democracy,* ch. 5; and Russell J. Dalton, "Parties Without Partisans: The Decline of Party Identifications Among Democratic Publics," (Irvine: University of California at Irvine, 1998). Independents are much less attentive to politics and public affairs and much less likely to participate. See Angus Campbell, Philip E. Converse, Warren E. Miller, and Donald E. Stokes, *The American Voter* (New York: John Wiley & Sons, 1960), and Miller and Shanks, *The New American Voter.*

7. Participation has declined in presidential election years more than in midterm years. Roughly half of the decline in presidential year activities and virtually all of the downward trend in midterm activities are due to generational replacement. Two other forms of campaign involvement are also measured in the National Election Studies: (1) displaying one's political preferences, by wearing a button, putting a campaign sticker on one's car, or putting up a sign at one's house; and (2) making a campaign contribution. Both show irregular changes, due in part perhaps to changes in question wording.

8. John Aldrich and Richard G. Niemi, "The Sixth American Party System: Electoral Change, 1952–1992," in *Broken Contract: Changing Relationships Between Americans and Their Government,* ed. Stephen C. Craig (Boulder, Colo.: Westview Press, 1995), 87–109.

9. In 1947 the median American adult had completed nine years of formal schooling; in 1998 that figure was about thirteen. According to the Census Bureau, the fraction of adults who had completed high school rose from 31 percent in 1947 to 82 percent in 1998.

10. Though this bon mot is widely attributed to Wilde, I have been unable to confirm that attribution.

11. Joseph Schumpeter, *Capitalism, Socialism, and Democracy* (London: Harper and Brothers, 1942).

12. Jefferson to Kercheval, July 12, 1816, in Merrill Peterson, ed., *Writings* (New York: Library of America, 1984), 1227, quoted in James P. Young, *Reconsidering American Liberalism* (Boulder, Colo.: Westview Press, 1996), 86.

13. Alexis de Tocqueville, *Democracy in America,* ed. J. P. Mayer, trans. George Lawrence (Garden City, N.Y.: Doubleday, 1969), 511.

14. See, for example, Peter L. Berger and Richard John Neuhaus, *To Empower People: From State to Civil Society* (Washington, D.C.: AEI Press, 1977; 1996).

15. Tocqueville, *Democracy in America,* 190.

16. Tocqueville, *Democracy in America,* 515.

17. William Kornhauser, *The Politics of Mass Society* (Glencoe, Ill.: Free Press, 1959), 73.

18. Verba, Schlozman, Brady, *Voice and Equality,* 378.

19. Frederick C. Harris, "Religious Institutions and African American Political Mobilization," in Paul Peterson, ed., *Classifying by Race* (Princeton, N.J.: Princeton University Press, 1995), 299. The evidence suggests that churches organized congregationally, such as Protestant denominations, tend to provide more opportunities for parishioners to build civic skills than do hierarchically organized churches, including Catholic and evangelical denominations. Protestants are three times as likely as Catholics to report opportunities to exercise civic skills. Verba, Schlozman, Brady, *Voice and Equality,* 321–322, 329.

20. Verba, Schlozman, Brady, *Voice and Equality,* 385.

21. Jon Elster, ed., *Deliberative Democracy* (Cambridge, UK: Cambridge University Press, 1998); Amy Gutmann and Dennis Thompson, *Democracy and Disagreement* (Cambridge, Mass.: Harvard University Press, 1996); J. Bohman, *Public Deliberation* (Cambridge, Mass.: MIT Press, 1996); C. Nino, *The Constitution of Deliberative Democracy* (New Haven, Conn.: Yale University Press, 1996).

22. Amy Gutmann, "Freedom of Association: An Introductory Essay," in Amy Gutmann, ed., *Freedom of Association* (Princeton, N.J.: Princeton University Press, 1998), 25.

23. See, for example, Will Kymlicka, "Ethnic Associations and Democratic Citizenship," in Gutmann, *Freedom of Association,* 177–213.

24. See Michael Walzer, "The Civil Society Argument," in Ronald Beiner, ed., *Theorizing Citizenship* (Albany: State University of New York Press, 1995).

25. Michael Hanks, "Youth, Voluntary Associations, and Political Socialization," *Social Forces* 60 (1981): 211–223.

26. David Sally, "Conversation and Cooperation in Social Dilemmas: A Meta-Analysis of Experiments from 1958 to 1992," *Rationality and Society* 7, no. 1 (1995): 58–92.

27. Gutmann and Thompson, *Democracy and Disagreement,* 52–53.

America's Civic Condition: A Glance at the Evidence

WILLIAM A. GALSTON
AND PETER LEVINE

T
he publication of Robert Putnam's "Bowling Alone" in 1995 sparked a vigorous but often murky debate about America's civic condition. Some of the confusion arose from the inconclusiveness of the available data and some from a failure to draw certain basic distinctions.

It is not always recognized that civic health may be measured along several dimensions: participation in electoral politics, political and social trust, voluntary sector activity, and attitudes and conduct bearing on the moral condition of society, to name but a few. No one doubts that many forms of participation in official political institutions and activities have declined in recent decades or that Americans are less inclined to express trust in political leaders—and in one another. It is equally clear that in overwhelming numbers, Americans believe that their society is morally weaker than it once was. Whether they are right to believe this is a different, and more difficult, question. But the fact that they do has contributed to the surprising public salience of what might have remained an abstruse scholarly debate.

When we turn our attention to the voluntary sector, matters become less clear. Here again, some basic distinctions prove useful. Voluntary sector activities include formal organizational membership, volunteering, charitable giving, and informal socializing. Evidence suggests that trends in these areas may be diverging. Moreover, civic trends have not been linear during the past generation. Some declines that began in the 1970s—in aggregate group membership, volunteering, and philanthropy—appear to have halted and even reversed themselves in the late 1980s and early 1990s.

Group Membership

Judged against other industrialized nations, American civil society remains comparatively strong (though its relative standing may have fallen in recent decades). According to the 1990–91 World Values Survey, 82 percent of Americans belong to at least one voluntary association, a rate exceeded only in Iceland, Sweden, and the Netherlands. Furthermore, Americans belong to (and volunteer for) almost all types of groups at above-average rates. Only unions are relatively weak in the United States.

Existing methods for determining and comparing rates of group membership are far from perfect. For example, surveys have not typically asked people how many associations they belong to. Instead, they have asked whether people belong to various types of groups, and answers to these questions have been aggregated to produce a total number of memberships. This aggregate figure is misleading because anyone may belong to several groups of a particular type. Over time, Americans' memberships may have concentrated within certain categories, creating an illusion of decline.

Critics have identified two additional problems with established survey instruments. First, they point out that since strictly comparable poll questions have been asked only since the 1970s, it is hard to know whether aggregate group membership has declined since earlier decades. Second, they argue that existing surveys are unlikely to have captured all recent changes in U.S. associational life—for example, the proliferation of faith-based informal "small groups" that Robert Wuthnow has so painstakingly documented.

Still, there is no evidence that the average rate of membership has increased in the last quarter century. This is a surprise, because in the past rising levels of education have been linked with increased associational activity. It appears that two trends over the past quarter century have roughly counterbalanced each other: the proportion of high school and college graduates in the population has grown larger, but civic participation at every educational level has declined. People with high school diplomas but no college education have become about 32 percent less likely to join any associations, while there has been an increase in the proportion of people who belong to no organizations at all.

Trends among racial and ethnic groups reflect their distinctive history and condition. To take just one example, African Americans have traditionally combined formal political acts, such as registering people to vote, with group membership and protest tactics. Overall, there has been little decline in these forms of civic engagement since the "activist" 1960s, but African Americans have typically shifted their attention from civil rights struggles to quality-of-life issues in local communities. And as Frederick C. Harris has noted, African Americans without much formal education have, like their white counterparts, largely dropped out of community-oriented activities as well as formal political life.

Another way to break down aggregate measures of civil society is to look at types of organizations. Most categories have seen little change since 1972, when the General Social Survey first asked relevant poll questions. For instance, religious associations, sports leagues, and youth organizations have had stable membership levels. However, millions of people have left labor unions and fraternal societies such as the Elks and Masons, and similar numbers have joined professional associations. Membership in school service groups has substantially increased, perhaps because of recent efforts to link community service and learning. Finally, as Everett C. Ladd has pointed out, there has been a huge shift from mainline Protestant denominations to evangelical churches.

Not All Groups Are Created Equal

These changes may prove significant for the future of democracy in America. Throughout American history, voluntary associations have been valued because they are thought to build civic virtue, foster trust, encourage cooperation, and promote political participation. But on closer inspection, it turns out that not all associations promote democratic health in the same way or to the same extent.

Unions, for instance, are important sources of solidarity among working people. They have core functions that attract members, but they also offer social activities, information, and mutual assistance. They also offer a measure of political power to workers, thereby increasing pluralism and encouraging participation. Members of union households are 8 percent more likely than other people to vote. Though John Brehm and Wendy Rahn have found that union membership is a relatively weak predictor of overall associational membership, Eric Uslaner's research shows that unionized workers join more voluntary organizations and make more charitable contributions than other people do. The dramatic decline in union membership over the past 40 years has been exacerbated by factors—automation, international competition, the relocation of factories to nonunion states, and changes in federal labor law enforcement—that do not directly affect other associations.

Fraternal organizations and women's auxiliaries have suffered deep losses in membership since 1974. As Theda Skocpol has demonstrated, these groups traditionally had deep roots in their communities, and they offered men and women of different classes an opportunity to talk and cooperate more or less as equals—something that professional associations, which have grown in recent decades, do not do. The important question is what (if anything) will replace the cross-class local organizations that flourished through most of American history.

Church-affiliated groups are the backbone of civil society in America, involving almost half the population (compared with just 13 percent in the average industrialized democracy). Religious associations offer ways for people to give money, receive aid, hold meetings, recruit members for other associations, and learn about public issues. As Sidney Verba, Kay Lehman Schlozman, and Henry E. Brady have found, they are especially valuable for people with little income or education, who tend not to join other groups. Polls show that membership in such groups correlates with voting, volunteering, charity, and political activity.

Evangelical denominations are no exception. The experience, values, and personal networks that they develop transfer easily to politics. They have little hierarchy, and they demand intense participation from their members. For example, as part of their church activities, Baptists are much more likely to plan meetings and make presentations than are Catholics. The growth of evangelical denominations has introduced many people, especially lower-income people, to the political process and given them powerful tools for mutual aid.

Even as fundamentalist denominations encourage the faithful to rely on one another, however, there is evidence that they promote distrust of outsiders. This practice, ironically, helps voter turnout, because a fervent dislike for others motivates people to vote. The broader point, however, is that increased mutual reliance and trust within groups is not necessarily correlated with increased trust among groups.

Mailing-list associations, from the National Rifle Association to the Children's Defense Fund, have grown since 1970. Members of these groups contribute dues to support professional staff; but they do not donate much time or effort. Presumably, writing a check improves one's skills, knowledge, and interpersonal trust much less than attending a meeting or organizing a grass-roots movement.

But mailing-list organizations must not be stereotyped. The Sierra Club, for instance, has been described as a group whose members merely write checks and read newsletters. But as George Pettinico has noted, in one May weekend, the Los Angeles chapter alone organized 39 events, from classes to camping excursions, that were cooperative and participatory.

The controversy over contemporary national check-writing organizations raises broader historical and political issues about the relationship between top-down and bottom-up activities. Theda Skocpol argues that classic voluntary associations such as the PTA and the American Legion succeeded in creating both effective national lobbying arms and vital chapters or affiliates at the state and local levels, with close communication between the various tiers. It should also be said that even pure mailing-list organizations can be effective political actors, thereby freeing members to perform other civic tasks.

Still, a large shift from grass-roots groups to national membership organizations would be grounds for concern. In general, today's associations offer relatively few opportunities for local leadership and deliberation. The past 25 years have seen a marked decline in the share of people who belong to committees and serve as officers of local groups, a trend that parallels declines in such forms of local political activity as attending school board meetings and participating in political parties.

Associational Life and Healthy Democracy

Recent scholarship suggests complex links between associational activities and key political variables such as political participation, social trust, and confidence in government. Controlling for education and income, members of church groups, neighborhood associations, and sports leagues are especially likely to follow politics and vote—a correlation that supports the hypothesis that political participation is significantly more attractive for individuals who belong to social networks. It's not hard to see why. Making a meaningful decision at the polls requires a big investment of time and attention. Because members of voluntary groups have many opportunities to discuss politics, they can easily acquire information, and they are sometimes persuaded to vote by each other or by local politicians and activists who gravitate to organizations. By urging fellow members to support particular candidates or causes, citizens can multiply their political power.

Most studies find that associational membership is also linked to trust in other people. But researchers differ on the strength of the relationship and on the direction of the causal arrow between the two. A recent poll of Philadelphians by the Pew Research Center for the People and the Press showed no strong direct link between trust and participation in voluntary activities. However, Philadelphians who believed that they could "make a difference" tended to be trusting; they were also especially likely to volunteer.

Interpersonal trust and confidence in government tend to go together. Some research suggests that disenchantment with official institutions is an important cause of wariness toward other people. When political leaders let us down, we draw negative conclusions about human nature in general. The reverse is presumably true as well: wariness toward other people (stemming from crime, family dysfunction, and other sources) may affect our confidence in politicians.

Yet trust in government has fallen more precipitously than interpersonal trust. Much of the decline took place in 1963–75, an era defined largely by Vietnam and Watergate. And perhaps, to a significant extent, the decline was justified. But there now exists, at least at the extremes, evidence of paranoia rather than healthy distrust. According to a recent study by the University of Virginia's Post-Modernity Project, a fifth of Americans believe that the governing elite is "involved in a conspiracy." Widespread fear of major public institutions not only creates generalized distrust thereby discouraging group membership—but may also cause people to favor exclusive and inward-looking organizations. As noted by Warren E. Miller and J. Merrill Shanks, excessive cynicism about politics and government may well discourage voting and other forms of political participation. A presumption that politicians are unworthy keeps many honorable people out of the field. And a belief in conspiracies prevents citizens from making critical distinctions among leaders, organizations, and ideologies.

A Refuge from Politics?

The evidence now available does not permit firm conclusions about the overall condition of associational life in America. But it does seem that voluntary activities are on balance healthier than are formal political institutions and processes. Indeed, citizens, particularly the youngest, seem to be shifting their preferred civic involvement from official politics to the voluntary sector. If so, the classic Tocquevillian thesis would have to be modified: local civic life, far from acting as a school for wider political involvement, may increasingly serve as a refuge from (and alternative to) it. The consequences for the future of our democracy could be significant.

DISCUSSION QUESTIONS

1. How many voluntary organizations do you belong to? Are they mainly political or civic? What is the main reason you do not join more?

2. Is it better if people trust the government more, or is it better to be skeptical of the government and constantly question its actions?

3. Do you think young people today are less civically involved than their parents? Does society today make it more difficult to get involved than, say, thirty years ago? Do young people today use voluntary commitments as a substitute for political participation, as Galston and Levine suggest?

4. Advertising stimulates us to consume more and earn more money. In your opinion, would advertisements that tried to make civic involvements sexy or cool be effective? What is the best way to stimulate greater civic participation?

5. What effect did the terrorist attacks have on your attitudes toward government and civic voluntarism? Are you concerned that the surge in patriotism that followed the attacks of 9/11 will result in the loss of civil liberties or in unjustified use of military force abroad?

SUGGESTED READINGS AND INTERNET RESOURCES

Robert Putnam's *Bowling Alone: The Collapse and Revival of American Community* (New York: Simon & Schuster, 2000) is an excellent starting point to enter the debate on the condition of American civil society. For an upbeat account of how Americans are renewing civil society, see Putnam and Lewis M. Fieldstein, *Better Together: Restoring the American Community* (New York: Simon & Schuster, 2003). The most extensive factual critique of Putnam's thesis is Everett Carll Ladd's *The Ladd Report* (New York: Free Press, 1999). An influential early statement of the thesis that big government is responsible for the decline of civil society is Peter L. Berger and Richard John Neuhaus, *To Empower People: The Role of Mediating Structures in Public Policy* (Washington, D.C.: American Enterprise Institute for Public Policy Research, 1977). An excellent collection of articles from both ends of the political spectrum is E. J. Dionne Jr., *Community Works: The Revival of Civil Society in America* (Washington, D.C.: Brookings Institution Press, 1998). One of the best collections of scholarly articles on civil society is Theda Skocpol and Morris P. Fiorina, eds., *Civic Engagement in American Democracy* (Washington, D.C.: Brookings Institution Press, 1999).

Civil Society International
www.civilsoc.org
This is the website of an organization dedicated to strengthening civic organizations and democratic institutions all over the globe.

Center for Civil Society Studies
www.jhu.edu/~ccss
The Center for Civil Society Studies is housed at the Johns Hopkins University Institute for Policy Studies. Its website reports on research designed to help philanthropies and nonprofits carry out their missions.

Informal Education Encyclopedia/Forum
www.infed.org/thinkers/putnam.htm
This site provides background on Robert D. Putnam and a bibliography that gives hyperlinks to his works as well as to other publications examining the civil society debate.

CHAPTER 5

Political Economy: How Democratic Is the Free Market Economy?

At first glance, democratic politics and free market economics seem to go together. The liberty to speak, to practice any religion or none at all, and to participate in politics has often come to be associated with the right to make as much money as we can, to succeed or fail according to our own merits in a free marketplace. Free enterprise seems as unintimidating as a yard sale or a bazaar, with many buyers and sellers, colorful haggling, and a variety of products from which to choose. In contrast, big, intrusive government, with its taxes, police, laws, and bureaucracy, appears to present the greatest threat to all these rights. The equation of democracy with free market capitalism seems, especially since the demise of communism, the best and now the only economic game in town. After all, aren't the most prosperous countries in the world also the most free from governmental control? And even if there are sometimes problems, what would be an alternative to what we have?

At closer inspection, though, the marriage between democracy and contemporary capitalism continues to be a contentious one everywhere. In Singapore and China, and arguably in many states of the former USSR, for instance, the rise of the market economy has hardly led to political freedom. And in America, free enterprise capitalism and political democracy may exist at the same time, but their relationship is hardly cozy. Everywhere, free market capitalism seems to generate enormous wealth, but also wrenching instability and inequalities. *Political economy* is the study of the relationship between the two in the very different countries around the globe. The two essays that follow ask what the roles of government, citizens, corporations, workers, and consumers actually *are* in America and also what they *should* be to best serve the public interest.

Perhaps the most important debate in political economy concerns the relationship among democracy, equality, and economic efficiency. Aristotle wrote that democracy couldn't tolerate extremes of wealth and poverty; large inequalities destroyed the spirit of self-sacrifice and fellowship necessary in a democracy. Politics became less the search for the common good than the single-minded pursuit of material interests by rich and poor alike. While the wealthy fell into luxury and decadence, the poor would sink into ignorance and envy.

For those who believe that economic equality and social equality are important for democratic politics, recent trends in our political economy are indeed ominous. Despite impressive economic growth, the U.S. economic system at the beginning of the millennium features high levels of income and wealth inequality. The income and wealth gap has widened continually at the expense of what was once a very large and politically predominant middle class. While the economy has produced new jobs and vast new wealth, workers in the most rapidly expanding areas (home health aides, orderlies, restaurant workers) are paid very low wages and are largely deprived of health and pension benefits. In 2003, nearly half the national income went to just 20 percent of the population, and the top 20,000 income earners accumulated as much as the bottom 96 million! Most U.S. wage earners have been facing increased insecurity, as waves of corporate mergers, downsizing, outsourcing, and other "innovations" make companies leaner but also meaner. Is the free market really free? If it produces such results, can democracy survive such new extremes?

Many corporations and individuals as well as ordinary Americans defend such inequalities by pointing to the efficiency, growth, and technological innovation that they say are consequences of the free enterprise system. They argue that it is healthier to divide a very large economic pie unequally than to have no pie to divide at all; they go on to say that many of the new changes represent necessary and inevitable adjustments to the realities of the new global economy. The market, its many defenders claim, also preserves liberty by allowing each individual to compete fairly and consumers to choose among a wide range of new products. Free market economies are said to be meritocracies, rewarding the industrious with wealth and punishing the lazy with hardship. In George Gilder's words: "A successful economy depends on the proliferation of the rich, on creating a large class of risk-taking men who are willing to shun the easy channels of a comfortable life in order to create new enterprise, win huge profits, and invest them again."

The two essays that follow not only offer opposing views about the meanings of American democracy and capitalism; they also differ about the meaning of freedom, individual liberty, and equality. They disagree profoundly about what role government actually does play in relationship to the U.S. market economy as well as about what role it should play.

The first essay is excerpted from *Capitalism and Freedom*, by Nobel Prize winner Milton Friedman. It was originally written in 1962 and has since been reissued in many editions. Friedman describes himself as a "classic liberal" and tries to restore the original doctrine's political and moral meanings. Classic liberals like Friedman advocate maximum individual freedom in the face of government's tendency to tyrannize. The market economy, Friedman argues, "remov[es] the organization of economic activity from the control of political authority," thereby "eliminat[ing] this source of coercive power." Since liberty is synonymous with democracy, Friedman argues that government has only two legitimate roles. It must defend the national territory and act as an umpire, deciding the rules of the market "game" and interpreting them as necessary when free individuals compete with one another.

In the second essay, Samuel Bowles, Frank Roosevelt, and Richard Edwards deny Friedman's claim that market capitalism and small government go together. They argue that "the expansion of the role of government in the United States is not something that happened in *opposition* to capitalism" but something that happened "in *response* to the development of capitalism." Bowles, Roosevelt, and Edwards go on to claim that a capitalist market economy is hardly a meritocracy; political power and economic power are linked and establish biased rules. Unlike Friedman, they say that the marketplace concentrates both kinds of power. Hierarchical corporations determine the investments and life circumstances for workers and communities and severely limit the meaning and scope of democratic government and citizenship themselves. For these writers, growing economic inequality spells the effective denial of liberty to the many. Corporate power often buys undue political influence, whether through campaign contributions or corporate ownership of the mass media.

The authors of both essays base their arguments on a defense of democracy. While reading them, ask the following questions: How would Friedman have defended himself against the charge that the market economy produces corporations that exercise unchecked and undemocratic power? What would Bowles, Roosevelt, and Edwards say to Friedman's charge that government often poses a threat to individual freedom and choice and thus to democratic liberty? How do both essays deal with voters and citizens and their potential role in controlling the production and distribution of economic resources? How would our political economy change if each author had his way? How would it stay the same?

Capitalism and Freedom

MILTON FRIEDMAN

Introduction

The free man will ask neither what his country can do for him nor what he can do for his country.[1] He will ask rather "What can I and my compatriots do through government" to help us discharge our individual responsibilities, to achieve our several goals and purposes, and above all, to protect our freedom? And he will accompany this question with another: How can we keep the government we create from becoming a Frankenstein that will destroy the very freedom we establish it to protect? Freedom is a rare and delicate plant. Our minds tell us, and history confirms, that the great threat to freedom is the concentration of power. Government is necessary to preserve our freedom, it is an instrument through which we can exercise our freedom; yet by concentrating power in political hands, it is also a threat to freedom. Even though the men who wield this power initially be of good will and even though they be not corrupted by the power they exercise, the power will both attract and form men of a different stamp.

How can we benefit from the promise of government while avoiding the threat to freedom? Two broad principles embodied in our Constitution give an answer that has preserved our freedom so far, though they have been violated repeatedly in practice while proclaimed as precept.

First, the scope of government must be limited. Its major function must be to protect our freedom both from the enemies outside our gates and from our fellow-citizens: to preserve law and order, to enforce private contracts, to foster competitive markets. Beyond this major function, government may enable us at times to accomplish jointly what we would find it more difficult or expensive to accomplish severally. However, any such use of government is fraught with danger. We should not and cannot avoid using government in this way. But there should be a clear and large balance of advantages before we do. By relying primarily on voluntary co-operation and private enterprise, in both economic and other activities, we can insure that the private sector is a check on the powers of the governmental sector and an effective protection of freedom of speech, of religion, and of thought.

---

1. Friedman is referring to John F. Kennedy's 1961 inaugural address.

The second broad principle is that government power must be dispersed. If government is to exercise power, better in the county than in the state, better in the state than in Washington. If I do not like what my local community does, be it in sewage disposal, or zoning, or schools, I can move to another local community, and though few may take this step, the mere possibility acts as a check. If I do not like what my state does, I can move to another. If I do not like what Washington imposes, I have few alternatives in this world of jealous nations. . . .

Government can never duplicate the variety and diversity of individual action. At any moment in time, by imposing uniform standards in housing, or nutrition, or clothing, government could undoubtedly improve the level of living of many individuals; by imposing uniform standards in schooling, road construction, or sanitation, central government could undoubtedly improve the level of performance in many local areas and perhaps even on the average of all communities. But in the process, government would replace progress by stagnation, it would substitute uniform mediocrity for the variety essential for that experimentation which can bring tomorrow's laggards above today's mean. . . .

The Relation Between Economic Freedom and Political Freedom

It is widely believed that politics and economics are separate and largely unconnected; that individual freedom is a political problem and material welfare an economic problem; and that any kind of political arrangements can be combined with any kind of economic arrangements. . . . The thesis of this chapter is . . . that there is an intimate connection between economics and politics, that only certain combinations of political and economic arrangements are possible, and that in particular, a society which is socialist cannot also be democratic, in the sense of guaranteeing individual freedom.

Economic arrangements play a dual role in the promotion of a free society. On the one hand, freedom in economic arrangements is itself a component of freedom broadly understood, so economic freedom is an end in itself. In the second place, economic freedom is also an indispensable means toward the achievement of political freedom.

The first of these roles of economic freedom needs special emphasis because intellectuals in particular have a strong bias against regarding this aspect of freedom as important. They tend to express contempt for what they regard as material aspects of life, and to regard their own pursuit of allegedly higher values as on a different plane of significance and as deserving of special attention. For most citizens of the country, however, if not for the intellectual, the direct importance of economic freedom is at least comparable in significance to the indirect importance of economic freedom as a means to political freedom. . . .

Viewed as a means to the end of political freedom, economic arrangements are important because of their effect on the concentration or dispersion of power. The kind of economic organization that provides economic freedom directly, namely, competitive capitalism, also promotes political freedom because it separates economic power from political power and in this way enables the one to offset the other.

Historical evidence speaks with a single voice on the relation between political freedom and a free market. I know of no example in time or place of a society that has been marked by a large measure of political freedom, and that has not also used something comparable to a free market to organize the bulk of economic activity.

Because we live in a largely free society, we tend to forget how limited is the span of time and the part of the globe for which there has ever been anything like political freedom: the typical state of mankind is tyranny, servitude, and misery. The nineteenth century and early twentieth century in the Western world stand out as striking exceptions to the general trend of historical development. Political freedom in this instance clearly came along with the free market and the development of capitalist institutions. So also did political freedom in the golden age of Greece and in the early days of the Roman era.

History suggests only that capitalism is a necessary condition for political freedom. Clearly it is not a sufficient condition. Fascist Italy and Fascist Spain, Germany at various times in the last seventy years, Japan before World Wars I and II, tzarist Russia in the decades before World War I— are all societies that cannot conceivably be described as politically free. Yet, in each, private enterprise was the dominant form of economic organization. It is therefore clearly possible to have economic arrangements that are fundamentally capitalist and political arrangements that are not free.

Even in those societies, the citizenry had a good deal more freedom than citizens of a modern totalitarian state.[2] . . . Even in Russia under the Tzars, it was possible for some citizens, under some circumstances, to change their jobs without getting permission from political authority because capitalism and the existence of private property provided some check to the centralized power of the state. . . .

Historical evidence by itself can never be convincing. Perhaps it was sheer coincidence that the expansion of freedom occurred at the same time as the development of capitalist and market institutions. Why should there be a connection? What are the logical links between economic and political freedom? In discussing these questions we shall consider first the market as a direct component of freedom, and then the indirect relation between market arrangements and political freedom. A by-product will be an outline of the ideal economic arrangements for a free society.

---

2. A totalitarian state is a political order in which state power is held by a single political party, with no political rights accorded to individuals. Friedman here is referring to the former Soviet Union and to other communist countries.

As liberals, we take freedom of the individual, or perhaps the family, as our ultimate goal in judging social arrangements. Freedom as a value in this sense has to do with the interrelations among people; it has no meaning whatsoever to a Robinson Crusoe on an isolated island. . . . Robinson Crusoe on his island is subject to "constraint," he has limited "power," and he has only a limited number of alternatives, but there is no problem of freedom in the sense that is relevant to our discussion. Similarly, in a society freedom has nothing to say about what an individual does with his freedom; it is not an all-embracing ethic. Indeed, a major aim of the liberal is to leave the ethical problem for the individual to wrestle with. The "really" important ethical problems are those that face an individual in a free society—what he should do with his freedom. There are thus two sets of values that a liberal will emphasize—the values that are relevant to relations among people, which is the context in which he assigns first priority to freedom; and the values that are relevant to the individual in the exercise of his freedom, which is the realm of individual ethics and philosophy.

The liberal conceives of men as imperfect beings. He regards the problem of social organization to be as much a negative problem of preventing "bad" people from doing harm as of enabling "good" people to do good; and, of course, "bad" and "good" people may be the same people, depending on who is judging them.

The basic problem of social organization is how to co-ordinate the economic activities of large numbers of people. Even in relatively backward societies, extensive division of labor and specialization of function is required to make effective use of available resources. In advanced societies, the scale on which co-ordination is needed, to take full advantage of the opportunities offered by modern science and technology, is enormously greater. Literally millions of people are involved in providing one another with their daily bread, let alone with their yearly automobiles. The challenge to the believer in liberty is to reconcile this widespread interdependence with individual freedom.

Fundamentally, there are only two ways of co-ordinating the economic activities of millions. One is central direction involving the use of coercion—the technique of the army and of the modern totalitarian state. The other is voluntary co-operation of individuals—the technique of the market place.

The possibility of co-ordination through voluntary co-operation rests on the elementary—yet frequently denied—proposition that both parties to an economic transaction benefit from it, *provided the transaction is bilaterally voluntary and informed.*

Exchange can therefore bring about co-ordination without coercion. A working model of a society organized through voluntary exchange is a *free private enterprise exchange economy*—what we have been calling competitive capitalism.

In its simplest form, such a society consists of a number of independent households—a collection of Robinson Crusoes, as it were. Each household uses the resources it controls to produce goods and services that it exchanges for goods and services produced by other households, on terms mutually acceptable to the two parties to the bargain. It is thereby enabled to satisfy its wants indirectly by producing goods and services for others, rather than directly by producing goods for its own immediate use. The incentive for adopting this indirect route is, of course, the increased product made possible by division of labor and specialization of function. Since the household always has the alternative of producing directly for itself, it need not enter into any exchange unless it benefits from it. Hence, no exchange will take place unless both parties do benefit from it. Co-operation is thereby achieved without coercion.

Specialization of function and division of labor would not go far if the ultimate productive unit were the household. In a modern society, we have gone much further. We have introduced enterprises which are intermediaries between individuals in their capacities as suppliers of service and as purchasers of goods. And similarly, specialization of function and division of labor could not go very far if we had to continue to rely on the barter of product for product. In consequence, money has been introduced as a means of facilitating exchange, and of enabling the acts of purchase and of sale to be separated into two parts.

Despite the important role of enterprises and of money in our actual economy, and despite the numerous and complex problems they raise, the central characteristic of the market technique of achieving co-ordination is fully displayed in the simple exchange economy that contains neither enterprises nor money. As in that simple model, so in the complex enterprise and money-exchange economy, co-operation is strictly individual and voluntary *provided:* (*a*) that enterprises are private, so that the ultimate contracting parties are individuals and (*b*) that individuals are effectively free to enter or not to enter into any particular exchange, so that every transaction is strictly voluntary. . . .

So long as effective freedom of exchange is maintained, the central feature of the market organization of economic activity is that it prevents one person from interfering with another in respect of most of his activities. The consumer is protected from coercion by the seller because of the presence of other sellers with whom he can deal. The seller is protected from coercion by the consumer because of other consumers to whom he can sell. The employee is protected from coercion by the employer because of other employers for whom he can work, and so on. And the market does this impersonally and without centralized authority.

Indeed, a major source of objection to a free economy is precisely that it does this task so well. It gives people what they want instead of what a particular group thinks they ought to want. Underlying most arguments against the free market is a lack of belief in freedom itself.

The existence of a free market does not of course eliminate the need for government. On the contrary, government is essential both as a forum for determining the "rules of the game" and as an umpire to interpret and enforce the rules decided on. What the market does is to reduce greatly the range of issues that must be decided through political means, and thereby to minimize the extent to which government need participate directly in the game. The characteristic feature of action through political channels is that it tends to require or enforce substantial conformity. The great advantage of the market, on the other hand, is that it permits wide diversity. It is, in political terms, a system of proportional representation. Each man can vote, as it were, for the color of tie he wants and get it; he does not have to see what color the majority wants and then, if he is in the minority, submit.

It is this feature of the market that we refer to when we say that the market provides economic freedom. But this characteristic also has implications that go far beyond the narrowly economic. Political freedom means the absence of coercion of a man by his fellow men. The fundamental threat to freedom is power to coerce, be it in the hands of a monarch, a dictator, an oligarchy, or a momentary majority. The preservation of freedom requires the elimination of such concentration of power to the fullest possible extent and the dispersal and distribution of whatever power cannot be eliminated—a system of checks and balances. By removing the organization of economic activity from the control of political authority, the market eliminates this source of coercive power. It enables economic strength to be a check to political power rather than a reinforcement.

Economic power can be widely dispersed. There is no law of conservation which forces the growth of new centers of economic strength to be at the expense of existing centers. Political power, on the other hand, is more difficult to decentralize. There can be numerous small independent governments. But it is far more difficult to maintain numerous equipotent small centers of political power in a single large government than it is to have numerous centers of economic strength in a single large economy. There can be many millionaires in one large economy. But can there be more than one really outstanding leader, one person on whom the energies and enthusiasms of his countrymen are centered? If the central government gains power, it is likely to be at the expense of local governments. There seems to be something like a fixed total of political power to be distributed. Consequently, if economic power is joined to political power, concentration seems almost inevitable. On the other hand, if economic power is kept in separate hands from political power, it can serve as a check and a counter to political power. . . .

In a capitalist society, it is only necessary to convince a few wealthy people to get funds to launch any idea, however strange, and there are many such persons, many independent foci of support. And, indeed, it is not even necessary to persuade people or financial institutions with available funds of the soundness of the ideas to be propagated. It is only necessary to persuade them that the propagation can be financially successful; that the newspaper or magazine or book or other venture will be profitable. The competitive publisher, for example, cannot afford to publish only writing with which he personally agrees; his touchstone must be the likelihood that the market will be large enough to yield a satisfactory return on his investment. . . .

The Role of Government in a Free Society

. . . From this standpoint, the role of the market is that it permits unanimity without conformity. . . . On the other hand, the characteristic feature of action through explicitly political channels is that it tends to require or to enforce substantial conformity. . . . The typical issue must be decided "yes" or "no"; at most, provision can be made for a fairly limited number of alternatives. . . .

The use of political channels, while inevitable, tends to strain the social cohesion essential for a stable society. The strain is least if agreement for joint action need be reached only on a limited range of issues on which people in any event have common views. Every extension of the range of issues for which explicit agreement is sought strains further the delicate threads that hold society together. If it goes so far as to touch an issue on which men feel deeply yet differently, it may well disrupt the society. Fundamental differences in basic values can seldom if ever be resolved at the ballot box; ultimately they can only be decided, though not resolved, by conflict. The religious and civil wars of history are a bloody testament to this judgment.

The widespread use of the market reduces the strain on the social fabric by rendering conformity unnecessary with respect to any activities it encompasses. The wider the range of activities covered by the market, the fewer are the issues on which explicitly political decisions are required and hence on which it is necessary to achieve agreement. In turn, the fewer the issues on which agreement is necessary, the greater is the likelihood of getting agreement while maintaining a free society. . . .

Government as Rule-Maker and Umpire

. . . Just as a good game requires acceptance by the players both of the rules and of the umpire to interpret and enforce them, so a good society requires that its members agree on the general conditions that will govern relations among them, on some means of arbitrating different interpretations of these conditions, and on some device for enforcing compliance with the generally accepted rules. . . . In both games and society also, no set of rules can prevail unless most participants most of the time conform to them without external sanctions; unless that is, there is a broad underlying social consensus. But we cannot rely on custom or on this consensus alone to interpret and to enforce the rules; we need an umpire. These then are the basic roles of government in a free society: to provide a means whereby we can modify the rules, to mediate differences among us on the meaning of the rules, and to enforce compliance with the rules on the part of those few who would otherwise not play the game.

The need for government in these respects arises because absolute freedom is impossible. However attractive anarchy may be as a philosophy, it is not feasible in a world of imperfect men. Men's freedoms can conflict, and when they do, one man's freedom must be limited to preserve another's— as a Supreme Court Justice once put it, "My freedom to move my fist must be limited by the proximity of your chin.". . .

Action Through Government on Grounds of Technical Monopoly and Neighborhood Effects

The role of government . . . is to do something that the market cannot do for itself, namely, to determine, arbitrate, and enforce the rules of the game. We may also want to do through government some things that might conceivably be done through the market but that technical or similar conditions render it difficult to do in that way. These all reduce to cases in which strictly voluntary exchange is either exceedingly costly or practically impossible. There are two general classes of such cases: monopoly and similar market imperfections, and neighborhood effects.

Exchange is truly voluntary only when nearly equivalent alternatives exist. Monopoly implies the absence of alternatives and thereby inhibits effective freedom of exchange. In practice, monopoly frequently, if not generally, arises from government support or from collusive agreements among individuals. With respect to these, the problem is either to avoid governmental fostering of monopoly or to stimulate the effective enforcement of rules such as those embodied in our anti-trust laws. However, monopoly may also arise because it is technically efficient to have a single producer or enterprise. I venture to suggest that such cases are more limited than is supposed but they unquestionably do arise. . . .

A second general class of cases in which strictly voluntary exchange is impossible arises when actions of individuals have effects on other individuals for which it is not feasible to charge or recompense them. This is the problem of "neighborhood effects." An obvious example is the pollution of a stream. The man who pollutes a stream is in effect forcing others to exchange good water for bad. These others might be willing to make the exchange at a price. But it is not feasible for them, acting individually, to avoid the exchange or to enforce appropriate compensation. . . .

Parks are an interesting example because they illustrate the difference between cases that can and cases that cannot be justified by neighborhood effects, and because almost everyone at first sight regards the conduct of National Parks as obviously a valid function of government. In fact, however, neighborhood effects may justify a city park; they do not justify a national park, like Yellowstone National Park or the Grand Canyon. What is the fundamental difference between the two? For the city park, it is extremely difficult to identify the people who benefit from it and to charge them for the benefits which they receive. If there is a park in the middle of the city, the houses on all sides get the benefit of the open space, and people who walk through it or by it also benefit. To maintain toll collectors at the gates or to impose annual charges per window overlooking the park would be very expensive and difficult. The entrances to a national park like Yellowstone, on the other hand, are few; most of the people who come stay for a considerable period of time and it is perfectly feasible to set up toll gates and collect admission charges. This is indeed now done, though the charges do not cover the whole costs. If the public wants this kind of an activity enough to pay for it, private enterprises will have every incentive to provide such parks. And, of course, there are many private enterprises of this nature now in existence. I cannot myself conjure up any neighborhood effects or important monopoly effects that would justify governmental activity in this area.

Considerations like those I have treated under the heading of neighborhood effects have been used to rationalize almost every conceivable intervention. In many instances, however, this rationalization is special pleading rather than a legitimate application of the concept of neighborhood effects. Neighborhood effects cut both ways. They can be a reason for limiting the activities of government as well as for expanding them. . . .

Action Through Government on Paternalistic Grounds

Freedom is a tenable objective only for responsible individuals. We do not believe in freedom for madmen or children. The necessity of drawing a line between responsible individuals and others is inescapable, yet it means that there is an essential ambiguity in our ultimate objective of freedom. Paternalism is inescapable for those whom we designate as not responsible.

The clearest case, perhaps, is that of madmen. We are willing neither to permit them freedom nor to shoot them. It would be nice if we could rely on voluntary activities of individuals to house and care for the madmen. But I think we cannot rule out the possibility that such charitable activities will be inadequate, if only because of the neighborhood effect involved in the fact that I benefit if another man contributes to the care of the insane. For this reason, we may be willing to arrange for their care through government.

Children offer a more difficult case. The ultimate operative unit in our society is the family, not the individual. Yet the acceptance of the family as the unit rests in considerable part on expediency rather than principle. We believe that parents are generally best able to protect their children and to provide for their development into responsible individuals for whom freedom is appropriate. But we do not believe in the freedom of parents to do what they will with other people. The children are responsible individuals in embryo, and a believer in freedom believes in protecting their ultimate rights.

To put this in a different and what may seem a more callous way, children are at one and the same time consumer goods and potentially responsible members of society. The freedom of individuals to use their economic resources as they want includes the freedom to use them to have children—to buy, as it were, the services of children as a particular form of consumption. But once this choice is exercised, the children have a value in and of themselves and have a freedom of their own that is not simply an extension of the freedom of the parents.

The paternalistic ground for governmental activity is in many ways the most troublesome to a liberal; for it involves the acceptance of a principle—that some shall decide for others—which he finds objectionable in most applications and which he rightly regards as a hallmark of his chief intellectual opponents, the proponents of collectivism in one or another of its guises, whether it be communism, socialism, or a welfare state. Yet there is no use pretending that problems are simpler than in fact they are. There is no avoiding the need for some measure of paternalism. . . .

Conclusion

A government which maintained law and order, defined property rights, served as a means whereby we could modify property rights and other rules of the economic game, adjudicated disputes about the interpretation of the rules, enforced contracts, promoted competition, provided a monetary framework, engaged in activities to counter technical monopolies and to overcome neighborhood effects widely regarded as sufficiently important to justify government intervention, and which supplemented private charity and the private family in protecting the irresponsible, whether madman or child—such a government would clearly have important functions to perform. The consistent liberal is not an anarchist. . . .

Is it an accident that so many of the governmental reforms of recent decades have gone awry, that the bright hopes have turned to ashes? Is it simply because the programs are faulty in detail?

I believe the answer is clearly in the negative. The central defect of these measures is that they seek through government to force people to act against their own immediate interests in order to promote a supposedly general interest. They seek to resolve what is supposedly a conflict of interest, or a difference in view about interests, not by establishing a framework that will eliminate the conflict, or by persuading people to have different interests, but by forcing people to act against their own interest. They substitute the values of outsiders for the values of participants; either some telling others what is good for them, or the government taking from some to benefit others. These measures are therefore countered by one of the strongest and most creative forces known to man—the attempt by millions of individuals to promote their own interests, to live their lives by their own values. This is the major reason why the measures have so often had the opposite of the effects intended. It is also one of the major strengths of a free society and explains why governmental regulation does not strangle it.

Corporate Capitalism Hurts American Democracy

SAMUEL BOWLES,
FRANK ROOSEVELT,
AND RICHARD EDWARDS

A capitalist economy operates on the basis of a set of principles—rules of the game—designed to organize commodity production for profit using wage labor and privately owned capital goods. Governments, on the other hand, are organized according to different principles, a different set of rules. These rules make possible collective action, and involve a compulsory relationship between citizens and their government. Governments—or government leaders—act on behalf of the entire population of a nation, and their actions can be enforced on all of its residents.

The principles of democratic government are very different from those that govern the capitalist economy. Generally, the employees of a corporation do not elect its leaders—the management—and neither does the community in which the corporation is located. In fact, corporate leaders are not elected at all in the sense that is usually attached to the word *election*. The people who own the corporation select them, with each owner having as many votes as the number of shares of stock he or she owns. Similarly, freedom of speech and other civil liberties guaranteed in the political sphere are often limited in the workplace. Many businesses enforce dress codes, and employees are generally not free to post information such as appeals from labor unions.

These two sets of rules—the rules of democratic government and the rules of a capitalist economy—exist side by side in our society. Both affect the economy, and they each conflict. Why has government grown and what does it have to do with the capitalist economy? Do citizens or capitalists have power in politics? Below, we address these questions.

The Expansion of Government Economic Activity

During the past century, the economic importance of the government has grown dramatically. Because its role has expanded qualitatively as well as quantitatively, and because not all government activities are equally important in relation to the economy, there is no single measure by which the expansion of the government's role can be adequately gauged. Measured in dollars, however, federal, state, and local government spending in the

United States increased from 7.7 percent of the total output of the economy in 1902 to 31 percent of it in 2002.

In the United States, increases in military, Social Security, and health-related programs in the twentieth century led to substantial growth of expenditures at the level of the federal government. Expansion of such direct services as public schools, municipal hospitals, and police and fire protection led to even more rapid growth of employment at the state and local levels.

Although government expenditures at all levels in the United States increased greatly during the past century, the sum of such expenditures, as a share of the nation's total output of goods and services, is smaller than the comparable percentages of national output spent by governments in other advanced capitalist countries.

The reasons for the increased economic importance of the government are much debated. Some people see growing government as a triumph by the ordinary citizen over the self-serving interests of business. Others see the growth as a triumph of the bureaucratic mentality, which assumes that if there is a problem its solution must take the form of a government program. Still others see big government and the free market economy as opposites.

But there is a more persuasive explanation for the increasing role of government in economic life: **The survival and workability of capitalism as an economic system has required the government to grow.** The ceaseless search for extra profits and the ensuing social, technical, and other changes . . . have created conditions that have led to demands for a more active government. These demands, as we will see, have come as often from businesspeople as from workers, as often from the Chamber of Commerce as from the AFL-CIO, as often from Republicans as from Democrats. The expansion of the role of government in the United States is not something that happened in *opposition* to capitalism; rather, it is something that has happened in *response* to the development of capitalism. In what specific ways did this expansion occur?

Economic Concentration

Much of the growth of governmental economic activity can be explained by the growth of large corporations and the decline of small producers. The enormous power of modern corporations in the United States has allowed their owners to lobby the government for favors and to influence the formation of public opinion. Thus, big business is able to induce the government do things that enhance profit making. Examples of this would include subsidies for the nuclear power industry and exorbitant purchases of military hardware. U.S. corporate leaders have also supported the expansion of government regulation in those many situations in which they wanted protection from competitive pressures that might lower profits. Examples of such situations include regulation of the quality of meat and other food to prevent competition from companies that would lower the quality of such products. In addition, consumers and workers have supported the expansion of the economic role of the government, in part to protect themselves from the power of the giant corporations. Passage of the Sherman Antitrust Act (1890), the Clean Air Act (1970), and the Consumer Product Safety Act (1973) are examples of this.

International Expansion

The increasingly global reach of large American corporations has contributed to the development of a conception of "U.S. interests" around the world. As corporations expanded from national to international businesses, they changed from wanting the government to impose tariffs to keep out goods made abroad to insisting that the government protect U.S. investments around the world. They have promoted the development of an increasingly expensive military establishment to defend these interests. Preparations for war and the payment of interest on the national debt—much of which was borrowed to pay for past wars—have accounted for much of the growth in federal expenditures. Capitalism did not invent war, but the degree of international economic interdependence and rivalry produced by the expansion of capitalism did make *world* wars more likely. After World War II, high levels of military expenditure became a permanent feature of the U.S. economy. In 2002 military expenditures amounted to nearly one-half of the "discretionary spending" part of the U.S. federal budget—the part not already committed to paying for "entitlements" such as Social Security and Medicare. In the aftermath of the terrorist attack on the World Trade Center in 2001 the role of government has increased still further with the creation of the Department of Homeland Security and with the government now empowered to monitor private individuals' e-mail communications and to bypass some of the rights of privacy that Americans had long taken for granted.

Economic Instability

The increasing instability of the economy, marked by periods of severe unemployment and dramatized by the worldwide Great Depression of the 1930s, has been another reason for the growing economic importance of the government. The stabilization of the U.S. economy was a major objective of the businessmen who promoted the formation of the Federal Reserve System in 1913 and the Securities and Exchange Commission in 1935. An even more significant impetus for governmental intervention was the persistence of the Great Depression until military expenditures brought about full employment at the beginning of World War II. During the depressed 1930s, radical political movements of both the left and the right spread around the world generating political instability as people responded in different ways to the failure of capitalist economies to provide for their livelihoods.

In many countries, broad coalitions of employers and workers pushed the government to take greater responsibility for maintaining economic growth, profits, and employment through its activities as a macroeconomic regulator. Immediately following World War II, organizations such as the Committee for Economic Development in the United States were successful in gaining congressional passage of the Employment Act of 1946. This legislation committed the U.S. federal government, at least in principle, to insuring that there would be adequate job opportunities for everyone in the labor force.

The post–World War II growth of total government expenditures has increased the ability of the government to stabilize employment. Some government programs (such as unemployment insurance) act as built-in stabilizers that automatically raise government spending when the economy slows down, thus helping to maintain enough total demand to avoid severe recessions. Other more deliberate macroeconomic regulation such as new tax policies or changes in the rate of interest may also counteract the economy's tendency to provide too few jobs. Except during the Korean War, the Vietnam War, and the late 1990s, however, such policies have not succeeded in bringing about full employment in the United States. In part this is because, despite the Employment Act of 1946, the elimination of unemployment has never actually been the objective of the government's macroeconomic regulation. Alben Barkley, a U.S. senator at the time of its passage, drew attention to the inadequacy of the Full Employment Act by saying that the new law "promised anyone needing a job the right to go out and look for one."

Income Support

During the Great Depression, many Americans became convinced that those unable to make an adequate living should be supported, at least at some minimal level, by the government. Government programs to support poor people replaced informal support systems and private charity, both because people who fell on hard times could no longer count on their families or neighbors to tide them over and because private charities did not have sufficient funds to take care of them. In the 1930s unemployment compensation, general relief, and Social Security were established. With the numerical growth and political mobilization of the aged population and of single parent families during the 1960s and early 1970s, benefits and beneficiaries expanded.

In recent years, however, the idea of government support for those in need has come under serious attack from political forces on the right. From the early 1970s through the 1990s, the expansion of income support programs was halted and, in some cases, reversed. In the 1990s, for example, the average weekly unemployment insurance benefit payment was lower in real terms (corrected for inflation) than it had been twenty years earlier.

With the 1996 "welfare reform" legislation passed by the Republican-dominated Congress and signed into law by President Clinton, the federal role in maintaining income support through Aid to Families with Dependent Children (AFDC) was eliminated altogether. Under the Temporary Assistance to Needy Families (TANF) legislation, blocks of aid were granted to states, which then became solely responsible for providing relief. From 1996 to 2002 welfare roles were further cut back by new regulations requiring all able-bodied former recipients to work at menial jobs in order to qualify for aid. It is too soon to judge whether this recent curtailment of federal support will have beneficial or harmful economic consequences for America's neediest citizens over the long term.

Changing Patterns of Family Life

The combination in the late 1960s of a slowdown in the growth of real wages and an upsurge of women's demands for equality had the effect of altering relationships between women and men both in the household and in the economy as a whole. The two developments have made it less likely that men will be the sole "breadwinners" while their wives stay home to take care of the children, cook the meals, and clean the house. In 1900, only 20 percent of American women worked outside the home; by 2000, the percentage of women between the ages of 25 and 64 in the paid labor force had increased to 73.5 percent.

In the face of wage stagnation from the late 1960s to the mid-1990s, more and more families found that they needed to have both husband and wife in the paid labor force in order to support their living standards. At the same time, the women's movement changed people's consciousness in ways that led at least some men to take more responsibility for household tasks and allowed many more women to take full-time jobs and have careers. Of course these changes have been accompanied by an increasing commodification of household tasks: more children are now taken care of in daycare centers or by paid "nannies," more meals are eaten out or ordered in, and more housecleaning is done by paid "help."

Increases in the labor force participation of women and the broader changes in society's gender roles became yet another set of factors making for expansion of the government's role in the economy. To break down barriers to women's equality in the workplace, new laws and new enforcement activities were required. In the United States, the Civil Rights Act of 1964 created the Equal Employment Opportunity Commission (EEOC) to secure the rights of women as well as members of minority groups to equal opportunities in the workplace. To help both women and men combine paid work with family responsibilities, the U.S. Congress passed and President Clinton signed the 1993 Family and Medical Leave Act. Although compliance with these laws has been less than perfect, they are both significant in bringing U.S. policies closer to those in other advanced industrial nations.

However, citizens in Japan and many Western nations have long had rights to government-funded childcare, to health care for children as well as adults, and to paid parental leave as well as generous required vacation time. In contrast, the U.S. government has been reluctant to formulate comprehensive policies for the support of families, the only exception being for families at or below the poverty line.

Still, the passage of the U.S. Family and Medical Leave Act in 1993 was at least a small step in the direction of governmental support for working families. The Act requires that all workers in firms with more than fifty employees be allowed to take up to twelve weeks of unpaid leave at the time of the birth or adoption of a child or when an ill family member needs to be cared for. Both women and men are covered by the Act. Although their leave is unpaid, employees retain their health benefits while they are on leave and are assured of an equivalent position within their firm when they return to work. What both the Equal Employment Opportunity Commission and the Family and Medical Leave Act do, then, is to assign greater responsibility to the U.S. government for regulating relationships between employers and their employees.

Public Safety

Many groups have demanded that government mediate the conflict between profitability and public safety. While competition generally pushes firms to develop the most profitable technology, the resulting technological advancements do not always result in net benefits to society. The pharmaceutical industry provides an example of the danger of leaving economic decision making solely up to firms seeking to maximize their profits. Certain drugs may be very profitable for the companies, but their side effects, though often complicated and long delayed, may ultimately be damaging to people's health. The chemical industry offers another example of the conflict between profit making and public safety. Some highly profitable production processes in this industry may cause brain damage, sterility, or cancer in the workers who run them; such effects may become known only after many years of exposure. . . .

Environmental Protection

Another issue that has aroused public demands for governmental intervention is the growing need to protect the natural environment from the effects of industrial production. Our natural surroundings—our land, fresh water, air, and oceans—are not only being used, they are being used up or contaminated as corporations compete to produce goods more cheaply. Historically, there have been no prices charged for the use—or misuse—of air and water, and the result has been the pollution of the elements that sustain life. In many cases the most profitable way of disposing of wastes—even very hazardous ones—has been simply to throw them away, using our natural environment as a free dumping ground. Incidents such as the burning of Ohio's Cuyahoga River in 1969, the poisoning of the Love Canal residential area outside of Buffalo in the 1970s, and the 1989 Exxon *Valdez* oil spill off the coast of Alaska have dramatized the need for more adequate controls. The creation of the Environmental Protection Agency and the passage of the Clean Air Act and the Water Pollution Control Act in the early 1970s were important steps in this direction.

Discrimination

Over the last three decades people have come to realize that the unrestricted exercise of private property rights can result in racial and sexual discrimination against both customers and workers. The lunch-counter sit-ins that set off the civil rights movement in the early 1960s brought the issue into sharp relief: should the owners of restaurants and lunch counters have the right to do whatever they please with their property, even if it involves the exclusion of black customers? Or do black people have a right to be treated equally in public places? Since 1964 the U.S. Civil Rights Commission has brought suits against companies, unions, and other institutions to force them to abandon discriminatory practices.

Many of the causes of expanded government economic activity discussed above may be understood as responses to particular aspects of the accumulation process of the capitalist economy. Thus the growth of government regulation has been as much a part of capitalist economic development as the growth of investment or the growth of technology.

But if government has had to grow to repair the problems and hardships caused by the development of the economy, it does not follow that such growth has always succeeded in meeting human needs. It is debatable whether people are today more secure economically than they were a hundred years ago, or better protected from the arbitrary power of giant corporations, or less susceptible to environmental or natural disaster, or less likely to encounter health hazards in their workplace or in their food. Many of the political battles during the last century have been about the extent to which the government can or should be called on to solve social problems caused by economic forces beyond the control of individuals.

Just as we should not overrate the impact of the government's economic activities, we should not exaggerate their extent. Government employment, including the military, is only 15 percent of the total labor force, and of greater significance is the fact that the most important determinant of the future course of the economy—investment—is still almost entirely in private hands. . . .

Government and Corporate Profits

While there is much controversy over the amount of government participation in the economy, the more essential question might be the ways in which government activity and taxation policy affect corporate profits. In general, when it comes to governmental intervention and the corporate profit rate, the power of ordinary citizens and workers is often sacrificed to the needs and political power of large companies and their biggest shareholders. Government can have a huge impact on both the pre-tax profit rate and, through taxation, on how much the after-tax profit rate of corporations rewards shareholders.

Government can improve corporate profits through relatively noncontroversial means, such as promoting research. Yet most other activities provide benefits to some groups and classes and harm others. Consider work regulations and the minimum hourly wage; minimal work regulation and a low minimum wage—both current policies—provide a higher profit rate by cutting corners with safety and by causing higher levels of job insecurity. Current policies permit employers to pay relatively low wages compared to other wealthy countries, speed up work, and obtain other concessions from workers without the time and expense of bargaining with them. These measures are all contrary to what workers generally want—higher wages, safer and less stressful working conditions, and more job opportunities. . . .

Businesses themselves may have contradictory goals for government. Each firm is not so concerned about the economy-wide profit rate as it is about its own profit rate. Thus businesses are often ready to urge the government to adopt policies that will raise their own profit rates even though such policies may push down the profit rates of other businesses. Individual firms lobby the government to reduce their own taxes, to obtain subsidies, or to be allowed to set high prices for their output. Big oil companies benefit enormously from tax credits for foreign royalties paid. The Boeing Corporation has regularly obtained support through government-subsidized cheap credit for the company's foreign customers. Companies in the oil industry were quite happy when the government lifted its controls on oil prices, permitting the price of oil (a raw material input for most other companies) to go up, not down. The oil companies' support of decontrol seemed unaffected by the fact that this policy inflicted big losses on the auto industry, whose high-profit gas guzzlers fell from favor among consumers as gasoline prices rose. Most businesses would be happy to promote government policies that would allow them to pay their own workers less while forcing other firms to pay more. In all these ways, businesses lobby for special benefits that are often in conflict with policies to raise the general profit rate.

Workers, too, have divided interests concerning what the government should do, although often for quite different reasons. Workers in the automobile industry, for example, may want government policies to limit imports of cars produced elsewhere; other workers may want to save money by purchasing a cheaper automobile made in, say, Japan. To take another example, unions that have mainly white male members may be less enthusiastic about government programs designed to secure equal employment opportunities for women and minority workers than unions with substantial minority and female memberships.

Our understanding of government policy is further complicated by the fact that employers and workers are not the only players in the game. Government leaders have their own objectives and face their own constraints. Most of all, they must find ways of getting reelected or reappointed. Such concerns may necessitate appealing to large numbers of voters, an objective that itself may require a combination of two strategies: adopting policies that are in the interest of a majority of voters, and instituting policies that appeal to individuals who can make substantial financial contributions to election campaigns. Only a combination of these strategies would improve one's chance of being reelected: politicians who faithfully serve the interests of the majority but cannot finance election campaigns are just as surely losers as the ones who too blatantly favor the few at the expense of the many.

Government leaders, like businesspeople, may thus find that their objectives work at cross-purposes. To gain favor with business, government leaders may want to cut taxes on profits or high incomes. But raising other taxes to maintain sufficient government revenues may incur the wrath of the broader electorate. And with lower taxes all around, it may be impossible for government leaders to offer public services that are considered essential by a majority of voters.

The three-way tug of war among government leaders, citizens (including workers), and business executives is illustrated, in the following section, by the problem of macroeconomic regulation of the unemployment rate. . . .

The Limits of Democratic Control of the Capitalist Economy

If government has often grown in response to the needs of the capitalist economy, might the economic powers of government be used instead to achieve economic growth that would benefit everyone? Can the citizens of a democratic society control the economy in ways that will promote their own well-being?

. . . The ability of voters—even large majorities of them—to alter the course of economic events is quite limited as long as the economy remains capitalist.

To understand the limits on government, think of our economy as a game in which there are two different sets of rules. One set of rules—the rules of a capitalist economy—confers power and privilege on those who own and control the capital goods used in production, particularly on the owners and managers of the largest corporations. The other set of rules—the rules of democratic government—confers substantial power on the electorate, that is, on the majority of adult citizens. Thus our social system gives rise to two types of power: the *power of capital* and the *power of the citizenry*.

Those powers are often at loggerheads, as when citizens want to restrict the power of capitalists to sell dangerous or environmentally destructive products. In most such conflicts, capitalists have immense and often overwhelming advantages, despite the fact that the owners of businesses (and particularly the owners of large businesses) are greatly outnumbered in the political arena. There are three explanations for their political power—one obvious, the other two not so obvious.

One reason capitalists have a significant amount of political power is that economic resources can often be translated *directly* into political power. Businesses or wealthy individuals can contribute to political campaigns; they can buy advertisements to alter public opinion; they can hire lawyers, expert witnesses, and others to influence the detailed drafting and implementation of legislation; and they can use their economic resources in other ways—engaging in outright bribery, for example—to influence the political system. In all these ways corporate control of economic resources makes it possible for businesspeople to influence government officials and economic policies.

A second reason for the disproportionate political power of business leaders is more indirect. The owners of today's media conglomerates control the TV stations, newspapers, publishing houses, and other capital goods used in the media that shape public opinion. Even "public" radio and TV now depend heavily on corporate contributions. The constitutional rights to freedom of speech and of the press (which includes TV and radio) guarantee that people can say, and journalists can write, whatever they please. However, the private ownership of the capital goods used in the TV industry, for example, guarantees that what is broadcast is in the end controlled by corporate leaders—either the owners of the stations or the owners of the major corporations that buy the advertising for the programs. These are people who generally have little interest in promoting citizen power because increases in such power may jeopardize their profits.

A third way in which money brings power has to do with the fact that capitalists control investment and therefore can influence what happens in the economy of any particular area. If businesspeople see an area as having a bad investment climate, meaning that they may have difficulty making profits there, they will not invest in that area but will choose instead to invest somewhere else (if they invest at all). If they do not invest in a particular area, the result will be unemployment, economic stagnation, and probably a decline in living standards. This explains why political leaders in particular areas are apt to be easily influenced by the demands of business leaders. If the former do not go along with the wishes of the latter, the population of the area will suffer economic hardships and, placing at least part of the blame for their difficulties on their political leaders, will vote the incumbents out in the next election.

Something like the same process plays a role in the political business cycle. When there has been a long expansion, government leaders are usually willing to go along with the demands of business leaders to bring about a recession that will raise the rate of unemployment. Why is this? It is because, in this situation, government officials can anticipate that business leaders will blame them for any decline in profit rates that might result from increases in the power of workers. If the profit rate was in fact threatened, business leaders would not only withhold their investment, thereby causing economic hardships that would lead people to express their anger in the next election; they would also deny the current political leaders the financial support the latter would need in order to finance a re-election campaign.

When business leaders refuse to invest in a particular area, whether it is a locality, an area such as a state in the United States, or an entire nation, the area will experience what is referred to as a *capital strike*. When workers strike, they refuse to do their part in the economy: they do not work. When capitalists strike, they also refuse to do their part: they do not invest. But here the similarity between the strikes of workers and those of capitalists ends. When workers strike they must organize themselves so that they all strike together. A single worker cannot go on strike (that would be called quitting). By contrast, when capital goes on strike, no coordination is needed. . . . Each corporation routinely studies the economic and other conditions relevant to its decision to invest. If the executives of the corporation do not like what they see, they will not invest. Nobody organizes a capital strike. Such strikes happen through the independent decisions of corporate leaders. If things look bad to a significant number of corporations, the effect of their combined withholding of investment will be large enough to change the economic conditions of a whole area.

The potential for a capital strike severely limits what citizen power can accomplish when citizen power conflicts with the power of capital. A hypothetical scenario will make this clear. It is currently the policy in the United States that unemployed workers are entitled to receive unemployment insurance checks for 26 weeks after they lose their jobs. But imagine what would happen if the government of a particular state—let's call it "Anystate, USA"—were to decide to provide longer-lasting unemployment benefits so that workers could continue to receive unemployment insurance checks as long as they are unemployed. And let's say that these payments are financed by heavy taxes on the profits of firms that pollute the environment. If a majority of Anystate's citizens support these policies, the state government will adopt them, paying the additional benefits to unemployed workers and collecting the "pollution taxes" to pay for them.

Now imagine that you are the chief executive officer (CEO) of a large multinational corporation—let's call it "MNC Enterprises, Inc."—that employs large numbers of workers in Anystate. Assume that you are considering investing in Anystate, say, by building a new plant there. Not only will you worry about the potential taxes (applicable to any production process that pollutes the environment); you will also be uncertain, first, about how much power you will have over your employees and, second, about how hard they will work, knowing that they are entitled to receive unemployment insurance checks for a long period if you fire them.

You may even ask yourself what the citizenry will vote for next—and you will certainly think twice before investing in Anystate, not necessarily because you personally do not like the new laws, but because your profit rate, both before and after taxes, would most likely be lower in Anystate than it might be elsewhere. Not only would a low profit rate make it difficult for MNC Enterprises to maintain its competitive position relative to other corporations; it would also have additional consequences. Once it became known that the company's profit rate was falling, the price of the company's stock in the stock market would fall. This, in turn, might cause the stockholders to sell their shares, putting more downward pressure on the price of the stock. It is also possible that the Board of Directors of the company, in response to its poor "performance," would begin thinking about replacing you with a new CEO. Anticipating all this, you will probably put any new plant somewhere else, perhaps in a state that actively advertises its favorable investment climate.

Quite independently, other businesspeople will, no doubt, come to the same conclusion. Some may even close plants or offices in Anystate and move them elsewhere. The cumulative effect of these independently made decisions will be increasing unemployment and lower incomes for the people of Anystate.

The hard times may bring on a state financial crisis. As unemployment increases, state expenditures on unemployment insurance will rise, as will the costs of other income support programs. As people's incomes fall, the state's tax revenues will also fall, and a deficit will appear in the state's budget. (Most states are required by their state constitutions to balance their budgets.)

But the problems have only just begun. In order to spend more money than taxes are currently bringing in, the state government will be forced to raise taxes further or to borrow money from banks or individuals willing to make loans to the state or buy bonds (IOUs) issued by the state government. Because of the decline in Anystate's economy, the banks cannot be sure that their loans will be paid back promptly or that they will ever be paid back. If they agree to lend money to the state, they will do so only at high interest rates (to cover the risk of lending to the state). Similarly, investors will be willing to buy the state's newly issued bonds only if they are guaranteed high rates of interest. If the loans are granted and the bonds are bought, the state will have more money to finance its current expenditure, but its fundamental problems will only be put off. They will return with greater intensity when the high interest charges have to be paid, adding to the other demands on state revenues. The resulting vicious cycle, now evident in many U.S. states, is called a *state fiscal crisis*.

There are two likely outcomes. First, with repayment increasingly uncertain, the banks may refuse further loans until the state government changes its policy. If the state government is on the verge of bankruptcy—which means breaking contracts with state employees and not paying wages or bills—the bank's policy recommendations may be quite persuasive. Second, the sovereign citizens of Anystate may decide to elect a new government, in order to have the laws revoked. In either case the new laws will be repealed.

Our example was for a single state, but in fact the process we have out-lined could well occur in any state or even in any nation. After all, MNC Enterprises did not have to locate any of its factories in the United States.

Let's go back over our "Anystate" example. Were the citizens' voting rights or civil liberties violated? No. Did capitalists collude to deliberately undermine citizen power? No, they acted independently and in competi-tion with each other. Did they use campaign contributions or lobbyists to influence government officials or elections? They might have but they did not need to.

Did the citizens exercise control over the economy? That is a much harder question. The capitalist economy certainly imposed limits on what they could do. The citizens could vote for any policy they wanted, but they could not force businesses to invest in Anystate, and that fact severely lim-ited the political outcomes.

Where did they go wrong? The example could have turned out very differently.

One course the citizens of Anystate could have followed would have been to limit their expectations; they could have instructed their govern-ment to concentrate only on those programs that would benefit citizens but at the same time *raise*—or at least not lower—the profit rates of companies in the state. In other words, they might have accepted from the outset the fact that they were not "sovereign" in economic matters. This would have allowed them to make the best of a less-than-ideal situation.

Thus, for example, the citizens might have concentrated solely on elim-inating the forms of air pollution that push down property values by reduc-ing profits in recreation businesses. They might have designed programs to give economic security to the elderly, but not to current workers. They might have tried to increase employment and equality of opportunity by giving all children more business-oriented schooling. And they might have voted to finance these programs by taxes that did not affect profits. If they had adopted any or all of these policies, many Anystate citizens would have benefited, and those who were adversely affected might not have been in a position to block the adoption of them. Specifically, capitalists might have looked favorably or at least indifferently at such policies and might not have brought about economic decline in the state by withholding or with-drawing their investments.

Again, our Anystate example is hypothetical, but it is in fact similar to a process that actually occurred in Wisconsin early in the twentieth century. Wisconsin was a leader in trying out programs to make the most of citizen power while operating within the limits of a capitalist economy. Moreover, the federal government and a number of state and local governments now engage in many beneficial economic activities that also fit this description. Providing for social needs within the general framework of a capitalist econ-omy has been the aim of European nations such as Sweden and Austria, where social democratic governments have been in power during much of the last century. As beneficial as these programs have been, however, they are severely limited by the fact that many of the ways to improve living standards and the quality of life sooner or later also threaten the rate of profit.

There is yet another course that Anystate citizens could have followed, which, if not likely, is at least conceivable. When MNC Enterprises (or other companies) decided to close down their operations in Anystate, the plants could have been bought by their local communities, by their workers, or by the state government itself. When a business leaves a community, what it takes with it, usually, is just its money. The plant, equipment and machinery—not to mention the workers—are left behind. If a way could be found to purchase the firm and sell its output, there is no reason why the workers who held jobs in the MNC Enterprises plant could not continue working there. They could do this by forming a community-owned enterprise, a worker-owned firm, or some other type of democratic organization.

We may conclude from our Anystate example that citizen power is severely limited in its ability to alter fundamental economic policies. These limits can only be overcome if citizens commit themselves to altering the rules of a capitalist economy. . . . The rules of a capitalist economy are not the same as those of democratic government. To achieve a democratic *society*—not just a democratic *government*—decision making in the economy, as well as in the government, would have to be made accountable to a majority of its participants.

DISCUSSION QUESTIONS

1. Some people have called the Bush administration's policies the most conservative since the administration of Herbert Hoover. Yet the Bush administration has expanded federal spending, runs large budget deficits, and is interested in certain forms of social regulation (e.g., stem cell research). How might the author(s) of each article deal with this apparent contradiction?

2. Friedman stresses the point that the market economy is made up of *voluntary exchanges.* No one is forced to buy a particular product or to work for a particular company. What would Bowles, Roosevelt, and Edwards say about Friedman's argument?

3. There is a substantial amount of income inequality in the United States. As long as all citizens still maintain equal political rights, is such inequality necessarily harmful to democracy? How much inequality is a threat to a democratic society and why? How much inequality is justified, and on what grounds?

4. Friedman argues that the free market promotes individual liberty. Yet many citizens in democratic countries use their liberty to support government programs that limit and regulate the scope and power of the marketplace itself. How might Friedman have responded to this reality?

SUGGESTED READINGS AND INTERNET RESOURCES

How democratic is the U.S. capitalist system? What is and what should be the roles of government and democratic citizens in the creation and distribution of economic resources? How "free" is our market system and how "equal" its citizens? Two excellent introductions to the answers of these questions are Joseph Schumpeter, *Capitalism, Socialism, and Democracy* (New Haven, Conn.: Yale University Press, 1984), and Charles Lindblom, *The Market System: What It Is, How It Works, and What to Make of It* (New Haven, Conn.: Yale University Press, 2002). An excellent account of the Clinton versus Bush approach to the political economy is Robert Pollin, *Contours of Descent* (New York: Verso Books, 2003). For a mainstream account of a new, healthy globalized economy, see Thomas Friedman, *The Lexus and the Olive Tree* (New York: Anchor Books, 2000). A brilliant treatment of how wealth inequality translates into political inequality is William Domhoff, *Who Rules America? Power and Politics in the Year 2000* (Mountain View, Calif.: Mayfield Publishing, 1999).

The Policy Action Network
www.movingideas.org
This is the best site for extensive data on and analyses of current economic policy issues and for study of income and wealth trends. Click onto the internal links to the Economic Policy Institute or Center for Budget and Policy Priorities for an analysis of current issues, or use the topic search engine. This site is sponsored by *The American Prospect,* a liberal opinion magazine.

The Heritage Foundation
www.heritage.org
This site contains economic news and policy prescriptions from the premier ultraright think tank, as well as good links to other conservative foundations and public policy lobbies.

The Left Business Observer
www.leftbusinessobserver.com
A spirited, iconoclastic newsletter by corporate critic Doug Henwood, this website has interesting statistics and many links to unconventional left- and right-wing websites.

The Cato Institute
www.cato.org
Here are speeches, research, and opinion from the leading libertarian think tank in the United States. This site provides economic data and opinion supportive of privatization of now-public functions, from social security to environmental protection and education.

6

Civil Liberties and War: Debating the USA Patriot Act

The terrorist attacks in New York and Washington on September 11, 2001, suddenly hurled a nation that had been enjoying peace and prosperity into a fearful new climate of war. As the U.S. government prepared to strike at the shadowy al Qaeda terrorist network around the globe, it also produced plans to find and stop terrorists from operating on American soil. Six weeks after September 11, Congress passed and President George W. Bush signed the USA Patriot Act (Uniting and Strengthening America by Providing Appropriate Tools Required to Intercept and Obstruct Terrorism Act of 2001), which was de- signed to arm federal authorities with stronger means of surveillance, detention, and punishment against those engaged in terrorist activities. The provisions of the Patriot Act were touted by the Bush administration as indispensable in making America safer, but they aroused fears among critics that the gains in homeland security would be outweighed by the loss of fundamental American liberties. The Patriot Act became the most controversial and widely debated feature of President Bush's war on terrorism.

With the onset of a war, pressures to strengthen government's powers build quickly. Proponents of these powers typically argue that the wide latitude of liberty that prevails in peacetime must be narrowed somewhat during wartime for the sake of security. Opponents of these powers typically argue that the measures adopted to strengthen government exceed the requirements for security and curtail legitimate dissent against the president and his policies.

Throughout the course of American history, civil liberties have frequently been restricted during periods of war or crisis. In 1798, only seven years after the adoption of the Bill of Rights, the Federalists passed the Alien and Sedition Acts to silence Jeffersonian opponents of the "quasi war" with France. During the Civil War, President Abraham Lincoln suspended the writ of habeas corpus and his generals subjected civilians to trials by military courts. Using another Sedition Act passed during World War I, President Woodrow Wilson imprisoned or deported radical critics of his war policies. Soon after the United States entered World War II, Japanese Americans were forced to leave their homes on the West Coast and relocate to internment camps for the duration of the conflict. The early Cold War years produced the anti-communist crusades by Senator Joseph McCarthy and his allies, damaging the careers and lives of many individuals accused of "subversive" activities.

After the crises have passed, many Americans have had second thoughts, regarding most of these wartime measures as excessive in boosting the power of government at the expense of the rights of citizens. The Alien and Sedition Acts stand as the principal black mark on the historical record of President John Adams. Lincoln's suspension of habeas corpus has been viewed as justified by most scholars, but in the case of *Ex parte Milligan* (1866), a unanimous Supreme Court struck down the Civil War conviction of a civilian by a military court in Indiana, declaring that the Constitution is "a law for rulers and people, equally in times of war and peace." President Wilson's crackdown on dissent during World War I is viewed by many historians as undermining his claim that he was fighting a war to "make the world safe for democracy." The internment of Japanese Americans in World War II was such an egregious violation of civil liberties that Congress later passed a resolution officially apologizing for the measure and providing financial compensation for surviving internees. McCarthyism has become a synonym for a hysterical climate of intolerance and repression.

Does the USA Patriot Act, along with sundry other measures adopted by the Bush administration at the same time, resemble these historical precedents, or is it a more narrowly and carefully tailored set of measures meant to assist law enforcement in combating an insidious enemy whose destructive aims have nothing to do with civil dissent? Among the more controversial provisions are (1) expanding the powers of the federal government to inquire into such private activities of individuals as surfing the Internet or obtaining reading matter from libraries or bookstores; (2) allowing federal officials to listen in on conversations between individuals detained in relation to suspected terrorist activities and their lawyers; (3) permitting the federal government to detain noncitizens on the basis of suspicion, holding them without trials or immigration hearings for many months and keeping their names secret; (4) facilitating various government practices, previously limited by law, of gathering evidence that can be used in a wide range of cases, some of which may involve criminal activity unrelated to terrorism. To Patriot Act proponents, these provisions are necessary to detect and detain terrorists before they strike again. To critics, they exploit the legitimate security concerns of Americans to establish excessive and unchecked executive powers.

From the time it was first proposed by the Bush administration, the Patriot Act has drawn fire from an unusual coalition, composed of liberals concerned about a danger to civil liberties and conservatives concerned about an ominous growth of the federal government. The initial criticisms have only grown over time: as of September 2003, the states of Alaska, Hawaii, and Vermont, along with more than 150 communities around the nation, had passed official resolutions critical of the Patriot Act. Numerous organizations have assailed the act; for example, the American Library Association condemned its provision allowing government inquiries into reading matter as "a present danger to the constitutional rights and privacy rights of library users." Yet public opinion polls have shown continuing majority support for the Patriot Act and related security measures. Arguing that criticisms of the act have been hysterical and ill-informed, President Bush's attorney general, John Ashcroft, has mounted an unusual public campaign to defend it, speaking on its behalf in eighteen cities during the summer of 2003 and establishing a Department of Justice website to explain its successes. Believing that an even further expansion of federal powers of surveillance and detention is needed in the battle against terrorists, Ashcroft's Justice Department has proposed a second Patriot Act.

Our two essays on the Patriot Act reveal the chief dimensions of this debate. Viet Dinh, who came to the United States as a refugee from Vietnam at age ten, is a professor of law at Georgetown University. While serving as an assistant attorney general under John Ashcroft, Dinh was the principal drafter of the Patriot Act. Dinh's essay disputes the idea that Americans face a trade-off between liberty and security, because liberty cannot exist without order. In the post–September 11 climate, Americans will not be able to enjoy cherished freedoms by living in a constant state of fear. It is in the defense of liberty, then, that the Justice Department has pursued, through the Patriot Act, an aggressive campaign to uncover and incarcerate the terrorists before they can launch another catastrophic attack on U.S. soil. Dinh discusses several of the controversial provisions in the Patriot Act and related measures, arguing that in each case the actions undertaken by the Bush administration have been consistent with the Constitution and the laws, and have been effective in countering the terrorist threat. The impassioned attack on the Patriot Act, he suggests, is rooted in unfounded fears of presidential abuses and has distracted Americans from a thoughtful discussion about the techniques that can defeat terrorists *and* preserve liberty.

Stephen Schulhofer, a professor of law at New York University, agrees with Dinh that extraordinary law enforcement measures are warranted after the horror of 9/11, but he argues that the Bush administration's response to the crisis has done too little to enhance homeland security and too much to endanger civil liberties. Schulhofer finds fault with the Patriot Act and other Bush policies in four distinct areas: domestic surveillance, excessive latitude for the FBI, detention of noncitizens, and the erosion of habeas corpus. From his vantage point, the consistent flaw in every phase of Bush's war on terror at home is a lack of checks and balances. Presidential authority has been increased at the expense of American liberties even in areas that are unrelated to the terrorist threat. Yet the implementation of these dangerous new executive powers, by an administration whose dedication to tax cuts has undercut its willingness to commit large financial resources to homeland protections, has not really made Americans much safer.

Dinh's essay updates the original elite democratic perspective that only a strong government can protect citizens against threats to their security. Schulhofer echoes the original popular democratic perspective in fearing government elites that amass too much power in their hands. How do you view the debate over the USA Patriot Act? Are its provisions vital in rooting out terrorists before they can again murder large numbers of Americans? Are they a burden only to a tiny minority, leaving the vast majority of Americans in possession of as much liberty as before 9/11? Or does the Patriot Act cut too deeply into American liberty while doing too little to protect us from terrorists? Are its provisions, by enhancing executive powers, dangerous for everyone's liberties, even when these provisions are applied only to the small number of individuals swept up in law enforcement efforts?

Defending Liberty Against the Tyranny of Terror

VIET DINH

I n the search for the elusive balance between liberty and security, commentators short of platitudes often resort to the stand-by dictum from Benjamin Franklin that "they that can give up essential liberty to obtain a little temporary safety deserve neither liberty nor safety." With this statement, there can be no disagreement. One should not trade liberty (let alone "essential liberty") for safety (let alone "a little temporary safety"). That is so because security should not be—and in our constitutional democracy, is not—an end in itself, but rather merely a means to the greater end of liberty.

Oft-quoted and incontrovertible, Franklin's truism is nevertheless not very illuminating. For the essential question is what does one mean by liberty. Here, I think Edmund Burke puts it best: "The only liberty I mean is a liberty connected with order; that not only exists along with order and virtue, but which cannot exist at all without them." Order and liberty, under this conception, are symbiotic; each is necessary to the stability and legitimacy that is essential for a government under law.

To illustrate this symbiotic relationship, consider liberty without order. Absent order, liberty is simply unbridled license: Men can do whatever they choose. It is easy enough to recognize that such a world of liberty without order is unstable, but I would argue that it is also illegitimate. The essence of liberty is the freedom from subjugation or the will of another. In a world of unbridled license, the strong do what they will and the weak suffer what they must. One man's expression of his desires will deprive another of his freedom. Liberty without order is illegitimate because one man may infringe, by force as necessary, another's freedom. True liberty only exists in an ordered society with rules and laws that govern and limit the behavior of men.

Just as liberty cannot exist without order, order without liberty is not only illegitimate but also unstable. The first of these propositions is widely accepted, so I will not dwell on it here. But it is important to recognize that where there is only order but not liberty, force must be exerted by men over men in an attempt to compel obedience and create a mirage of stability. Most people are familiar with Rousseau's dictum that "Man was born free, yet everywhere he is in chains." But often neglected is the sentence that immediately follows in *On the Social Contract:* "He who believes himself the master of others is nonetheless a greater slave than they. . . . For in recovering its freedom by means of the same right used to steal it, either the people is justified in taking it back, or those who took it away were not justified in doing so."

Order without liberty is unstable precisely because it is illegitimate. In an apparent order maintained by brute strength, the ruler has no greater claim to the use of force than his subject, and the master and slave are in a constant state of war—one trying to maintain the mirage of stability created by his use of force, the other seeking to use force to recover his lost freedom. Order and liberty, therefore, are not competing concepts that must be balanced against each other to maintain some sort of democratic equilibrium. Rather, they are complementary values that contribute symbiotically to the stability and legitimacy of a constitutional democracy. Order and liberty go together like love and marriage and horse and carriage; you can't have one without the other.

In his 1998 book, *The Structure of Liberty,* Randy Barnett distinguishes liberty structured by order from unbridled license by comparing it to a tall building, the Sears Tower. License permits thousands of people to congregate in the same space, but only with the order imposed by the structure of the building—its hallways and partitions, stairwells and elevators, signs and lights—would those thousands be endowed with liberty, each to pursue his own end without trampling on others or being trampled on. Like a building, every society has a structure that, by constraining the actions of its members, permits them at the same time to act to accomplish their ends. To illustrate the essential necessity of that structure, Barnett posits this hypothetical: "Imagine being able to push a button and make the structure of the building instantly vanish. Thousands of persons would plunge to their deaths."

Osama bin Laden pushed that button on September 11, and thousands of persons plunged to their deaths. Just as Barnett's building was only a metaphor for the structure of ordered liberty, al Qaeda's aim was not simply to destroy the World Trade Center. Its target was the very foundation of our ordered liberty.

Knowing what we now know about al Qaeda, it is easy to see that its radical, extremist ideology is incompatible with, and an offense to, ordered liberty. Al Qaeda seeks to subjugate women; we work for their liberation. Al Qaeda seeks to deny choice; we celebrate the marketplace of ideas. Al Qaeda seeks to suppress speech; we welcome open discussion.

More fundamental, however, is the proposition that al Qaeda or any other terrorist group, simply by adopting the way of terror, attacks the foundation of our ordered liberty. Terrorism, whomever its perpetrator and whatever his aim, poses a fundamental threat to the ordered liberty that is the essence of constitutional democracies.

The terrorist seeks not simply to kill, but to terrorize. His strategy is not merely to increase the count of the dead, but to bring fear to those who survive. The terrorist is indiscriminate in his choice of victims and indifferent about the value of his targets. He uses violence to disrupt order, kills to foment fear, and terrorizes to incapacitate normal human activity.

In this sense, the terrorist is fundamentally different from the criminal offender normally encountered by our criminal justice system. By attacking the foundation of order in our society, the terrorist seeks to demolish the structure of liberty that governs our lives. By fomenting terror among the masses, the terrorist seeks to incapacitate the citizenry from exercising the liberty to pursue our individual ends. This is not mere criminality. It is a war-like attack on our polity.

In waging that war, the terrorist employs means that fundamentally differ from those used by the traditional enemies we have faced on the battlefield according to the established rules of war among nations. Those rules clearly distinguish uniformed combatants who do battle with each other from innocent civilians who are off-limits, a distinction that is not only ignored but exploited by the terrorist to his advantage. In this war, the international terrorist differs even from the guerilla warriors who mingle among and, at times, target innocent civilians. The activities of the terrorist are not limited to some hamlet in Southeast Asia or remote village in Latin America. For the international terrorist, the world is his battleground, no country is immune from attack, and all innocent civilians are exposed to the threat of wanton violence and incapacitated by the fear of terror.

This, then, is the enemy we face: A criminal whose objective is not crime but fear; a mass murderer who kills only as a means to a larger end; a predator whose victims are all innocent civilians; a warrior who violates the rules of war; a war criminal who recognizes no boundaries and who reaches all corners of the world.

Many thoughtful experts are devoting their energies to finding the root causes of terrorism, but we need to be clear: A terrorist is not a social worker, but one who works to defeat the social order. And a terrorist is not a politician seeking to advance a political objective, but one who would coerce agreement with his ideology by mortally threatening the polity. After 9/11, the primary threat to America's freedom comes from al Qaeda and others who seek to annihilate America and her people, and not from the men and women of law enforcement who protect us from danger.

Why, then, the controversy? One reason may be that most of us in the debate adopt one or the other perspective. Those who are libertarians or human rights activists usually concentrate on the costs of action: that is, how does a particular government action or policy affect the rights of suspected terrorists and the expectation of the general public to be free from governmental intrusion.

The security experts, by contrast, would focus on the costs of inaction. Because their job is to ensure the security of America and the safety of her people, they live in dread that a preventable terrorist attack would happen under their watch, that they could have done more to protect the lives and liberties of those lost in the attack.

However, for the ultimate maker of decisions and the disinterested commentator judging those decisions, I think it is critical that we focus not just on the risk of action or the risk of inaction, but the relative risks of action versus inaction.

That is why, after the first National Security Council meeting on September 11, 2001, the president turned to the attorney general and said, "John, you make sure this does not happen again." Following this simple yet momentous directive, we in the Justice Department crafted and implemented what became the prevention paradigm: a strategy to identify and disrupt terrorist conspiracies before they can carry out their plans instead of waiting for terror to strike, picking up the pieces and counting the bodies.

Critical to this strategy was congressional passage of the USA Patriot Act. The 50 legislative proposals that the president submitted to Congress had three primary themes. First, they served to update the law to conform to new technology. The laws governing governmental intercept of criminal conversations were first drafted as Title III of the Omnibus Crime Act of 1968, at a time when communication was effected through analog lines and rotary telephones. The USA Patriot Act ensured that law enforcement has the same ability to monitor criminal and terrorist conspiracies in the digital and wireless world—with the same level of judicial authorization and supervision that pre-existed the Act.

Second, the USA Patriot Act authorized and in some cases required the sharing of information and coordination of activities among the law enforcement, intelligence, and military agencies of the federal government. Different persons in different agencies had isolated information about the various aspects of the 9/11 conspiracy, but a culture of segregation created by legal barriers prevented the compilation of such information. The USA Patriot Act relaxed those barriers and permitted all the pieces of the puzzle to be assembled at one table into a coherent mosaic of intelligence information about future terrorist threats.

Third, the USA Patriot Act made clear that terrorism was our nation's highest priority after 9/11. The authority to investigate and the penalties for certain crimes on the books, such as drug trafficking or health care fraud, at times exceeded those for terrorism. Congress acted swiftly to fix this anomaly.

Two years later, we can assess the Act through the results. According to the Department of Justice, the government has disrupted over 100 terrorist cells and incapacitated over 3,000 al Qaeda operatives worldwide. Two hundred eighty four persons linked to the 9/11 investigation have been criminally charged, 149 of whom have pled guilty or been convicted. Five hundred fifteen foreigners of interest to the 9/11 investigation have been deported for immigration violations. And the government has frozen $133 million in terrorist assets through 70 investigations and 23 convictions or guilty pleas. But perhaps the most telling statistic is a non-statistic: terrorists have not taken another life on American soil in two years despite the continuing threat everywhere else around the world.

These successes, according to a Department of Justice communication to Congress, "would have been much more difficult, if not impossibly so, without the USA Patriot Act." That Act, of course, owes its existence to the near unanimous vote of Congress after careful work by its Judiciary Committees. During the six weeks of deliberations that led to the passage of the Act, the drafters heard from and heeded the advice of a coalition of concerned voices urging caution and care in crafting the blueprint for America's security. That conversation was productive, and the USA Patriot Act benefited from the voices of concern.

The debate has since deteriorated, and the shouting voices ignore questions that are critical to both security and liberty. Lost among fears about what the government might be doing to threaten civil liberties are questions about what it is actually doing and what else it should be doing to protect security and safeguard liberty. And rhetoric over minor alterations has overshadowed profoundly important questions about fundamental changes in law and policy.

For example, consider the debate relating to section 215 of the Act, the so-called library records provision. Critics have rallied against the provision as facilitating a return to J. Edgar Hoover's monitoring of reading habits. The American Civil Liberties Union has sued the government, claiming that the provision, through its mere existence, foments a chilling fear among Muslim organizations and activists.

These fears are undoubtedly real, but they are also unfounded. Grand juries for years have issued subpoenas to businesses, including libraries and bookstores, for records relevant to criminal inquiries. Section 215 gives courts the same power, in national security investigations, to issue similar orders to businesses, from chemical makers to explosives dealers. Like its criminal grand jury equivalent, these judicial orders for business records conceivably could issue to bookstores or libraries, but section 215 does not single them out.

Section 215 is narrow in scope. The FBI cannot use it to investigate garden-variety crimes or even domestic terrorism. Instead, section 215 can be used only to "obtain foreign intelligence information not concerning a United States person," or to "protect against international terrorism or clandestine intelligence activities."

Because section 215 applies only to national security investigations, the orders are confidential. Such secrecy raises legitimate concerns, and thus Congress embedded significant checks in the process. First, they are issued and supervised by a federal judge. By contrast, grand jury subpoenas are routinely issued by the court clerk.

Second, every six months the government has to report to Congress on the number of times and the manner in which the provision has been used. The House Judiciary Committee has stated that its review of that information "has not given rise to any concern that the authority is being misused or abused." Indeed, the Attorney General has recently made public the previously classified information that section 215 has not been used since its passage.

It may well be that the clamor over section 215 reflects a different concern, that government investigators should not be able to use ordinary criminal investigative tools so easily to obtain records from purveyors of First Amendment activities, such as libraries and bookstores. Section 215, with its prohibition that investigations "not be conducted of a United States person solely upon the basis of activities protected by the first amendment of the Constitution of the United States," in this regard is more protective of civil liberties than ordinary criminal procedure.

Perhaps this limitation should be extended to other investigative tools. The attorney general's Guidelines governing criminal and terrorist investigations already require that "such investigations not be based solely on activities protected by the First Amendment or on the lawful exercise of any other rights secured by the Constitution or laws of the United States." Congress may well consider whether to codify this requirement, but that is a debate far different from the utility of section 215.

Among the most alarming episodes in the saga of the USA Patriot Act was the decision by the House of Representatives to approve the Otter Amendment, an appropriations rider that would have prohibited investigators from asking a court to delay notice of a search warrant. Had the provision become law, it would have been a mistake of momentous dimensions that threatened to cripple numerous federal criminal investigations. That is so because the rider would have taken away an investigative tool that pre-existed the USA Patriot Act and has proven critical in saving lives and preserving evidence.

Inherent in a federal judge's power to issue a search warrant is her authority to supervise the terms of its use, including the delay of any notice of the execution of the warrant. So firmly established is this authority that the Supreme Court in 1979 labeled as "frivolous" an argument that notice must be immediate. Even the notoriously permissive 9th Circuit Court of Appeals has consistently recognized that notice may be delayed for a reasonable period of time. The problem is that different judges exercised their discretion to delay notice differently, resulting in a mix of inconsistent standards, rules, and practices across the country.

Congress solved this problem in section 213 of the USA Patriot Act by adopting a uniform standard—that a judge may delay notice for a reasonable period upon showing of "reasonable cause" that immediate notification may have an adverse result such as endangering the life or physical safety of an individual, flight from prosecution, evidence tampering, witness intimidation, seriously jeopardizing an investigation, or unduly delaying a trial.

Under the USA Patriot Act, a judge must still approve the delayed notice and only for specified situations. And the uniform "reasonable cause" standard is similar to the Supreme Court's reasonableness test to judge the circumstances surrounding the service of a warrant. For example, the Court last month unanimously approved as reasonable police entry into a drug house 15 seconds after announcing their presence. Indeed, the reasonable cause standard is arguably more restrictive than the prevailing standard prior to the USA Patriot Act—that the government show "good reason" to delay notice of a warrant.

All the sound and fury over politically charged issues such as section 213 and section 215 has drowned out constructive dialogue about fundamental changes in policy. For instance, section 218 of the USA Patriot Act amended the Foreign Intelligence Surveillance Act to facilitate increased cooperation between agents gathering intelligence about foreign threats and investigators prosecuting foreign terrorists. I doubt that even the most strident of critics would want another terrorist attack to happen because a 30-year-old provision prevented the law enforcement and intelligence communities to communicate with each other about potential terrorist threats.

This change, essential as it is, raises important questions about the nature of law enforcement and domestic intelligence. The drafters grappled with questions such as whether the change comports with the Fourth Amendment protection against unreasonable searches and seizures (yes), whether criminal prosecutors should initiate and direct intelligence operations (no), and whether there is adequate process for defendants to seek exclusion of intelligence evidence from trial (yes). We were confident of the answers. But lawyers are not infallible, and the courts ultimately will decide. Meanwhile, better airing of these weighty issues would help the public understand the government's actions and appreciate their effects.

The coverage of and commentary on the government detention of Jose Padilla and Yasser Hamdi, U.S. citizens detained as enemy combatants, provides a good illustration. Contrary to popular belief, the detention of Padilla and Hamdi is not authorized by and indeed has nothing to do with the USA Patriot Act or any other congressional action since 9/11. Rather, they are detained through the exercise of the president's inherent constitutional authority as commander-in-chief of the armed forces in times of war.[1]

---

1. In June 2004, the Supreme Court rejected the president's claims in the Hamdi case.

This distinction, that the president detained Hamdi and Padilla not to enforce U.S. law against criminal offenders but to fight the continuing armed conflict against terrorists, is critical to understanding why they are not necessarily entitled to the due process that courts routinely provide to criminal defendants. Yasser Hamdi was captured on the battlefield and transferred to a military brig in South Carolina. Despite the vocal opposition to his detention, surely a military commander should have the power to incapacitate enemy combatants on the battlefield (think Eisenhower and the Nazis), and legal precedents confirm this common sense proposition.

The power to incapacitate enemy combatants extends to those who unlawfully target innocent civilians and who would make the streets of America their battlefield. Thus, the president properly designated Jose Padilla as an unlawful combatant. Padilla was captured in O'Hare Airport while engaged in an alleged plot to detonate a radioactive bomb in the United States. That plot is a crime, but it is also a battle plan to endanger the national security in time of armed conflict.

The more difficult question, one on which past cases provide less guidance, is whether the military can hold these enemy combatants indefinitely without any process at all. The initial government position, that it could hold Padilla for the duration of the conflict without any access to counsel and without any legal procedure to challenge the facts underlying his detention, was problematic.

The administration has since agreed for Hamdi to have access to lawyers, and promised to grant such access to Padilla in the near future. This is an important development because the government has always maintained that the courthouse doors are open to the detainees to challenge the legality of their detention. Access to counsel makes access to the courts truly meaningful, and strengthens the government's argument to a sustainable position.

The determination as to when and under what circumstances to grant access to counsel disruptive to the interrogation process necessarily rests with the executive in the first instance. Few would doubt that, if al Qaeda leaders like Khalid Sheik Mohammed were in U.S. custody, they would have continuing intelligence value and government efforts to extract information should not be disrupted. On the other hand, when access would not disrupt the intelligence flow, as the government has decided for Hamdi and Padilla, the government has no reason to bar detainees from speaking with their lawyers.

There is room for the administration to move into even safer harbor by providing, after a reasonable period, some legal procedure for Padilla and Hamdi to contest the underlying facts of their detention. It need not be full-dress judicial process. A military hearing to evaluate the information underlying the detention would suffice. The Supreme Court is more likely to defer to an executive judgment when the process by which it is arrived at is capable of inspection.

The developments in the Hamdi and Padilla cases should comfort those who fear executive authority because they suggest that the administration is exercising its discretion responsibly to accommodate changed circumstances. Likewise, those who support executive prerogative should applaud the administration for not pushing the envelope and risk a judicial backlash that would erode presidential authority. Just as President Clinton was criticized for unsuccessfully arguing that executive privilege extended to prevent the testimony of Secret Service agents, President Bush should be commended for protecting executive authority against unnecessary erosion.

The administration's action is especially noteworthy given Congress' silence on enemy combatants. After two years of unofficial criticism, especially from members with presidential aspirations, it is time for Congress to contribute its voice, either to affirm the president's authority or to suggest refinements to administration policy. As Judge Michael Chertoff, former head of the Justice Department's Criminal Division, has suggested, we need to discuss moving beyond case-by-case treatment of combatants and think more systematically about a sustainable architecture for determining when, why, and for how long someone may be detained as an enemy combatant.

Karl Llewellyn, a renowned professor of law, once observed: "Ideals without technique are a mess. But technique without ideals is a menace." In many ways our nation is navigating uncharted territory, provoked into a conflict with nihilistic terrorists instead of a traditional nation-state. During these times, when the foundation of liberty is under attack, it is critical that we both reaffirm the ideals of our constitutional democracy and also discern the techniques necessary to secure those ideals against the threat of terror.

No Checks, No Balances: Discarding Bedrock Constitutional Principles

STEPHEN J. SCHULHOFER

As expected, September 11 has prompted an expansion of law enforcement powers at almost every level. The domain of individual rights has contracted. And who would have it otherwise? For those of us who live and work in Manhattan, September 11 was not just a single horrific day but an extended nightmare. For weeks, kiosks, store windows, and parks displayed flyers by the thousands, pleading for information about loved ones still missing. National guard units seemed to be everywhere. Day after day, the air, gray and acrid, carried the smell of burning flesh.

No, the "war" metaphor is not just convenient political spin. And despite shameless hyping of so-called sleeper cells and color-coded threat levels, no responsible person can dismiss the danger of devastating future attacks. Actions to strengthen law enforcement are not simply the product of panic or paranoia.

But the particulars are troubling—and worse. Predictably, there has been overreaction and political grandstanding. More surprising is the neglect. Inexcusably, the administration of George W. Bush has swept aside urgent security needs while it continues to win public acclaim for toughness by targeting and scapegoating civil liberties.

An accounting of the state of our liberties should begin with the positives. To his credit, President Bush has preached tolerance and respect for our Muslim neighbors. Unlike previous wartime governments, this administration has not sought to prosecute dissenters for political speech, has not attempted anything comparable to the internment of Japanese Americans during World War II, and (technically, at least) has not tried to suspend the writ of habeas corpus.

But to measure performance by these standards is to set the bar terribly low; these were sorry historical embarrassments. And 9/11 has already produced several comparable missteps. The administration's efforts to stymie habeas corpus rival the civil liberties low points of prior wars, as does its determination (wholly without precedent) to hold American citizens indefinitely on disputed charges without affording them a trial in any forum whatsoever. Likewise without precedent are the oddly imbalanced means chosen to fight this war. Never before in American history has an administration claimed emergency powers while stinting on urgent national security expenditures and making tax cuts its top wartime priority. Conventional wisdom about "striking a balance" between liberty and security obscures the fact that responses to 9/11 are deeply flawed from *both* perspectives.

Specifically, the domestic security policies of this administration encroach on three principles that are fundamental to the preservation of freedom: accountability, checks and balances, and narrow tailoring of government's power to intrude into the lives of citizens. In each case, the administration has overlooked or dismissed alternative approaches that would strengthen the nation's security at least as effectively without weakening fundamental freedoms. The encroachments on bedrock principles, altogether unnecessary even in this perilous time, are especially evident in four realms of policy: domestic surveillance, new guidelines governing the Federal Bureau of Investigation, the detention of foreign nationals, and the erosion of habeas corpus.

Domestic Surveillance

Expanded surveillance powers have reduced privacy rights that most of us took for granted before September 11. Yet even without knowing the details, many Americans see no need to worry about the civil liberties impact of the new laws. They feel that law-abiding citizens should have nothing to hide, and they welcome rather than fear this enhancement of government surveillance powers. Others (a relatively small minority) argue that sacrificing any of our pre-9/11 privacy rights will simply make us less free without making us more secure and will amount to destroying our freedom in order to defend it. Neither of these positions captures the complex reality of the expanded surveillance powers.

Some of the provisions included in the October 2001 USA Patriot Act simply correct oversights in prior law or adapt technically worded statutes to new technologies and practices. For example, the authority included in the act for judges to permit surveillance of mobile phones in foreign intelligence investigations (a power long permitted in domestic law enforcement) and to issue search warrants with nationwide effect reflect legitimate law enforcement needs that raise no new privacy concerns.

But other new powers are more problematic. The Patriot Act undermines checks and balances by giving investigators new authority to track Internet usage and to obtain previously confidential financial records without having to demonstrate probable cause or obtain a judicial warrant. The Treasury Department expanded its authority to require banks, brokers, and other businesses to report cash transactions and "suspicious activities," which include any transaction that differs from ones the customer typically conducts. Though the Justice Department created a furor with its proposal for Operation TIPS to encourage voluntary snooping by private citizens, the Treasury Department's regulations *require* private citizens and businesses to become eyes and ears for the government—again without any oversight by the judicial branch. Compounding this problem, the new FBI and Treasury Department powers are not narrowly tailored to investigations potentially related to terrorism; the government can invoke most of these new powers even when it seeks only to investigate routine criminal offenses.

The Patriot Act also made especially important changes in the complex Foreign Intelligence Surveillance Act (FISA). The expanded FISA provisions now allow FBI agents to obtain business and educational records, without any need to certify that the targeted customer or student is considered a foreign agent or a suspect in any way. Before 9/11, FISA gave investigators access to the records of a narrow category of travel-industry businesses, provided that the person targeted was a foreign agent. The Patriot Act now permits FBI access to all the records of any business and any nonbusiness entity, apparently including noncommercial entities such as a synagogue or mosque. And the new authority (like that for financial and educational records) drops the requirement that the records pertain to a suspected foreign agent. Formerly confidential records concerning any American citizen are now available for FBI inspection on a clandestine basis whenever an investigator thinks they may be relevant to a terrorism investigation, whether or not the person concerned is a foreign agent or a suspected criminal offender. Again, this is the antithesis of government restraint: Judicial oversight is allowed no role as a check on the executive branch, and the powers granted extend far beyond the international terrorism suspects that are the legitimate targets of concern. . . .

The FISA changes, of course, are just one part of the multidimensional expansion of government surveillance powers, an expansion that encompasses the many new FBI and Treasury Department capabilities just mentioned. An overall assessment of these developments must begin by acknowledging that the counterterrorism payoff from the new powers, though not scientifically measurable, can't be dismissed as insignificant. And many Americans probably feel ready to sacrifice all the privacy interests that these new powers affect, if only to obtain even a small nugget of information about Al-Qaeda's plans. Nonetheless, the rollback of privacy rights has three flaws that should trouble us all.

First, worries about terrorism provide no reason to expand law enforcement power across the board. Yet FBI and Treasury agents can use most of their new powers to investigate allegations of prostitution, gambling, insider trading, and any other offense. Prosecutors can now use open-ended FISA surveillance powers to gather evidence for a conventional fraud or income-tax prosecution. Treasury regulations impose reporting obligations that can even be used to police compliance with ordinary government regulations. Far from respecting the imperative to tailor government power narrowly, even in times of peril, we have seen inexcusable opportunism on the part of the law enforcement establishment, which has exploited the momentum of 9/11 to expand government power to intrude on privacy in pursuit of wholly unrelated goals.

Second, accountability measures, though neglected in the rush to pass the Patriot Act, need not impair the usefulness of the new powers and, if well designed, will enhance them. The new provisions not only dilute traditional checks and balances; they neglect many of the internal supervision and control procedures that are staples of effective management in government and the private sector alike. The FBI's Carnivore system for spying on e-mail, for example, desperately needs procedures to preserve audit trails and ensure the accountability of agents who have access to it.

Finally, nuggets or even piles of telling information are useless unless our agencies have the capability to make sense of them. It is now well known that before September 11 the FBI and the Central Intelligence Agency had important clues to the plot in hand, but as one FBI agent put it, "We didn't know what we knew." Since a large part of what we lack is not raw data but the ability to separate significant intelligence from so-called noise, pulling more information into government files will not help and may aggravate the difficulty. Even before 9/11, Treasury officials complained to Congress that the staggering volume of reports they received (more than 1 million every month) was interfering with enforcement. Absent a substantial infusion of resources (which the Bush administration has not yet provided), powerful new surveillance tools can give us only a false sense of comfort.

New FBI Guidelines

In May 2002, headlines featured for days the startling news that during the summer of 2001, before the terrorist attacks, agents in Minneapolis and Phoenix had urged investigations of Zacharias Moussaoui and the flight schools, only to be stifled by FBI headquarters—an enormous blunder. In response, on May 30, 2002, Attorney General Ashcroft called a press conference to denounce "bureaucratic restrictions" that were preventing FBI agents from doing their jobs.

The rules he had in mind grew out of extensive FBI abuses in the 1950s and 1960s. Free to pursue random tips and their own hunches, FBI agents of that era intimidated dissidents, damaged the reputations of many who were not, and produced thousands of thick dossiers on public figures and private citizens. Agents spent years monitoring political groups of all stripes, from the Socialist Workers Party to the Conservative American Christian Action Council. They maintained files on student clubs, civil rights groups, antiwar groups, and other social movements. By 1975, FBI headquarters held more than a half-million domestic intelligence files.

Such sprawling dragnets are as inefficient as they are abusive, and rules to rein them in, adopted in 1976 under President Gerald Ford, were carried forward by every president since. Nonetheless, Attorney General Ashcroft ridiculed these guidelines as absurdly restrictive. He said, incorrectly, that the rules barred FBI agents from surfing the Internet and even from observing activities in public places. He announced that he was solving this problem by allowing FBI agents to operate with much less supervision.

The civil liberties community responded with furious criticism. But far from hurting the attorney general's popularity, the criticism reinforced his intended message: that law enforcement had been tied down by defendants' rights. The failure to pursue the flight school leads was in effect blamed on the American Civil Liberties Union, and the Justice Department presented itself as taking firm corrective action.

What actually occurred was rather different. One part of the rules the attorney general relaxed governs investigations of "general crimes"—gambling, theft, and other offenses *not* related to terrorism. The other rules he relaxed govern investigations of *domestic* terrorist groups. Unnoticed in the brouhaha, the rules that govern international terrorism cases—the ones that apply to Al-Qaeda—were not affected by the changes at all.

Behind the screen of this public relations maneuver, damage was inflicted in several directions. Public frustration with central oversight was understandable under the circumstances, but none of the previous guidelines, even the more restrictive domestic regimes, impeded the kinds of investigative steps the Minneapolis and Phoenix agents had urged. What the field offices needed was better supervision, not less of it. Yet Ashcroft's actions obscured responsibility for FBI missteps, and instead of censure, the FBI was rewarded with greater discretion. As in the case of the Patriot Act, fear of terrorism offered an occasion for the bait-and-switch: The guideline revisions are irrelevant to the concerns about Al-Qaeda that preoccupy the American public, yet they leave us with a large risk to civil liberties and large losses to effective management of the FBI.

Detention of Foreign Nationals

In the months following September 11, federal agents arrested approximately 1,200 foreign nationals. Hundreds were held for months before being cleared and released; others (the precise number is unknown) remain in detention, ostensibly to await deportation. Courts are still sorting out the many issues posed by these actions.

The length of these detentions and the absence of any judicial finding on the need for it are one of the primary concerns. Preventive detention is not unknown in American law, and the extraordinary uncertainties in the days after September 11 presented a virtually unique public safety emergency. Nonetheless, even making ample allowance for the pressure of circumstances, the outer boundaries of executive power in emergency situations were easily reached and exceeded in these roundups.

The most glaring of the problems posed is that the executive branch assumed the power to decide *unilaterally* who would be detained and for how long. Supreme Court decisions make clear that for preventive confinement to satisfy due process, measures like these be strictly confined to limited time periods, with adequate safeguards against the arbitrary exercise of executive power. At a minimum, there must be provision for prompt *independent* review of relevant evidence in an adversary hearing, and the judge must find a substantial government need, reasonably related to the nature and duration of the detention.

The 9/11 detentions of foreign nationals are sharply at odds with these norms. Without statutory authority—and in apparent violation of the extended seven-day period for precharge detention that the Patriot Act allows in terrorism cases—the Immigration and Naturalization Service held some of these suspects for months without affording hearings and without charging any violation of criminal or administrative law. Even after review by semi-independent administrative judges, immigration law violators who would normally be excused or deported were held, and are still being held, for preventive and investigative purposes without any independent review of the grounds for suspicion or the relation of government need to the individual hardship created. Aside from the relocation of Japanese Americans during World War II, the 9/11 detentions appear to be unprecedented in terms of the unilateral, unreviewable executive branch powers on which they rest.

Equally troubling is the extraordinary secrecy surrounding these sweeps. The government has refused to release the names of any of the detainees, and when they are charged and afforded immigration hearings, all hearings are closed to the press and even to their own families.

The government's justifications for secrecy are revealing. Secrecy, Attorney General Ashcroft stated, is necessary to protect the privacy of detainees. Since many of the detainees desperately wanted their names made public (so that aid organizations and lawyers could contact them), and since the Justice Department could have provided secrecy to detainees who requested it, the privacy claim was painfully disingenuous. In litigation, Justice Department lawyers added the argument that releasing the names of terrorists would give their cohorts clues about the progress of the investigation. This "road map" argument, though harder to dismiss outright, is still embarrassingly thin. Because all detainees have the right to make phone calls, and because gag orders have not been imposed on their family members or on their lawyers, the true terrorists among them can easily find ways to signal their confederates.

The shallow character of these arguments led the U.S. Court of Appeals for the Sixth Circuit to rule unanimously in August 2002 that the government's secrecy policy violates the First Amendment. The court accepted that secrecy might occasionally be warranted, when case-specific reasons for it were accepted by a judge. The crucial point was to provide an independent check on the supposed necessity and ensure that a closed-door policy did not become a cloak for government incompetence or abuse of power.

In October 2002, however, the U.S. Court of Appeals for the Third Circuit, in a 2–1 decision, reached the opposite conclusion, relying on the government's assertion that openness could damage national security. But as Judge Anthony Scirica (a Reagan appointee) noted in his dissent, the issue was not whether deportation hearings should be closed; at issue was only the question of who should make that determination. Closure of all proceedings, regardless of circumstances, was clearly unnecessary, he stressed, because a simple alternative to protect national security was available: Judges could determine national security needs on a case-by-case basis, in a closed proceeding if necessary, just as they do when national security matters arise in a formal criminal trial. In determining the need for secrecy, moreover, judges would of course give great weight to the national security interest and would extend great deference to executive branch expertise.

Secrecy across the board, without any obligation to present case-specific reasons for it to a court, has less to do with the war on terrorism than with the administration's consistent efforts, firmly in place before 9/11, to insulate executive action from public scrutiny. The cumulative effect of these efforts is an unprecedented degree of power—an attempt simultaneously to cut off the right to counsel, judicial review, and even any ability of the press to report what happens to individuals arrested on our own soil. As Judge Damon Keith wrote in the Sixth Circuit decision striking down the blanket secrecy order:

> The Executive Branch seeks to uproot people's lives, outside the public eye, and behind a closed door. Democracies die behind closed doors.
> The First Amendment, through a free press, protects the people's right

to know that their government acts fairly, lawfully, and accurately in deportation proceedings. . . . The Framers of the First Amendment "did not trust any government to separate the true from the false for us." They protected the people against secret government.

The Erosion of Habeas Corpus

. . . The case of Jose Padilla . . . also merits scrutiny from the standpoint of judicial review. Padilla, the so-called dirty bomber who allegedly planned to explode a bomb laced with radioactive material, was arrested at O'Hare International Airport in Chicago and held for a month as a material witness. Counsel was appointed for him, and he was due to be brought to court on June 11, 2002. Instead, two nights before the scheduled hearing, President Bush decided that Padilla was an "enemy combatant," a finding that the Justice Department tenaciously argues cannot be reviewed by any federal judge.

That night, without notice to his court-appointed counsel, Padilla was taken from federal detention in Manhattan, put on a military plane for South Carolina, and thrown into a Navy brig. That was on June 9, and Padilla has not been heard from since.[1] The government has refused to let him speak to the press or to his own attorney and has done everything in its power to deny him access to the courts.

Enemy infiltrators have posed acute threats to public safety before, notably during the Civil War. Abraham Lincoln, a straightforward man, responded by suspending the writ of habeas corpus.

That is not the Bush administration's style, however. When Padilla's lawyer, Donna Newman, tried to file a habeas petition on his behalf, the government suggested no need to suspend the writ. Its argument was the "narrow" one that the Padilla petition was invalid because he hadn't signed it. Having deliberately blocked all contact between Padilla and the outside world, the government told the court that a valid habeas petition required his signature, that Newman couldn't sign for him (how do we know that Padilla still wanted her to obtain his release?), and that she—his own lawyer—had no standing to ask the court's help because she had no "significant relationship" with him.

Federal Judge Michael Mukasey ultimately dismissed these arguments as frivolous. He ruled that Newman had to be granted access to her client and that he would review the enemy-combatant designation to be sure it was supported by "some evidence."

Mukasey's decision was announced on December 9, 2002; yet Padilla remains incommunicado. The government responded to Mukasey's order by demanding yet more time and finding several allegedly new reasons why Newman should be denied all contact with her client. In March 2003 Mukasey, finally losing patience, reaffirmed his original ruling and insisted

---

1. Padilla was not allowed to meet with lawyers until March 2004.

that a visit be permitted. Rather than comply, however, the government obtained yet another stay and appealed Mukasey's ruling to the U.S. Court of Appeals, a move that is certain to leave Padilla isolated for many more weeks, or, more likely, months.

The *New York Times* and the *Washington Post* praised Mukasey for his courage in standing up to the government. But we should take little comfort from his decision. Normally detention without a hearing becomes unconstitutional after forty-eight hours, and regardless of the context (civil, criminal, immigration, or military) detention incommunicado has never been permitted for any appreciable time at all. Yet, as of this writing, Padilla's detention (incommunicado, to boot) has continued without any judicial review for nearly a year.

More important, what is left of the writ of habeas corpus? Paradoxically, Padilla was lucky, because the government initially treated him as a material witness, and a judge appointed counsel to represent him. Next time, federal agents will be free to send the detainee straight to the Navy brig, without stopping first in a federal court. The Navy won't let him communicate with the outside world, and there won't be any Donna Newman to file a habeas petition for him. . . .

The other worry in Judge Mukasey's decision, for any case that gets to court, is the standard of review: "some evidence." The charge against Padilla is based on the affidavit of a Pentagon employee, Michael Mobbs. The so-called Mobbs declaration describes intelligence reports from confidential sources—captured Al-Qaeda operatives who were interrogated in detention. According to these sources, Padilla traveled to Pakistan, met with Al-Qaeda operatives, received training, and explored the possibility of setting off a radioactive dirty bomb. One of the government's sources cautioned that Padilla is not a "member" of Al-Qaeda. But informants claimed that Padilla "had significant and extended contacts with senior Al-Qaeda members and operatives" and that he "was sent to the United States to conduct reconnaissance and/or other attacks on their behalf."

Of course, it is currently impossible to cross-examine these informants to test their accusations. And although the declaration states that "certain aspects" of their reports have been corroborated, it says nothing about what those aspects were and whether the details corroborated related to Padilla in any way. As a result, the affidavit provides no basis for crediting the allegations that relate specifically to Padilla. To the contrary, the Mobbs declaration itself acknowledges (in a footnote) several grounds for concern about the informants' reliability. It concedes that "these confidential sources have not been completely candid" and that "some information provided by the sources remains uncorroborated and may be part of an effort to mislead or confuse U.S. officials." It also notes that while under interrogation, one of the sources was being given unspecified drugs "to treat medical conditions."

Information subsequently disclosed (but apparently not presented to the president or the court) reveals an even more troubling detail about drugs that this confidential source was *not* given: The informant against Padilla was interrogated while severely wounded; when he refused to cooperate, pain-killing medication was withheld until he agreed to talk and name names.

Confidential tips given under these circumstances obviously cannot provide proof of guilt beyond a reasonable doubt. They do not even establish probable cause sufficient to support a routine wiretap, because for that purpose the law requires that an affidavit provide a basis for trusting the reliability of an informant's tip. But there is *some* evidence.

If the Supreme Court upholds the "some evidence" standard, it won't matter whether detainees get to file habeas petitions. An unsupported tip from a confidential source is still some evidence, and that will be all it takes to require deference to a president's finding. That finding of enemy-combatant status, in turn, is enough in the administration's view to support detention for the long duration of this conflict, without any trial at all.

The government's approach is rooted, it says, in its need to continue incommunicado interrogation, for an indefinite period, in order to find out what Padilla knows. If he hasn't talked at this point, after almost a year of interrogation, it is hard to believe another six or twelve months will do the trick or that whatever Padilla knows has not gone stale. But we cannot completely rule out the possibility that after many months (or years) of isolation, a suspect might eventually reveal something useful.

The problem with that argument is the Constitution—not just its fine points but the very idea of a government under law. If the mere possibility of a useful interrogation is enough to support indefinite detention incommunicado, then no rights and no checks and balances are available at all, except when the executive chooses to grant them. If a ruler in any other country claimed unilateral powers of this sort, Americans would be quick to recognize the affront to the most basic of human rights.

Nonetheless, the government claims that two lines of precedent support its approach.

The first is *Ex parte Quirin,* the German saboteurs case. In World War II, eight German naval officers, one of whom claimed to be a U.S. citizen, landed secretly on beaches in the United States, buried their uniforms, and began preparations for sabotaging war production facilities. They were arrested; after conviction by a military tribunal, six were executed. The U.S. Supreme Court held that since they were acknowledged members of the German armed forces, the military had jurisdiction (just as it did over members of our own armed forces) to put them on trial. The Court said that military jurisdiction was permissible because the defendants were "admitted enemy invaders."

In the media and in court, the Bush administration argues that *Quirin* squarely settles its power over Padilla. They are right only if there is no important difference between being an admitted enemy and being an accused enemy. The argument boils down to the claim that since a person who admits guilt can be punished, the law should allow the same result when the president reviews a secret record and finds the crucial facts in the privacy of the Oval Office.

The government's other precedents are the cases holding that military discretion is unquestioned on the battlefield. And in this war on terror, they say, the entire nation is a battlefield. That analogy is not completely false, but if the military can do within the United States whatever it could do in Afghanistan, then again, checks and balances are over for the duration.

The American homeland has been threatened before. The Civil War brought four years of fighting on American soil, and Hawaii was a theater of active military operations throughout World War II. In both situations the military argued the need for displacing civilian courts, and in both situations the Supreme Court rejected that argument explicitly. "Martial law," the Court said in *Ex parte Milligan,* "cannot arise from a threatened invasion. The necessity must be actual and present, . . . such as effectually closes the courts. . . . If martial law is continued after the courts are reinstated, it is a gross usurpation of power."

The presumption against military detention, whenever civilian courts are functioning, is not merely a doctrinal technicality. The central premise of government under law is that executive officials, no matter how well intentioned, cannot be allowed unreviewable power to imprison a citizen. Even in times of dire emergency, the Supreme Court has been consistent and emphatic on this point. However much we respect the good intentions of the current attorney general and secretary of defense, such disregard for traditional checks and balances is a recipe for bad mistakes and serious abuses of power. Unchecked executive power of this sort, when exercised in other countries, is what we immediately recognize as a dangerous step in the direction of tyranny.

Perverse Logic

The Bush administration's counterterrorism strategy is not captured by the cliché about "shifting the balance" from liberty to security because so many of its actions encroach on liberty *without* enhancing security. Even within the executive branch, the rush to be tough, and to appear tough, has triggered disregard for accountability principles that lie close to the core of effective management. And the White House's determination to enlarge unilateral executive power has prompted unprecedented measures to bypass checks and balances that do not impede legitimate national security efforts. At the same time, the administration, brushing aside traditional commitments to narrow tailoring of intelligence-gathering power, has taken far too many steps that are demonstrably irrelevant to the Al-Qaeda threat; 9/11 opportunism in the law enforcement establishment has fueled successful efforts to expand investigative and surveillance powers wholly unrelated to terrorism.

Yet this lack of caution concerning encroachments on freedom coexists with great restraint in pursuing security needs that require the commitment of significant financial resources. The decision to blame civil liberties and to draw attention away from other aspects of an effective counterterrorism strategy is logical for an administration that puts tax cuts ahead of all other priorities. But for a nation facing unprecedented threats, it is a dangerous and indefensible choice.

DISCUSSION QUESTIONS

1. Is the USA Patriot Act an indispensable tool for law enforcement officials combating terrorists, or does the act do too much to limit American liberties and contribute little to preventing another catastrophic event like those of 9/11?

2. How might Viet Dinh respond to Stephen Schulhofer's charge that the Patriot Act does not contain sufficient checks and balances and thus invites the arbitrary power of presidents and their subordinates to invade the personal lives of citizens?

3. How might Stephen Schulhofer respond to Viet Dinh's claim that the Department of Justice has been faithful to the laws and the Constitution in carrying out the Patriot Act?

4. Do you think that some civil liberties might have to be temporarily sacrificed for the sake of homeland security until the terrorist threat has been defeated?

SUGGESTED READINGS AND INTERNET RESOURCES

The debate over the USA Patriot Act has been more one-sided in print than in politics: almost all of the books published on this subject have been critical of the act. For anthologies of essays by prominent critics of the Bush administration's domestic security policies, see Cynthia Brown, ed., *Lost Liberties: Ashcroft and the Assault on Personal Freedom* (New York: New Press, 2003), and Richard C. Leone and Greg Anrig Jr., eds., *The War on Our Freedoms: Civil Liberties in an Age of Terrorism* (New York: Public Affairs, 2003). In *Terrorism and the Constitution: Sacrificing Civil Liberties in the Name of National Security* (2d ed; New York: New Press, 2002), David Cole, James X. Dempsey, and Carole E. Goldberg argue that the Bush administration's post-9/11 security measures repeat the errors of past government programs that committed abuses against civil liberties. The denial of rights to foreign nationals detained under the Patriot Act is the subject of David Cole, *Enemy Aliens* (New York: New Press, 2003).

United States Department of Justice
www.lifeandliberty.gov
This website has been created by Attorney General Ashcroft's department to provide extensive materials that explain and support the USA Patriot Act.

Electronic Privacy Information Center
www.epic.org/privacy/terrorism/usapatriot
EPIC's website offers a detailed critical analysis of the Patriot Act and links to numerous articles and resources on the subject.

CHAPTER 7

Civil Rights:
How Far Have
We Progressed?

H alf a century after the U.S. Supreme Court ruled in *Brown* v. *Board of Education of Topeka* (1954) that racial segregation was a violation of the Constitution, where do relations between the races stand? And what kinds of public policies are still needed to address issues of racial inequity? Have we made considerable progress toward becoming "one nation, indivisible," as claimed by Stephan Thernstrom and Abigail Thernstrom, authors of the first selection that follows? Or do pervasive racial divisions continue to make us "a country of strangers," the title of our second selection, by David Shipler? Should we abandon affirmative action programs, as the Thernstroms recommend, because they impede progress toward a "colorblind" society, or do we need them, as Shipler suggests, because African Americans continue to face handicaps and prejudices in schools and workplaces?

Few Americans today question the landmark civil rights laws and court decisions of the 1950s and 1960s, even though they were enormously controversial in their day. After hundreds of years of slavery and racial segregation, this country has at last granted official status to the argument of the civil rights movement that racial discrimination is incompatible with democracy. But since its heroic phase ended in the late 1960s with the assassination of Martin Luther King Jr., the civil rights struggle has become embroiled in one bitter debate after another. Leaders and groups associated with the old civil rights movement have continued to call for strong legal measures to advance racial equality, including school busing and affirmative action in education and employment. Critics of the movement, black as well as white, challenge these measures, contending that they actually obstruct racial progress by undermining black self-help and by sowing fresh resentments among whites.

The dilemmas of race continued to trouble American society throughout the 1990s, as dramatically evidenced in the Los Angeles riots of 1992 and the antithetical reactions of African Americans and whites to the O. J. Simpson murder trial in 1994–1995. President Bill Clinton claimed that a top priority of his second term was a national dialogue focused on these dilemmas. But critics on the left disparaged Clinton's initiative on race as talk without action, while critics to the right saw it as merely a sounding board for bankrupt liberal nostrums such as affirmative action.

Affirmative action programs suffered a series of legal and political setbacks during the 1990s. In 1995, the U.S. Supreme Court ruled in *Adarand* v. *Peña* that government programs that provide preferential treatment on the basis of race are unconstitutional unless a pattern of prior discrimination against minorities can be demonstrated. In 1996, voters in California approved Proposition 209, which forbade public agencies and schools in the state from employing racial or gender preferences. That same year, a federal appeals court decided in *Hopwood* v. *Texas* that the state university could not continue to admit minorities with lower grades and test scores in the name of promoting diversity. In 1998, voters in the state of Washington approved a measure similar to California's Proposition 209.

However, affirmative action in higher education won qualified support from the U.S. Supreme Court in two cases decided in 2003. The affirmative action program for undergraduate admissions at the University of Michigan was rejected by a 6–3 majority because it awarded points to minority applicants on the basis of their race. But a 5–4 majority approved of the affirmative action program for law school admissions at the same university because the law school engaged, in the words of Justice Sandra Day O'Connor, in "a highly individualized, holistic review of each applicant's file. . . . " The Court's narrow majority emphasized the importance of diversity, one of the chief rationales for affirmative action, as vital to higher education's part in preparing the next generation for leading roles in American society.

How we view civil rights policies such as affirmative action depends in large part on how we understand and evaluate relations between the races in the United States today. Stephan and Abigail Thernstrom argue in our first selection that purveyors of racial gloom have distorted public debate, particularly by obscuring the evidence that racial attitudes in the United States have been growing more tolerant for decades. Relying heavily on public opinion surveys, the Thernstroms see whites and blacks as coming increasingly closer to one another since the days of Jim Crow segregation, even forming bonds of friendship across the boundaries of race. While not denying that African Americans suffer from higher rates of crime and poverty than do whites and score lower on various educational measures, the Thernstroms are most impressed by the signs of African-American advancement, such as the rise of a black middle class. The Thernstroms oppose affirmative action. Although it may spring from benevolent intentions, they argue, it has had pernicious consequences and has blocked further progress toward a "colorblind society."

David Shipler studies race relations differently from the Thernstroms and reaches very different conclusions. Shipler's work is based not on public opinion surveys but on interviews and observations about race relations in schools, workplaces, and communities around the nation. He believes that race continues to draw a line between white and black Americans, with uncertainty, discomfort, and anxiety on both sides. To Shipler, talk of "colorblindness" is unrealistic: "there is scarcely a consequential interaction between a black and a white in the United States in which race is not a factor."

Like many supporters of affirmative action, Shipler expresses some ambivalence, conceding that the policy can play into old racial stereotypes. But to him, affirmative action is needed so long as African Americans face educational and economic handicaps and subtle prejudices that undermine genuine equality of opportunity.

Race relations in the United States have profound implications for our understandings of democracy, freedom, and equality. How do you view the current state of American race relations? Are you more persuaded by the surveys cited by the Thernstroms that we are becoming a more tolerant interracial society or by the interviews and observations presented by Shipler that racial tensions and grievances continue to prevail along an American color line? What measures should our society take to deal with remaining racial inequalities? Is affirmative action still needed? If affirmative action were abolished, would we at last create a level playing field where everyone could compete on equal terms, or would white males reassert their traditional advantages?

One Nation, Indivisible

STEPHAN THERNSTROM
AND ABIGAIL THERNSTROM

In 1991, 13 percent of the whites in the United States said that they had generally "unfavorable" opinions about black Americans. In an ideal world, that number would be zero. But such a world is nowhere to be found. In Czechoslovakia that same year, 49 percent of Czechs had "unfavorable" attitudes toward the Hungarian ethnic minority living within the boundaries of their country. Likewise, 45 percent of West Germans disliked the Turks living in Germany; 54 percent of East Germans regarded Poles negatively; 40 percent of Hungarians frowned on the

Romanians who lived among them; and 42 percent of the French disdained Arab immigrants from North Africa. In only two of the dozen European countries surveyed—Britain and Spain—was the proportion of majority group members who expressed dislike for the principal minority group less than twice as high as in the United States. . . .

Against this yardstick the racial views of white Americans look remarkably good. But are seemingly tolerant whites simply more hypocritical than Czechs or French? Perhaps they have learned to keep their animus hidden from public view. We think not. Although different ways of framing questions about racial prejudice yield slightly different answers, the bulk of the evidence squares with the 1991 survey results: when it comes to intergroup tolerance, Americans rate high by international standards. . . .

America Since Myrdal

This is a profound change. When Gunnar Myrdal first trained his microscope on the American racial scene in the closing years of the Great Depression, he was struck by the radical difference between the status of immigrants and that of African Americans.[1] The United States stood out for its success in absorbing millions of immigrants from other lands into the melting pot. Myrdal believed that American social scientists were too preoccupied with "the occasional failures of the assimilation process" and the "tension" that immigration created in the society. They lacked the perspective available to "the outside observer," to whom the "first and greatest riddle to solve" was how "the children and grandchildren of these unassimilated foreigners" so quickly became "well-adjusted Americans." Part of the answer to the puzzle, Myrdal suggested, was "the influence upon the immigrant of a great national *ethos*, in which optimism and carelessness, generosity and callousness, were so blended as to provide him with hope and endurance."

In those days, the "optimism" and "generosity" Myrdal found did not extend to the descendants of enslaved Africans, though the "callousness" certainly did. Blacks had not been coaxed or coerced into the American melting pot; they had been forcibly kept out of it. Everyone was eager to "Americanize" the immigrants, Myrdal noticed, and viewed "the preservation of their separate national attributes and group loyalties as a hazard to American institutions." The recipe for African Americans was the reverse. They were "excluded from assimilation," and advised "even by their best friends in the dominant white group" to "keep to themselves and develop a race pride of their own."

In the South, where the large majority of African Americans lived, an elaborate legal code defined their position as a separate and inferior people.

---

1. Gunnar Myrdal was a Swedish social scientist who published a landmark study of U.S. race relations, *An American Dilemma: The Negro Problem and American Democracy,* in 1944.

Poorly educated in segregated schools, and confined to ill-paid, insecure, menial jobs, they were a subordinate caste in a society dedicated to white supremacy. Moreover, in countless ways blacks were daily reminded of their status as a lesser breed; they entered only the back door of a white home, never shook hands with a white person, and grown men were habitually addressed as "boy" or simply by their first names. In the North, blacks could vote, and the color line was less rigid and lacked the force of law. But many of the semiskilled and skilled industrial positions that gave immigrants the chance to climb out of poverty were off-limits, and blacks lived for the most part in a world separate from whites. A color line in the housing market confined black families to black neighborhoods; swimming in the "white" part of a public beach was dangerous; and many restaurants would not serve black customers. As Myrdal found, nine out of ten of even the most liberal and cosmopolitan northerners whom he encountered in the 1940s blanched at the thought of interracial marriage.

None of the public opinion surveys conducted in the Depression or World War II years included a specific question about whether whites had "favorable" or "unfavorable" opinions about blacks. But there can be no doubt about the answer such an inquiry would have yielded. The polling data we reviewed . . . demonstrated that large majorities of whites held strongly racist sentiments. African Americans were a stigmatized group, assumed to be a permanent caste that would forever remain beyond the melting pot.

That world has now vanished. In the spring of 1995, in the wake of attacks on affirmative action, Georgia congressman and one-time civil rights hero John Lewis complained that he sometimes felt as if he were reliving his life. "Didn't we learn?" he asked. He felt "the need to . . . tell people we've got to do battle again." But yesterday is not today, as many do recognize—including, we suspect, Lewis himself. "We black folk should never forget that our forefathers were slaves," Florida congresswoman Carrie P. Meek said in 1994. But then she added, "though my daughter says, 'Enough, Mom, enough of this sharecropper-slave stuff.'" Meek was born in 1926, and in her own lifetime the rigidly oppressive caste system delineated in *An American Dilemma* gave way to the far more fluid social order of today.

From rigid caste system to a more fluid social order . . . we reviewed decades of amazing change.

. . . We did not neglect the bad news. In 1995 half of all the murder victims in the United States were African Americans, though they comprised just one-eighth of the population; more than half of those arrested for murder were also black. The black poverty rate that same year was still 26 percent; 62 percent of children in female-headed families were poor. Perhaps most ominously, in 1994, on average, blacks aged seventeen could read only as well as the typical white child just thirteen years old. The racial gap in levels of educational performance permanently stacks the deck against too many African American youngsters as they move on to work or further schooling.

To stress the bad news is to distort the picture, however. Equally important is the story of enormous change, of much more progress than many scholars have recognized. For instance, between 1970 and 1995 the proportion of African Americans living in suburban communities nearly doubled, and residential segregation decreased in almost all the nation's metropolitan areas with the largest black populations. One of the best kept secrets of American life today is that over 40 percent of the nation's black citizens consider themselves members of the middle class. The black male unemployment rate has gotten much press, but, in fact, of those who are in the labor force (working or looking for work), 93 percent had jobs in 1995. We have let the underclass define our notion of black America; it is a very misleading picture.[2]

Over the last half century, the positions of African Americans thus improved dramatically by just about every possible measure of social and economic achievement: years of school completed, occupational levels, median incomes, life expectancy at birth, poverty rates, and homeownership rates. Much of the change took place before the civil rights movement. And while key decisions made by political and legal authorities in this early period were undeniably important (President Truman's order abolishing segregation in the armed forces, for example, and *Brown* v. *Board of Education*), the impersonal economic and demographic forces that transferred so many blacks from the southern countryside to the northern city were more fundamental.

In addition, white racial attitudes were gradually liberalized. Racist beliefs that were once firmly held by highly educated and uneducated whites alike lost all claim to intellectual respectability by the 1950s, and that changed racial climate finally opened doors. For instance, the door to the Brooklyn Dodgers' locker room. Had the visionary Branch Rickey believed Dodger fans were unreconstructed racists, he would not have put Jackie Robinson on the field and risked plunging ticket sales. As it was, his feel for changing racial attitudes brought championships to Brooklyn.

Social contact between the races has also increased enormously. By 1989, five out of six black Americans could name a white person whom they considered a friend, while two out of three whites said their social circle included someone who was black. By 1994 it had become not the least bit unusual for blacks and whites to have brought someone of the other race home to dine (a third of white families and a majority of the black families had done so), and most blacks and whites said someone of the other race lived in their neighborhood. When a sample of people in the Detroit metropolitan area were asked in 1992 whether they had contact on the job with people of the other race, 83 percent of blacks and 61 percent of whites said, yes. That same year, 72 percent of blacks and 64 percent of whites reported having interracial conversations on the job "frequently" or "sometimes." Even in the most intimate of relations, there had been substantial

---

2. *Underclass* refers to residents of the nation's poorest areas.

change. By 1993, 12 percent of all marriages contracted by African Americans were to a spouse of the other race.

Two Nations: Black and White, Separate, Hostile, Unequal, Andrew Hacker called his best-selling book. Our book is in many ways an answer to Hacker. *One* nation (we argue), no longer separate, much less unequal than it once was, and by many measures, less hostile. Moreover, the serious inequality that remains is less a function of white racism than of the racial gap in levels of educational attainment, the structure of the black family, and the rise in black crime.

We quarrel with the left—its going-nowhere picture of black America and white racial attitudes. But we also quarrel with the right—its see-no-evil view. It seems extraordinarily hard for liberals to say we have come a long way; the Jim Crow South is not the South of 1997. But it seems very hard for conservatives to say, yes, there was a terrible history of racism in this country, and too much remains.

Conservatives seem to think that they concede too much if they acknowledge the ugliness of our racial history and the persistence of racism (greatly diminished but not gone)—that if they do so, they will be committed to the currently pervasive system of racial preferences and indeed to reparations. And liberals, from their different perspective, also fear concession. To admit dramatic change, they seem to believe, is to invite white indifference. As if everything blacks now have rests on the fragile foundation of white guilt . . .

The Road to Progress

Much racial progress has been made. And much has *yet* to be made. How to keep moving forward? It is a question that can be answered only by knowing the route by which African Americans have come to where they are today.

There is no mystery as to how they got from there to here, most writing on racial change in recent decades assumes. The story began with the civil rights movement, which, with a boost from *Brown* v. *Board of Education,* created turmoil in the nation and forced Congress and the White House to act. The civil rights and voting rights legislation of the mid-1960s destroyed Jim Crow institutions and gave equal legal status to African Americans. These colorblind measures, however, failed to remedy deeper economic and social inequalities rooted in race. Color-conscious policies that set specific numerical goals and timetables attacked the underlying problems. In fact, only the adoption of preferential policies could have created a black middle class and brought about other economic and educational gains.

From this account, a simple policy conclusion flows: preferential policies are the key to future progress. And thus Supreme Court decisions and other actions that constrain the use of racial classifications by public authorities are viewed by some as truly dangerous—a threat to black well-being comparable to the end of Reconstruction.

Such alarm ignores the historical record, we have argued, although the great strides forward have since been somewhat obscured by the gains and disappointments of subsequent years. The civil rights revolution reached a climax in a burst of legislation that destroyed the Jim Crow system, but that legislation promised more than it could quickly deliver. As Dr. King and others understood, the legal fix would not tomorrow solve the problem of economic and educational inequalities so long in the making. Blacks were understandably impatient. They had already waited much too long—almost a century since the passage of the great Reconstruction Amendments to the Constitution. It was tempting to seek shortcuts, ways of accelerating social change, and thus the demand for "freedom now" soon became a call for "equality as a fact and as a result," as Lyndon Johnson put it in 1965.

That call for equality as a "fact" and "result" was the first step down the road to racial preferences. Much celebrated in the civil rights community for the benefits they have brought, preferences are in fact difficult to assess. . . . In 1995 the historian Roger Wilkins described himself as the happy recipient of racial preferences. "I'd rather be an assistant attorney general who was a beneficiary of affirmative action than a GS 14,"[3] he said. It's hard to believe Wilkins is really convinced he would have been languishing at the bottom of a bureaucratic heap had he not been rescued by preferential policies. His tale certainly does not square with the larger picture, as we understand it.

In a few respects the overall rate of black progress did accelerate after preferential policies were introduced. Rates of entry into law and medical schools are one example. But lawyers and doctors are a tiny fraction of the black middle class. And by many other measures progress slowed—and in some cases stopped altogether. One recent study found that the racial gap in median wages, labor-force participation, and joblessness was wider in 1992 than in 1967. As a consequence of the huge rise in female-headed households among African Americans, the ratio of black to white family income has fallen somewhat since the 1960s. And the poverty rate for blacks in the 1990s is about as high as it was a generation ago.

Thus, on many counts the socioeconomic gains made by African Americans in the affirmative action era have been less impressive than those that occurred before preferential policies. On the basis of that historical record, however, we cannot conclude that affirmative action did nothing significant. In the 1940s and 1950s, big strides forward were relatively easy to take—blacks were so far behind whites. Thereafter, the rate of progress naturally slowed. Moreover, preferential policies may indeed have benefited some African Americans (those with better educational credentials) without dramatically improving the position of the group as a whole.

The slower growth of the American economy since the early 1970s further complicates the task of assessment. Groups on the lower rungs of the

---

3. GS stands for General Schedule, the system that classifies federal civil servants; GS 14 denotes a middle-level position in the federal bureaucracy.

socioeconomic ladder usually find it far easier to improve their position when the economy is booming, as it was to an extraordinary degree in the 1950s and 1960s. And perhaps without affirmative action, the slow economy would have been even harder on African Americans than it was. It's a what-might-have-been argument that cannot be settled. But those who assume that ending affirmative action will end black progress must reconcile the history of pre-1970s progress with their fear of a future that returns to the past.

Even assuming that affirmative action rescued Roger Wilkins and others from professional oblivion, an important question remains: have the benefits outweighed the costs? The issue was implicitly raised in a surprising 1993 letter. The mayors of Minneapolis and four other large American cities wrote to Attorney General Janet Reno, calling for an end to the collection and dissemination of any crime statistics broken down by race. "We believe," the mayors said, "that the collection and use of racial crime statistics by the federal government perpetuate racism in American society." Such data, the mayors went on, were "largely irrelevant" and conveyed the erroneous impression that race and criminality were causally linked. "Racial classifications," the letter continued, were "social constructs" and had "no independent scientific validity." An earlier letter from the Minneapolis mayor had expressed concern about the "'we' vs. 'they' mentality" that racial classifications created.

The crime statistics had wonderfully concentrated the mayors' minds. Momentarily, at least, they recalled what liberals had always believed until the late 1960s but had chosen to forget when they were converted to affirmative action: racial classifications perpetuate racism. The mayors did not object to racial body counts on principle, as liberals once had. They were simply troubled by the publication of statistics that made African Americans look bad. Racial statistics showing that black poverty and unemployment rates were higher than those of whites, that our colleges and universities did not have "enough" African American students, and that our corporations were short on black executives: these racial classifications apparently were not mere "social constructs" with "no scientific validity." They were essential to enlightened public policy. It was only the black crime rate to which the mayors objected.

But racial data used to distribute benefits inevitably creates the we-versus-they outlook that worried them. American society has paid, it seems to us, a very high price for well-intentioned race-conscious policies. Particularly those built into our law, for the law delivers messages that ripple through both the public and private sectors. And thus unlike the mayors, we hold to Justice Harlan's belief that "our Constitution is color-blind, and neither knows nor tolerates classes among citizens."[4]

---

4. Justice John Marshall Harlan was the lone dissenter to the 1896 Supreme Court decision in *Plessy* v. *Ferguson* that legitimated the "separate-but-equal" system of racial segregation.

In 1896, Justice Harlan was under no illusion that American *society* was color-blind; his was a statement about how to read the Constitution. Nor did Thurgood Marshall in 1947 suppose the country had become oblivious to race when he argued that "classifications based on race or color have no moral or legal validity in our society."[5] We're not naïve; we don't think Americans have to think twice about the color of someone they meet. And we do know that for many whites color still carries important connotations: a young black man on an urban street in the evening appears much more menacing than one who is white. Even middle-class black neighbors may still seem less appealing than white ones to too many white families. It is, in fact, precisely the problem of ongoing racism and just plain color-consciousness that makes race-blind public policy so imperative. Policies that work to heighten the sense of racial separatism spell disaster in a nation with an ugly history of racial subordination and a continuing problem, albeit dramatically diminished, of racial intolerance.

Race-conscious policies make for more race-consciousness; they carry American society backward. We have a simple rule of thumb: that which brings the races together is good; that which divides us is bad. Of course, which policies have what effect is a matter of deep contention. To tear down affirmative action "could start a race war that would make Bosnia look like a kindergarten party," Arthur Fletcher, a former assistant secretary for employment standards, said in 1995. The . . . research we have frequently cited suggests quite a different picture: a racial divide widened by preferences. Others argue that "diversity" strategies bring whites and blacks together; it is not our view. Only those policies that recognize differences among *individuals* can create a true community.

A nation in which individuals are judged as individuals: it was the dream of the 1960s, and we still cherish it. "There *is* a proper object for all the loathing in this country," *New Republic* literary editor Leon Wieseltier has said. "That object is: race. Instead of race hatred, the hatred of race. Instead of the love of what is visible about the person, the love of what is invisible about the person." Does the Wieseltier view ask black Americans to turn their back on all things "black"—to deny all cultural differences associated with group membership? Of course not. Jews haven't; Armenians haven't; Ukrainians haven't. Many Americans arrange their private lives so as to spend much of their time with others of the same background. Purging all racial distinctions from our law and our public life would pose no threat to those who wish to live in a predominantly black neighborhood, attend an all-black church, and otherwise associate primarily or even exclusively with their fellow African Americans.

Racist Americans have long said to blacks, the single most important thing about you is that you're black. Indeed, almost the only important

---

5. Justice Thurgood Marshall was the principal lawyer in the battle by the National Association for the Advancement of Colored People (NAACP) against "separate-but-equal"; later he served on the U.S. Supreme Court.

thing about you is your color. And now, black and white Americans of seeming good will have joined together in saying, we agree. It has been— and is—exactly the wrong foundation on which to come together for a better future. "There can be no empathy and persuasion across racial lines," the economist Glenn C. Loury has said, unless we understand "that the conditions and feelings of particular human beings are universally shared. Such an understanding can be had, but only if we look past race to our common humanity." Ultimately, black social and economic progress largely depend on the sense that we are one nation—that we sink or swim together, that black poverty impoverishes us all, that black alienation eats at the nation's soul, and that black isolation simply cannot work. . . .

True Equality

"The contest between white suburban students and minority inner-city youths is inherently unfair," the chancellor of the University of California at Berkeley, Chang-Lin Tien, said in the summer of 1995. It was not a very persuasive argument for the racial double standards he was defending. If inner-city youngsters are educationally deprived, surely the real solution— indeed the only effective and just solution—has to be one that attacks the problem of K–12 education directly. But in any case, most of the beneficiaries were not the inner-city youths upon whom Tien chose to focus; 30 percent of the black students in the 1994–1995 freshmen class came from families with annual incomes over $70,000. In fact, the Berkeley admissions office, studying the question, found that preferences reserved only for students from low-income families would have reduced the black enrollment by two-thirds. Relatively privileged students—by the measure of economic well-being—had acquired privileges on the basis of the color of their skin.

Affirmative action is class-blind. Students who fall into the category of protected minority will benefit whatever the occupation and income of their parents. As the *Boston Globe* has put it, "officials at even the most selective schools recruit minority scholars with the zeal of a Big 10 football coach." The overwhelming majority of four-year institutions buy expensive lists of minority students and their scores from the Educational Testing Service. Admissions counselors and a network of thousands of alumni comb the country, visiting schools and the special preparatory programs that Phillips Academy in Andover and other private high schools run. Some universities, like Tufts, start the recruitment process in the elementary school years; others, like Boston College, have been known to bring minority students, all expenses paid, for a visit, complete with a chauffeured tour of the area. And if that student can already afford the air fare and more? That's not relevant. Until 1996, when the policy was changed, the African-American student whom the Harvard Graduate School wanted automatically qualified for a Minority Prize Fellowship—even if that student was the son or daughter of a black millionaire.

It's not a process likely to encourage its beneficiaries to work hard in high school. The message is clear: color is the equivalent of good grades. If you don't have the latter, the former will often do. When the University of California regents decided in July 1995 to abolish racial and ethnic preferences in admissions, the executive director of a YWCA college-awareness program told students that the UC vote meant that their "application would be sent in with everybody else's—people who are on college tracks and are prepared." One of the minority students at the session, Jesley Zambrano, reacted at first with anger: "The schools are mostly run by white people. If they don't help us get in, how are we going to get in?" she asked. But then she answered the question herself: "I guess I have to work harder," she said.

That was exactly the point Martin Luther King had made in a speech Shelby Steele heard as a young student in Chicago.[6] "When you are behind in a footrace," King had said, "the only way to get ahead is to run faster than the man in front of you. So when your white roommate says he's tired and goes to sleep, you stay up and burn the midnight oil." As Steele went on to say, "academic parity with all other groups should be the overriding mission of black students.... Blacks can only *know* they are as good as others when they are, in fact, as good.... Nothing under the sun will substitute for this." And nothing under the sun except hard work will bring about that parity, as King had said. Challenge the students academically rather than capitulate to their demands for dorms with an ethnic theme, Steele has urged universities. And dismantle the machinery of separation, break the link between difference and power. For as long as black students see themselves as *black* students—a group apart, defined by race—they are likely to choose power over parity.

A Country of Strangers

DAVID K. SHIPLER

line runs through the heart of America. It divides Oak Park from Chicago's West Side along the stark frontier of Austin Boulevard, splitting the two sides of the street into two nations, separating

---

6. Shelby Steele is an African-American scholar who has been one of the most prominent critics of affirmative action.

the carefully integrated town from the black ghetto, the middle class from the poor, the swept sidewalks from the gutters glistening with broken glass, the neat boutiques and trim houses from the check-cashing joints and iron-grilled liquor stores.

The line follows stretches of the Santa Monica Freeway in Los Angeles and Rock Creek Park in Washington, D.C. It runs along the white picket fence that divides the manicured grounds from the empty field where the slaves' shacks once stood at Somerset Place plantation in North Carolina. It cuts across the high, curved dais of the Etowah County Commission in Alabama, where one black member sits with five whites. It encircles the "black tables" where African-Americans cluster together during meals at Princeton University, Lexington High School in Massachusetts, and a thousand corporate cafeterias across the country.

At eleven o'clock Sunday morning, which has been called the most segregated hour in America, the line neatly separates black churches from white churches. It intertwines itself through police departments and courtrooms and jury rooms, through textbooks and classrooms and dormitories, through ballot boxes and offices, through theaters and movie houses, through television and radio, through slang and music and humor, and even through families. The line passes gently between Tony and Gina Wyatt of Florida; he is black, she is white, and they both reach gracefully across the border. It tangles the identity of their teenage son, Justin, who looks white but feels black.

"The problem of the Twentieth Century is the problem of the color-line," W. E. B. Du Bois wrote in 1901; the prophetic words became the opening declaration of his lyrical work *The Souls of Black Folk*.[1] In the succeeding decades, that line has been blurred and bent by the demise of legal segregation and the upward movement of many blacks through the strata of American opportunity. But it remains forbidding to black people left behind in poverty and to others, more successful, who may suddenly confront what Du Bois called a "vast veil"—the curtain of rejection drawn around those whose ancestors were brought in chains from Africa. Today, when sensibilities have been tuned and blatant bigotry has grown unfashionable in most quarters, racist thoughts are given subtler expression, making the veil permeable and often difficult to discern. Sometimes its presence is perceived only as a flicker across a face, as when a white patient looks up from her hospital bed to discover that an attending physician is an African-American.

And so, as the close of the century now approaches, I offer this journey along the color line. It is a boundary that delineates not only skin color and race but also class and culture. It traces the landscape where blacks and whites find mutual encounters, and it fragments into a multitude of fissures

---

1. W. E. B. Du Bois was a leading African-American scholar and political activist whose career stretched from the 1890s to the 1960s.

that divide blacks and whites not only from each other, but also among themselves.

Americans of my generation, who were youngsters when the civil rights movement began in the 1950s, grew up on awful, indelible images. I am haunted still by the cute little white girls who twisted their faces into screams of hatred as black children were escorted into schools. I saw for the first time that the face of pristine innocence could be merely a mask.

Here was the enemy. And the solution seemed obvious: Break down the barriers and let people mingle and know one another, and the importance of race would fade in favor of individual qualities. Blacks would be judged, as Martin Luther King Jr. was preaching, not by the color of their skin but by the content of their character. The perfect righteousness of that precept summoned the conscience of America. . . .

. . . As the Jim Crow segregation laws were overturned, less tractable problems were revealed, and they frustrated King toward the end of his life as he tried to bring his campaign to cities in the North. There, villainy was less easily identified. Rooted in the prejudices, the poverty, the poor education, and the culture of hopelessness that divided blacks and whites, the racial predicament proved too deeply embedded in the society to be pried out by mere personal contact and legal equality. Perhaps it was naïve to think that all that would have to happen was for people to look into each other's eyes, to give blacks as many opportunities as whites, to open the doors. I put this to Reverend Bill Lawson, the black pastor of the Wheeler Avenue Baptist Church in Houston, who had been in the movement and had a long perspective. . . .

. . . "I think that there has been a redefinition of relationships over the last, say, forty years," he said. "There has been, on the one hand, a push toward eliminating the old segregation laws and, on the other hand, a resistance to changing community and neighborhood patterns. So there has been a tension between what we felt was right and what we felt was expedient. There has been the allowance of public contacts. Blacks can ride in the fronts of buses or eat at lunch counters. There has not been a significant change in intimate, personal attitudes. There is still some feeling that we don't want to live too close together, that we don't want to have too many close connections in places [where] we worship, or that we don't want to have too much family contact. We still have some problems with dating and marriage. So in the more public relationships, there has been at least a tolerance that says, let's each one have our own freedom. But anything that becomes more intimate or personal, we tend to have a little bit more resistance."

In Birmingham, Alabama, an old civil rights warrior, Reverend Abraham Lincoln Woods of the St. Joseph Baptist Church, saw the movement's accomplishments as more cosmetic than substantive. "Birmingham has gone through tremendous changes," he said, "and the fact that we have gone from a city where blacks were shut out of the process to having a black mayor and a predominantly black city council—we now have black policemen, in fact we have a black chief now—many things have changed of that kind. But I find that in spite of what seems to be a tolerance of the races and a working together, I find still, somewhat beneath the surface, sometimes not too deeply, those same old attitudes."

But it is behavior, not attitudes, that concerns David Swanston, a white advertising executive whose wife, Walterene, is black. He sat in his handsome town house in McLean, Virginia, one evening and took the measure of America in terms of his own interracial marriage. "It was against the law in a number of states twenty-five years ago," he observed. "It just seems to me that this world was institutionally significantly more racist, overtly racist, than today. Now, each individual black and white within the country may be about the same place they were twenty-five years ago, as regarding interracial marriages and other issues. But it seems to me that's very secondary to the fact that institutionally, we are much beyond that—and it's the institutions that hurt you, that can have the impact on your lives. And by and large, if the twenty people we see in the mall don't like it, and those twenty people wouldn't have liked it twenty-five years ago, I don't really care. The fact that our marriage is recognized by the Commonwealth of Virginia, that we're not criminals, those are the areas where it just seems to me incredible change has been made." . . .

There is scarely a consequential interaction between a black and a white in the United States in which race is not a factor. Even as it goes unmentioned, as it normally does, race is rarely a neutral element in the equation. It may provoke aversion, fear, or just awkwardness, on the one hand, or, on the other, eager friendliness and unnatural dialogue. Even in easy contacts that are fleeting and impersonal—between a diner and a waiter, a customer and a salesperson, a passenger and a bus driver—race does not always drop to zero; it possesses weight and plays some role in the chemical reaction. "There's always something there," said a young white Princeton graduate working for the *National Journal,* a Washington magazine. "It can be mitigated or it can be worsened by a lot of other factors: social class, culture, the status hierarchy in the office." But it never quite goes away, as he realized when he observed how the mixture of race, class, and hierarchy led him to feel more comfortable with the white reporters than with the black secretaries and receptionists.

If race distorts individual relations, it also magnifies most major social and policy issues facing the American public. Poverty, crime, drugs, gangs, welfare, teenage pregnancy, chronic joblessness, homelessness, illiteracy, and the failure of inner-city public schools are usually viewed through the racial prism. They are seen as black problems or as problems created by blacks. The most popular solutions—cuts in welfare for teenage mothers and long sentences for repeat offenders—are codes for cracking down on blacks' misdeeds. Where race enters the realms of politics, health care, economic injustice, and occasionally foreign policy (as in Haiti and South Africa), the debates are charged with an additional layer of emotion. Despite the upheavals brought by the Supreme Court's 1954 ruling against segregated schools in *Brown* v. *Board of Education,* by the civil rights movement, and by the resulting 1964 Civil Rights Act and the 1965 Voting Rights Act, race is still central to the American psychological experience, as it has been for more than two hundred years.

Over their entire history on this continent, African-Americans have struggled as a people in every conceivable way, short of widespread armed insurrection, to share in the pursuit of happiness. By social reflex or by calculation, by happenstance or ideology, blacks have been servile and militant, passive and hardworking, dependent and self-sufficient. They have used the church, the mosque, the schoolhouse, the university, the military, and the corporation in an effort to advance. They have tried to go back to Africa, and they have tried to function within the political system of the United States. They have tried peaceful demonstrations and violent street riots. They have tried sweet reason and angry rhetoric, assimilation and separatism. They have appealed to the nation's conscience and to its fears. It would be wrong to say that none of this has worked: Individuals have succeeded. But neither deference nor defiance has been effective for black Americans as a whole. No degree of personal success quite erases the stigma of black skin, as many achieving blacks realize when they step outside their family, neighborhood, or professional environment into a setting where their rank and station and accomplishments are not known. "I didn't come from a deprived family," says Floyd Donald, who owns a small radio station in Gadsden, Alabama. "I grew up with books. I grew up with china. I grew up with silver. My background is impeccable, so far as my education and my parents' education and their positions in life and their abilities and so forth. So I had that advantage. However, out of my community, I was just another black. You see, it doesn't make much difference about the status that a black achieves. He is black in America."

In five years of crisscrossing the country to research this book, I was struck by the ease with which most blacks I interviewed were able to discuss race and the difficulty most whites had with the subject. . . .

. . . [B]lack Americans were enormously generous of spirit and time in reaching into their experiences to lay them out for me. Gradually, I came to understand what should have been obvious at the outset: that a black person cannot go very long without thinking about race; she has already asked herself every question that I could possibly pose.

By contrast, most whites rarely have to give race much thought. They do not begin childhood with advice from parents about how to cope with racial bias or how to discern the racial overtones in a comment or a manner. They do not have to search for themselves in history books or literature courses. In most parts of America, their color does not make them feel alone in a crowd; they are not looked to as representatives of their people. And they almost never have to wonder whether they are rejected—or accepted— because of their genuine level of ability or the color of their skin. As a result, few whites I interviewed had considered the questions I put to them. Many struggled to be introspective, but most found that I was taking them into uncharted territory, full of dangers that they quickly surrounded with layers of defensiveness. . . .

Many whites are confused over how they should be thinking about racial issues now. Some adopt an air of smooth indifference, an emotional distance. They often hesitate to say what's on their minds, lest they be accused of racism. Others work quietly, sometimes in frustration, to improve blacks' opportunities in their companies or universities or military units; indeed, I have discovered that more sincere effort goes on than ever gets reflected in press portrayals of America's racial problems. But nothing adds up to a neat sum anymore. How does a white person—even a liberal—sort out the anti-white prejudices, the black self-segregation, the manipulation of history, the endless message of white guilt, the visible achievements of prominent blacks coupled with the deepening poverty and violence of the inner cities? Across much of the spectrum of white America run common themes of distress and impatience with the subject of race, a national mood of puzzlement and annoyance. . . .

The question most often asked me by whites is whether racial matters are getting better or worse. It is an odd inquiry for people to make about their own country. I am used to being asked by Americans how things are going in Russia or in the Middle East, where I have lived and traveled and they perhaps have not.[2] But to have so little feel for the situation right at home betrays the corrosive nature of our racial legacy: how it eats away at our equilibrium, our sense of direction, our navigational skills. We simply do not know where we are, and we are not even quite sure where we have been.

What's more, there is no neat answer to the question. Sometimes I ask in return, "What is your reference point? Slavery? Jim Crow? The height of the civil rights movement? The last five years? Are we measuring economic success or personal attitudes? Are we counting black college graduates or anti-black hate crimes? And what if we decide that pockets of hopefulness are tucked into the midst of despair? Shall we feel virtuous and relax?"

If any sum can be reckoned, it is one of acute contradiction. In the 1920s, the Ku Klux Klan had about two million members; by the mid-1990s, the estimated membership was down to between 2,500 and 3,000, out of 20,000 or 25,000 altogether in various hate groups, including skinheads and militias. Furthermore, prospects have improved for blacks with high skills or advanced degrees in the sciences, business, law, medicine, and other professions as more and more white-run institutions have grown eager to find talented African-American men and women to serve diverse constituencies, improve profits, and demonstrate a commitment to "equal opportunity." But other black people, dragged down by the whirlpool of

---

2. Shipler was a foreign correspondent for the *New York Times.*

poverty and drugs, have fewer and fewer exits. The United States has more black executives and more black prison inmates than a decade ago.

The answer may be that things are getting better and worse at the same time. Racially, America is torn by the crosscurrents of progress and decay. Practically every step forward is accompanied by a subtle erosion of the ground beneath. . . .

On a late summer day in the early 1990s, the dean, who was white, rose to welcome the black and Hispanic students entering one of the country's leading law schools. They had been invited a week early for special orientation, and he had a delicate message for them. His remarks were born of anguish, for he knew something that they did not: They had been admitted with lower average scores than their white classmates had earned on the Law School Aptitude Test.

He wanted to warn them but not defeat them. He could not tell them of the disparities in test scores, because his school, like virtually all others, tried to keep such information secret. So he took an oblique approach. He himself had come from a small town, not an intellectual background, he told the new students. To overcome that deprivation, he had been forced to apply enormous effort, and so would they. "If you work extremely hard," he remembered himself saying, "you can make up for differences in past credentials."

His talk was as welcome as an earthquake. "I was deeply criticized by a number of faculty who felt I had hurt these people on their first day at the institution," he said. "I felt terrible."

The issue confronted him more directly when a group of Hispanic students approached him for reassurance. They were being tormented by white classmates who insisted that Hispanics had scored lower than whites on the LSAT and did not deserve to be there. They wanted the smear refuted. "I tried to be very candid with them," the dean recalled. It was true, he told them: Their scores had been somewhat lower, but with hard work they could erase the deficiencies of their pasts.

An awful silence descended. "I just looked into their eyes as I was talking," the dean remembered, "and I thought, 'I can't bear this; it's too painful.' Their hopes and expectations about what would be said were defeated. There was just a feeling of betrayal."

So goes the conversation about one of the most critical methods used to pry open doors long locked against Hispanics, blacks, and other minorities. The truth cannot be told on any campus without stigmatizing those being aided, without giving a weapon to conservative opponents of such efforts. This law school cannot be identified, the dean cannot be named. He cannot be quoted, except anonymously, as he reveals that if only scores and not race were taken into account, only five or six blacks would be admitted each year instead of forty or fifty. A full and honest discussion of how colleges and graduate schools increase the numbers of African-Americans in their ranks cannot be had.

But why not? How shameful can it be, after generations of imprisonment in inferior educational systems, to score lower on a standardized test? How unfair can it be, after three hundred years of white advantage, to spend thirty years redressing the imbalance? And how unwise can it be, after failing to tap the vast resources of black America, to search affirmatively past the sterile test scores into a rich human potential not easily measured? . . .

Although SAT scores are reliable predictors of freshman grades, they forecast later achievement less accurately. Harvard studied alumni in its classes of '57, '67, and '77 and found that graduates with low SAT scores and blue-collar backgrounds displayed a high rate of "success"—defined by income, community involvement, and professional satisfaction. Here is where race and socioeconomic background mix; some admissions officers believe that if affirmative action were aimed particularly at lower-class students, it would generate less opposition. But it would also yield fewer blacks, since two-thirds of eighteen-year-olds below the poverty line are white. Furthermore, giving preference to students who need financial aid would cost more in scholarships than most colleges have. Consequently, some universities seek upper-middle-class blacks, who can bring diversity and also afford the tuition. However, other elite schools, such as Dartmouth, Harvard, and the Massachusetts Institute of Technology, do give a nod to lower-class applicants. "We have particular interest in students from a modest background," said Marlyn McGrath Lewis, director of admissions for Harvard and Radcliffe. "Coupled with high achievement and a high ambition level and energy, a background that's modest can really be a help. We know that's the best investment we can make: a kid who's hungry."

The two words "affirmative action" were first put together during the inauguration of President John F. Kennedy in 1961, when Vice President Lyndon Johnson, standing in a receiving line, buttonholed a young black attorney named Hobart Taylor Jr. and asked him to help advisers Arthur Goldberg and Abe Fortas write Executive Order 10925 barring federal contractors from racial discrimination in hiring. "I was searching for something that would give a sense of positiveness to performance under that executive order, and I was torn between the words 'positive action' and the words 'affirmative action,' " Taylor recalled in an interview for the Lyndon Baines Johnson Library. "And I took 'affirmative action' because it was alliterative."

From that poetic genesis has come an array of requirements and programs that stir resentment in most of white America. An elastic concept with many definitions, affirmative action is broadly seen as unnatural and unfair, yet it has begun to work its way into the standard practices of so many universities, corporations, and government agencies that it seems sustained as much now by habit and ethic as by law. Even as the courts whittle away at affirmative action's constitutional rationales, more and more institutions are following the military's lead in justifying racial diversity as pragmatic, not merely altruistic. They strive to avoid not only legal punishment but the punishment of a marketplace that is producing fewer and fewer white males as a percentage of workers and customers. As the Pentagon realized after the draft ended in 1973, if the armed services were to compete for good people and tap the entire reservoir of potential recruits, those who were not white men would have to be convinced that unfettered opportunities existed in the ranks. Some corporations have experienced a similar epiphany of self-interest, and at many universities, an admissions officer observed, "success in minority recruitment has become a kind of coin of the realm to indicate institutional success." . . .

. . . [T]he problem created by the solution of affirmative action is this: It allows whites to imagine themselves as victims. Polls find about two-thirds of Americans believing that a white has a smaller chance of getting a job or a promotion than an equally or less qualified black does. When asked why they think this, however, only 21 percent can say that they have seen it at work, 15 percent that it has happened to a friend or relative, and just 7 percent that they have experienced it personally. "With blacks, who are such a small fraction of the population," says Barbara Bergmann, an economist at American University, "the lost opportunities to white men are really minuscule."

Furthermore, some of the personal experience is suspect. Affirmative action transports long-standing biases against blacks into the realm of reasonable discussion: It gives whites permission to affirm the stereotype of blacks as less competent by saying, or thinking, that this or that African-American was not good enough to have been admitted, hired, or promoted without a racial preference. Unscrupulous white supervisors contribute to the slander either by hiring less qualified blacks, just to get their numbers up and avoid discrimination suits, or by disingenuously telling whites, "Gee, I'd love to promote you, but I have to take a black or a woman." Affirmative action thus becomes, in the first case, an excuse for sloppy recruiting and, in the second, a handy pretext to spare a manager the discomfort of telling a white colleague why he doesn't deserve to be promoted.

These are perversions of affirmative action's purpose, and they undermine its viability. In its many forms, from intensive recruiting to hiring goals to set-aside contracts for minority-owned businesses, the effort is designed to remedy unjustified exclusion by seeking out qualified people from the excluded groups and accepting the best of them. It recognizes that passive color blindness is not enough, that people do not deal with one another purely as individuals, and that even if overt discrimination is eliminated, the handicaps of poor schooling and impoverished family life, of subtle prejudice and institutional intolerance, remain severe obstacles to advancement by African-Americans.

DISCUSSION QUESTIONS

1. What is the best way to obtain information and insight into American race relations? What are the advantages and disadvantages of using public opinion surveys to gauge race relations? What are the advantages and disadvantages of using interviews and observations to gauge race relations?

2. One point of contention between the Thernstroms and Shipler concerns inter-racial friendships. Looking at the campuses or workplaces with which you are familiar, do you think that whites and blacks have grown more comfortable with one another on a personal level, or do you think that racial separatism is growing?

3. If laws and other measures bar racial discrimination, has American society treated both races with justice? Or do further steps need to be taken to compensate for past racial injustices and to counteract subtly persisting prejudices?

4. Do affirmative action programs only encourage greater white prejudice against blacks? Or do they bring whites into contact with blacks and allow them to see real individuals rather than racial stereotypes?

5. What would American society look like today if affirmative action programs had never been instituted? What would it look like tomorrow if affirmative action programs were abolished?

SUGGESTED READINGS AND INTERNET RESOURCES

Shelby Steele's *The Content of our Character* (New York: St. Martin's Press, 1990) is a passionate call for personal responsibility and an attack on affirmative action by a black scholar. Black journalist Ellis Cose provides a sober critique of the anti-affirmative-action position in *Color-Blind: Seeing Beyond Race in a Race-Obsessed World* (New York: HarperCollins, 1997). For an extensive assault on affirmative action by a former member of the Reagan administration, see Terry Eastland, *Ending Affirmative Action: The Case for Colorblind Justice* (New York: Basic Books, 1996). A detailed case for affirmative action, for women as well as racial minorities, can be found in Barbara Bergmann, *In Defense of Affirmative Action* (New York: Basic Books, 1996). As the title suggests, *Two Nations: Black and White, Separate, Hostile, Unequal* (New York: Ballantine Books, 1993), by political scientist Andrew Hacker, offers a grim account, laden with numerous statistics, of American racial divisions.

Center for Equal Opportunity
www.ceousa.org
A conservative organization for the promotion of "colorblind" public policies, the Center for Equal Opportunity concentrates on the issues of racial

preferences, immigration, and multicultural education; its site provides commentary and extensive access to articles and links on these issues.

National Association for the Advancement of Colored People
www.naacp.org
The nation's oldest civil rights organization's official site provides commentary on current civil rights controversies and offers research tools.

American Civil Liberties Union
www.aclu.org/issues/racial/hmre.html
This site of a section of the ACLU that focuses on race relations and civil rights provides current news and extensive research tools and links.

CHAPTER

Public Opinion: The American People and War

I n the aftermath of September 11, the Bush administration retaliated with invasions of Afghanistan and Iraq, and pledged the United States to engagement in a "war on terrorism" of uncertain duration and consequences, requiring the commitment of U.S. troops and money around the globe. New doctrines of "preemptive war" against "rogue" states prompted a transformation of U.S. policies, and not a little dissent among many of America's traditional allies. Federal budget priorities shifted from dividing up a surplus accumulated in the late 1990s to a new era of deficit spending, fueled by massive new war expenditures, billions for homeland security, and tax cuts designed to spur a sputtering economy. New federal laws, including the Patriot Act, preventive detention of undocumented workers, and increased security measures in public places, shifted the nation's focus from individual freedom to order.

How, if at all, has the new "war on terrorism," including the ongoing U.S. occupation of Iraq, changed the basic political opinions of the American people? Have long-standing views about America's role in the world changed? What about the war's potential ripple effects on Americans and their opinions about the political parties, the corporate and global economy, civil liberties, and alliances with other nations? Students of public opinion have observed that fundamental public attitudes about the roles of government, partisanship, and social policies usually change fairly slowly. At the same time, the present war on terrorism and its attendant cultural climate may just shock the public into altering these fundamental perceptions. President Bush has claimed that the war on terrorism is a different kind of war from those America has fought before, not the least because it is fought on many fronts, against a shadowy, dangerous, and elusive enemy, and with no perceivable end to it.

164

For elite and popular democrats alike, this new war presents a dilemma. In the immediate aftermath of the September 11 attacks, stirring and novel examples of national community, unity, and resolve were commonplace. In New York City, the heroism of residents, firefighters, and police officers inspired the nation. Charitable organizations were flooded with donations and volunteers, as many Americans engaged in new civic commitments. Government, scorned as inefficient, bloated, and wasteful by many throughout the 1980s and 1990s, seemed to gain new respect. In mounting the case for a strike against Iraq in early 2003, the Bush administration attempted to tap into this solidarity, and with some success: public support for the war to remove Saddam Hussein was high, especially after the invasion was launched in March.

For many others, however, there was a manipulative and even antidemocratic cynicism to these evocations of a new American patriotism, placed in stark evidence by the preparations and execution of the U.S. invasion and occupation of Iraq. For those who care about civil liberties, measures like the Patriot Act, the detention of "enemy combatants" without rights to attorneys or trials, and the detention of immigrants initiated by the Bush administration and passed by Congress threatened the very basic civil liberties of freedom of speech and equality before the law, heralded as cornerstones of U.S. and western democracies. The mass media generally provided unquestioning support of the Bush administration's case for war against Iraq, even as later revelations demonstrated that the case for war was based on faulty intelligence and assumptions. The massive antiwar protests, the largest in U.S. history, were virtually ignored by the media and dismissed by President Bush as a mere "focus group." Worse, many observers were concerned that the general climate of fear and emphasis on war were shields for a whole host of new Bush policies on the environment, taxes, regulation, and spending that furthered procorporate interests and hurt American wage-earners.

The two essays reprinted here present startlingly contrasting pictures of the American people and their opinions since the "war on terrorism" and in Iraq began. Greg Shafer, a Mott College English professor, sees wartime as a test of the strength of U.S. democratic values and the toleration and encouragement of lively debate. Before the Iraq war, Shafer observes a nation engaged in healthy debate about the implications and morality of war. In the aftermath of the invasion of Iraq, Shafer finds the emergence of a government- and media-sponsored censorship that both openly and subtly stifles dissent, discussion, and protest, distorting and manipulating public opinion through fear and a false brand of patriotism. How, Shafer asks, can a democracy flourish if the people aren't given the facts, and dissent is rendered unpatriotic by both the media and government? Shafer observes that there is plenty of democratic energy in the American citizenry, but that it continually is obstructed by a government- and corporate-sponsored censorship inimical to core democratic values.

David Brooks, a former senior editor of the conservative *Weekly Standard* and now a new *New York Times* columnist, argues that the war has generated a new popular consensus supporting the aggressive use of American state power at home and abroad. The serious threat posed to world order by Islamic terrorists, Brooks contends, has transformed the soft, antiwar reflexes that have heretofore pervaded U.S. society in the aftermath of the very different war in Vietnam. A new tough-mindedness predominates in U.S. public opinion, he argues. The average American, born after the Vietnam war, is repelled by Arabists, European "elitists," and "Bush haters." In a nation under threat, Brooks argues that ordinary Americans reject the "dream palace" of a rational world that can be ruled without conflict or force.

While reading these two provocative essays, you might ask the following: How might Shafer respond to Brooks's argument that average Americans support the war not because opinions are censored, but because they are "realists"? For Brooks, young people are more likely to be sympathetic to the new "war on terror." Is this assertion justified? In both essays, democratic public opinion is said to be an essential political value. How might Shafer and Brooks define the idea differently in their essays?

Lessons from the U.S. War on Iraq

GREG SHAFER

U npopular during even the happiest of stock-market booms, in time of war dissent attracts the attention of the police. The parade marshals regard any wandering away from the line of march as unpatriotic and disloyal.

Something unsettling happened as bombs began to rain down on Baghdad during the U.S. war on Iraq. Where before there had been healthy and quintessentially democratic debate on the morality of bombing a nation because it might harbor terrorists and have weapons of mass destruction, suddenly there was an uneasy silence as many Americans were told to behave and support President George W. Bush. For a nation that boasted the right to liberate Iraq and bring American values to the repressive nation, this bit of polite censorship was ironic and contradictory. Patriotic Americans have failed to defend celebrities' right to speak out against the war, and a New York lawyer was even harassed, asked to leave a mall, and then arrested for donning an antiwar T-shirt. All across the nation, people warily removed antiwar stickers from their cars in fear of vandalism. Therefore, without ever being officially censored, Americans began to feel pressure to support U.S. troops and cease their skepticism about the war. Radio disk jockeys announced with incredible constancy that it was time to stand behind U.S. fighting soldiers and be "good Americans." For many, it was no longer patriotic to question the bombing and bloodshed of an international conflict. Fealty had replaced undiluted American expression as the nation began to censor its people.

Through it all, as "smart" bombs continued to explode in the streets around innocent Iraqi citizens, revelations began to stir unrest and suspicion among Americans. Was this really a war to end terrorism or was it about imperialism and transnational profits? While the president ignored the intrepid few who continued to march in protest, a collection of alternative news magazines uncovered disconcerting contradictions about this so-called war for democracy. Many wondered why Iraq was suddenly so dangerous and such an imminent threat to the United States when there was virtually no talk of "liberating" it during the 2000 presidential election. Was Iraq not the same nation that was bombed into submission just ten years earlier, and was this not the nation that had been dealing with sanctions and constant inspections by a United Nations team? Was this a war to end terror or was it more about the fount of oil that flowed under the Iraqi sand? Finally, was it about a president and vice-president who wanted peace or a piece of the action?

Fundamental to a successful democracy is the ability of its people to be given honest and accurate information about their government and the actions that government takes on their behalf. Americans can't participate in a system that only feeds them a steady diet of propaganda and mendacity, leading them to believe what isn't true or is only part of a larger story. At the same time, to be truly free, Americans must be able to reject the policies of their president and practice civil disobedience when they see nefarious policies coming to fruition and hurting others. This was the centerpiece of Henry David Thoreau's night in a Concord, Connecticut, jail and his essay *Civil Disobedience*. This, we must remember, is the essence of a real, robust republic—one that is governed for and by the people. And yet, as the first week of the war passed in a blaze of explosions and death—with twelve British and American soldiers dying in a helicopter crash—Americans felt increasingly pressured to decide between supporting the war and being depicted as un-American.

Democracy, we must always remember, is never a stable and fixed entity. As with any dynamic, it is the product of tenacious struggle and unremitting pursuit. Blacks weren't granted their right to emancipation but had to win it through the crucible of a Civil War and another century of civil disobedience in the streets of the South and urban North. The right to vote was denied to women until their voices were heard in fractious speeches and aggressive political campaigns. Heroines of the era weren't respected in their own time because the prevailing wisdom suggested that it wasn't feminine or moral for women to march for suffrage or demand the right to decent contraception. Even today, few Americans know about the intrepid heroism of Frederick Douglass, Margaret Sanger, or Elizabeth Cady Stanton. Progress, it seems, is almost never embraced during the time that it is proposed—few wanted a Civil War to emancipate blacks and even fewer saw any real utility in extending the right to vote to women. Entrenched power likes the status quo or, as Howard Zinn writes in *Declarations of Independence*, "What normally operates day by day is the quiet dominance of certain ideas, ideas we are expected to hold by neighbors, our employers, and our political leaders; the ones we learn are the most acceptable. The result is an obedient, acquiescent, passive citizenry—a situation that is deadly to democracy."

Such has been the case with the U.S. war on Iraq. As soon as Bush chose to ignore the UN's recommendations—and the voices of millions of protesting Americans as well as others throughout the world—to allow nuclear weapons inspections, there was a dramatic change in the political terrain of the U.S. landscape. Instead of Americans being free to voice their dissent about a questionable war, many found that they were virtually forced to accept the conflict or be branded anti-military. Much like abolitionists over a century before, advocates for peace were increasingly given the moniker of apostates, of radicals who didn't love their country, of people who didn't appreciate the sacrifice of their soldiers. Morning talk radio—always a reflection of what is most sordid and lurid in the American psyche—trumpeted the might of the U.S. military and excoriated the "traitors" and "cowards" who would rather protest war than stand behind U.S. troops. Pathetic jingles were created to lampoon Saddam Hussein and his imminent demise, while disk jockeys with limited vision and respect vilified those who refused to support the "American cause." Gradually, the American right to dissent and disagree was evaporating like morning dew as stridency supplanted debate and war became the mantra for those in power.

Consider the example of Stephen Downs, who was arrested for wearing a T-shirt that had on the front the innocuous mantra of "give peace a chance" and on the back "peace on earth." When asked why Downs was arrested, Tim Kelley, the executive of the company that manages the Crossgates mall [near Albany, N.Y.], suggested that Downs was being "disruptive." When pushed to define what he did to be depicted as "disruptive," Kelly admitted that the expulsion from the mall had been prompted by the T-shirt. . . . [The *Miami Herald*'s Leonard] Pitts says in his analysis of the situation, "There's something chilling in the very act of Downs' arrest. Especially in light of local media reports that this isn't the first time Crossgates has ejected shoppers wearing antiwar T-shirts."

What is perhaps most chilling about the arrest—and the swirl of raging patriotism—is the fact that many Americans seem to have forgotten what is unique about their freedoms. When Americans burn a flag, march in protest, or wear T-shirts that declare their contempt for a leader, they are engaging in acts that define them as a people that revere free expression, especially since these acts are often punished harshly in other countries. The United States becomes yet another repressive regime when it penalizes the voices of the minority and tries to squelch those who expose its peccadilloes. The United States becomes little better than the countries it seeks to "liberate" when it stifles dissent and stymies protest.

Some Americans have confused the United States with an abstract idea of set, venerated, and dynamic principles—ones that make American's collective culture unique. Burning a flag isn't an action that should be outlawed but one that should be protected and inspired since it symbolizes expression and active engagement in the search for justice. Without dispute and rebellion, human beings become obedient machines, saluting a flag that ceases to epitomize the right to be free. Indeed, if Americans can't safely express their opinions, to what, exactly, are they pledging allegiance?

Isn't the essence of American freedom rooted in the right to express disapproval and to articulate the basis for that dispute? I was educated to believe that Americans are a restless, demanding people—ones who don't brook injustice and who are quick to have their voice heard. Americans don't have their tongues chopped off for speaking their minds and deriding their president, as in other nations. However, what does it say about Americans if their opinions are punished with the destruction of compact disks that represent a musician's livelihood? For some, it seems that iconoclasm isn't American if it conflicts with the U.S. government's point of view. . . .[1]

Of course, the United States has always fancied itself to be a bastion of free speech and unbridled expression. History, however, recalls a more sordid and checkered story. During World War I, hundreds of people were arrested for simply criticizing the war effort while, during the Cold War, celebrities had their livelihood wrested away from them by being labeled communists. The blacklists, which made Joseph McCarthy infamous, were a lamentable symbol of what can happen when antiwar emotions collide with ensconced power.

Sometimes it doesn't matter if one is antiwar. Sometimes simply telling the truth can result in a collision with so-called patriots. Perhaps this is why the case of Peter Arnett is so important. During the 1991 Gulf War, the CNN reporter and Pulitzer Prize winner was labeled a traitor by many Americans, including Senator Alan Simpson (Republican, Wyoming), for simply reporting the bombing of an Iraqi milk factory by U.S. aircraft. The accusations were curious since Arnett, by all accounts, had reported the bombing faithfully and with the professionalism that earned him a Pulitzer Prize for his efforts in Vietnam. Indeed, a building that clearly appeared to be producing milk had been destroyed. However, as the condemnations began to grow, it seemed clear that Simpson and other Americans weren't angry because Arnett was a traitor but simply because he had revealed an unpleasant truth about U.S. practices. In the days after Arnett's report, letters demanded his dismissal while others accused CNN owner Ted Turner of being sympathetic to the enemy. Suddenly Turner was being branded with the moniker of "Baghdad Ted" because he allowed Arnett to chronicle the ugly side of U.S. war tactics. Telling the truth in time of war was seemingly no longer allowed. It was yet another example of the United States displaying its fear of freedom and its

---

1. Shafer is writing about the burning of CDs produced by the "Dixie Chicks," who had come out against the Iraq war.

unwillingness to reveal the shadowy side of its policy. Indeed, while Arnett and others were being vilified, one wonders why other journalists had refused to uncover the carnage, why they refused to tell the whole story. . . .

This timidity is a blemish on U.S. democracy and a reflection of how impotent Americans' freedoms really are when they are tested in times of crisis. Much like the U.S. war on Iraq, when citizens were pressured to support their troops and president, Arnett and others were being castigated for failing to follow a narrow patriotic line. In many ways, they are a reminder of the proclivity in the United States to react in despotic ways when people question national policy. Americans are often not as free as they think they are—or as they should be.

Of course, the blacklists were a generation ago, but today the United States has the Patriot Act, which seems to have the same chilling and paralyzing effect. Passed in the frenetic days after the September 11, 2001, terrorist attacks, the law makes it easier to stifle dissent, creating a nation that is more tentative, more reticent, and less outspoken. While it began as a response to terrorism, the Patriot Act permits the U.S. government to collect information about people who use the Internet, whether they are doing so for a library research paper or simply to engage in personal enlightenment. For example, the act makes it easier for government officials to collect information about Web browsing and e-mail accounts without meaningful judicial review. Government officials can simply suggest that they are investigating possible terrorism and begin to use the Patriot Act as a ruse for government intimidation. The American Civil Liberties Union decried Attorney General John Ashcroft, the Patriot Act, and its potential for limiting rights and said, "He's supposed to defend the Constitution, not rewrite it."

Lamentably, the string of special rights granted to the Federal Bureau of Investigation isn't limited to people's computers. . . . In the April 2003 issue of *Harpers* magazine, Lewis Lapham says, "The USA Patriot Act has been reinforced so many times since it was first passed by Congress in October 2001 that by now the country's law agencies have been equipped with as many powers as they choose to exercise—random search, unwarranted seizure, arbitrary arrest."

In exploring the specifics of the Patriot Act, one can quickly appreciate . . . Lapham's concerns and the relevance they have to the United States' diminution of democracy. Where before there were constitutional protections in what one researched, wrote, and observed on the Internet, there is now an easy means for the government to intimidate those who might undermine its policies. If a teacher wants to explore the ways to protest an unjust war—as Thoreau did over a century ago—they could have their homes searched without prior notice. It becomes an easy way to thwart free expression, to scuttle the voices of those who are unhappy with the government. In the end, it is yet another example of liberties becoming attenuated in what is supposed to be a free society. . . .

Of course, there will always be those who wonder why anyone should worry—why essays should be written about the U.S. government's long and sinewy arms of investigation. The U.S. government tells Americans that they should trust in their president and have faith that he will do what is best. Such incredible romanticism has been repeated several times as news programs blithesomely carry out report after report on the heroism of American troops and the inherent goodness of removing Saddam Hussein and his supposed weapons of mass destruction. In times of war, the mainstream media becomes an organ, a willing toady of the government, reverting to the role of glorified cheer-leaders for the home team rather than engaging in a skeptical investigation of what is right. Zinn writes:

> There are two false assumptions about experts. One is that they see more clearly and think more intelligently than ordinary citizens. Sometimes they do, sometimes not. The other assumption is that these experts have the same interests as ordinary citizens, want the same things, hold the same values, and, therefore, can be trusted to make decisions for all of us.

Zinn's declaration is especially pungent when compared to news anchors like CBS's Dan Rather, who told a caller on "Larry King Live" that he trusts his president and believes in his wisdom and choices. Where is the scrutiny of the media when they are compliantly trusting in a president—a former oil executive—who is invading a nation with more oil reserves than in all of North America?

During the U.S. war with Iraq, nightly programs—and mainstream newspapers—became little more than chroniclers for the daily travails of the marching soldiers. Gone from the discourse was the watching, observing eye of the critical press. Gone from the discussion were questions of why the United States is invading another country and killing people to liberate them. What if Bush was lying in his reasons for launching a war in Iraq? What if his motivations aren't to bring democracy to the Iraqi people but, rather, to obtain access to their oil?

On May 1, 2003, Bush stood on the *USS Abraham Lincoln* aircraft carrier and declared, "Major combat operations in Iraq have ended. In the battle of Iraq, the United States and our allies have prevailed. I am honored to be your commander in chief." Between the backslapping and handshakes, there was never a mention of the 138 U.S. casualties, the 32 British deaths, or the estimated 2,300 Iraqi[2] fatalities. All of this is expected in a war that seeks to protect persecuted people and subjugated populations. However, what if this war was about political gain? What if this was simply an attempt to divert attention from a failed domestic policy, and what if the deaths of these brave soldiers were driven by a lust for Iraqi oil? would Americans be as willing to send their children to die if they knew the whole story about the U.S. invasion into Iraq? More importantly, can Americans

---

2. By Election Day 2004, American combat deaths had reached 1,100 and Iraqi fatalities an estimated 20,000.

call the United States democratic if its media stops asking these questions and treats the war as a moral inevitability?

News headlines on April 3, 2003, discussed an interesting fact: Bush's approval rating had jumped to over 70 percent. War, it seems, is often good for presidents. It unites a nation and asks citizens to choose between their leader and the dark nemesis thousands of miles away. The question Americans must ask, however, is whether it is ethical for a president to use war— and the deaths of innocent and brave people—to plunder another country's oil or to bolster their own political popularity. Moreover, without a curious and investigative media, how can U.S. democracy ever expose this unpleasant possibility?

According to Eric Alterman, [writing in] the *Nation,* Bush has consistently lied about his motivation for attacking Iraq. Alterman suggests that Bush lied as a pretense for committing troops to a war, using mendacity in exaggerating the military might of Hussein and his ability to launch missiles. Alterman says, "Most particularly, [Bush] has lied consistently about Iraq's nuclear capabilities as well as its missile-delivery capabilities." Alterman says the result is that the United States will again dive into a war that will cost it lives and respect. Much like previous incursions in Vietnam, it subverts U.S. democracy when the media supplants information and skepticism with propaganda and prevarication. He is provocative in his conclusion:

> Reporters and editors who protect their readers and viewers from the truth about Bush's lies are doing the nation—and ultimately George W. Bush—no favors. Take a look at the names at that long black wall on the mall. Consider the tragic legacy of LBJ's failed presidency. Ask yourself just who is being served when the media allow Bush to lie, repeatedly, with impunity, in order to take the nation into war.

The foundation of a democracy is in many ways rooted in the kind of information that Alterman discusses. Americans can't make educated decisions about their lives if the nightly news does nothing more than describe military victories and provide a running death count. The nation can't feel truly empowered if news anchors like Peter Jennings and Dan Rather subscribe to the notion that it would make people too uncomfortable to hear the darker, more shadowy side of U.S. foreign policy.

The failures of the media in investigating the untold story of the Iraqi war—and the U.S. involvement in the Middle East—could also include questions of whether or not Bush and Vice-President Dick Cheney actually wanted to invade Afghanistan and Iraq long before terrorist attacks killed U.S. civilians. According to Gore Vidal in his book *Dreaming War,* the oil company Unocal proposed to construct in 1997 a pipeline across much of Afghanistan in an attempt to develop the rich resources of the Caspian Sea. The plan was to ignore Afghanisttan's atrocities and repression of human rights, its abject misogyny, and use Afghanistan for its oil. However, when Osama bin Laden became a bigger player in the Middle East, Vidal suggests that the United States turned its back on the Taliban and suddenly became interested in the Taliban's violations of human rights as a pretext to overthrow its government. Vidal says, "By 1999 it was clear that the Taliban could never provide the security we need to protect our fragile pipelines. The arrival of Osama as a warrior for Allah on the scene refocused, as it were, the bidding. New alliances were now being made."

Frederick Starr, chair at Johns Hopkins University at Baltimore, Maryland, said in a 2000 *Washington Post* article, "The United States has quietly begun to align itself with those in the Russian government calling for military action against Afghanistan and has toyed with the idea of a new raid to wipe out Osama bin Laden." Therefore, Vidal suggests, the attack on Afghanistan wasn't about ending terrorism but about solidifying the area for oil. He adds that much the same is happening in Iraq where there is more oil than in any country except Saudi Arabia. The conquest of the oil-rich Middle East, he intimates, isn't about peace and democracy but about oil, power, and influence.

Michael Niman's article in the March/April 2003 issue of the *Humanist* shows how the American media has also kept the public in the dark about the role the U.S. government played in originally arming Iraq with weapons of mass destruction. According to Niman:

> When Iraq presented its weapons declaration to the United Nations in December 2002, the Bush administration immediately attacked the report as incomplete. . . . But that's because the United States removed over 8,000 pages of information from the 11,800-page document before passing it on. The missing pages implicated . . . the successive Ronald Reagan and George [H. W.] Bush administrations in connection with the illegal supplying of Saddam Hussein's Iraqi goverment with myriad weapons of mass destruction and training to use them.

Niman suggests that U.S. companies supplied much of the chemical and biological weaponry obtained by Hussein. This occurred with the assistance and knowledge of people like Cheney, whose company (Halliburton) received the contract to rebuild Hussein's oil fields after the Gulf War, and Secretary of Defense Donald Rumsfeld, who could be seen as culpable in the use of the chemical weapons used in the slaughter of Iraqi Kurds. Indeed, it was Rumsfeld, acting as an envoy for then-President Ronald Reagan in 1983, who went to Baghdad and discussed Iraq's war against Iran. Niman says, "In 1984 Iraq used chemical weapons against Iran. In 1988 it used them against one of its own oppressed ethnic minorities, the Iraqi Kurds." During the entire series of murderous episodes, the United States stood mute. When the UN Security Council condemned Iraq's use of chemical weapons, the Untied States stood alone as the only nation not censoring Iraq.

So why didn't the mainstream press report or even discuss this, and what does this curious neglect suggest about U.S. democracy? Niman writes, "Clearly, there is a desire—whether for love of country or love of money—to keep certain history a secret." Therefore, how can a democracy flourish if the people aren't told about the underhanded deals and duplicitous motives of their government—a goverment that will send its children to war?

Only time will reveal the mendacity of the U.S. government and the neglect of the media. However, as the soldiers fight and die, and the journalists eschew the more thorny issues of U.S. government deceit, too many Americans remain patriotically stupid, waving flags and marching for a war they fail to understand. Is there an axis of evil? And if there is, do the American people—the citizens of a great democracy—appreciate their government's complicity in making it a reality?[3]

The Collapse of the Dream Palaces

DAVID BROOKS

George Orwell was a genuinely modest man. But he knew he had a talent for facing unpleasant facts. That doesn't seem at first glance like much of a gift. But when one looks around the world, one quickly sees how rare it is. Most people nurture the facts that confirm their worldview and ignore or marginalize the ones that don't, unable to achieve enough emotional detachment from their own political passions to see the world as it really is.

Now that the war in Iraq is over, we'll find out how many people around the world are capable of facing unpleasant facts. For the events of recent months confirm that millions of human beings are living in dream palaces, to use [commentator] Fouad Ajami's phrase. They are living with versions of reality that simply do not comport with the way things are. They circulate and recirculate conspiracy theories, myths, and allegations with little regard for whether or not these fantasies are true. And the events of the past month have exposed them as the falsehoods they are.

There is first the dream palace of the Arabists. In this dream palace, it is always the twelfth century, and every Western incursion into the Middle East is a Crusade. The Americans are always invaders and occupiers. In this dream palace, any Arab who hates America is a defender of Arab honor, so Osama bin Laden becomes an Arab Joe Louis, and Saddam Hussein, who probably killed more Muslims than any other person in the history of the world, becomes the champion of the Muslim cause.

In this dream palace, the problems of the Arab world are never the Arabs' fault. It is always the Jews, the Zionists, the Americans, and the imperialists who are to blame. This palace reeks of conspiracies—of Israelis who

_____

3. By late 2004, numerous investigations concluded that Iraq held no weapons of mass destruction at the time of the invasion.

blew up the World Trade Center, of Jews who put the blood of Muslim children in their pastries, of Americans who fake images of Iraqis celebrating in Baghdad in order to fool the world. . . .

In this palace, old men really do shoot down Apache helicopters with AK-47s. Saddam's torture chambers are invisible, the hundreds of thousands of Iraqis he murdered go unmentioned, [Saddam's] fedayeen who shot their own refugees are ignored, but every civilian casualty caused by an American bomb is displayed in all its bloody agony. In this dream palace, rage is always the proper emotion, victimhood the pleasure most indulged. Other people—Iraqis, Palestinians, suicide bombers—are always called upon to fight the infidels to the death so that the satellite TV–watching Arabists, safe in their living rooms, can have something to cheer about.

Then there is the dream palace of the Europeans. In this palace, America is a bigger threat to world peace than Saddam Hussein. America is the land of rotting cities, the electric chair, serial killers, gun-crazed hunters, shallow materialists, religious nuts, savage capitalists, the all-powerful Jewish lobby, the oil lobby, the military-industrial complex, and bloodthirsty cowboy-presidents.

In this dream palace, the Hollywood clichés are taken to be real. George Bush really is Rambo, Clint Eastwood, and John Wayne rolled into one. American life really is *NYPD Blue* and *Baywatch.* In this dream palace, Oliver Stone is as trustworthy as the *Washington Post,* Michael Moore accurately depicts the American soul, *Dr. Strangelove* is a textbook of American government, and Noam Chomsky tells it like it is.

In the European dream palace, Americans are terminally naive, filled with crazy notions like the belief that Arabs are capable of democracy. In this vision of reality, Americans are at once childish, selfish, and trigger-happy, but Arabs live just this side of savagery. Any action that might rile them will cause the Arab street to explode, and will lead to a thousand more bin Ladens. In this dream palace, history is tragic, and teaches us it is always prudent to do nothing—to do nothing about Bosnia, to do nothing about Kosovo, to do nothing about Rwanda, to do nothing about the slow-motion holocaust unleashed in Iraq by Saddam.

Finally, there is the dream palace of the American Bush haters. In this dream palace, there is so much contempt for Bush that none is left over for Saddam or for tyranny. Whatever the question, the answer is that Bush and his cronies are evil. What to do about Iraq? Bush is evil. What to do about the economy? Bush is venal. What to do about North Korea? Bush is a hypocrite.

In this dream palace, Bush, Cheney, and a junta of corporate oligarchs stole the presidential election, then declared war on Iraq to seize its oil and hand out the spoils to Halliburton and Bechtel. In this dream palace, the warmongering Likudniks [supporters of Israeli Prime Minister Ariel Sharon] in the administration sit around dreaming of conquests in Syria, Iran, and beyond. In this dream palace, the boy genius Karl Rove[1] hatches schemes to use the Confederate flag issue to win more elections, John Ashcroft wages

1. Karl Rove is George W. Bush's chief political consultant.

holy war on American liberties, Donald Rumsfeld, Paul Wolfowitz, and his cabal of neoconservatives long for global empire. In this dream palace, every story of Republican villainy is believed, and all the windows are shuttered with hate.

These dream palaces have taken a beating over the past month.[2] As the scientists would say, they are conceptual models that failed to predict events. But as we try to understand the political and cultural importance of the war in Iraq, the question is this: Will they crumble under the weight of undeniable facts? Will the illusions fall, and the political landscape change?

My first guess is that the dream palace of the Arabists will temporarily sag. As happened after the Six Day War back in 1967, the newspapers and TV networks that depicted glorious Arab victories and failed to prepare their audiences for the crushing defeat that came will see their credibility suffer. The radicals who preach eternal war with the infidel will seem stale, architects of a failed vision. As happened after Desert Storm [the 1991 Persian Gulf War] the Arabs who preach reform and modernization will begin to seem more attractive. There will be some restlessness, some searching for a fresh start and a different way, and thus a window of opportunity will open for democratization and peace, but that opening will have a termination date. The window will close if, a year or two hence, millions of Arabs continue to feel humiliated by their region's backwardness. They will go looking again for conspiracy theories, victimhood, and rage.

My second guess is that Europeans will not shake off their clichéd image of America. The stereotypes are entrenched too deeply. But official Europe will go through one of its periodic phases of gloomy and self-lacerating introspection. There will be laments about European impotence, continental divisions, the need to build a common European alternative. But this self-criticism will not spark any fundamental change, just summits, conferences, and books.

My third guess is that the Bush haters will grow more vociferous as their numbers shrink. Even progress in Iraq will not dampen their anger, because as many people have noted, hatred of Bush and his corporate cronies is all that is left of their leftism. And this hatred is tribal, not ideological. And so they will still have their rallies, their alternative weeklies, and their Gore Vidal[3] polemics. They will still have a huge influence over the Democratic Party, perhaps even determining its next presidential nominee. But they will seem increasingly unattractive to most moderate and even many normally Democratic voters who never really adopted outrage as their dominant public emotion.

In other words, there will be no magic "Aha!" moment that brings the dream palaces down. Even if Saddam's remains are found, even if weapons of mass destruction are displayed, even if Iraq starts to move along a winding, muddled path toward normalcy, no day will come when the enemies of this endeavor turn around and say, "We were wrong. Bush was right." They will just extend their forebodings into a more distant future. Nevertheless,

---

2. Brooks wrote this essay one month after the U.S. invasion of Iraq.
3. Gore Vidal, a prominent writer, is a noted opponent of the war.

the frame of the debate will shift. The war's opponents will lose self-confidence and vitality. And they will backtrack. They will claim that they always accepted certain realities, which, in fact, they rejected only months ago.

But there is another, larger group of people whose worldviews will be permanently altered by the war in Iraq. Members of this group were not firm opponents of the war. Indeed, they were mild supporters, or they were ambivalent. They were members of the vast, nervous American majority that swung behind the president as the fighting commenced.

These people do not have foreign policy categories deeply entrenched in their brains. They don't see themselves as hawks or doves, realists or Wilsonians. They don't see each looming conflict either through the prism of Vietnam, as many peaceniks do, or through the prism of the 1930s and the Cold War, as many conservatives do. They don't attract any press coverage or much attention, because they seldom take a bold stand either way. Their foreign policy instincts are unformed. But they are the quiet people who swing elections.

What lessons will they draw from the events of the past month? How will the fall of Saddam affect their voting patterns, their approach to the next global crisis? One way to think about this is to conduct a thought experiment. Invent a representative 20-year-old, Joey Tabula-Rasa,[4] and try to imagine how he would have perceived the events of the past month.

Joey doesn't know much about history; he was born in 1983 and was only 6 when the Berlin Wall fell.

He really has no firm idea of what labels like liberal and conservative mean. But now he is in college, and he's been glued to the cable coverage of the war and is ready to form some opinions. Over the past months, certain facts and characters have entered his consciousness, like characters in a play he is seeing for the first time.

The first character is America itself. He sees that his country is an incredibly effective colossus that can drop bombs onto pinpoints, destroy enemies that aren't even aware they are under attack. He sees a ruling establishment that can conduct wars with incredible competence and skill. He sees a federal government that can perform its primary task—protecting the American people—magnificently.

These are obviously not the things Joey would have seen if he had come of age in 1972, and his mentality is likely to be radically different from that of many people of the sixties generation. He is likely to feel confident about American power. He is likely to assume that when America projects its might, it is not only great, but good. Its pilots fly low, at some risk to themselves, to reduce civilian casualties. Teams of lawyers vet bombing targets to minimize unnecessary damage. Efforts are made to spare enemy soldiers who don't want to fight. The military, moreover, is fundamentally open to the press, allowing embedded reporters to wander amidst the troops. The ruling

---

4. Tabula rasa is Latin for "blank slate."

class is reasonably candid about the war's progress. The anonymous people in the corridors of power basically seem to know what they are doing.

The American system of government, moreover, is clearly the best system. In Joey's eyes, the United Nations is a fractious debating society. The European Union is split. The French are insufferable, the Germans both hostile and pacifist. The Arab ruling class is treacherous. Billions of people around the world seem to hate us, and while Joey is aware that there are some reasons to be suspicious of the United States, he resents the way so many people are over the top in their resentment, fury, and dislike. In short, Joey does not look around and assume that the world is moving toward some world government or global unity. When the chips are down, there are very few nations you can trust. Joey is both more trusting of America, and more suspicious of the world, than he would have been if he had formed his worldview in the 1990s.

The second great character on Joey's mind is the American soldier. When Joey thinks of youthful idealism, he doesn't think of college students protesting in the streets, he thinks of young soldiers risking their lives to liberate a people. These are the men and women Joey saw interviewed by the dozen on TV. They seemed to enjoy being in the military. They seemed to believe in their mission. They seemed to be involved in something large and noble even at a young age.

In Joey's eyes, the people who get to do the most exciting things are not members of the meritocratic elite—Harvard and Stanford alums who start software companies. They are the regular men and women of the armed forces, or, as he remembers from the days after 9/11, they are firemen and cops. They are people without prestigious degrees and high income prospects.

Joey naturally feels that while those soldiers are liberating a country and talking about duty and honor, all he is doing is preparing for business school. That doesn't mean he necessarily wants to enlist, but he is aware that there is something lacking in his pampered private life. He also sees, in the example the soldiers set, that discipline, neatness, professionalism, and openly expressed patriotism are kind of cool.

The third character Joey sees is the terrorist. He sees the people who blew up the World Trade Center. In Iraq, people like that piled into pickups and suicidally attacked tanks. They wore those black fedayeen gowns. In Israel, they strap bombs to their waists and blow up buses. Joey is aware that there are a lot of people, especially in the Arab world, who are just batshit crazy. There is no reasoning with these people. They understand only force, and they must be crushed.

Joey sees that some regimes around the world are sadistic and evil. They torture and mutilate their own people. They ignore the basic rules of warfare and civilization. Conflict with these people is inevitable. They lurk in the dark corners of the globe, and for some reason they think they should take out their problems on us. You always have to be on guard, because there really is evil about.

When Joey looks at the talking heads on TV, he begins to form judgments about this country's political divides. First, he sees the broad majority of people who support the war, who, it seems to him, deserve to be called the progressives. These people talk optimistically of spreading democracy and creating a new Middle East. They have a very confident approach to what America can achieve in the world. People in this political movement include Christopher Hitchens, Dennis Miller, Paul Wolfowitz, Joseph Lieberman, John McCain, Richard Holbrooke, Charles Krauthammer, the staff of Fox News, Bernard Lewis, and George W. Bush.

These people tend to endorse progressive interventionism, not only in Iraq, but in places like Kosovo. They use the explicitly moral language of good and evil. Joey is a little nervous that they are not realistic about what can actually be achieved in this messy world. He's afraid they might bite off more than they can chew. But he gives them credit for their idealism, their hope, their grand vision.

The second group Joey sees he calls the conservatives. These people are far more skeptical of the war and grand endeavors of that sort. They emphasize all the things that could go wrong. They seem more prudent and less idealistic or visionary. They were not necessarily implacably opposed to the effort in Iraq, but they thought it imprudent. . . .

When Joey listens to these conservatives, he thinks they raise some valid concerns. They serve as a useful brake on the progressives, but they are not exactly inspiring or hopeful, and their prognostications on Iraq proved more wrong than right.

The final group Joey sees on the political landscape are the marchers. These people are always in the streets with their banners and puppets. They march against the IMF and World Bank one day, and against whatever war happens to be going on the next. Joey is not sure what these people are for. They don't seem to have any alternative to globalization. They don't seem to know how to deal with the Taliban or Saddam. They just march against. Joey figures it must be part of their personality.

Joey knows that this is what people did in the 1960s, and he regards the marchers as vaguely archaic. He knows that they tend to come from Hollywood and academia. Joey is not hostile to those worlds. He loves movies and likes many of his professors. He just senses that they are cloistered worlds, removed from day-to-day reality, and he doesn't plan on spending his life there. Marching for peace is something people in those worlds do, just as Mormons devote a few years of their lives to missionary work, or Jews keep kosher. It does not occur to Joey to enter the subculture of the protesters, and what they say is not likely to affect him one way or another.

Joey likes to think of himself as fundamentally independent. He looks at the people living in their dream palaces—the Arabists, the European elites, the Bush haters—and he knows he doesn't want to be like them. He doesn't want to be so zealous and detached from reality. He's not even into joining political movements at home. But he is less independent than he thinks. He has started to acquire certain assumptions over the past months, which will shape his thinking in years to come. As a rule, these assumptions are the exact opposite of the assumptions he would have formed if he had been watching the Vietnam war unfold. His politics will be radically different from those of the Vietnam generation.

Moreover, new categories are crystallizing in his mind. These categories—who is progressive, who is conservative, who is reactionary—do not comport with the categories in the minds of people who came of age during the civil rights era, or even the Cold War.

Joey isn't one of a kind. There are millions of Joeys, and variations on Joey. Inevitably, then, in ways subtle and profound, the events of the past month will shape our politics for the rest of our lives.

DISCUSSION QUESTIONS

1. Brooks creates a fictional ordinary person, Joey Tabula-Rasa, to stand in for the views of young people who didn't experience the Cold War. How convincing is Brooks's portrayal of Joey, given the young people you know who are enrolled in college?

2. Since these essayists wrote these articles, U.S. public opinion has become evenly divided about the Iraq war and whether it should have been started at all. How would Brooks explain this development? How would Shafer? What's changed in American life to account for the shift?

3. For Brooks and Shafer, where do the antidemocratic impulses in U.S. culture and politics come from? Is there a way to reconcile their apparently contrasting views about the foundations of truly democratic public opinion?

4. Shafer argues that the news media was largely supportive of the war, while Brooks has doubts on that score. How would we know who might have the better case?

SUGGESTED READINGS AND INTERNET RESOURCES

The two selections by Brooks and Shafer are based on what has changed about U.S. public opinion since September 11. One comprehensive book about this subject is Robert Erikson and Kent Tedin, *American Public Opinion* (Boston: Allyn and Bacon, 2001). For public opinion during wartime, see the brilliant anthology edited by W. Lance Bennett and David Paletz, *Taken by Storm: The Media, Public Opinion, and U.S. Foreign Policy in the Gulf War* (Chicago:

University of Chicago Press, 1994). Two contrasting works about Iraq war American politics are Joe Conason, *Big Lies: The Right Wing Propaganda Machine and How It Distorts the Truth* (New York: Thomas Dunne/St. Martin's, 2003), and William Bennett, *Why We Fight: Moral Clarity and the War on Terrorism* (New York: Regnery Publishing, 2003).

Pew Center for the People and the Press
www.people-press.org
Pew, an independent opinion research group that conducts surveys about the media, foreign policy, partisanship, and global issues, is known for its in-depth analyses of long-term trends in public opinion. See especially its "2004 Electoral Landscape" site, and its mammoth survey of global attitudes toward U.S. foreign policy.

Policy.com
www.policy.com
This is perhaps the most comprehensive site for all political news; click on "polling" in the subject column for links to all major international and national polling organizations.

Public Agenda
www.publicagenda.org
This is an outstanding source for all kinds of polling data, along with helpful assessments about how to read surveys and their results critically and comparatively.

9

The New Media and the Internet: Corporate Wasteland or Democratic Frontier?

I t is a cliché to say that we live in an age saturated with information. A billion websites are available to the digerati at the click of a mouse, and hundreds of cable television stations compete with satellite radio and the long-established television networks, newspapers, and magazines for mass attention.

Yet this information doesn't come to us unmediated: even on a website, someone is structuring a particular version of facts, is setting an agenda for discussion, is including some information while excluding a vast tidal wave of those facts that may confict with a particular viewpoint. Most of us are dependent on the mass media for knowledge of phenomena of which we have little direct experience. In a democratic society, we can only hope that all citizens are exposed to a variety of information and ideas. Yet we also hope that the media somehow mirrors ourselves as well as others, that it reflects and expresses a wide range of views, and that at some level at least parts of the media speak "truth to power." While any single media source can be deemed biased and incorrect, a diverse mass media is supposed to provide assurance that conflicting versions of political truth emerge and can be rationally debated.

Just how have the mass media performed these democratic tasks? According to a chorus of critics, not all that well. The media's most vocal critics lampoon the media for liberal or conservative biases. Others accuse the news media of crass commercialism and "cheerleading." During the early days of the

Iraq war, leading news commentators donned U.S.–flag lapel pins, frankly supported the invasion, and, perhaps more seriously, rarely challenged what turned out to be Bush administration false assertions about Iraq's weapons of mass destruction. The rationale was often caused by the ratings race; network news was more interested in pleasing the audience than in informing it. On the other hand, "new media" and "streaming" fueled the antiwar movement. Activists streamed the BBC and searched out dissident websites to supply information counter to that found in the U.S. networks. Is the media "glass" half empty or half full?

Contemporary U.S. and global media are dominated by two major trends, which seem to run at cross-purposes. First, and as noted above, there seem to be more media outlets to choose from than at any time in human history. However, concentrated corporate ownership of the mass media means that most people see programming, read books, and listen to music produced by just six or seven mega-corporations with a global reach. The paradox of diversity and increased corporate concentration in firms like the News Corporation, Disney, and Viacom raises fundamental questions about how noncommercial, non-self-interested voices can ever be heard.

Still, the case for a wide and increasingly democratic and participatory marketplace of ideas seems bolstered by the growth of digital communication and the World Wide Web. On the Internet, every person and group can set up as a media source, sending out opinion and fact seemingly at the speed of light. Low start-up costs allow millions of people to exchange ideas and information below the radar screen of corporate life and government—those using such sites as moveon.org and meetup.com can even arrange impromptu demonstrations if they so desire.

Does the era of digital communication really distinguish itself from corporate and government concentration of influence and ownership? In the two essays that follow, the authors agree about the Internet's democratic potential. Yet agreement leads to debate when it comes to the real consequences. In the first article, University of Chicago law professor Cass Sunstein heralds the World Wide Web but worries that individuals and groups will use it to insulate themselves from the larger realm of public political life and dialogue. Sunstein argues that individual consumer and citizen choices will mesh with emerging technologies to produce a "Daily Me"—choosing those Internet sites that tend to favor the extremes in cultural and political life by promoting a kind of "marination" in what one already believes. Without having to confront alternate views, democratic life stagnates.

Robert McChesney shares some of Sunstein's concerns about the isolating aspects of the Internet. Yet he argues that corporate control poses a much greater threat. McChesney asks whether corporate power and its relentless quest for higher profits create a nation of passive consumers. Commercial values and their prominence throughout the media may be extended to the Internet. People don't so much create a "Daily Me" they respond to Internet portals and links controlled by major corporations and advertisers. For all its supposed diversity, the Internet, according to McChesney, is going the way of traditional media.

Both writers point to public policies and new ideas that may help the Internet to become a more democratic medium. While reading these two essays, you might ask the following questions: How would each author define a democratic standard for mass media and for the Internet? How do the authors see the role of government, public policy, and civil society in creating a "democratic" Internet? In what ways is the Internet a corporate-controlled market; in what ways is it not?

The Daily We

CASS R. SUNSTEIN

Is the Internet a wonderful development for democracy? In many ways it certainly is. As a result of the Internet, people can learn far more than they could before, and they can learn it much faster. If you are interested in issues that bear on public policy—environmental quality, wages over time, motor vehicle safety—you can find what you need to know in a matter of seconds. If you are suspicious of the mass media, and want to discuss issues with like-minded people, you can do that, transcending the limitations of geography in ways that could barely be imagined even a decade ago. And if you want to get information to a wide range of people, you can do that via email and websites; this is another sense in which the Internet is a great boon for democracy.

But in the midst of the celebration, I want to raise a note of caution. I do so by emphasizing one of the most striking powers provided by emerging technologies: the growing power of consumers to "filter" what they see. As a result of the Internet and other technological developments, many people are increasingly engaged in a process of "personalization" that limits their exposure to topics and points of view of their own choosing. They filter in, and they also filter out, with unprecedented powers of precision. Consider just a few examples:

1. Broadcast.com has "compiled hundreds of thousands of programs so you can find the one that suits your fancy. . . . For example, if you

want to see all the latest fashions from France 24 hours of the day you can get them. If you're from Baltimore living in Dallas and you want to listen to WBAL, your hometown station, you can hear it."

2. Sonicnet.com allows you to create your own musical universe, consisting of what it calls "Me Music." Me Music is "A place where you can listen to the music you love on the radio station YOU create. . . . A place where you can watch videos of your favorite artists and new artists."

3. Zatso.net allows users to produce "a personal newscast." Its intention is to create a place "where you decide what's news." Your task is to tell "what TV news stories you're interested in," and Zatso.net turns that information into a specifically designed newscast. . . .

4. George Bell, the chief executive officer of the search engine Excite, exclaims, "We are looking for ways to be able to lift chunks of content off other areas of our service and paste them onto your personal page so you can constantly refresh and update that 'newspaper of me.'" . . .

Of course, these developments make life much more convenient and in some ways much better: we all seek to reduce our exposure to uninvited noise. But from the standpoint of democracy, filtering is a mixed blessing. An understanding of the mix will permit us to obtain a better sense of what makes for a well-functioning system of free expression. In a heterogeneous society, such a system requires something other than free, or publicly unrestricted, individual choices. On the contrary, it imposes two distinctive requirements. First, people should be exposed to materials that they would not have chosen in advance. *Unanticipated encounters,* involving topics and points of view that people have not sought out and perhaps find irritating, are central to democracy and even to freedom itself. Second, many or most citizens should have a range of *common experiences.* Without shared experiences, a heterogeneous society will have a more difficult time addressing social problems and understanding one another.

Individual Design

Consider a thought experiment—an apparently utopian dream, that of complete individuation, in which consumers can entirely personalize (or "customize") their communications universe.

Imagine, that is, a system of communications in which each person has unlimited power of individual design. If some people want to watch news all the time, they would be entirely free to do exactly that. If they dislike news, and want to watch football in the morning and situation comedies at night, that would be fine too. If people care only about America, and want to avoid international issues entirely, that would be very simple; so too if they care only about New York or Chicago or California. If people want to restrict themselves to certain points of view, by limiting themselves to conservatives, moderates, liberals, vegetarians, or Nazis, that would be entirely feasible with a simple point-and-click. If people want to isolate themselves, and speak only with like-minded others, that is feasible too.

At least as a matter of technological feasibility, our communications market is moving rapidly toward this apparently utopian picture. A number of newspapers' websites allow readers to create filtered versions, containing exactly what they want, and no more. . . . To be sure, the Internet greatly increases people's ability to expand their horizons, as millions of people are now doing; but many people are using it to produce narrowness, not breadth. Thus MIT professor Nicholas Negroponte refers to the emergence of the "Daily Me"—a communications package that is personally designed, with components fully chosen in advance.

Of course, this is not entirely different from what has come before. People who read newspapers do not read the same newspaper; some people do not read any newspaper at all. People make choices among magazines based on their tastes and their points of view. But in the emerging situation, there is a difference of degree if not of kind. What *is* different is a dramatic increase in individual control over content, and a corresponding decrease in the power of general interest intermediaries, including newspapers, magazines, and broadcasters. For all their problems, and their unmistakable limitations and biases, these intermediaries have performed some important democratic functions.

People who rely on such intermediaries have a range of chance encounters, involving shared experience with diverse others and exposure to material that they did not specifically choose. You might, for example, read the city newspaper and in the process come across a range of stories that you would not have selected if you had the power to control what you see. Your eyes may come across a story about Germany, or crime in Los Angeles, or innovative business practices in Tokyo, and you may read those stories although you would hardly have placed them in your "Daily Me." . . . Reading *Time* magazine, you might come across a discussion of endangered species in Madagascar, and this discussion might interest you, even affect your behavior, although you would not have sought it out in the first instance. A system in which you lack control over the particular content that you see has a great deal in common with a public street, where you might encounter not only friends, but a heterogeneous variety of people engaged in a wide array of activities (including, perhaps, political protests and begging).

In fact, a risk with a system of perfect individual control is that it can reduce the importance of the "public sphere" and of common spaces in general. One of the important features of such spaces is that they tend to ensure that people will encounter materials on important issues, whether or not they have specifically chosen the encounter. When people see materials that they have not chosen, their interests and their views might change as a result. At the very least, they will know a bit more about what their fellow citizens are thinking. As it happens, this point is closely connected with an important, and somewhat exotic, constitutional principle.

Public (and Private) Forums

In the popular understanding, the free speech principal forbids government from "censoring" speech of which it disapproves. In the standard cases, the government attempts to impose penalties, whether civil or criminal, on political dissent, and on speech that it considers dangerous, libelous, or sexually explicit. The question is whether the government has a legitimate and sufficiently weighty basis for restricting the speech that it seeks to control.

But a central part of free speech law, with large implications for thinking about the Internet, takes a quite different form. The Supreme Court has also held that streets and parks must be kept open to the public for expressive activity. Governments are obliged to allow speech to occur freely on public streets and in public parks—even if many citizens would prefer to have peace and quiet, and even if it seems irritating to come across protesters and dissidents whom one would like to avoid. . . .

The public forum doctrine serves three important functions. First, it ensures that speakers can have access to a wide array of people. If you want to claim that taxes are too high, or that police brutality against African Americans is common, you can press this argument on many people who might otherwise fail to hear the message. Those who use the streets and parks are likely to learn something about your argument; they might also learn the nature and intensity of views held by one of their fellow citizens. Perhaps their views will be changed; perhaps they will become curious, enough to investigate the question on their own.

Second, the public forum doctrine allows speakers not only to have general access to heterogeneous people, but also to specific people, and specific institutions, with whom they have a complaint. Suppose, for example, that you believe that the state legislature has behaved irresponsibly with respect to crime or health care for children. The public forum ensures that you can make your views heard by legislators simply by protesting in front of the state legislature building.

Third, the public forum doctrine increases the likelihood that people generally will be exposed to a wide variety of people and views. When you go to work, or visit a park, it is possible that you will have a range of unexpected encounters, however fleeting or seemingly inconsequential. You cannot easily wall yourself off from contentions or conditions that you would not have sought out in advance, or that you would have chosen to avoid if you could. Here, too, the public forum doctrine tends to ensure a range of experiences that are widely shared—streets and parks are public property—and also a set of exposures to diverse circumstances. . . .

. . . Society's general interest intermediaries—newspapers, magazines, television broadcasters—can be understood as public forums of an especially important sort, perhaps above all because they expose people to new, unanticipated topics and points of view.

When you read a city newspaper or a national magazine, your eyes will come across a number of articles that you might not have selected in advance, and if you are like most people, you will read some of those articles. Perhaps you did not know that you might have an interest in minimum wage legislation, or Somalia, or the latest developments in the Middle East. But a story might catch your attention. And what is true for topics of interest is also true for points of view. You might think that you have nothing to learn from someone whose view you abhor; but once you come across the editorial pages, you might read what they have to say, and you might benefit from the experience. . . .

Television broadcasters have similar functions. Most important in this regard is what has become an institution: the evening news. If you tune into the evening news, you will learn about a number of topics that you would not have chosen in advance. Because of their speech and immediacy, television broadcasts perform these public forum–type functions more than general interest intermediaries in the print media. The "lead story" on the networks is likely to have a great deal of public salience; it helps to define central issues and creates a kind of shared focus of attention for millions of people. . . .

None of these claims depends on a judgment that general interest intermediaries are unbiased, or always do an excellent job, or deserve a monopoly over the world of communications. The Internet is a boon partly because it breaks that monopoly. So too for the proliferation of television and radio shows, and even channels, that have some specialized identity. (Consider the rise of Fox News, which appeals to a more conservative audience.) All that I am claiming is that general interest intermediaries expose people to a wide range of topics and views and at the same time provide shared experiences for a heterogeneous public. Indeed, intermediaries of this sort have large advantages over streets and parks precisely because they tend to be national, even international. Typically they expose people to questions and problems in other areas, even other countries.

Specialization and Fragmentation

In a system with public forums and general interest intermediaries, people will frequently come across materials that they would not have chosen in advance—and in a diverse society, this provides something like a common framework for social experience. A fragmented communications market will change things significantly.

Consider some simple facts. If you take the ten most highly rated television programs for whites, and then take the ten most highly rated programs for African Americans, you will find little overlap between them. Indeed, more than half of the ten most highly rated programs for African Americans rank among the ten *least* popular programs for whites. With respect to race, similar divisions can be found on the Internet. Not surprisingly, many people tend to choose like-minded sites and like-minded discussion groups. Many of those with committed views on a topic—gun control, abortion, affirmative action—speak mostly with each other. It is exceedingly rare for a site with an identifiable point of view to provide links to sites with opposing views; but it is very common for such a site to provide links to like-minded sites.

With a dramatic increase in options, and a greater power to customize, comes an increase in the range of actual choices. Those choices are likely, in many cases, to mean that people will try to find material that makes them feel comfortable, or that is created by and for people like themselves. This is what the Daily Me is all about. Of course, many people seek out new topics and ideas. And to the extent that people do, the increase in options is hardly bad on balance; it will, among other things, increase variety, the aggregate amount of information, and the entertainment value of actual choices. But there are serious risks as well. If diverse groups are seeing and hearing different points of view, or focusing on different topics, mutual understanding might be difficult, and it might be hard for people to solve problems that society faces together. . . .

We can sharpen our understanding of this problem if we attend to the phenomenon of *group polarization*. The idea is that after deliberating with one another, people are likely to move toward a more extreme point in the direction to which they were previously inclined, as indicated by the median of their predeliberation judgments. With respect to the Internet, the implication is that groups of people, especially if they are like-minded, will end up thinking the same thing that they thought before—but in more extreme form.

Consider some examples of this basic phenomenon, which has been found in over a dozen nations. (a) After discussion, citizens of France become more critical of the United States and its intentions with respect to economic aid. (b) After discussion, whites predisposed to show racial prejudice offer more negative responses to questions about whether white racism is responsible for conditions faced by African Americans in American cities. (c) After discussion, whites predisposed not to show racial prejudice offer more positive responses to the same question. (d) A group of moderately profeminist women will become more strongly profeminist after discussion. . . .

The phenomenon of group polarization has conspicuous importance to the current communications market, where groups with distinctive identities increasingly engage in within-group discussion. If the public is balkanized, and if different groups design their own preferred communications packages, the consequence will be further balkanization, as group members move one another toward more extreme points in line with their initial tendencies. At the same time, different deliberating groups, each consisting of like-minded people, will be driven increasingly far apart, simply because most of their discussions are with one another. . . .

Group polarization is a human regularity, but social context can decrease, increase, or even eliminate it. For present purposes, the most important point is that group polarization will significantly increase if people think of themselves . . . as part of a group having a shared identity and a degree of solidarity. If . . . a group of people in an Internet discussion group think of themselves as opponents of high taxes, or advocates of animal rights, their discussions are likely to move toward extreme positions. As this happens to many different groups, polarization is both more likely and more extreme. Hence significant movements should be expected for those who listen to a radio show known to be conservative, or a television program dedicated to traditional religious values or to exposing white racism. . . .

Group polarization is occurring every day on the Internet. Indeed, it is clear that the Internet is serving, for many, as a breeding ground for extremism, precisely because like-minded people are deliberating with one another, without hearing contrary views. Hate groups are the most obvious example. Consider one extremist group, the so-called Unorganized Militia, the armed wing of the Patriot movement, "which believes that the federal government is becoming increasingly dictatorial with its regulatory power over taxes, guns and land use." A crucial factor behind the growth of the Unorganized Militia "has been the use of computer networks," allowing members "to make contact quickly and easily with like-minded individuals to trade information, discuss current conspiracy theories, and organize events." . . .

Of course we cannot say, from the mere fact of polarization, that there has been a movement in the *wrong* direction. Perhaps the more extreme tendency is better; indeed, group polarization is likely to have fueled many movements of great value, including the movement for civil rights, the antislavery movement, the movement for sex equality. All of these movements were extreme in their time, and within-group discussion bred greater extremism; but extremism need not be a word of opprobrium. If greater communications choices produce greater extremism, society may, in many cases, be better off as a result. . . .

The basic issue here is whether something like a "public sphere," with a wide range of voices, might not have significant advantages over a system in which isolated consumer choices produce a highly fragmented speech market. The most reasonable conclusion is that it is extremely important to ensure that people are exposed to views other than those with which they currently agree, that doing so protects against the harmful effects of group polarization on individual thinking and on social cohesion. This does not mean that the government should jail or fine people who refuse to listen to others. Nor is what I have said inconsistent with approval of deliberating "enclaves," on the Internet or elsewhere, designed to ensure that positions that would otherwise be silenced or squelched have a chance to develop. Readers will be able to think of their own preferred illustrations. . . .

Consider in this light the ideal of "consumer sovereignty," which underlies much of contemporary enthusiasm for the Internet. Consumer sovereignty means that people can choose to purchase, or to obtain, whatever they want. For many purposes this is a worthy ideal. But the adverse effects of group polarization show that, with respect to communications, consumer sovereignty is likely to produce serious problems for individuals and society at large—and these problems will occur by a kind of iron logic of social interactions.

The phenomenon of group polarization is [also] closely related to the widespread phenomenon of "social cascades." Cascade effects are common on the Internet, and we cannot understand the relationship between democracy and the Internet without having a sense of how cascades work.

It is obvious that many social groups, both large and small, seem to move both rapidly and dramatically in the direction of one or another set of beliefs or actions. These sorts of "cascades" often involve the spread of information; in fact they are driven by information. If you lack a great deal of private information, you may well rely on information provided by the statements or actions of others. A stylized example: If Joan is unaware whether abandoned toxic waste dumps are in fact hazardous, she may be moved in the direction of fear if Mary seems to think that fear is justified. If Joan and Mary both believe that fear is justified, Carl may end up thinking so too, at least if he lacks reliable independent information to the contrary. If Joan, Mary, and Carl believe that abandoned toxic waste dumps are hazardous, Don will have to have a good deal of confidence to reject their shared conclusion.

The example shows how information travels, and often becomes quite entrenched, even if it is entirely wrong. The view, widespread in some African-American communities, that white doctors are responsible for the spread of AIDS among African Americans is a recent illustration. Often cascades of this kind are local, and take different form in different communities. Hence one group may end up believing something and another group the exact opposite, and the reason is the rapid transmission of one piece of information within one group and a different piece of information in the other. In a balkanized speech market, this danger takes a particular form: different groups may be led to quite different perspectives, as local cascades lead people in dramatically different directions. The Internet dramatically increases the likelihood of rapid cascades, based on false information. Of course, low-cost Internet communication also makes it possible for truth, and corrections, to spread quickly as well. But sometimes this happens much too late. In the event, balkanization is extremely likely. As a result of the Internet, cascade effects are more common than they have ever been before. . . .

I hope that I have shown enough to demonstrate that for citizens of a heterogeneous democracy, a fragmented communications market creates considerable dangers. There are dangers for each of us as individuals; constant exposure to one set of views is likely to lead to errors and confusions, or to unthinking conformity (emphasized by John Stuart Mill). And to the extent that the process makes people less able to work cooperatively on shared problems, by turning collections of people into non-communicating confessional groups, there are dangers for society as a whole.

Common Experiences

In a heterogeneous society, it is extremely important for diverse people to have a set of common experiences. Many of our practices reflect a judgment to this effect. National holidays, for example, help constitute a nation, by encouraging citizens to think, all at once, about events of shared importance. And they do much more than this. They enable people, in all their diversity, to have certain memories and attitudes in common. At least this is true in nations where national holidays have a vivid and concrete meaning. In the United States, many national holidays have become mere days-off-from-work, and the precipitating occasion—President's Day, Memorial Day, Labor Day—has come to be nearly invisible. This is a serious loss. With the possible exception of the Fourth of July, Martin Luther King Day is probably the closest thing to a genuinely substantive national holiday, largely because that celebration involves something that can be treated as concrete and meaningful—in other words, it is *about* something.

Communications and the media are, of course, exceptionally important here. Sometimes millions of people follow the presidential election, or the Super Bowl, or the coronation of a new monarch; many of them do so because of the simultaneous actions of others. The point very much bears on the historic role of both public forums and general interest intermediaries. Public parks are places where diverse people can congregate and see one another. General interest intermediaries, if they are operating properly, give a simultaneous sense of problems and tasks.

Why are these shared experiences so desirable? There are three principal reasons:

1. Simple enjoyment is probably the least of it, but it is far from irrelevant. People like many experiences more simply because they are being shared. Consider a popular movie, the Super Bowl, or a presidential debate. . . .
2. Sometimes shared experiences ease social interactions, permitting people to speak with one another, and to congregate around a common issue, task, or concern, whether or not they have much in common with one another. In this sense they provide a form of social glue. They help make it possible for diverse people to believe that they live in the same culture. Indeed they help constitute that shared culture, simply by creating common memories and experiences, and a sense of common tasks.
3. A fortunate consequence of shared experiences—many of them produced by the media—is that people who would otherwise see one another as unfamiliar can come to regard one another as fellow citizens, with shared hopes, goals, and concerns. This is a subjective good for those directly involved. But it can be objectively good as well, especially if it leads to cooperative projects of various kinds. . . .

How does this bear on the Internet? An increasingly fragmented communications universe will reduce the level of shared experiences having salience to a diverse group of Americans. This is a simple matter of numbers. When there were three television networks, much of what appeared would have the quality of a genuinely common experience. The lead story on the evening news, for example, would provide a common reference point for many millions of people. To the extent that choices proliferate, it is inevitable that diverse individuals, and diverse groups, will have fewer shared experiences and fewer common reference points. It is possible, for example, that some events that are highly salient to some people will barely register on others' viewscreens. And it is possible that some views and perspectives that seem obvious for many people will, for others, seem barely intelligible.

This is hardly a suggestion that everyone should be required to watch the same thing. A degree of plurality, with respect to both topics and points of view, is highly desirable. Moreover, talk about "requirements" misses the point. My only claim is that a common set of frameworks and experiences is valuable for a heterogeneous society, and that a system with limitless options, making for diverse choices, could compromise the underlying values.

Changing Filters

My goal here has been to understand what makes for a well-functioning system of free expression, and to show how consumer sovereignty, in a world of limitless options, could undermine that system. The point is that a well-functioning system includes a kind of public sphere, one that fosters common experiences, in which people hear messages that challenge their prior convictions, and in which citizens can present their views to a broad audience. I do not intend to offer a comprehensive set of policy reforms or any kind of blueprint for the future. . . . But it will be useful to offer a few ideas, if only by way of introduction to questions that are likely to engage public attention in coming years.

In thinking about reforms, it is important to have a sense of the problems we aim to address, and some possible ways of addressing them. If the discussion thus far is correct, there are three fundamental concerns from the democratic point of view. These include:

(a) the need to promote exposure to materials, topics, and positions that people would not have chosen in advance, or at least enough exposure to produce a degree of understanding and curiosity;
(b) the value of a range of common experiences;
(c) the need for exposure to substantive questions of policy and principle, combined with a range of positions on such questions. . . .

Drawing on recent developments in regulation generally, we can see the potential appeal of five simple alternatives. Of course, different proposals would work better for some communications outlets than others. I will speak here of both private and public responses, but the former should be favored: they are less intrusive, and in general they are likely to be more effective as well.

Disclosure: Producers of communications might disclose important information on their own, about the extent to which they are promoting democratic goals. To the extent that they do not, they might be subject to disclosure requirements (though not to regulation). In the environmental area, this strategy has produced excellent results. The mere fact that polluters have been asked to disclose toxic releases has produced voluntary, low-cost reductions. Apparently fearful of public opprobrium, companies have been spurred to reduce toxic emissions on their own. . . .

The same idea could be used far more broadly. Television broadcasters might, for example, be asked to disclose their public interest activities. On a quarterly basis, they might say whether and to what extent they have provided educational programming for children, free air time for candidates, and closed captioning for the hearing impaired. They might also be asked whether they have covered issues of concern to the local community and allowed opposing views a chance to speak. The Federal Communications Commission has already taken steps in this direction; it could do a lot more. . . .

Self-Regulation: Producers of communications might engage in *voluntary self-regulation.* Some of the difficulties in the current speech market stem from relentless competition for viewers and listeners, competition that leads to a situation that many broadcast journalists abhor about their profession, and from which society does not benefit. The competition might be reduced via a "code" of appropriate conduct, agreed upon by various companies, and encouraged but not imposed by government. In fact, the National Association of Broadcasters maintained such a code for several decades, and there is growing interest in voluntary self-regulation for both television and the Internet. The case for this approach is that it avoids government regulation while at the same time reducing some of the harmful effects of market pressures. Any such code could, for example, call for an opportunity for opposing views to speak, or for avoiding unnecessary sensationalism, or for offering arguments rather than quick soundbites whenever feasible. . . .

Subsidy: The government might *subsidize speech,* as, for example, through publicly subsidized programming or publicly subsidized websites. This is, of course, the idea that motivates the Public Broadcasting System. But it is reasonable to ask whether the PBS model is not outmoded. Other approaches, similarly designed to promote educational, cultural, and democratic goals, might well be ventured. Perhaps government could subsidize a "Public.net" designed to promote debate on public issues among diverse citizens—and to create a right of access to speakers of various sorts.

Links: Websites might use links and hyperlinks to ensure that viewers learn about sites containing opposing views. A liberal magazine's website

might, for example, provide a link to a conservative magazine's website, and the conservative magazine might do the same. The idea would be to decrease the likelihood that people will simply hear echoes of their own voices. Of course many people would not click on the icons of sites whose views seem objectionable; but some people would, and in that sense the system would not operate so differently from general interest intermediaries and public forums. . . .

Public Sidewalk: If the problem consists in the failure to attend to public issues, the most popular websites in any given period might offer links and hyperlinks, designed to ensure more exposure to substantive questions. Under such a system, viewers of especially popular sites would see an icon for sites that deal with substantive issues in a serious way. It is well established that whenever there is a link to a particular webpage from a major site, such as MSNBC, the traffic is huge. Nothing here imposes any requirements on viewers. People would not be required to click on links and hyperlinks. But it is reasonable to expect that many viewers would do so, if only to satisfy their curiosity. The result would be to create a kind of Internet "sidewalk" that promotes some of the purposes of the public forum doctrine. . . .

These are brief thoughts on some complex subjects. My goal has not been to evaluate any proposal in detail, but to give a flavor of some possibilities for those concerned to promote democratic goals in a dramatically changed media environment. . . .

Beyond Anticensorship

My principal claim here has been that a well-functioning democracy depends on far more than restraints on official censorship of controversial ideas and opinions. It also depends on some kind of public sphere, in which a wide range of speakers have access to a diverse public—and also to particular institutions, and practices, against which they seek to launch objections.

Emerging technologies, including the Internet, are hardly an enemy here. They hold out far more promise than risk, especially because they allow people to widen their horizons. But to the extent that they weaken the power of general interest intermediaries and increase people's ability to wall themselves off from topics and opinions that they would prefer to avoid, they create serious dangers. And if we believe that a system of free expression calls for unrestricted choices by individual consumers, we will not even understand the dangers as such. Whether such dangers will materialize will ultimately depend on the aspirations, for freedom and democracy alike, by whose light we evaluate our practices. What I have sought to establish here is that in a free republic, citizens aspire to a system that provides a wide range of experiences—with people, topics, and ideas—that would not have been selected in advance.

The Power
of the Producers

ROBERT McCHESNEY

More than forty years ago, C. Wright Mills published *The Power Elite*. In his book, Mills discusses the paradox of the postwar United States. On the one hand, it is a nation abuzz with technology, celebrity and commercialism, a radical society in which tradition has been torn asunder and all that is solid melts into air. On the other hand, it is a highly depoliticized society—only formally democratic in many key respects—where most important political decisions are made by the few for the few, with public relations to massage the rabble should they question their status.

We are today dazzled by a mind-boggling explosion of new technologies, seemingly lifted from the pages of a science fiction novel, that promise unprecedented consumer choice. On the other hand, the clear tendencies of our media and communication world tend toward ever greater corporate concentration, media conglomeration, and hypercommercialism. There is really no paradox in this, as Mills knew: the illusions of consumer choice and individual freedom merely provide the ideological oxygen necessary to sustain a media system that serves the few while making itself appear accountable and democratic. The digital revolution and the Internet seem less a process of empowering the less powerful than a process that will further the corporate and commercial penetration and domination of life in the United States.

Cass Sunstein has done a great service by raising the anti-democratic implications of the emerging wired world. Much of his critique is on target, and I found myself nodding my head vigorously time after time. In two fundamental areas, however, my train of thought diverges from his. One is a matter of contextualization: In what kind of political and social contexts do people feel the need to construct what Sunstein calls a "Daily Me"? The second is a disagreement over a core assumption: Sunstein seems to assume that consumer sovereignty actually exists, yet I would argue that there are many reasons for doubt on this score.

It may be true, as Sunstein says, that people will tend to look for opinions that reinforce what they already believe. Yet the desire to construct a Daily Me that threatens democracy may not be inherent in the species. Nothing in our genetic code makes the bulk of us, especially those among us who are poorer and younger, narrowly self-obsessed and depoliticized in the ways Sunstein describes. In my view it is fairly clear that since the advent of universal adult suffrage powerful interests have worked tirelessly to promote depoliticization and social demoralization. Sometimes these interests seem to have liberal concerns, or at other times they are frankly elitist, but the point is always the same: it is best for the unwashed not to have too much interest in politics or too much control over important decisions. To the liberals, an active and democratic public will lead to outcomes offensive to the educated; to the elitists, it will lead to outcomes offensive to the wealthy. In either case—and the two groups tend to overlap on core issues—nothing good comes from too much democracy.

A viable democracy depends upon minimal social inequality and a sense that an individual's welfare is determined in large part by the welfare of the general community. It is difficult to imagine an inegalitarian social order like the United States surviving as a democracy if the bottom half of the population put as much interest into political affairs as the top 5 or 10 percent. What better example of this than the 2000 presidential election, where exit polls showed that the richest 20 percent of Americans accounted for about one-half of all voters.

How this process of depoliticizing people plays out is of course tremendously complex; my own work has emphasized the role that the commercial media system has played in making the world safe for vibrant capitalism and weak democracy. It does this partly through a vapid journalism. Because investigative journalism or coverage of foreign affairs makes no economic sense for profit-driven media, it is discouraged as being too expensive. There is appalling schlock journalism for the masses, based upon lurid tabloid-style-type stories. For the occasional serious story, there is the mindless regurgitation of press releases from one source or another, with the range of debate mostly limited to what is being debated among the elites. As with entertainment, at times the corporate media giants generate first-rate journalism, but it is a minuscule fraction of their output and often causes just the sort of uproar that corporate media firms prefer to avoid.

At another level, however, the hypercommercial entertainment culture has been the result of, and necessary condition for, the rise of a global market for goods and services dominated by a few hundred trans-national corporations. The global commercial media system and the growth and emergence of a global economy are predicated upon pro-business deregulation policies worldwide. Just following rational market calculations, the media system exists to provide light escapist entertainment. Dominated by a handful of massive firms, advertisers, and the firms' billionaire owners, the whole media system is spinning in a hypercommercial frenzy with little trace of public service or public accountability.

Is the Internet any different? I believe that Sunstein exaggerates the extent of "consumer sovereignty" on the Internet. Recall the countless pronouncements of the 1990s that the rise of the Internet would spell the doom of the media giants, as entrepreneurs would use the Internet to launch commercially viable competitors to the conglomerates. Supposedly, Internet users could pick from billions of choices, and were there any modicum of demand for something that did not exist, a plucky entrepreneur would surely respond. Hundreds of millions, even billions, of dollars were invested to seize the opportunity to introduce online competition to the media industries. And guess how many commercially viable Internet content providers this flurry of investment generated?

Zero.

It is true that anyone can start a website at a nominal expense and that there may well be billions of websites in the coming decades. It is also true that one can access the global media instantaneously on the Web, which breaks down barriers of time and space. While these are truly astonishing and world-historical developments, they do not however lead to consumer sovereignty, which requires intense competition among producers. Ironically, the evidence suggests that the effect of the Internet on our media culture may well be, strangely enough, to generate even greater *producer* sovereignty.

How can this be?

The principal reason is that the two dozen or so media firms that rule the U.S. media system have spectacular advantages over nascent online competitors. Firms like AOL-Time Warner have digital programming already and need not create something entirely new; they have known brand names; they can advertise their Web activities in their traditional media, a striking advantage over someone who has to pay for that level of promotion. They can bring their advertisers over to their websites; they get "pole position" from browsers, portals, and search engines. Plus, the media giants have a much longer time horizon with regard to the Web. They will take huge losses every year because they know that by doing so they can make sure no one can use the Internet to destroy their existing empires. An investor without an existing media empire to protect recognizes early on that there are better locations for profitable investment. Indeed, the Internet may well be likely to increase concentration rather than competition in the media and other industries as they move online. This is the lesson of Amazon.com: whoever gets the jump on an online industry, because the margins are low, requires massive scale to make a profit. Once the scale reaches a certain point, it is virtually impossible for newcomers to invade the market. Just recently, Borders has thrown in the towel as an Internet bookseller. If Borders, with its massive warehouses of books, cannot compete with Amazon, who can?

So, when individuals are selecting from billions of websites to construct their Daily Me, as Sunstein suggests they are doing, they will not be exercising consumer sovereignty. More than likely, they will be selecting from a much smaller group of options directed by the largest media firms in the world. While the Internet will permit the occasional interloper to break a story, and it will change many aspects of political organizing, the journalism that receives the funding and attention will do so under the same commercial auspices and terms that offline journalism operates under. In my view, that is bad news for the sort of informed, participatory democracy that both Sunstein and I advocate.

The simple truth is that for those atop our economy success is based in large part on *eliminating* competition, not encouraging it. I am being somewhat facetious, because in the end capitalism is indeed a war one against all, since every capitalist is in competition with all the others. But competition is also something successful capitalists learn to avoid like the plague. The less competition a firm has, the less risk it faces and more profitable it tends to be. In general, most markets in the United States in the twentieth century have gravitated not to monopoly but to oligopolistic status. This means that a small handful of firms—this ranges from two to three to as many as a dozen or so—thoroughly dominate the market's output and maintain barriers to entry that effectively keep new market entrants at bay.

So how should we expect the Internet to develop? Exactly as it has so far. Despite now having the technological capacity to compete, the largest firms are extremely reticent about entering new markets and forcing their way into highly lucrative communications markets. It is safe to say that *some* new communications giants will be established during the coming years, much as Microsoft attained gigantic status during the 1980s. But most of the great new fortunes will be made by start-up firms who develop a profitable idea and then sell out to one of the existing giants. Witness Microsoft, which spent over $2 billion between 1994 and 1997 to purchase or take a stake in some fifty communications companies.

The market system may "work" in the sense that goods and services are produced and consumed, but it is no means fair in any social or political or ethical sense of the term. Wealthy individuals have significant advantages over poor or middle class individuals in terms of participating as capitalists. A tremendous amount of talent simply never gets an opportunity to develop and contribute to the economy. It is unremarkable that "self-made" billionaires like Bill Gates, Ted Turner, Michael Eisner, Rupert Murdoch, and Sumner Redstone all come from privileged backgrounds. And on the demand side of the market, power is determined by how much money an individual has; it is a case of one dollar, one vote, rather than one person, one vote. In this sense, the political system to which the media and Internet market is most similar is the limited suffrage days of pre-twentieth century democracies, where propertyless adults could not vote and their interests were studiously ignored.

What this all means is clear. To have the Internet contribute to a democratization of our society requires that we work to democratize our political economy and reform our media system. The most important area of political activity ultimately is to organize to change media policies. The core problem with the U.S. media systems relates to how it is owned, its profit motivation, and its reliance upon advertising. Corporate media power must be confronted directly, and reduced. Here are some suggestions:

1. *Building nonprofit and commercial media.* The starting point for media reform is to build up a viable, nonprofit, noncommercial media sector. Such a sector currently exists in the United States, and produces much

of value, but is woefully small and underfunded. It can be developed independently of changes in laws and regulations—foundations and organized labor could and should contribute far more to nonprofit media. Government subsidies and policies have played a key role in establishing lucrative commercial media; now new policies could also foster a nonprofit media sector.

2. *Public broadcasting.* Establishing a strong nonprofit sector to complement the commercial media giants is not enough. Therefore, it is important to establish and maintain a noncommercial, nonprofit, public radio and television system, which could include national networks, local stations, public access television, and independent community radio stations. Every community should also have a stratum of low power television and micropower radio stations.

3. *Regulation.* A third main plank is to increase regulation of commercial broadcasting in the public interest. Experience in the U.S. and abroad indicates that if commercial broadcasters are not held to high public service standards, they will generate the easiest profits by resorting to the crassest commercialism and overwhelm the balance of the media culture. The solution to this problem is clear: Commercial broadcasters should receive their government licenses for only eighteen hours per day. The remaining six hours should be taken out of their control and dedicated to public service.

4. *Antitrust.* Break up the largest firms and establish more competitive markets, thus shifting some control from corporate suppliers to citizen consumers. The contemporary political power implied in the consolidation of media into a handful of corporate behemoths rivals that of the great trusts of the Gilded Age. We need a new media antitrust statute, which emphasizes the importance of ideological diversity and noncommercial editorial content.

There are, of course, some specific policy reforms we should seek for the Internet: for example, guaranteeing universal public access at low rates, perhaps for free. But in general terms, we might do better to regard the Internet as the corporate media giants regard it. It is part of the emerging media landscape, not its entirety. So when we create more and smaller media firms, when we create public and community radio and television networks and stations, when we create a strong public service component to commercial news and children's programming, when we use government policies to spawn a nonprofit media sector, all these will have a tremendous effect on the Internet's development. Why? Because websites will not be worth much if they do not have the resources to provide a quality product. And all the new media that result from media reform will have websites as a mandatory aspect of their operations, much like the commercial media. By creating a vibrant and more democratic traditional media culture, we will go a long way toward creating a more democratic cyberspace.

DISCUSSION QUESTIONS

1. Both authors suggest alternatives to the present Internet system in the name of increasing democracy. Yet maybe the Internet is already democratic and diverse. Which of the reforms suggested by either author seem to restrict democracy, and why? Which seem to further democracy, according to your definition?

2. McChesney attacks corporate media mergers as leading to a mass media system dominated by commercialism and the search for profits. Yet in 2003, the once-momentous merger between AOL and Time Warner broke up, with Time Warner executives concerned about the failing profit margins and reputation of the world's largest online provider. Is corporate control of Internet access inevitable? Can't the capitalist marketplace itself defeat corporate efforts to control Internet access and content?

3. Because almost anyone with minimal expertise can set up a website, the Internet has been heralded as the ultimate participatory medium. In what ways is the Internet an extension of the established traditional media of newspapers, TV, and radio? In what ways is it a departure?

4. Sunstein fears that individuals will only confirm their own prejudices through the "Daily Me." Yet aren't any efforts to control individual use of the Internet through the proposals he advocates in themselves censorship?

SUGGESTED READINGS AND INTERNET RESOURCES

Debates about the Internet's impact on a corporate-dominated media system depend, in large part, on how one characterizes the traditional media system. When it comes to governmental and corporate power, are the media watchdogs or lapdogs? How diverse are the traditional news media, and what new influences might shape the news coverage of networks, cable stations, and newspapers?

One book that makes a comprehensive assessment of these questions is W. Lance Bennett, *News: The Politics of Illusion* (New York: Longman, 2003). See also the outstanding anthology by Robert Entman and W. Lance Bennett, *Mediated Politics: Communication in the Future of Democracy* (New York: Cambridge University Press, 2001). One book that debates the dilemma of commercial pressures for working journalists is Kristina Borjesson, ed., *Into the Buzzsaw* (Amherst, N.Y.: Prometheus Books, 2002). The role of the Internet in U.S. politics and culture has spawned vastly different perspectives. See Howard Rheingold, *Smart Mobs: The Next Social Revolution* (New York: Basic Books, 2003), and Diana Saco, *Cybering Democracy: Public Space and the Internet*

(Minneapolis: University of Minnesota Press, 2002). For mainstream accounts, see Elaine Kamarck and Joseph Nye, eds., *Governance.com: Democracy in the Internet Age* (Washington, D.C.: Brookings Institution Press, 2002), and David Anderson, Michael Cornfield, and Christopher Arterton, eds., *The Civic Web: On-line Politics and Democratic Politics* (New York: Rowman and Littlefield, 2002).

Media Reform—Free Press
www.mediareform.net
This group is among the most active in efforts to roll back corporate concentration and commercialism in television and radio, and has won several important battles against the FCC's efforts to loosen ownership restrictions. There are great links to numerous groups who work on public media.

Fairness and Accuracy in Reporting (FAIR)
www.fair.org
This New York–based watchdog group reports inaccuracies and biases in mainstream news programs, with an emphasis on the undemocratic effects of corporate control.

Pew Research Center for the People and the Press
www.people-press.org
This website contains excellent polling information on the changing patterns of media use by Americans. Use the archives selection.

C H A P T E R

10

Political Parties and Elections: Are Voters United or Divided?

The electoral system is often trumpeted as the defining feature of U.S. political identity. There is good reason for such a declaration. Since the founding of this country, regular elections between competing candidates and parties have provided a stable and dignified way in which the people's voice is heard.

Yet elections between competitive political parties are not always truly democratic. Women, African Americans, and the propertyless were excluded by law and custom from the polls throughout much of the nineteenth century and in some cases well into the twentieth century. Only with much blood, sweat, and tears did great social movements expand the voting franchise, and Jim Crow laws were struck down only as recently as the 1960s. In the 2000 presidential election, Americans learned that they must still struggle to be heard. Although Al Gore beat George W. Bush by over half a million votes nationwide, Bush won the White House when the Supreme Court intervened to certify Bush's victory in Florida. Investigations by the Federal Civil Rights Commission revealed that many African-American voters were effectively disenfranchised through intimidation at polling places, while many others were deceived by "butterfly ballots" and voting machines that didn't work. In 2004, the same issues remain in Florida and elsewhere. Voting problems are compounded by frankly undemocratic aspects of the American electoral system, such as the electoral college, a "winner-take-all" system that rewards all power to those groups that win a plurality, and a reapportionment system for the House of Representatives that draws electoral districts in a way that rewards incumbents. Since 2000, none of these features has changed.

Are American elections broadly representative of the conflicts, divisions, and aspirations of the U.S. population? From a popular democratic viewpoint, there are problems beyond mechanical failures of voting machines. Only about half the electorate votes in presidential elections, and there's a decided middle- and upper-class skew to the voting population. The young vote much less often than do the middle-aged and elderly, and people with college degrees are more likely to vote than those with less formal education. Compared with other wealthy countries, even the new democracies in the former USSR, the United States ranks near the bottom in voting participation rates. The kinds of people who don't vote are most likely to be those who lack other means to influence politics. They have less money to contribute to campaigns, less time to study the issues, and less contact with other people who talk about politics.

From an elite democratic perspective, however, there are few reasons for real concern. Since the 1960s, voter registration rules have eased, and people have ample opportunities to become involved in politics, even if many choose not to do so. According to most surveys, nonvoters generally hold public policy and partisan views similar to those who do vote. For them, these factors suggest that U.S. elections do reflect the citizenry's real choices and diversity in all their complexity.

Much of the debate about the democratic breadth of U.S. elections is related to the question of our two dominant political parties and what kinds of people they organize and represent. For the most part, Democrats and Republicans define our electoral landscape; third parties are sometimes important but they have rarely done more than influence the two dominant parties. Since the late 1960s, and especially since Ronald Reagan's election in 1980, the voting electorate has been sharply and closely divided between the two parties. In the 2000 election, the Gore/Bush race divided the electorate almost in half, and most observers see the close partisan divide as one likely to shape our electoral landscape for a long time to come.

In this chapter, the essayists explore several key questions: How well does the partisan divide between Republicans and Democrats reflect the social, economic, and cultural divisions and aspirations of the American people? Are there forms of consensus and unity between Americans, despite the apparent partisan warfare? Can the Democrats regain control of the Congress and the White House, or is there a new Republican majority in the making?

The two excerpts reprinted here reflect very different perspectives on the 2000, 2002, and 2004 elections and their meaning. In the first, former *Weekly Standard* editor and present *New York Times* conservative columnist David Brooks writes about the genuine differences between "Blue" and "Red" America (in the 2000 election, the news media colored states that Gore had won blue, and those that Bush had won red). In his journeys as a columnist, Brooks finds two Americas, which are divided from each other by consumption preferences and cultural attitudes toward life, work, and religion. Brooks argues that the Republican Party, with its emphasis on low taxes, religious faith, and wide-open spaces, best embodies a future majority, as well as dominant U.S. social and demographic trends. In the second selection, former President Bill Clinton takes issue with many of Brooks's formulations and details how it is that the Democrats can once again become the majority party. In contrast to Brooks's argument stressing cultural differences, Clinton argues that increasing economic inequality and the needs of working people for affordable health insurance, housing, and quality education can promote a Democratic resurgence, if the Democrats choose to make an aggressive case.

   While reading Brooks's essay and Clinton's interview with *American Prospect* editor Michael Tomasky, you might think about the following: Does either one address the question of voter nonparticipation in U.S. elections? For both Brooks and Clinton, what are the fundamental divisions in U.S. society, and what is the role of political parties in trying both to express them and to resolve them? What would be common points of consensus between the citizens of Blue and Red America?

One Nation, Slightly Divisible

DAVID BROOKS

Sixty-five miles from where I am writing this sentence is a place with no Starbucks, no Pottery Barn, no Borders or Barnes & Noble. . . . The place I'm talking about goes by different names. Some call it America. Others call it Middle America. It has also come to be known as Red America, in reference to the maps that were produced on the night of the 2000 presidential election. People in Blue America, which is my part of America, tend to live around big cities on the coasts. People in Red America tend to live on farms or in small towns or small cities far away from the coasts. Things are different there. . . .

   Different sorts of institutions dominate life in these two places. In Red America churches are everywhere. In Blue America Thai restaurants are everywhere. In Red America they have QVC, the Pro Bowlers Tour, and hunting. In Blue America we have NPR, Doris Kearns Goodwin, and socially conscious investing. In Red America the Wal-Marts are massive, with parking lots the size of state parks. In Blue America the stores are small but the markups are big. . . .

   We in the coastal metro Blue areas read more books and attend more plays than the people in the Red heartland. We're more sophisticated and cosmopolitan—just ask us about our alumni trips to China and Provence, or our interest in Buddhism. But don't ask us, please, what life in Red America is like. We don't know. . . .

All we know, or all we think we know, about Red America is that millions and millions of its people live quietly underneath flight patterns, many of them are racist and homophobic, and when you see them at highway rest stops, they're often really fat and their clothes are too tight. . . .

Crossing the Meatloaf Line

Over the past several months . . . I have every now and then left my home in Montgomery County, Maryland, and driven sixty-five miles northwest to Franklin County, in south-central Pennsylvania. Montgomery County is one of the steaming-hot centers of the great espresso machine that is Blue America. It is just over the border from northwestern Washington, D.C., and it is full of upper-middle-class towns inhabited by lawyers, doctors, stockbrokers, and establishment journalists like me—towns like Chevy Chase, Potomac, and Bethesda (where I live). Its central artery is a burgeoning high-tech corridor with a multitude of sparkling new office parks housing technology companies such as United Information Systems and Sybase, and pioneering biotech firms such as Celera Genomics and Human Genome Sciences. When I drive to Franklin County, I take Route 270. After about forty-five minutes I pass a Cracker Barrel—Red America condensed into chain-restaurant form. I've crossed the Meatloaf Line; from here on there will be a lot fewer sun-dried-tomato concoctions on restaurant menus and a lot more meatloaf platters.

Franklin County is [Bush's] Red America. It's a rural county, about twenty-five miles west of Gettysburg, and it includes the towns of Waynesboro, Chambersburg, and Mercersburg. . . .

I shuttled back and forth between Franklin and Montgomery Counties because the cultural differences between the two places are great, though the geographic distance is small. The two places are not perfect microcosms of Red and Blue America. The part of Montgomery County I am here describing is largely the Caucasian part. Moreover, Franklin County is in a Red part of a Blue state: overall, Pennsylvania went for Gore. And I went to Franklin County aware that there are tremendous differences within Red America, just as there are within Blue. Franklin County is quite different from, say, Scottsdale, Arizona, just as Bethesda is quite different from Oakland, California.

Nonetheless, the contrasts between the two counties leap out, and they are broadly suggestive of the sorts of contrasts that can be seen nationwide. When Blue America talks about social changes that convulsed society, it tends to mean the 1960s rise of the counterculture and feminism. When Red America talks about changes that convulsed society, it tends to mean World War II, which shook up old town establishments and led to a great surge of industry. . . .

[In Red America] there . . . seems to be an important distinction between men who work outdoors and men who work indoors. The outdoor guys wear faded black T-shirts they once picked up at a Lynyrd Skynyrd concert and wrecked jeans that appear to be washed faithfully at least once a year. They've got wraparound NASCAR sunglasses, maybe a NAPA auto parts cap, and hair cut in a short wedge up front but flowing down over their shoulders in the back—a cut that is known as a mullet, which is sort of a cross between Van Halen's style and Kenny Rogers's, and is the ugliest hairdo since every hairdo in the seventies. . . .

The guys who work indoors can't project this rugged proletarian image. It's simply not that romantic to be a bank-loan officer or a shift manager at the local distribution center. So the indoor guys adopt a look that a smart-ass, sneering Blue American might call Bible-academy casual—maybe Haggar slacks, which they bought at a dry-goods store best known for its appliance department, and a short-sleeved white Van Heusen shirt from the Bon-Ton. . . .

The kinds of distinctions we make in Blue America are different. In my world the easiest way to categorize people is by headroom needs. People who went to business school or law school like a lot of headroom. They buy humongous sport-utility vehicles that practically have cathedral ceilings over the front seats. They live in homes the size of country clubs, with soaring entry atriums so high that they could practically fly a kite when they come through the front door. These big-headroom people tend to be predators: their jobs have them negotiating and competing all day. . . .

Small-headroom people tend to have been liberal-arts majors, and they have liberal-arts jobs. They get passive-aggressive pleasure from demonstrating how modest and environmentally sensitive their living containers are. They hate people with SUVs, and feel virtuous driving around in their low-ceilinged little Hondas, which often display a RANDOM ACTS OF KINDNESS bumper sticker or one bearing an image of a fish with legs, along with the word "Darwin," just to show how intellectually superior to fundamentalist Christians they are.

Some of the biggest differences between Red and Blue America show up on statistical tables. Ethnic diversity is one. In Montgomery County 60 percent of the population is white, 15 percent is black, 12 percent is Hispanic, and 11 percent is Asian. In Franklin County 95 percent of the population is white. White people work the gas-station pumps and the 7-Eleven counters. (This is something one doesn't often see in my part of the country). Although the nation is growing more diverse, it's doing so only in certain spots. . . .

Another big thing is that, according to 1990 census data, in Franklin County only 12 percent of the adults have college degrees and only 69 percent have high school diplomas. In Montgomery County 50 percent of the adults have college degrees and 91 percent have high school diplomas. The education gap extends to the children. . . .

Because the information age rewards education with money, it's not surprising that Montgomery County is much richer than Franklin County. According to some estimates, in Montgomery County 51 percent of households have annual incomes above $75,000, and the average household income is $100,365. In Franklin County only 16 percent of households have incomes above $75,000, and the average is $51,872.

A major employer in Montgomery County is the National Institutes of Health, which grows like a scientific boomtown in Bethesda. A major economic engine in Franklin County is the interstate highway Route 81. Trucking companies have gotten sick of fighting the congestion on Route 95, which runs up the Blue corridor along the northeast coast, so they move their stuff along 81, farther inland. Several new distribution centers have been built along 81 in Franklin County, and some of the workers who were laid off when their factories closed, several years ago, are now settling for $8.00 or $9.00 an hour loading boxes.

The two counties vote differently, of course—the differences, on a nationwide scale, were what led to those red-and-blue maps. Like upscale areas everywhere, from Silicon Valley to Chicago's North Shore to suburban Connecticut, Montgomery County supported the Democratic ticket in last year's presidential election, by a margin of 63 percent to 34 percent. Meanwhile, like almost all of rural America, Franklin County went Republican, by 67 percent to 30 percent. . . .

"The People Versus the Powerful"

There are a couple of long-standing theories about why America is divided. One of the main ones holds that the division is along class lines, between the haves and the have-nots. This theory is popular chiefly on the left. . . .

According to this theory, during most of the twentieth century gaps in income between the rich and the poor in America gradually shrank. Then came the information age. The rich started getting spectacularly richer; the poor started getting poorer, and wages for the middle class stagnated, at best. Over the previous decade, these writers emphasized, remuneration for top-level executives had skyrocketed: now the average CEO made 116 times as much as the average rank-and-file worker. Assembly-line workers found themselves competing for jobs against Third World workers who earned less than a dollar an hour. Those who had once labored at well-paying blue-collar jobs were forced to settle for poorly paying service-economy jobs without benefits.

People with graduate degrees have done well over the past couple of decades: their real hourly wages climbed by 13 percent from 1979 to 1997. . . . But those with only some college education saw their wages fall by nine percent, while those with only high school diplomas saw their wages fall by 12 percent, and high school dropouts saw a stunning 26 percent decline in their pay.

Such trends have created a new working class . . . not a traditional factory-and-mill working class but a suburban and small-town working class, made up largely of service workers and low-level white-collar employees. . . .

[Pollster] Stanley Greenberg tailored Al Gore's presidential campaign to appeal to such voters. Gore's most significant slogan was "The People Versus the Powerful," which was meant to rally members of the middle class who felt threatened by "powerful forces" beyond their control, such as HMOs, tobacco companies, big corporations, and globalization, and to channel their resentment against the upper class. Gore dressed down throughout his campaign in the hope that these middle-class workers would identify with him.

Driving from Bethesda to Franklin County, one can see that the theory of a divide between the classes has a certain plausibility. . . .

When the locals are asked about their economy, they tell a story very similar to the one that . . . the wage-stagnation liberals recount. There used to be plenty of good factory jobs in Franklin County, and people could work at those factories for life. But some of the businesses, including the textile company J. Schoeneman, once Franklin County's largest manufacturer, have closed. Others have moved offshore. The remaining manufacturers, such as Grove Worldwide and JLG Industries, which both make cranes and aerial platforms, have laid off workers. The local Army depot, Letterkenny, has radically shrunk its work force. The new jobs are in distribution centers or nursing homes. People tend to repeat the same phrase: "We've taken some hits."

And yet when they are asked about the broader theory, whether there is class conflict between the educated affluents and the stagnant middles, they stare blankly as if suddenly the interview were being conducted in Aramaic. I kept asking, Do you feel that the highly educated people around, say, New York and Washington are getting all the goodies? Do you think there is resentment toward all the latte sippers who shop at Nieman Marcus? Do you see a gulf between high-income people in the big cities and middle-income people here? I got only polite, fumbling answers as people tried to figure out what the hell I was talking about.

When I rephrased the question in more-general terms, as Do you believe the country is divided between the haves and the have-nots?, everyone responded decisively: yes. But as the conversation continued, it became clear that the people saying yes did not consider themselves to be among the have-nots. Even people with incomes well below the median thought of themselves as haves.

What I found was entirely consistent with the election returns from November of last year [2000]. Gore's pitch failed miserably among the voters it was intended to target: nationally he lost among non-college-educated white voters by 17 points and among non-college-educated white men by 29 points. But it worked beautifully on the affluent, educated class: for example, Gore won among women with graduate degrees by 22 points. The lesson seems to be that if you run a campaign under the slogan "The People Versus the Powerful," you will not do well in the places where "the people" live, but you will do fantastically well in the places where "the powerful" live. This phenomenon mirrors, on a larger scale, one I noted a couple of years ago, when I traveled the country for a year talking about *Bobos in Paradise,* a book I had written on upscale America. The richer the community, the more likely I was to be asked about wage inequality. In middle-class communities the subject almost never came up.

Hanging around Franklin County, one begins to understand some of the reasons that people there don't spend much time worrying about economic class lines. The first and most obvious one is that although the incomes in Franklin County are lower than those in Montgomery County, living expenses are also lower—very much so. . . .

The biggest difference is in real-estate prices. In Franklin County one can buy a nice four-bedroom split-level house with about 2,200 square feet of living space for $150,000 to $180,000. In Bethesda that same house would cost about $450,000. . . .

Some of the people I met in Franklin County were just getting by. Some were in debt and couldn't afford to buy their kids the Christmas presents they wanted to. But I didn't find many who assessed their own place in society according to their income. Rather, the people I met commonly told me that although those in affluent places like Manhattan and Bethesda might make more money and have more-exciting jobs, they are the unlucky ones, because they don't get to live in Franklin County. They don't get to enjoy the beautiful green hillsides, the friendly people, the wonderful church groups and volunteer organizations. They may be nice people and all, but they are certainly not as happy as we are.

Another thing I found is that most people don't think sociologically. They don't compare themselves with faraway millionaires who appear on their TV screens. They compare themselves with their neighbors. . . . One man in Mercersburg, Pennsylvania, told me about a friend who had recently bought a car. "He paid twenty-five thousand dollars for that car!" he exclaimed, his eyes wide with amazement. "He got it fully loaded." I didn't tell him that in Bethesda almost no one but a college kid pays as little as $25,000 for a car.

Franklin County is a world in which there is little obvious inequality, and the standard of living is reasonably comfortable. Youth-soccer teams are able to raise money for a summer trip to England; the Lowe's hardware superstore carries Laura Ashley carpets; many people have pools, although they are almost always above ground; the planning commission has to cope with an increasing number of cars in the county every year, even though the population is growing only gradually. But the sort of high-end experiences that are everywhere in Montgomery County are entirely missing here. . . .

No wonder people in Franklin County have no class resentment or class consciousness; where they live, they can afford just about anything that is for sale. (In Montgomery County, however—and this is one of the most striking contrasts between the two counties—almost nobody can say that. In Blue America, unless you are very, very rich, there is always, all around you, stuff for sale that you cannot afford.) And if they sought to improve their situation, they would look only to themselves. If a person wants to make more money, the feeling goes, he or she had better work hard and think like an entrepreneur. . . .

People do work extremely hard in Franklin County—even people in supposedly dead-end jobs. You can see it in little things, such as drugstore shelves. The drugstores in Bethesda look the way Rome must have looked after a visit from the Visigoths. But in Franklin County the boxes are in perfect little rows. Shelves are fully stocked, and cans are evenly spaced. The floors are less dusty than those in a microchip-processing plant. The nail clippers on a rack by the cash register are arranged with a precision that would put the Swiss to shame.

There are few unions in Franklin County. People abhor the thought of depending on welfare; they consider themselves masters of their own economic fate. . . .

In sum, I found absolutely no evidence that a Stanley Greenberg–prompted Democratic Party (or a Pat Buchanan–led Republican Party) could mobilize white middle-class Americans on the bias of class consciousness. I found no evidence that economic differences explain much of anything about the divide between Red and Blue America. . . .

Pew has conducted a broad survey of the differences between Red and Blue states. The survey found that views on economic issues do not explain the different voting habits in the two regions. There simply isn't much of the sort of economic dissatisfaction that could drive a class-based political movement. Eighty-five percent of Americans with an annual household income between $30,000 and $50,000 are satisfied with their housing. Nearly 70 percent are satisfied with the kind of car they can afford. Roughly two thirds are satisfied with their furniture and their ability to afford a night out. These levels of satisfaction are not very different from those found in upper-middle-class America.

The Pew researchers found this sort of trend in question after question. Part of the draft of their report is titled "Economic Divide Dissolves."

A Lot of Religion but Few Crusaders

This leaves us with the second major hypothesis about the nature of the divide between Red and Blue America, which comes mainly from conservatives: America is divided between two moral systems. Red America is traditional, religious, self-disciplined, and patriotic. Blue America is modern, secular, self-expressive, and discomfited by blatant displays of patriotism. Proponents of this hypothesis in its most radical form contend that America is in the midst of a culture war, with two opposing armies fighting on behalf of their views. . . .

The values-divide school has a fair bit of statistical evidence on its side. Whereas income is a poor predictor of voting patterns, church attendance . . . is a pretty good one. Of those who attend religious services weekly (42 percent of the electorate), 59 percent voted for Bush, 39 percent for Gore. Of those who seldom or never attend religious services (another 42 percent), 56 percent voted for Gore, 39 percent for Bush.

The Pew data reveal significant divides on at least a few values issues. Take, for example, the statement "We will all be called before God on Judgment Day to answer for our sins." In Red states 70 percent of the people believe that statement. In Blue states only 50 percent do. . . .

Chambersburg and its vicinity have eighty-five churches and one synagogue. The Bethesda–Chevy Chase area, which has a vastly greater population, has forty-five churches and five synagogues. Professors at the local college in Chambersburg have learned not to schedule public lectures on Wednesday nights, because everybody is at prayer meetings. . . .

Life is complicated, however. Yes, there are a lot of churches in Franklin County; there are also a lot of tattoo parlors. And despite all the churches and bumper stickers, Franklin County doesn't seem much different from anywhere else. People go to a few local bars to hang out after softball games. Teenagers drive recklessly along fast-food strips. Young women in halter tops sometimes prowl in the pool halls. The local college has a gay-and-lesbian group. One conservative clergyman I spoke with estimated that 10 percent of his congregants are gay. He believes that church is the place where one should be able to leave the controversy surrounding this sort of issue behind. Another described how his congregation united behind a young man who was dying of AIDS. . . .

Franklin County is probably a bit more wholesome than most suburbs in Blue America. (The notion that deviance and corruption lie underneath the seeming conformism of suburban middle-class life, popular in Hollywood and in creative-writing workshops, is largely nonsense.) But it has most of the problems that afflict other parts of the country: heroin addiction, teen pregnancy, and so on. Nobody I spoke to felt part of a pristine culture that is exempt from the problems of the big cities. . . .

If the problems are the same as in the rest of America, so are many of the solutions. Franklin County residents who find themselves in trouble go to their clergy first, but they are often referred to psychologists and therapists as part of their recovery process. Prozac is a part of life.

Almost nobody I spoke with understood, let alone embraced, the concept of a culture war. Few could see themselves as fighting such a war, in part because few have any idea where the boundary between the two sides lies. People in Franklin County may have a clear sense of what constitutes good or evil (many people in Blue America have trouble with the very concept of evil), but they will say that good and evil are in all neighborhoods, as they are in all of us. People take the Scriptures seriously but have no interest in imposing them on others. One finds little crusader zeal in Franklin County. For one thing, people in small towns don't want to offend people whom they'll be encountering on the street for the next fifty years. Potentially controversial subjects are often played down. . . .

Certainly Red and Blue America disagree strongly on some issues, such as homosexuality and abortion. But for the most part the disagreements are not large. For example, the Pew researchers asked Americans to respond to the statement "There are clear guidelines about what's good or evil that apply to everyone regardless of their situation." Forty-three percent of people in Blue states and 49 percent of people in Red states agreed. Forty-seven percent of Blue America and 55 percent of Red America agreed with the statement "I have old-fashioned values about family and marriage." Seventy percent of the people in Blue states and 77 percent of the people in Red states agreed that "too many children are being raised in day-care centers these days." These are small gaps. And, the Pew researchers found, there is no culture gap at all among suburban voters. In a Red state like Arizona suburban voters' opinions are not much different from those in a Blue state like Connecticut. The starkest differences that exist are between people in cities and people in rural areas, especially rural areas in the South.

The conservatism I found in Franklin County is not an ideological or a reactionary conservatism. It is a temperamental conservatism. People place tremendous value on being agreeable, civil, and kind. They are happy to sit quietly with one another. They are hesitant to stir one another's passions. They appreciate what they have. They value continuity and revere the past. They work hard to reinforce community bonds. Their newspapers are filled with items about fundraising drives, car washes, bake sales, penny-collection efforts, and auxiliary thrift shops. Their streets are lined with lodges: VFW, Rotarians, Elks, Moose. Luncheons go on everywhere. Retired federal employees will be holding their weekly luncheon at one restaurant, Harley riders at another. . . .

These are the sorts of things that really mobilize people in Franklin County. Building community and preserving local ways are far more important to them than any culture war.

The Ego Curtain

The best explanation of the differences between people in Montgomery and Franklin Counties has to do with sensibility, not class or culture. If I had to describe the differences between the two sensibilities in a single phrase, it would be conception of the self. In Red America the self is small. People declare in a million ways, "I am normal. Nobody is better, nobody is worse. I am humble before God." In Blue America the self is more commonly large. People say in a million ways, "I am special. I have carved out my own unique way of life. I am independent. I make up my own mind."

In Red America there is very little one-upmanship. Nobody tries to be avant-garde in choosing a wardrobe. The chocolate-brown suits and baggy denim dresses hanging in local department stores aren't there by accident; people conspicuously want to be seen as not trying to dress to impress.

For a person in Blue America the blandness in Red America can be a little oppressive. But it's hard not to be struck by the enormous social pressure not to put on airs. If a Franklin County resident drove up to church one day in a shiny new Lexus, he would face huge waves of disapproval. If one hired a nanny, people would wonder who died and made her queen. . . .

I sometimes think that Franklin County takes its unpretentiousness a little too far. I wouldn't care to live there, because I'd find it too unchanging. I prefer the subtle and not-so-subtle status climbing on my side of the Ego Curtain—it's more entertaining. Still, I can't help respecting the genuine modesty of Franklin County people. It shows up strikingly in data collected by Mediamark Research. In survey after survey, residents of conservative Red America come across as humbler than residents of liberal Blue America. About half of those who describe themselves as "very conservative" agree with the statement "I have more ability than most people," but nearly two thirds of those who describe themselves as "very liberal" agree. Only 53 percent of conservatives agree with the statement "I consider myself an intellectual," but 75 percent of liberals do. Only 23 percent of conservatives agree with the statement "I must admit that I like to show off," whereas 43 percent of liberals do. . . .

[Thus far, I have been concerned with the divisions between Red and Blue America, crystallized in Franklin and Montgomery counties.] Yet there is another trend at work as well. That is the rise of Sprinkler Cities. Sprinkler Cities are the fast growing suburbs, mostly in the South and West that are the homes of the new style American Dream. They stand at the peripheries of older suburbs, at the borders between rural and urban America. Douglas County, Colorado, which is the fastest growing county in America between Denver and Colorado Springs, is a Sprinkler City. So is Henderson, Nevada, just outside of Las Vegas. So is Loudoun County, Virginia, near Dulles Airport. So are Scottsdale, Arizona, and Union County, North Carolina.

The growth of these places is astronomical, as middle-class families, and retirees—yuppie geezers who still like to grill, swim, and water ski—flock to them from all over. People move to Sprinkler Cities from places like Montgomery County for the same reasons people came to America or headed out west. They want to leave behind the dirt and toxins of their former existence—the crowding and inconvenience, the precedents, and the oldness of what suddenly seems to them a settled and unpromising world. They want to move to some place that seems fresh and new and filled with possibility. Sprinkler city immigrants are not leaving cities to head out to suburbia. They are leaving older suburbs—which have come to seem as crowded, expensive, and stratified as cities—and heading for newer suburbs, for the suburbia of suburbia.

Say you grew up in some southern California suburb in the 1970s. You're making $65,000 a year, far more than you ever thought you would, but back in Orange County you find you can't afford to live anywhere. You paid $356,000 for a 1962 four-bedroom split-level with a drab kitchen, low ceilings, and walls that are chipped and peeling.

And then you visit a Sprinkler City in Arizona, Nevada, or Colorado— far from the coast and deep into exurbia—and what do you see? Bounteous roads! Free traffic lanes! And those real estate prices! In, say, Henderson,

Nevada, you could get a home that's brand new, twice the size of your old one, and three times as beautiful for $299,000.

Plus, if you moved to a Sprinkler City there would be liberation of a subtler kind. The old suburbs have become socially urbanized. They've become stratified. Two sorts of people have begun to move in and ruin the middle-class equality you grew up in: the rich and poor. First there are the poor immigrants from Mexico, Vietnam, and the Philippines. They come in, a dozen to a house, and they introduce an element of unpredictability to what was a comforting milieu. They shout. They're less tidy. Suddenly you feel you will lose control of your children, and begin to feel a new level of anxiety in the neighborhood.

And then there are the rich. Suddenly many of the old ramblers are being knocked down by lawyers who erect 4,000-square-foot, arts-and-crafts bungalows with two-car garages for their Volvos. And these new people, while successful and upstanding, are also . . . snobs. They went to fancy colleges and they consider themselves superior to you if you sell home-security systems or if you are a mechanical engineer.

I recently interviewed a woman in Loudoun County who said she had grown up and lived most of her life in Bethesda, Maryland, in Montgomery County. When I asked why she left Bethesda, she hissed, "I hate it there now." And as we spoke, it became clear that it was precisely the "improvements" she hated: the new movie theater that shows only foreign films, the explosion of French, Turkish, and new wave restaurants.

Sprinkler Cities are generally the most Republican areas of the country. In some of the Sprinkler City congressional districts, Republicans have a 2 or 3 or 4 to 1 registration advantage over the Democrats. As cultural centers, they represent the beau ideal of Republican selfhood, and are becoming the new base—the brains, heart, guts, and soul—of the emerging Republican Party. Their values are not the same as those found in either old-line suburbs like Greenwich, Connecticut, where a certain sort of Republican used to dominate, or traditional conservative bastions, such as the old South This isn't even the more modest conservatism found in the Midwestern farm belt. In fact, the rising prominence of these places heralds a new style of suburb v. suburb politics, with the explosively growing Republican outer suburbs vying the slower-growing and increasingly Democratic inner suburbs for control of the center of American political gravity.

A Cafeteria Nation

These differences in sensibility don't in themselves mean that America has become a fundamentally divided nation. As the sociologist Seymour Martin Lipset pointed out in *The First New Nation* (1963), achievement and equality are the two rival themes running throughout American history. Most people, most places, and most epochs have tried to intertwine them in some way.

Moreover, after bouncing between Montgomery and Franklin Counties, I became convinced that a lot of our fear that America is split into rival camps arises from mistaken notions of how society is shaped. Some of us still carry the old Marxist categories in our heads. We think that society is like a layer cake, with the upper class on top. And, like Marx, we tend to assume that wherever there is class division there is conflict. Or else we have a sort of *Crossfire* model in our heads: where would people we meet sit if they were guests on that show?

But traveling back and forth between the two counties was not like crossing from one rival camp to another. It was like crossing a high school cafeteria. Remember high school? There were nerds, jocks, punks, bikers, techies, druggies, God Squadders, drama geeks, poets, and Dungeons & Dragons weirdoes. All these cliques were part of the same school: they had different sensibilities; sometimes they knew very little about the people in the other cliques; but the jocks knew there would always be nerds, and the nerds knew there would always be jocks. That's just the way life is.

And that's the way America is. We are not a divided nation. We are a cafeteria nation. We form cliques (call them communities, or market segments, or whatever), and when they get too big, we form subcliques. Some people even get together in churches that are "nondenominational" or in political groups that are "independent." These are cliques built around the supposed rejection of cliques.

We live our lives by migrating through the many different cliques associated with the activities we enjoy and the goals we have set for ourselves. Our freedom comes in the interstices; we can choose which set of standards to live by, and when.

We should remember that there is generally some distance between cliques—a buffer zone that separates one set of aspirations from another. People who are happy within their cliques feel no great compulsion to go out and reform other cliques. The jocks don't try to change the nerds. . . .

What unites the two Americas, then, is our mutual commitment to this way of life—to the idea that a person is not bound by his class, or by the religion of his fathers, but is free to build a plurality of connections for himself. . . .

Never has this been more apparent than in the weeks following the September 11 attacks. . . .

. . . If I had to boil down all the conversations I have had in Franklin and Montgomery Counties since September 11, the essence would be this: A horrible thing happened. We're going to deal with it. We're going to restore order. We got through Pearl Harbor. We're going to get through this. . . .

If the September 11 attacks rallied people in both Red and Blue America, they also neutralized the political and cultural leaders who tend to exploit the differences between the two. Americans are in no mood for a class struggle or a culture war. The aftermath of the attacks has been a bit like a national Sabbath, taking us out of our usual pleasures and distractions and reminding us what is really important. Over time the shock will dissipate. But in important ways the psychological effects will linger, just as the effects of John F.

Kennedy's assassination have lingered. The early evidence still holds: although there are some real differences between Red and Blue America, there is no fundamental conflict. There may be cracks, but there is no chasm. Rather, there is a common love for this nation—one nation in the end.

The Clinton Formula

MICHAEL TOMASKY

MICHAEL TOMASKY:—I'd like to begin by talking about the historical moment. Karl Rove[1] wants to create a realignment along the lines of that which coalesced around the New Deal. This realignment would undo a lot of the work of the last 60 years, including, of course, a lot of your work. Do you think we're at such a turning point?

BILL CLINTON:—I do think it's a very important moment. Essentially, Karl Rove's politics are a combination of efforts by the increasingly conservative Republican Party to recover from the '64 election and assume a dominant position in America—through the advocacy of ideas and policies that were designed to have more appeal to the middle class, through the use of socially conservative issues that were designed to get people to vote for them for reasons other than economic ones, and through the extraordinary ability to increase their dominance in the mainstream press [and to] have a competing right-wing press and label Democrats . . . almost turn them into cartoons in a way that got them votes from people who otherwise never would have voted for them. And that's basically been their strategy.

So they believe those things, coupled with their extraordinary ability to raise money from the people they're helping financially with the government, will enable them to pursue policies which are way to the right of where the American people are.

I don't think we're headed for a realignment. If anything, we should be realigning in the direction I took the country. When I left office we had a 65 percent job approval, or something like that, so two-thirds of the people favored my policies. And that's why they attacked me personally so much, why they tried to attack Al Gore and make him look dishonest. And to say that compared to President Bush, and their backgrounds in public life, that Gore was dishonest was ludicrous. But they got away with it.

---

1. Karl Rove is President George W. Bush's senior political adviser.

And if you look at these tax cuts, they got a good return for their investment. I mean, people say, "Gosh, how did Bush raise $200 million, $300 million?" I say it's peanuts compared to the tax cuts he gave. It's not even a tithe, you know? Not even 1 percent!

MT:—They continue to get away with it. . . .

BC:—Well, they do, but I think that we as a country, including the press and the political opposition, were profoundly traumatized by what happened on [September 11], and we were angered and we wanted to be united. And we were collectively prepared to check our critical judgment in a deep freeze somewhere for a period of time.

And in that period, they actually had a chance to effect their realignment. But instead, they chose to use the moment to try to consolidate their power, to extend the secrecy of government and to move the country way, way to the right. And there was a slow but building reaction to it. . . . And no democracy can go without debate for very long. So it was inevitable that one by one, the American people would go back to the deep freeze and get their brains back and start thinking, and that's basically what's happening now.

MT:—But the Democrats participated in this lack of debate for far too long.

BC:—I think that the only place where we really were derelict was in not being tougher in the last six, eight weeks of the [midterm] election cycle. Because that's the only time it could have been made manifest to the voters what [the Republicans] were doing. I mean, the idea that they could be against the homeland-security bill for seven, eight months and then decide that . . . I can just hear Rove now; I mean, it's impressive. Going in there and saying, "You know, we can't make any security votes against the Democrats. One-hundred percent of them are with us in Afghanistan, and two-thirds of them are with us in Iraq. We've got to have some issue, so let's be for this bill we've been against. And let's put a poison pill or two in there that'll give the Democrats some pause, and hope it doesn't get passed by election day, and call everybody a virtual traitor that's not for a bill that we weren't for either until yesterday. Let's just do that. See if we can make *that* work!"

MT:—And they did, and part of the reason that they did is that the Democrats didn't do what you're saying. Why not?

BC:—I just think a lot of people were just unsure how to proceed after 9-11, and they were somewhat intimidated by the president's big poll numbers. But we always do that in a wartime when we feel threatened. But you know, Max Cleland,[2] the idea that his patriotism could be questioned after he left three limbs in Vietnam, and questioned by a man who had a deferment like

---

2. Max Cleland, a severely wounded Vietnam veteran, was elected to the U.S. Senate from Georgia in 1996. He was defeated for reelection in 2002, with his Republican opponent attacking his patriotism.

I did . . . you know, it's just unbelievable to me. [Then] the Bush people took a compromise on the public-employee issue as soon as the election was over. It was just a scam. One of the great scams of modern American history, the way they did that homeland-security bill.

But we shouldn't whine about that. Their job is to beat us. Our job is to beat them. If they come at us with a deal we think is a scam, we ought to be smart enough to expose it. So I'm not mad at them. That's their job.

MT:—Let me ask you about the schism within the Democratic Party. The liberals and the centrists, when you talk with them, express a lot of contempt for each other. At times, the rhetorical tone has crossed the line from reasoned argument to mockery. And this has happened more from the centrists toward the liberals than the other way around—

BC:—Yeah, and I think it's a big mistake. And I'd like to say why.

First of all, I think the differences in most cases are overrated. And I'd like to give some examples. When I was president and we did welfare reform, I vetoed the first two bills because they eliminated the guarantee of nutrition, food stamps and health care to poor children. I signed the third bill even though it had restrictions I didn't like on immigrants because I thought that this was a historic opportunity to get a bill that emphasized work over welfare and dependence without hurting poor kids. Now, when I did that we had over two-thirds of the House members and about three-quarters of the Senate voting for it. So we were sort of together.

If you listen to the debate now among the presidential candidates, to take another issue, on fiscal responsibility, there isn't that much difference between the liberals and the conservatives. I reached a judgment that with the baby boomers retiring in a few years, we couldn't keep running these huge deficits and raiding Social Security, and middle-class people were better off having low interest rates in a growing economy. And that would create more revenues, which we could then spend on poor people. And that's exactly what happened. So we developed a consensus around fiscal responsibility.

I make these two points, just to use welfare reform and fiscal responsibility, to point out that I think it is very easy to overstate the differences.

Now: If there are differences, there's a better way to get them out than having our candidates dump on each other. I have no objection in this [2004] primary season [to] Candidate X saying, "I'm for that," and Candidate Y saying, "I'm against it." You've got to have a little of that. But I don't believe that either side should be saying, "I'm a real Democrat and the other one's not," or, "I'm a winning Democrat and the other one's not."

It oversimplifies the issue. The public is operationally progressive and rhetorically conservative. The more they believe that you're careful with tax money and responsible in the way you run the programs and require responsibility from citizens, the more the public in general is willing to be liberal in the expenditure of tax money. The more the public believes the Democrats can be trusted with the national security of America, to protect and defend the country against terror and weapons of mass destruction, the more free they are emotionally to think about the other issues.

Therefore I think it is highly counterproductive to spend a great deal of time trying to identify the wings of the party and [having] each wing criticize the other. I think it's fine to explore specific differences among the candidates. We can't win if people think we're too liberal. But we can't get our own folks out if people think we have no convictions. So the trick is to get them both.

I thought in the [Democratic primary] debate, to be fair to our crowd, they were much better about avoiding these kind of ad hominem attacks, which I think are dead-bang losers.

MT:—How do you get both? You, in 1992, given where the Democratic Party had been, made certain steps in the direction of showing you were willing to reject some old nostrums. But is that as necessary a politics today as it was in 1992?
BC:—No, I think it has to be done differently today.

MT:—How?
BC:—Well, first of all I think the Democrats ought to all pocket some of the gains I made. They ought to say, "We're the party that gave you responsible welfare reform. We're the party that gave you fiscal responsibility, low interest rates and high growth. And we're the party that gave you the weapons systems and the training programs that won in Iraq and Afghanistan." The question is, what do we do now?

[The Republicans'] argument to their base is gonna be, "We kept our promises. We promised to cut taxes as much on wealthy people as we could, and we did it. We promised to weaken environmental controls, and we did it. We promised to weaken labor regulations and put less money into workers' safety and more money into investigating unions. We promised to put right-wingers on the court, and we've done it every chance we got. We promised to get rid of Saddam Hussein, and we did it, and we promised to undo everything Bill Clinton did, and we did a lot of that." So that's their promises to their base.

The only promises they have broken so far are promises to swing voters. So [Bush is] gonna say, "I kept my promises to my base. How am I gonna get the others? The same way I got them in 2002. By convincing people the Democrats can't be trusted with national security."

So what we have to say is, "You can trust us with the national security. If America has to fight, we ain't gonna lose, because we've got the only military in the world. And they won in Afghanistan and Iraq with the training programs and the weapons systems developed during the Clinton years. So what you need a good president for is not to win a war. It's for when you don't fight, for a good diplomacy and a good domestic policy. And we don't agree with the diplomacy or the domestic policy."

But to go back to '92, I don't think we have to do as much conscious adding to the base in the way I did it. I was never against wealth and business creation. My theory was that class warfare wouldn't take us very far, but that if we were growing jobs and growing the economy, the government then should make extra efforts to help the poor. And we did a lot of that.

Now what we should say is that they, not we, have brought class warfare back to America. You know, every time I complain about these tax cuts some conservative says I'm practicing class warfare. I am not. I pay these taxes. And I live in New York state and Westchester County, so I think I probably pay as high [of] rates as anybody in America. And I should. Nobody makes me live in this country. America has been good to me. And I think for somebody to give me a tax cut and then turn around and say, "We've gotta have $87 billion spent in Iraq, but we're gonna kick 300,000 kids out of after-school programs, 84,000 kids out of student loans . . . 25,000 uniformed police *off the street?* We're gonna kick a coupla thousand police off the street in New York City who put their lives on the line on September the 11th, and they're gonna give me a tax cut?" That's class warfare! And I think we ought to say that!

And the other thing I think is, we can smile when we say that. I don't want our side ever to treat the Republicans with the sort of personal animosity and contempt with which Hillary and I and Al were treated. I don't like that, I don't believe that, I don't think that's necessary. But we *got* to argue. And we got to fight hard. Otherwise they'll run right over us like they did in 2002.

MT:—How vulnerable is this administration? What are the main targets of opportunity?
BC:—Well, I think the economy is a target of opportunity. I think the fact that most of the world doesn't trust us anymore is a target of opportunity. I think the assault on the environment is a target of opportunity. I think giving me a tax cut and then [trying to take] overtime away from 8 million workers is a target of opportunity. . . . We're gonna spend $87 billion in Iraq. We're gonna give the 400 wealthiest Americans an average tax cut of $8-and-a-half million. $8-and-a-half million! And that's just a start. And they tried to get rid of the children's health-insurance program. That's 5 million kids' health insurance.

Man, if we can't sell that, we ought to get in another line of work! Either that or I don't live in the country I think I live in.

MT:—Is part of the problem that when Bush says, "It's your money, you deserve it back," that that's so emotionally compelling—
BC:—It is.

MT:—What is a good emotional counterargument to that? I believe that Democrats should be willing to make a more direct case for government than they make.

BC:—Oh, I do, too. I think we should say, "It *is* your money. And the government should only take your money to do those things which you need done collectively, which we have to do as a community—"

MT:—Which neither the private sector nor the states—

BC:—Yes, which the private sector won't do in the economy, and which charity can't do. And those things are plainly national security, basic infrastructure, law enforcement, environmental protection, education and health care for the elderly, for poor children, the disabled and others for whom it is inaccessible. Just to start there. And we have a government, and we raise taxes because we think that we rise or fall together, and we want to live in a country where everybody has a chance to live their dreams.

And so, to say that it's your money does not answer any question. That's a demagogic statement that every Democrat could say as well as every Republican. Of *course* it's their money! It's all their money. But the question is, who's doing what with the money? They made a decision to give me a tax cut with the money and kick 300,000 kids out of after-school programs. I haven't met a single person in my income group, Republican or Democrat, who believes that we should get the check and the kids should get the boot. Not one! And I ask a bunch of them. So I think we ought to say, "It's your money, and it's your *country*. What kind of country do you want?"

I also think we ought to say, "It's not like they're not spendin' money! They're creating a big lie here. They're spending the money and giving you a tax cut and printing money to pay the bills." And let me just say, I didn't object to the president's running deficits after 9-11. He didn't make those conditions. But they did decide how to respond to them. And to give a big tax cut in 2001 before we knew what our income, expense or emergency [costs] were gonna be was not responsible. Except to those who believe it was ideologically dictated. So in 2003 we come back, and usually when you find yourself in a hole you're supposed to quit digging, but people who are ideologically inclined will only ask for a bigger shovel. So the 2003 tax cut was the bigger shovel.

MT:—One of the problems liberals have had is they haven't found a compelling way to deliver their message. I've been reading lately some scholars who talk about conservatism and liberalism not only as ideologies but as psychological belief systems.

BC:—Yeah, I read some of that.

MT:—It says basically [that] conservatives believe in authority, they do see things in black and white, and that makes it easier for them to get their message out—it's stark, it's more reducible to the five-second sound bite. Liberals tend to see more nuance, tend to be more skeptical of authority, and it makes it harder, especially in this media climate, to get the message out.

BC:—I think that's right. And I think the psychological setting after 9-11 helped them. Because we all wanted to see things in black and white for a while. A grievous thing had been done to us, and we wanted to stand united against it.

But we think there are some things that are not open to debate. One is the historic mission of America, to form a more perfect union. What does that mean? It means widening the circle of opportunity, deepening the meaning of freedom and strengthening the bonds of community. And we feel passionately about that. We feel just as strongly as the Republicans do.

And we are not gonna demonize them the way they demonize us. We will never have the talk-show people saying things about them without regard to whether they're true or not. That's not who we are. But we do show up to fight. We think you're worth fighting for. We think your future's worth fighting for. And we need to use the rhetoric of passion, commitment and combat on behalf of ordinary people without ever slipping into the kind of vicious, personal, evidence-free—to use my wife's phrase—assaults that they're so good at.

We don't have to do that. And it doesn't really sell all that well with our crowd. But people have to believe that we wake up in the morning just as passionately committed to what we believe as they are. And in the process of conducting ourselves in that way, people get the sense intuitively that we're strong enough to defend the country.

This is a contact sport. They're supposed to try to beat us. Now, they do things by and large that we don't think are legitimate. And lord knows they did while I was president. But . . . nobody *gags* us! The press has moved way, way, way to the right. And the mainstream press was incredibly supine in the face of all this secrecy, you know, covering up the [Ronald] Reagan and [George] Bush [Senior] records, covering up the [Miguel] Estrada legal opinions, covering up the 9-11 report, covering up the global-warming deal and the air-quality issue down there [in lower Manhattan]. And it all started with putting the governor's records in the Bush presidential library. And [the press] just laid down and let it happen. But we don't have to contribute to it.

Now, let me just close on an upbeat note here I don't entirely buy the Ruy Teixeira [and John B. Judis][3] analysis about the natural Democratic majority. On the other hand, there is *something* to it.

[Lyndon] Johnson wins big in '64 cuz he marginalizes [Barry] Goldwater. They never got over it and they've been trying to do it to us ever since. By '68, Nixon wins by a point, but we all know he would have beaten [Hubert] Humphrey handily if [George] Wallace hadn't been in the race. So there was a traumatic coalescing of a culturally conservative majority in the Republican Party between '64 and '68, ratified by the '72 election, OK? So essentially

---

3. John Judis and Ruy Teixeira are the authors of *The Emerging Democratic Majority* (New York: Scribner, 2002).

from '68 forward the Republican Party had a hardcore base of roughly 45 percent. The Democrats had a hardcore base of roughly 40 percent.

So in '80, Reagan wins 51-to-41, and [John] Anderson gets, what, [6 percent], [7 percent], whatever he got? Then in '84, [Reagan] wins 6-to-4. And in '88, they win 54-to-46, which means they won 9 points of the undecided vote and we won 6 points. In '92, because of the campaign I ran, if no [Ross] Perot had been in there, all the analyses show that it would have been 52 [percent], 53 percent. In '96, if no Perot had been in there and we'd had a normal turnout, it would have been about 55 percent. [So] by 2000, sometime between '92 and 2000, because of immigration, urbanization and the suburbanite voters developing a more communitarian ethic, both parties had a base of about 45 percent. And what happened in 2000 is they were fighting over an effective 10 percent, and they fought to a draw.

So that means that we're in every race. You start with 45 percent, you're in a race. I don't care what anybody says. So sometime between 1992 and 2000, for the first time—probably in the last four years, for the first time since 1964—we were no longer at a cultural disadvantage in our base. So both parties go into this next election with a natural base of about 45 percent. So in 2004, this race will be about—it goes back to your question about the Democrats' dilemma and our division. We have to improve our turnout to their level, as we did in '98 and 2000 but not in 2002. And then we have to win the votes among the other 10 percent. That's eminently doable.

But we've got to fight. And we gotta look like we're havin' a good time doing it.

DISCUSSION QUESTIONS

1. How would Brooks comment on Clinton's contention that the Bush administration's tax cuts hardly benefit most voters—that, in fact, the top two hundred income earners each get $8 million in tax savings?

2. According to Brooks, what factors motivate middle-income earners to move to "Sprinkler City"? Why wouldn't low-cost housing and open space also be issues that could benefit Democratic candidates?

3. Clinton argues that "they [the GOP], not we [the Democrats], have brought class warfare back to America." Yet if Brooks is correct, voters in "Red" America just don't respond to class appeals. How important electorally has social class been in recent elections or in the appeals of candidates to voters?

4. Democrats are generally given high marks for their domestic policies favoring equality, while Republicans score high on issues of national security. How would both Brooks's and Clinton's arguments take into account this apparent disparity?

SUGGESTED READINGS
AND INTERNET RESOURCES

A now-classic work on the state of political participation in America is Sidney Verba, Kay Lehman Schlozman, and Henry Brady, *Voice and Equality* (Cambridge, Mass.: Harvard University Press, 1995). For the specifics about the 2000 election, see E. J. Dionne and William Kristol, eds., *Bush v. Gore: The Court Cases and the Commentary* (Washington, D.C.: Brookings Institution Press, 2001). A recent, less academic account of the parties and the electorate is Stanley Greenberg, *The Two Americas: Our Current Political Deadlock and How to Break It* (New York: Thomas Dunne Books, 2004). For a critical look at the Democrats, see Zell Miller, *A National Party No More: The Conscience of a Conservative Democrat* (Atlanta: Stroud and Hall, 2003).

Center for Voting and Democracy
www.fairvote.org
This is the site of a broad-based electoral reform group, with archives on new forms of representation, innovative and inclusive ballot proposals, and other measures to increase political participation.

Rock the Vote
www.rockthevote.org
This is the site of the leading organization trying to mobilize young people to vote.

Democracy Corps
www.democracycorps.com
This survey research site has massive amounts of data on the electorate. Democracy Corps was founded by James Carville and Stanley Greenberg, leading Democratic consultants and pollsters.

Project Vote Smart
www.vote-smart.org
Targeted at young voters, this site includes highly accessible information on political parties and candidates for public office.

Democratic Party
www.democrats.org

Republican Party
www.rnc.org

Green Party
www.greens.org

Reform Party
www.reformparty.org

11

Campaigns and Elections: Organized Money Versus (Dis)Organized People?

From the nineteenth century's camp meetings and torchlight parades to today's sound bites and attack ads, political campaigns are part of the American democratic landscape. Despite their hoopla and hype, electoral campaigns are serious business. Without them, voters wouldn't have a choice, couldn't get organized, and would judge their would-be rulers from a standpoint of ignorance and isolation.

Today, however, a chorus of critics complains about campaigns. Campaigns often seem to be personality contests that trivialize issues rather than engage the electorate. Supercharged accusations fly between candidates, without much sense of their truth value. The media often compound the problem through sensationalized coverage. Campaign professionals and spin doctors seem to orchestrate images and manipulate voters rather than respond to their deeper aspirations. Sensing that they're being used, many citizens become cynical spectators or withdraw from the electoral process entirely.

While there are few unqualified fans of modern campaigns, there are some defenders of the process. Most of the voters, most of the time, seem to learn something from campaigns, and when voters care enough to participate, the democratic debate seems to improve. The 1992 and 1994 electoral contests, some say, were more substantive because many voters demanded precision and substance from the candidates and the parties. Perhaps campaigns are no better or worse than the society from which they emerge.

Expensive campaigns are inevitable. Old-style, door-to-door campaigning just isn't possible in a country of 280 million people, whose attention is constantly distracted from politics by the burdens of work and family and the diversions of entertainment. Politicians and parties have to rely on costly and sophisticated advertising, focus groups, and public opinion polls because it is impossible to know every voter and because there is considerable competition for attention. In any case, perhaps campaigns are no worse than they used to be; competitive elections have always been messy affairs, and perhaps today's critics romanticize the past. And many say that the intense grassroots efforts of presidential contender Howard Dean in 2004 show that money *and* grassroots enthusiasm can mix.

Nonetheless, there are some notable developments in modern election campaigns that deserve extended scrutiny. Successful campaigns have always had ample amounts of cash, but today the new technology of politics—polls, advertising, and image-makers—requires money in amounts that seem to utterly exclude the unconnected or the unrich. Today, political campaigns may be monopolized by interests and candidates concerned less with addressing the needs of voters than those of the privileged, that slender slice of American society that contributes the cash that makes campaigns effective.

Raising money has almost always mattered in modern U.S. electoral campaigns, but elections since the 1980s witnessed a quantum leap in expenditures. In 2000, the total cost of federal elections soared to $3 billion. The presidential contest's price was $250 million, while winning House candidates spent an average of $900,000 apiece—double the 1992 amount. To get around federal caps on contributions to individual candidates, the major political parties have pioneered new ways to collect and disperse funds. The parties spent over $480 million in so-called soft money in 2000, and interest groups spent an estimated (and undisclosed) $300 million in so-called issue advocacy efforts.

The vast bulk of the growing cash pile is donated by very affluent individuals, corporations, and trade associations organized into political action committees. This phenomenon has sparked an intense movement for reform, spurred in part by Arizona senator John McCain, a Republican, and leading House and Senate Democrats.

After six years of procedural maneuvering and delay in early 2002, both houses of Congress passed, and President Bush reluctantly signed, a major revision of campaign finance laws. The new law banned soft money contributions, raised the allowable limits for individual contributions to candidates, and called for a ban on political ads sponsored by interest groups. Campaign finance reformers relished this long-sought victory. Yet many labeled the "McCain-Feingold" bill only a modest first step toward a more extensive reform. In the wake of campaign finance reform, many loopholes appeared. So-called "527 organizations," independent of candidates and parties, collected unrestricted amounts of cash in the 2004 election.

Is the cost of money-driven campaigns too high? Or is the right to contribute money to candidates an expression of a lively democracy? Answers to these questions provide judgment about the state of American democracy itself. For people who believe in popular democracy, today's campaigns have to be judged by how well or poorly they promote talk and participation by ordinary voters. While money, advertising, polling, and professional marketing may never disappear from contemporary campaigns, do these drown out democratic activity by volunteers and organizations that have little money to give? Popular democrats look to a historical standard by which to judge modern campaigns. Which is more important: organized money or organized people? Do modern campaigns mean that only candidates who are wealthy or backed by wealthy people can succeed? And does money undermine the egalitarian spirit of one citizen, one vote, which is supposed to be the basis of democracy itself?

For elite democrats, money's corrupting role is far from clear. Money is said to promote effective free speech, for to be heard requires resources and organization. Reformers, in their zeal to create a wall between money and politics, don't understand why generations of reformers have been ineffective; no matter what the laws intend, organized money in a free society will always find a way to be heard. The best that we can hope for in a free society is that the sources of money be made known to the electorate. Existing laws passed in the 1970s could be beefed up to further disclosure, and there are already ample laws on the books to limit the size of contributions to individual candidates. Anything more than that, elite democrats say, would be a violation of the democratic norm of free speech and would backfire on democracy itself.

The two essays reprinted here both articulate and expand on these arguments. Bradley Smith, an Ohio law professor and a GOP appointee to the Federal Election Commission, provides a persuasive case against further efforts to regulate campaign contributions. He finds little evidence to support the charges of people who believe that campaign donations corrupt the political process and much evidence that limits on campaign spending would prevent full debate and discussion of contentious political issues. Sociologists Dan Clawson, Alan Neustadtl, and Mark Weller respond with a careful study of what corporate contributors expect from politicians as they hand out the cash. These authors argue that business campaign contributions "subvert democracy" for numerous reasons, and they propose a system of public financing of campaigns to level the playing field. Such systems are already working in three states—Arizona, Vermont, and Maine.

While reading these essays, you might think about the following questions: How would the "Dollars and Votes" authors respond to Smith's charge that regulating campaign money never works? How would Smith deal with the problem of the amount of time politicians must devote to fund-raising? All the authors rely on a historical standard of democracy to defend their claims. What do the authors of each essay mean by the term?

Free Speech Requires Campaign Money

BRADLEY A. SMITH*

I n 1974, Congress passed amendments to the Federal Elections Campaign Act that, for the first time in our nation's history, seriously undertook to regulate political campaigns. Most states followed suit, and virtually overnight, politics became a heavily regulated industry.

Yet we now see, on videotape and in White House photos, shots of the President of the United States meeting with arms merchants and drug dealers; we learn of money being laundered through Buddhist nuns and Indonesian gardeners; we read that acquaintances of the President are fleeing the country, or threatening to assert Fifth Amendment privileges to avoid testifying before Congress.[1] Regulation, we were told two decades ago, would free our elected officials from the clutches of money, but they now seem to devote more time than ever before to pursuing campaign cash. The 1974 reforms, we were promised, would open up political competition, yet the purely financial advantage enjoyed by incumbents in congressional races has increased almost threefold. Regulation was supposed to restore confidence in government, yet the percentage of Americans who trust their government to "do what is right most of the time" is half what it was before the 1974 act, and campaigns themselves seem nastier and less informative.

Well, say apologists for the law, if we have failed, it is only because our labors have just begun. If our goals seem further away, we must redouble our efforts. We must ban political action committees (PAC's). We must prevent "bundling," a procedure whereby a group collects contributions from its members and delivers them all at once to a candidate's election committee. We must ban large contributions to political parties ("soft money"). . . .

If existing regulation has failed so spectacularly, and existing laws are being broken seemingly at will, is more regulation the solution? Before we rush off on another round, it may be worthwhile to examine the premises on which the impulse to regulate campaign finance is based. Each of them is severely flawed. . . .

---

* Smith is now the GOP-appointed chair of the Federal Election Commission, the agency charged with enforcement of campaign finance laws.

1. Smith is writing about allegations regarding the Clinton White House's fund-raising practices during the 1996 election.

II

The first assumption underlying proposals for campaign-finance regulation is that too much money is being spent on political campaigning. The amounts are often described in near-apocalyptic terms. Candidates, we are informed, amass "huge war chests" from "fat cats" who "pour their millions" into campaigns and "stuff the pockets" of representatives in an "orgy" of contributions. Expenditures "skyrocket," leaving legislators "awash" in "obscene" amounts of cash.

Hyperbole aside, however, the amount spent each year on all political activity in the United States, from every ballot referendum to races for every office from dog catcher to President, is less than the amount spent on potato chips. Total spending on congressional races in 1995–96 was less than what is spent annually on Barbie dolls. Total PAC contributions in federal elections in 1995–96 were just about equal to the amount needed to produce the most recent *Batman* movie.

On a per-voter basis, our expenditures are equally low: less than $2.50 per eligible voter per year, or about the cost of a single video rental, for all congressional races, including all primaries. . . .

Perhaps more relevant than any of these comparisons are the amounts spent on political campaigning versus other types of advertising. In 1996, the Home Depot corporation alone spent more on advertising than federal law allowed Bill Clinton, Bob Dole, and Ross Perot put together to spend on the general election. Although Michael Huffington was roundly criticized for "exorbitant" spending in his 1994 race for a Senate seat from California, it cost him less than what Sony International spent in the same year to promote a single compact disc by Michael Jackson. . . .

The plain truth is that it costs money to communicate, and there is no reason to expect that political communication should come free. This is the crucial insight of the Supreme Court's 1976 decision in *Buckley* v. *Valeo,* a case issuing from a challenge to the 1974 Federal Elections Campaign Act by a broad coalition of groups ranging from the ACLU to the Conservative and Libertarian parties. There the Court struck down mandatory limits on campaign spending as well as limits on what a candidate could spend from his own personal funds. The Court did not say, as its critics have alleged, that money equals speech; rather, it recognized that limits on spending can restrict speech just as surely as can a direct prohibition. Imagine, for example, if newspapers were limited to $100,000 a year for publishing costs: most would go out of business, and those that remained would become very thin indeed. . . .

Spending on political advertisements is important to educate voters, increasing their interest in elections and their knowledge of candidates and issues. Repetition plays an important part in this process: the electorate's hatred of 30-second campaign ads is surpassed only by its desire to get its political information by means of those same ads. And the ads cost money.

Although campaign-finance reformers often appeal to the public's unhappiness with negative ads, negativity has long been a feature of political campaigns, and money is not the source of it. (As long ago as 1796, the

presidential candidate Thomas Jefferson was attacked as "an atheist, anarchist, demagogue, coward, mountebank, trickster, and Francomaniac." . . .)
In fact, if the goal is to have positive campaigns, even *more* money would be needed, for the simple reason that positive ads are less memorable than negative ones and hence need to be repeated more frequently. Besides, a limit on spending would mean that candidates would have to depend more on the media to get their message across, and the press is often more negative in its campaign coverage than the contestants themselves.

There is, finally, no objective criterion by which to measure whether "too much" is being spent on political campaigns. But as we have seen, spending in this country is not high. Considering the vital importance of an informed electorate to democratic government, it is hard to discern why it should be lower.

The hidden premise behind the idea that too much is being spent on campaigns is that money "buys" election results—a second assumption of reformers. It is true that the candidate who spends the most money wins most of the time. But the cause-and-effect relationship between spending and victory is nowhere near so straightforward as this might suggest.

For one thing, the formulation neglects the desire of donors to give to candidates likely to win. In other words, it may be the prospect of victory that attracts money, not the other way around. . . . Or a candidate's fundraising edge may simply reflect the relative status of his popularity, later to be confirmed or disconfirmed at the polls.

Even when the ability to raise and spend money actually succeeds in changing the outcome of a race, it is ballots, not dollars, that ultimately decide who wins, and ballots reflect the minds of voters. All that spending can do is attempt to change those minds. It would be a strange First Amendment that cut off protection for speech at the point where speech began to influence people's views, and it reflects a remarkable contempt for the electorate to suggest that it is incapable of weighing the arguments being tendered for its consideration.

Indeed, there is ample evidence that the electorate does so discriminate, and that higher spending in behalf of a losing argument will not necessarily translate into electoral triumph. In the Republican takeover of Congress in 1994, for example, the 34 victorious challengers spent, on average, just two-thirds of the amount spent by their Democratic opponents, who also enjoyed the inherent advantage of incumbency. By contrast, in the 1996 race for the Republican presidential nomination, Phil Gramm, who raised the most money, was the first to have to drop out. As Michael Malbin of the Rockefeller Institute of Government has observed, "Having money means having the ability to be heard; it does not mean that voters will like what they hear."

The key variable in elections is not which candidate spends the most, but whether or not challengers are able to spend enough to overcome the advantage of incumbency and make their names and issues known to voters.

Once they reach this threshold, races are up for grabs. For example, in the 1996 House races, 40 percent of challengers who spent over $600,000 won, as opposed to just 3 percent who spent less than $600,000. Once the threshold was crossed, it mattered little whether or not the challenger was outspent, or by how much. The problem, if it can be called that, is not that some candidates "buy" elections by spending too much, but that others spend too little to get their message to the voters.

Still another assumption of reformers is that, if we truly cared about self-government and participatory democracy, we would be better off if campaigns were funded by many small contributors rather than by fewer large ones.

In fact, the burden of financing political campaigns has *always* fallen to a small minority, both in the United States and in other democracies. Nearly eighteen million Americans now make contributions to a political party, candidate, or PAC during an election cycle. Although this figure is higher than at any other time in American history, and represents a broader base of voluntary public support than has been enjoyed by any other system of campaign funding anywhere, it still comes to less than 10 percent of the voting-age population.

Which sorts of candidates are typically able to raise large sums of money in small amounts, as the reformers prefer? In the years prior to federal funding of presidential campaigns, the two most successful in this respect were Barry Goldwater and George McGovern. The former raised $5.8 million from over 400,000 contributors in 1964, only to suffer a landslide defeat, while the latter, who raised almost $15 million from donors making average contributions of about $20, lost in an even bigger landslide eight years later. More recently, Oliver North raised approximately $20 million, almost all from small contributors, for his 1994 U.S. Senate race, outspent his rival by almost four to one, and still lost to a candidate plagued by personal scandal—primarily because the electorate, rightly or wrongly, viewed him as too "extreme."

What these examples suggest is that the ability to raise large sums in small contributions can be a sign less of broad public support, as reformers assert, than of fervent backing by an ideological minority. Other groups positioned to exert influence by this means tend to be those (like unions) in possession of an ongoing structure for mobilizing their constituents or those we usually call "special interests." It is the inchoate, grass-roots public that more often fails to make its interests known, and is therefore frequently reliant on individuals with large fortunes to finance movements that will represent it. . . .

Ironically, the banning of large contributions, which means that no single gift is likely to make much difference in a political race, gives potential donors little incentive to become involved. A radical campaign can overcome this difficulty: its supporters tend to be motivated more by ideology than by rational calculations of a candidate's chances of winning. But this just further underscores the way in which banning large contributions can help render the political system more rather than less vulnerable to forces on the fringes of the mainstream—hardly, one presumes, the result the reformers have in mind.

A corollary fallacy entertained by reformers is that the financial resources placed at a candidate's disposal should ideally reflect his level of popular support. But this is to confuse the purpose of elections with the purpose of campaigns. The former do measure popular support. The latter, however, are about something else: persuading voters, and *improving* one's level of support. This, as we have seen, requires monetary expenditures, and it is a sign of health in a democracy when such expenditures are forthcoming. . . .

Perhaps no belief is more deeply rooted in the psyche of reformers—and of the public at large—than that the money drawn into the system through political campaigns corrupts not only the campaigns themselves but, once a candidate is elected, the entire legislative process. Many office-holders have themselves complained about the influence of money in the legislature. But political scientists and economists who have studied this matter have consistently concluded otherwise. As John Lott and Stephen Bronars, the authors of one such study, conclude: "Our tests strongly reject the notion that campaign contributions buy politicians' votes. . . . Just like voters, contributors appear able to sort [out] politicians who intrinsically value the same things that they do." . . .

This makes perfect sense. Individuals who enter politics usually do so because they have strong views on political issues; party support is almost always more important to election than any one contribution; and, to repeat, a legislator wins with votes, not dollars. For a politician to adopt an unpopular or unwise position that will cost him voter support in exchange for a $5,000 campaign contribution—the maximum amount allowed under federal law—would be counterproductive, to say the least.

This is not to say that other factors never come into play. A legislator may be concerned about how his vote will be reported in the press, or whether an opponent can easily caricature him in a negative ad. Personal friendships may affect a voting decision, as may the advice of aides and staff, itself often influenced by ideology. Money is another such secondary factor, but it is only one, and not necessarily the political commodity of greatest value. Many of the most influential Washington lobbying groups, including the American Association of Retired Persons, the National Education Association, and the American Bar Association, do not make political contributions. The NRA does have a large PAC, but it also has nearly two million members who care intensely about its issues. Although gun-control advocates complain that the NRA outspends them, the more important fact is that it also outvotes them.

Finally, most issues find well-financed lobbies on both sides. A seemingly dull proposal to introduce a one-dollar coin, for example, may line up metal companies, vending-machine manufacturers, and coin laundries on one side, paper and ink companies on the other. Similarly with higher-profile issues like tort reform, where well-financed insurance interests take one position and equally well-financed trial lawyers the other. At least one set of these contributors, and often both, will suffer enormous *losses* in the legislative process, a fact often ignored by reformers.

When push comes to shove, even the most ardent reformers are rarely able to point to a specific instance of corruption. Ask a reformer to name which of our 535 Congressmen and Senators are acting contrary to what they believe to be the public good, or to what their constituents desire, because of campaign contributions, and the answer every time is some variation of "It's the system that's corrupt." But if we cannot name individuals corrupted by the system, on what basis are we to conclude that corruption is a problem intrinsic to the "system"?

III

When it came time to fight the American Revolution, the founders of this nation did not go to the king seeking matching funds with which to finance their revolt. Instead, in the Declaration of Independence, they pledged their fortunes as well as their lives and sacred honor.

Today, in order to cure the alleged problem of fortunes in politics, reformers offer a variety of complex schemes aimed at *preventing* private citizens from demonstrating their commitment to democratic political change. Former Senator Bill Bradley and [former] House Minority Leader Richard Gephardt claim that we need a constitutional amendment to overturn the *Buckley* decision. In Gephardt's sweeping formulation, there is a "direct conflict" between "freedom of speech and our desire for healthy campaigns in a healthy democracy," and "you can't have both." Their proposed amendment, if enacted, would grant a greater degree of protection to commercial speech, flag burning, and Internet porn than to the discussion of political candidates and issues.

Meanwhile, "moderate" reformers continue to push the McCain-Feingold bill, lately shorn of a ban on PAC's that even its sponsors admit was "probably" unconstitutional. Even so, this bill would place vast new limits on the freedom of political discussion, ban most contributions to political parties to pay for voter registration, slate cards, rallies, and get-out-the-vote drives, and restrict speech in ways directly prohibited by standing Supreme Court decisions.[2]

If it is not the case that too much money is spent on campaigns, or that money, rather than the character of a handful of elected officials, is the source of political corruption, or that large contributors buy elections or in some way frustrate "true democracy," why should we tolerate such gross infringements of traditional First Amendment freedoms? What would be accomplished by measures like those being proposed by the reformers that would not be better accomplished by minimal disclosure laws that simply require the reporting of all sources of financial support?

---

2. Opposition from Senate Republicans and Senate Majority Leader Trent Lott (R-Mississippi) prevented the McCain-Feingold bill from reaching the Senate floor in 1998. In early 2002, a modified version of McCain-Feingold was passed by Congress and signed by President Bush.

Of course, disclosure laws may also be broken, as they appear to have been in the 1996 campaign. Character matters, and the rule has yet to be invented that someone will not succeed in violating. But what all the reformers overlook, from the most extreme to the most moderate, is that we already have, in the First Amendment, a deeply considered response to the problems inherent in democratic elections—and one that is far superior to the supposedly enlightened system of regulation with which we are now saddled.

By assuring freedom of speech and the press, the First Amendment allows for exposure of government corruption and improper favors, whether these consist of White House meetings with drug dealers or huge tax breaks for tobacco companies. By keeping the government out of the electoral arena, it allows for robust criticism of government itself, and prevents incumbents from manipulating the election-law machinery in their own favor. It frees grass-roots activists and everyday speech alike from suffocating state regulation, thereby furthering the democratic aim of political discussion. And it allows candidates to control their own message rather than having to rely on the filters of the press or the vagaries of bureaucrats and judges called upon to decide which forms of speech are to be limited as "endorsements or attacks," and which allowed as "genuine debate."

In the vast muddle that has been made by our decades-old regulatory folly, the only real question concerns whose logic we will now follow: the logic of those who gave us our existing campaign-finance laws and who, despite a disastrous record, now want license to "reform" them still further, or the logic of the founders who gave us the First Amendment. For most Americans, I suspect, the choice would be an easy one.

Dollars and Votes

DAN CLAWSON,
ALAN NEUSTADTL, AND
MARK WELLER

Imagine the November election is just a few weeks away, and your friend Sally Robeson is seriously considering running for Congress two years from now. This year the incumbent in your district, E. Chauncey DeWitt III, will (again!) be reelected by a substantial margin, but you and Sally hate Chauncey's positions on the issues and are convinced that with the right campaign he can be beaten. Sally is capable, articulate, well informed, respected in the community, politically and socially connected, charming, good at talking to many kinds of people, and highly telegenic. She has invited you and several other politically active friends to meet with her immediately after the election to determine what she would need to do to become a viable candidate.

The meeting that takes place covers a host of topics: What are the key issues? On which of these are Sally's stands popular, and on which unpopular? What attacks, and from what quarters, will be launched against her? What individuals or groups can she count on for support? How, why, and where is the incumbent vulnerable? But lurking in the background is the question that cannot be ignored: *Can Sally (with the help of her friends and backers) raise enough money to be a contender?*

This is the *money primary, the first, and, in many instances, the most important round of the contest.* It eliminates more candidates than any other hurdle. Because it eliminates them so early and so quietly, its impact is often unobserved. To make it through, candidates don't have to come in first, but they do need to raise enough money to be credible contenders. Although having the most money is no guarantee of victory, candidates who don't do well in the money primary are no longer serious contenders. . . .

How much is needed? If Sally hopes to win, rather than just put up a good fight, she, you, and the rest of her supporters will need to raise staggering amounts. (At least they are staggering from the perspective of most Americans. . . .) In order to accumulate the *average* amount for major-party congressional candidates in the general election, you will collectively need to raise $4,800 next week. And the week after. And *every* week for the next two years.

But even that is not enough. The average amount includes many candidates who were never "serious"; that is, they didn't raise enough to have a realistic hope of winning. If you and your friends want to raise the average amount spent by a *winning* candidate for the House, you'll have to come up with $6,730 next week and every single week until the election, two years away.[1]

Well, you say, your candidate is hardly average. She is stronger, smarter, more politically appealing, and more viable than the "average" challenger. You think she can win even if she doesn't raise $6,730 a week. Let's use past experience—the results of the 1996 elections—to consider the likelihood of winning for challengers, based on how much money they raised. In 1996 more than 360 House incumbents were running for reelection; only 23 of them were beaten by their challengers. The average successful challenger spent $1,045,361—that is, he or she raised an average of over $10,000 every week for two years. What were the chances of winning without big money? Only one winning challenger spent less than $500,000, 12 spent between a half-a-million and a million dollars, and 10 spent more than a million dollars. Furthermore, 13 of the 23 winning challengers outspent the incumbent. A House challenger who can't raise at least a half-million dollars doesn't have a one percent chance of winning. . . .

---

1. In 2000, the figure was around $9,000, and in 2002 rose to $11,000 weekly.

In the Senate, even more money is needed. Suppose your candidate were going to run for the Senate, and started fundraising immediately after an election, giving her six years to prepare for the next election. How much money would she need to raise each and every week for those *six* years? The average winning Senate candidate raised approximately $15,000 per week.

For presidential candidates, the stakes are, of course, much higher: "The prevailing view is that for a politician to be considered legitimate, he or she must collect at least $20 million by the first of January 2000." Presumably any candidate who does not do so is "illegitimate" and does not belong in the race.[2]

If you collectively decide that the candidate you plan to back will need to raise $7,000 per week (for the House; $15,000 per week for the Senate), how will you do it? Suppose you hold a $10-per-person fundraiser—a barbecue in the park on Memorial Day or Labor Day. Even if 500 people attend, the affair will gross only $5,000, and net considerably less, no matter how cheap the hot dogs and hamburgers. And that takes no account of the problems of persuading 500 people to attend—just notifying them of the event is a major undertaking—or what it would mean to hold such an event every week, not just on Labor Day. In order to get through the money primary, an alternative strategy is needed, so candidates, especially incumbents, increasingly prefer to raise money at "big ticket" events. Selling 10 tickets for a $1,000-per-person fundraiser brings in more than twice as much as the 500-person barbecue in the park.

Who is likely to cough up a thousand bucks to attend a fundraiser? . . . A disproportionate number of such contributors are corporate political action committees (PACs), executives, and lobbyists. One typical version of the $1,000-per-person fundraiser is a breakfast: The candidate and 10 to 30 PAC officers and lobbyists from a particular industry (trucking, banking, oil and gas exploration). Even with a lavish breakfast, the candidate's net take is substantial. If enough lobbyists and corporate executives can be persuaded to come, perhaps the candidate could get by on one fundraiser every couple of weeks.

Coming up with the money is a major hassle; even for incumbents, it requires constant effort. *National Journal,* probably the single most authoritative source on the Washington scene, reports that "there is widespread agreement that the congressional money chase has become an unending marathon, as wearying to participants as it is disturbing to spectators," and quoted an aide to a Democratic senator as observing, "During hearings of Senate committees, you can watch senators go to phone booths in the committee rooms to dial for dollars." . . .

Long before the 1996 election, politicians felt that they had no choice: The Senate majority leader reported that "public officials are consumed with the unending pursuit of money to run election campaigns." Senators not only leave committee hearings for the more crucial task of calling people to beg for money. They also chase all over the country, because their

---

2. By June 2004, President Bush's reelection campaign had raised over $240 million and John Kerry's close to $160 million.

reelection is more dependent on meeting rich people two thousand miles from home than on meeting their own constituents. Thomas Daschle, the current Democratic leader in the Senate, reports that, in the two years prior to his election to the Senate, he "flew to California more than 20 times to meet with prospective contributors," going there almost as often as he went to the largest city in his home state of South Dakota. . . .

Not only is it necessary to raise lots of money; it is important—for both incumbents and challengers—to raise it early. Senator Rudy Boschwitz, Republican of Minnesota, was clear about this as a strategy. He spent $6 million getting reelected in 1984, and had raised $1.5 million of it by the beginning of the year, effectively discouraging the most promising Democratic challengers. After the election he wrote, and typed up himself, a secret evaluation of his campaign strategy:

> "Nobody in politics (except me!) likes to raise money, so I thought the best way of discouraging the toughest opponents from running was to have a few dollars in the sock. *I believe it worked. . . . From all forms of fundraising I raised $6 million plus and got 3 or 4 (maybe even 5) stories and cartoons that* irked me," he said. "In retrospect, I'm glad I had the money. . . ."

The Contributors' Perspective

Candidates need money, lots of it, if they are to have any chance of winning. The obvious next question . . . is who gives, why, and what they expect for it.

Contributions are made for many different reasons. The candidate's family and friends chip in out of loyalty and affection. Others contribute because they are asked to do so by someone who has done favors for them. People give because they agree with the candidate's stand on the issues, either on a broad ideological basis or on a specific issue. Sometimes these donations are portrayed as a form of voting—people show that they care by putting their money where their mouth is, anyone can contribute, and the money raised reflects the wishes of the people. Even for these contributions, however, if voting with dollars replaces voting at the ballot box, then the votes will be very unequally distributed: the top 1 percent of the population by wealth will have more "votes" than the bottom 90 percent of the population. In the 1996 elections, less than one-fourth of one percent of the population gave contributions of $200 or more to a federal candidate. PACs and large contributors provide most of the money, however; small contributors accounted for under one-third of candidate receipts.

It is not just that contributions come from the well-to-do. Most contributors have a direct material interest in what the government does or does not do. Their contributions, most of them made directly or indirectly by business, provide certain people a form of leverage and "access" not available to the rest of us. The chair of the political action committee at one of the twenty-five largest manufacturing companies in the United States explained to us why his corporation has a PAC:

The PAC gives you access. It makes you a player. These congressmen, in particular, are constantly fundraising. Their elections are very expensive, and getting increasingly expensive each year. So they have an ongoing need for funds. . . .

You know, some congressman has got X number of ergs of energy and here's a person or a company who wants to come see him and give him a thousand dollars, and here's another one who wants to just stop by and say hello. And he only has time to see one. Which one? So the PAC's an attention getter.

So-called soft money, where the amount of the contribution is unlimited, might appear to be an exception: Isn't $100,000 enough to buy a guaranteed outcome? . . . It is *not,* at least not in any simple and straightforward way. PAC contributions are primarily for members of Congress; they are for comparatively small amounts, but enough to gain access to individual members of Congress. The individual member, however, has limited power. Soft money donations are best thought of as a way of gaining access to the president, top party leaders, and the executive branch. These individuals are more powerful than ordinary members of Congress, so access to them comes at a higher price. . . . It does not—and is not expected to—*guarantee* a quid pro quo. . . .

Why Business?

In business-government relations most attention becomes focused on instances of scandal. The real issue, however, is not one or another scandal or conflict of interest, but rather the *system* of business-government relations, and especially of campaign finance, that offers business so many opportunities to craft loopholes, undermine regulations, and subvert enforcement. . . .

Business and the way it uses money and power . . . subverts the democratic process. This runs counter to the conventional wisdom, which treats all campaign contributions as equally problematic. A "balanced" and "objective" approach would, we are told, condemn both business and labor; each reform that primarily restricts business should be matched by one that restricts labor. We've heard these arguments, thought them over, and rejected them. They assume that what we have now is "balance" and that all changes should reinforce the existing relations of power. We see no reason to accept that as an a priori assumption.

Why are business campaign contributions more of a problem than contributions by labor (or women, or environmentalists)? First, because business contributes far more money. According to a study by the Center for Responsive Politics, in [1996] business outspent labor by an 11 to 1 margin.[3]

---

3. The disparity was 14 to 1 in 2000, and early signs indicated it could be over 20 to 1 in 2004.

Most reports about campaign finance give the impression that labor contributes roughly as much as business—a distortion of the reality.

Second, . . . beyond the world of campaign finance, business has far more power than labor, women's groups, or environmentalists.

Third, business uses campaign contributions in a way few other groups do, as part of an "access" process that provides corporations a chance to shape the details of legislation, crafting loopholes that undercut the stated purpose of the law. Other groups do this on rare occasions; business does so routinely. Businesses are far more likely than other donors to give to *both* sides in a race; nearly all the soft money donors who gave to both sides were corporations. . . .

Fourth, there is a fundamental difference between corporate and labor PAC contributions. That difference is democracy; unions have it, corporations don't. This overwhelmingly important distinction is concealed by almost all public discussion. No one talks about it, no one seems to take it seriously. There is a virtual embargo on any mention of this fact, but it merits serious consideration.

The original legislation ratifying the creation of PACs, passed in 1971 and amended in 1974 after Watergate, intended that corporations and labor unions be treated in parallel fashion. In each case, the organization was permitted a special relationship to the group that democratically controlled it—stockholders in the case of corporations, members in the case of labor unions. The organization was permitted to communicate with those individuals and their families on any issue (including political issues), to conduct registration and get-out-the-vote campaigns, and to ask those people for voluntary contributions to a political action committee.

In the 1975 SUN–PAC decision, the Federal Election Commission, for almost the only time in its existence, took a bold step. In fact, it essentially threw out a key part of the law and then rewrote it, permitting corporations to solicit PAC contributions not just from their stockholders but also from their managerial employees. This had two consequences. First, corporate PACs—but no others—are able to coerce people to contribute. Second, corporate PACs are not, even in theory, democratically controlled. Each of these consequences needs to be examined.

Neither stockholders nor union members can be coerced to contribute—the organization doesn't have power over them, they have power over the organization. Managers, however, can be coerced. As a result, virtually all corporate PAC money comes from employees rather than stockholders. If your boss comes to you and asks for a contribution, saying he or she hopes that all team players will be generous, it's not easy for you, an ambitious young manager, to say no. Some companies apparently do not pressure employees to contribute, but others do. For example, at one company we studied, the head of government relations told us that each year he and the company's lobbyist go to each work unit and hold an employee meeting: "We talk about the PAC and what it means to the company and what it means to them as individuals, and we solicit their membership; if they are members, we solicit an increase in their gift." Then the employees' boss is asked "to get up and say why they are members and why they think it's important for an employee to be a member." The upper-level manager clearly has no confidentiality, which in itself sends a key message to others. A number of coercive elements converge in this solicitation: The meeting is public, employees are to commit themselves then and there in the public meeting, the boss recommends that subordinates contribute, and an impression is probably conveyed that the boss will be evaluated on the basis of his or her employees' participation rate. . . . No one is told they will be fired for failing to contribute, but it seems probable that they will assume their boss will be disappointed and that their contribution or noncontribution will be remembered at promotion time.

The second consequence of the 1975 SUN–PAC decision is even more important. Corporate PACs are *not* democratic. Many corporations have steering committees that vote to decide to whom the PAC will contribute, but the committees are appointed, the corporate hierarchy selects individuals who are expected to take the corporate purpose as their own, and managers know that they will be evaluated on their performance on the committee. As one senior vice president explained: "Policy is made by the top of the company, and it filters down. They tell you what they want, and you do it."

The internal functioning of corporate PACs suggests how they relate to and value democracy. Most aspects of the political system are beyond the *direct* control of corporations, but they *can* determine how their PACs operate and make decisions. As a result, in all but a handful of corporate PACs democratic control is not even a theoretical possibility. . . .

The only corporation that reported having *some* contested elections agreed that, in general: "It is an elected-appointive; it's kind of a pseudo-election I guess is what it amounts to."

We might expect those ideological corporations that stress general principles of support for democracy and the "free" enterprise system to be exceptions to the undemocratic organization of corporate PACs. Not at all. At one corporation that boasted about its wholehearted support of the "free enterprise system," the chair of the PAC Committee matter-of-factly noted: "If our [company] chairman said we are going to have a certain kind of PAC, then we'd have an option of resigning or doing it the way he wanted." . . .

The nondemocratic character of corporate PACs is consistent with the principles guiding the corporation as a whole. Corporations are not run on democratic principles; employees don't vote on corporate leadership or policies. Many corporate executives are dubious about democracy in general. [Journalists] Leonard Silk and David Vogel attended a set of meetings organized by the Conference Board for top executives. They concluded:

> While critics of business worry about the atrophy of American democracy, the concern in the nation's boardrooms is precisely the opposite. For an executive, democracy in America is working all too well—*that is the problem.*

Campaign contributions are (part of) the solution to the "problem" of democracy. . . .

Business Is Different

Power, we would argue, is not just the ability to force someone to do something against their will; it is most effective (and least recognized) when it shapes the field of action. Moreover, business's vast resources, influence on the economy, and general legitimacy place it on a different footing from other campaign contributors. Every day a member of Congress accepts a $1,000 donation from a corporate PAC, goes to a committee hearing, proposes "minor" changes in a bill's wording, and has those changes accepted without discussion or examination. The changes "clarify" the language of the bill, legalizing higher levels of pollution for a specific pollutant, or exempting the company from some tax. The media do not report this change and no one speaks against it. On the other hand, if a PAC were formed by Drug Lords for Cocaine Legalization, no member would take their money. If a member introduced a "minor" wording change to make it easier to sell crack without bothersome police interference, the proposed change would attract massive attention, the campaign contribution would be labeled a scandal, the member's political career would be ruined, and the changed wording would not be incorporated into the bill. Drug Lords may make an extreme example, but approximately the same holds true for many groups: At present, equal rights for gays and lesbians could never be a minor and unnoticed addition to a bill with a different purpose.

Even groups with great social legitimacy encounter more opposition and controversy than business faces for proposals that are virtually without public support. One example is the contrast between the largely unopposed commitment of tens or hundreds of billions of dollars for the savings and loan bailout, compared to the sharp debate, close votes, and defeats for the rights of men and women to take *unpaid* parental leaves. The classic term for something non-controversial that everyone must support is "a motherhood issue," and while it costs little to guarantee every woman the right to an *unpaid* parental leave, this measure nonetheless generated intense scrutiny and controversy—going down to defeat under [the first] President Bush, passing under President Clinton, and then again becoming a focus of attack after the 1994 Republican takeover of Congress. Few indeed are the people publicly prepared to defend pollution or tax evasion. Nonetheless, business is routinely able to win pollution exemptions and tax loopholes. . . .

Corporations are unlike other "special interest" groups not only because business has far more resources, but also because of its acceptance and legitimacy. When people feel that "the system" is screwing them, they tend to blame politicians, the government, the media—but rarely business. In terms of campaign finance, while much of the public is outraged at the way money influences elections and public policy, the issue is almost always posed in terms of politicians, what they do or don't do. This is part of a pervasive double standard that largely exempts business from criticism. We, however, believe it is vital to scrutinize business as well. . . .

. . . Corporations are so different, and so dominant, that they exercise a special kind of power, what Antonio Gramsci called hegemony. Hegemony can be regarded as the ultimate example of a field of power that structures what people and groups do. It is sometimes referred to as a worldview, a way of thinking about the world that influences every action, and makes it difficult to even consider alternatives. But in Gramsci's analysis it is much more than this, it is a culture and set of institutions that structure life patterns and coerce a particular way of life. . . .

. . . Today business has enormous power and exercises effective hegemony, even though (perhaps because) this is largely undiscussed and unrecognized. *Politically,* business power today is similar to white treatment of blacks in 1959—business may sincerely deny its power, but many of the groups it exercises power over recognize it, feel dominated, resent this, and fight the power as best they can. At least until very recently, *economically,* business power was more like gender relations in 1959: Virtually no one saw this power as problematic. The revived labor movement is beginning to change this, and there are signs that a movement is beginning to contest corporate power. Nonetheless, if the issue is brought to people's attention, many still don't see a problem: "Well, so what? how else could it be? maybe we don't like it, but that's just the way things are." . . .

Everyone is talking about campaign finance reform. But what kind of reform? The answer varies. If the problem is occasional abuses by renegade fundraisers, then the only change needed is a system of improved enforcement. . . . If the problem is that the public has (momentarily? irrationally?) lost faith in the system, and now sees democracy for sale, then the solution is to address the most visible symbol of this—soft money—and make cosmetic changes elsewhere, loudly proclaiming that this is a thorough reform. For campaign finance insiders—a tiny fraction of the population, but crucial for policy decisions—the problem is that politicians are having to work too hard to raise money. The solution is to find some way to reduce the cost of campaigns (typically, through limited free television time), while seeing to it that the margin of success continues to depend on campaign contributions from big-money donors, which is, after all, the system that put these politicians into office. Most campaign finance experts analyze the issue in ways generally similar to the political insiders. Academic "expertise," and certainly media punditry, generally depends on possessing views certified as "reasonable" by those with power—that is, by politicians, the media, business, and big-money campaign contributors. For most members of the American public—and for us—the problem is an entire system that is institutionally corrupt, that coerces politicians to put dollars over voters, that buys off democracy. The solution, therefore, must be a complete overhaul and the introduction of a fundamentally new system. . . .

Public Financing

. . . As long as our society continues to have vast inequalities of wealth, income, and power, the people with the most money will be able to find ways around restrictive rules. Virtually all current [reform] proposals are intended to limit the ways in which money can be funneled into campaigns. It is extremely difficult to impose limitations, because however many rules and barriers are erected, the ingenuity of the rich, or their hirelings, will always find ways to evade the regulations. Clinton's Deputy Chief of Staff Harold Ickes explains, "Money is like water. . . . If there is a crack, water will find it. Same way with political money." Moreover, virtually no meaningful penalties are imposed on those caught violating the rules. As a result, the regulators are always one step behind the evaders and shysters.

The alternative approach is to cut the Gordian knot of restrictions by instituting public financing of election campaigns. In the early 1990s, such proposals seemed utopian. In 1992, we argued that Congress and the president would not institute public financing unless a popular movement put a gun to their heads. As we predicted, Washington didn't budge, but state-level referendum campaigns may do what Congress would never do. In 1996, Maine voters adopted a public financing system, and Public Campaign, a new organization dedicated to taking special interest money out of elections, is spearheading a movement around the country to bring about public campaign financing, one state at a time, if necessary. Real reform, with full public financing, is no longer a utopian dream—it's on today's political agenda. Other proposals are of course possible, but Public Campaign's model law is an excellent framework, *and* it has helped mobilize and coordinate a major grassroots campaign. Our discussion therefore focuses on this proposal.

Public Campaign, and its Clean Money Campaign Reform (CMCR), are—at least for now—bypassing Congress, which has shown an amazing ability to sidetrack and frustrate reform efforts, and focusing instead on state-by-state efforts, most notably by putting referendum questions on the ballot. By taking the issue directly to the voters in a ballot referendum, it's possible to pass a full reform proposal. The normal legislative process is highly likely to bury reform in committee and then change "just a few" details in order to make the proposal "more realistic"—that is, to be sure that special interest money continues to provide a decisive margin in most contests.

State-level campaigns necessarily mean that there will be minor variations from one place to another. And any effort to present a campaign finance proposal confronts a dilemma: Readers want enough detail to be sure the proposal is viable—that it won't encounter an insoluble contradiction—but don't want to be bogged down in minor provisions of interest only to technocrats and political junkies. In its broad outlines, Clean Money Campaign Reform limits campaign spending, prohibits special interest contributions to those candidates who participate in the system, provides public financing for participating candidates, and guarantees a level playing field. The system is completely voluntary. . . .

The arguments in favor of [public financing of campaigns] are . . . powerful. . . . Elections would be far more competitive. Although challengers would still have less name recognition than incumbents, they would have enough money to mount credible campaigns, and for the first time challengers as a group would have as much to spend as incumbents.

Special interests could no longer use campaign money to increase their access and win benefits for themselves. It is not only that a member would not be indebted for a past donation. Members would also know they would never need to depend on a future donation and could never gain a campaign advantage by soliciting or accepting such a donation. Corporations would continue to have substantial clout based on their wealth, power, and respectability, their ability to maintain a staff of lobbyists, their advocacy advertising, their networks, connections, and friendships. But *one* of their major special interest weapons would have been eliminated.

The guarantee of public funding for campaigns would give members of Congress more time to spend on legislation and on keeping in touch with constituents who are *not* campaign contributors. . . .

People sometimes argue that such reforms only make the system more stable and resistant to change. Perhaps that is true in some instances. In other instances, what Andre Gorz called a "non-reformist reform" provides immediate benefits to people *and* makes it easier to win future reforms. Did the auto safety campaign Nader launched produce a significant change in the way people think about business? Yes. Did it make people more or less willing to consider additional reforms? Obviously, much more willing.

We would argue that Clean Money Campaign Reform is also a "nonreformist reform." It proposes a reform that can be won, and one that if won will substantially weaken business power. By itself, will it transform American society? No. Will it have an impact? Yes. Will the end of corporate campaign contributions and the emergence of public financing make it easier or more difficult to make future political changes? Clearly, easier. Will continued struggle be necessary to elect good people and to fight business power? Certainly. Will electoral politics be enough? No. Business exercises power on many different fronts and that power must be opposed on every front.

DISCUSSION QUESTIONS

1. Smith claims that campaign contributors don't buy favors or votes from candidates but that contributions simply register support for candidates' political positions. How would Smith deal with the contention that contributions buy privileged access to candidates?

2. In *Buckley* v. *Valeo* (1976), the U.S. Supreme Court seemed to agree with Smith's idea that campaign contributions are protected by the First Amendment as free speech. Are proposals for public financing of campaigns such as those submitted by the authors of "Dollars and Votes" a violation of free speech?

3. In 1999 and 2000, the House leadership blocked campaign reform initiatives from coming to a vote. If money is such a corrupting influence in campaigns, why aren't voters more supportive of the kinds of initiatives

proposed to limit its effects? What are the obstacles to forming a grassroots movement that supports campaign finance reform?

4. During the 2004 primary election, former Vermont Governor Howard Dean raised an unprecedented amount of money, most of it from small donations. At the same time, Dean's campaign used it to mobilize an army of grassroots volunteers. What would the advocates of public financing of campaigns say about the Dean campaign's combination of both money and democratic energy?

SUGGESTED READINGS AND INTERNET RESOURCES

A comprehensive look at the recent campaign finance reform law is supplied in Michael Malbin, ed., *Life After Reform: When the Bipartisan Campaign Reform Act Meets Politics* (New York: Rowman and Littlefield, 2003). A devastating look at the effects of private money on electoral politics is in Charles Lewis, *The Buying of the President, 2004* (New York: Perennial, 2004). See also Arianna Huffington, *Fanatics and Fools: The Game Plan for Winning Back America* (New York: Miramax Books, 2004). A short and effective set of proposals for public financing of campaigns can be found in David Donnelly, Janice Fine, and Ellen Miller, *Money and Politics* (Boston: Beacon Press, 1999).

Federal Election Commission (FEC)
www.fec.gov
The FEC's site provides access to the financial reports of all candidates for federal offices and press releases summarizing monthly trends in campaign fund-raising.

Center for Responsive Politics
www.opensecrets.org
This is the most comprehensive site for data and analysis of FEC data, with a concentration on the role of monied interests and their effects on the political process.

Public Campaign
www.publiccampaign.org
Here are news and views from the major advocacy organization favoring public financing of political campaigns.

Democracy Network
www.dnet.org
This League of Women Voters–sponsored site provides state-by-state access to candidate information and ways to contact and interact with campaign organizations.

Campaign Finance Institute
www.cfinst.org
This nonpartisan institute's mission is to assess the effectiveness of campaign finance reform. The institute's website features reports on pending legislation, easy access to donor lists, and news of key congressional races where money is the chief factor.

CHAPTER 12

Debating the Deficit and the Size of Government

T he 2000 presidential election showed how evenly the nation is divided along partisan lines. Americans disagree about many issues, including when to go to war, trade policy, and gay marriage. A big issue underlying the partisan divide is the size of government. Simply put, Americans disagree about how big government, especially the federal government, should be. With the exception of the military, Republicans want to scale back the federal government and turn its functions over to state and local governments, the private sector, and nonprofits, including churches. Democrats defend a vigorous role for the federal government, especially to protect the environment, children, workers, minorities, and the elderly.

Debates over the size of government intensify when budget deficits soar. After a short period of federal budget surpluses (1998–2001), the federal government racked up the largest budget deficits in history in 2003 and 2004. Reflecting their very different views on the size of government, Republicans and Democrats proposed contrasting approaches for dealing with the deficit: Republicans wanted to cut spending; the Democrats proposed increasing taxes, especially on those earning more than $200,000. At the beginning of the twenty-first century, the democratic debate on deficits and the size of government has rarely been hotter.

It has not always been this way. At various points in our history, Americans seemed to be approaching a consensus on the size of government. Driven by Franklin Roosevelt's New Deal and World War II, the size of the federal government grew tremendously during the 1930s and 1940s. Military spending declined rapidly right after World War II, but the Cold War with the

Soviet Union caused it to shoot up again. When Republican Dwight Eisenhower won the presidency in 1952, he did not try to roll back the New Deal but accepted the broad contours of the welfare state. In the 1960s, Lyndon Johnson's Great Society expanded the size of federal government with new programs aimed both at the poor (Medicaid) and the elderly of all classes (Medicare). Despite his reputation as a conservative, Richard Nixon supported a large federal government, although he tried to reform many federal programs by giving more power over them to state and local governments.

The broad acceptance of a muscular federal government was supported by the belief that government could smooth out the business cycle and prevent depressions, like the one that crippled the U.S. economy in the 1930s. Known as Keynesian economics, this idea was developed by English economist John Maynard Keynes (1883–1946). Keynes argued that economic downturns are caused by inadequate consumer spending. As the economy begins to tumble into a recession, Keynes recommended that the government deliberately engineer deficits, spending more than it takes in from taxes. By pumping money into the economy, government spending, Keynes argued, would get the economy moving again toward full employment. By the 1960s, it was widely accepted that federal fiscal policy could prevent depressions and help keep unemployment low. Reflecting the consensus, Richard Nixon was quoted in a 1971 *Newsweek* cover story as saying, "We are all Keynesians now."

The election of Ronald Reagan in 1980 shattered the illusion that Americans agreed on the need for a large federal government. In his Inaugural Address, Reagan famously charged that "government is not the solution to our problems; government is the problem." In 1981, Reagan succeeded in enacting one of the largest tax cuts in American history.

Reagan's tax cuts were supported by an intellectual challenge to Keynesian economics known as supply-side economics. Supply-siders argue that economic stagnation is not caused by inadequate consumer spending but by problems on the supply (or production) side—basically, inadequate capital investment. High tax rates, they maintain, reduce the incentive to work and invest. (Ronald Reagan was fond of telling the story of how he quit making movies during World War II when the marginal tax rate hit 94 percent.)

Supply-siders go further, saying that reducing tax rates can actually lead to *greater* tax revenues by fueling economic growth. This idea is based on the Laffer curve, first proposed in 1974 by economist Arthur B. Laffer. The basic idea is that when tax rates are at low levels, tax revenues go up with higher rates. But at higher tax rates the curve slopes downward as more people decide not to work or invest because of high taxes, thus reducing revenues even though rates are higher. When we are at this point on the Laffer curve, we can actually increase revenues by lowering tax rates because the lower rates will stimulate economic growth.

The Reagan administration was more successful at cutting taxes than at reducing the size of government. As a result, budget deficits soared in the 1980s. Debate continued on whether the tax cuts helped the economy. Defenders of Reaganomics argued that the soaring deficits were not caused by the tax cuts but by the unwillingness of Democrats in Congress to cut spending.

Following Reagan's lead, at the 1988 Republican convention George H. W. Bush made his famous "no new taxes" pledge—memorialized by the refrain "read my lips." As president, Bush came under tremendous pressure to deal with soaring deficits, and in 1990 he signed a budget bill that included modest tax increases. By agreeing to tax increases, Bush undermined his credibility, contributing to his defeat by Bill Clinton in 1992.

Early in his own presidency, Clinton narrowly passed a tax increase that fell almost entirely on the wealthy and he tried, but failed, to pass a major new expansion of the federal government to provide universal health insurance. Partly because of opposition to the tax increase and national health insurance, in 1994, for the first time in forty years, the Republicans won control of both houses of Congress. For the remainder of his time in office, Clinton proposed no major new federal initiatives. He supported turning welfare policy over to the states and contented himself with smaller targeted initiatives like Americorps and urban empowerment zones. In his 1995 State of the Union address Clinton seemed to embrace a new centrist view of a more modest role for the federal government when he declared, "The era of big government is over."

Thanks primarily to the economic boom of the 1990s, George W. Bush came to office with the prospect of trillions of dollars of surpluses in the years ahead. However, record surpluses turned into record deficits within a few years. The causes of these deficits are subject to dispute, but everyone agrees that the economic recession played a role, as did the added expenses of the war on terrorism and the occupations of Afghanistan and Iraq. Also, during his first year in office, President Bush succeeded in passing a ten-year, $1.35 trillion tax cut that contributed significantly to the deficit. Bush defended his budget deficits by saying that they were partly caused by the war on terrorism and maintaining, on supply-side grounds, that economic growth, stimulated by tax cuts, would cut the deficit in half within five years. As we go to press, the budget deficit for fiscal year 2004 is projected to reach a record $477 billion. Even without a third-party candidate like Ross Perot, who succeeded in putting deficits on the agenda in the 1992 presidential election, deficits are certain to be an issue in the 2004 campaign.

Our first selection is by Stephen Moore, president of the Club for Growth, a 9,000-member organization headquartered in Washington, D.C., which lobbies and campaigns on behalf of smaller government. The Club for Growth got media attention recently for giving campaign contributions to Republican candidates who are running in primaries against moderate Republicans who do not fully support cutting taxes. In his essay, Moore provides a thoughtful defense of supply-side economics—and, by implication, Bush's tax cuts. Moore focuses not so much on the size of government as on high tax rates, which he argues stifle economic initiative and investment. He challenges those who argue that tax cuts cause high deficits that, in turn, damage the economy by driving up interest rates and cutting productive investment. The real damage to the economy, Moore argues, comes from wasteful spending programs, not deficits. If we want to improve the economy, we should cut federal spending, not rescind tax cuts.

Jonathan Chait, a senior editor at the *New Republic,* a well-respected weekly magazine with a liberal bent, vigorously attacks President Bush's tax cuts, which he blames for soaring deficits. Chait argues that the supply-side economics behind the tax cuts is flawed. Instead of boosting the economy, Chait asserts, the tax cuts will harm the economy by increasing the national debt and soaking up private capital that otherwise would be available for productive investment. Chait charges Bush and the Republicans with deliberately engineering deficits in a "starve-the-beast" strategy, designed to force liberals to support spending cuts. The result, argues Chait, is a game of chicken in which neither side backs down, resulting in soaring deficits that damage the entire nation.

The debate on the size of government and deficits often seems to hinge on technical issues, such as the disincentive effects of marginal tax rates and the impact of deficits on interest rates. But underlying the debate are value-laden questions. Supply-siders argue that cutting taxes on high incomes will stimulate more investment than will cutting taxes on working people. But are tax cuts for the wealthy fair—even if they do stimulate economic growth? Similarly, if you value negative freedom (see the Introduction to this book) then you will want government to be as small as possible. But if you think that positive freedom requires an active government, you will see an enlarged federal government as a potential friend of liberty. The debate on the size of government and deficits resonates with many of the same value conflicts found in Chapter 3 on federalism and Chapter 5 on political economy.

Tax Policy: The Theory Behind the Supply-Side Model

STEPHEN MOORE

In 2003 President George W. Bush called for one of the largest tax cuts in American history in order to help revitalize the lagging U.S. economy. President Bush called for reducing income taxes, taxes on stocks, and taxes on businesses. He argued that this tax plan would "free up resources in the American economy to create more jobs, higher incomes, and more economic growth." Although the initial indicators are positive, it is still too early to assess whether that tax cut was a success or not; what is clear is that the idea that tax policy can impact family finances and the direction of the U.S. economy is now firmly entrenched in the economics debate at the federal level and in many states as well.

So where did this controversial idea come from? Some say the idea came from Ronald Reagan. In 1981 the newly elected President Reagan enacted a cut in income tax rates of roughly 30 percent in order to get the American economy out of the lingering recession of the 1970s. By doing so, Reagan wrote a new history of modern economics, sometimes called "supply-side economics." The Reagan program of cutting taxes, reducing government spending, curing runaway inflation, and deregulating key sectors of the economy was ridiculed by the media and Reagan's political opponents as "voodoo economics." But it turns out that the idea of cutting tax rates to grow the economy was not so new and not so radical as critics believe. As far back as the 1920s and since then, presidents of both political parties have relied on tax rate reductions to help pump steroids into the economy and put unemployed Americans back to work. And in many cases, this economic game plan has worked quite successfully.

There are many definitions of supply-side economics, but the one that fits the theory best is the basic idea that human beings respond to incentives. This is a lesson everyone learns as a young child. If the child misbehaves, he might get a swat on the behind; but if the child does a good deed, he is rewarded with an Oreo cookie or a warm smile. Incentives matter in life. As Arthur Laffer, an economist who is often regarded as the Godfather of supply-side economics, once put it: "When you tax something, you get less of it. And when you tax something less, you get more of it." Income taxes are levies imposed on work, savings, investment, risk taking—that is, all of the activities that cause an economy to grow. That is why normally societies tax bad things or behavior they want to avoid. We tax cigarettes because we want to discourage people from smoking. We tax alcohol to discourage excessive drinking. The income tax is a strange and potentially economically debilitating tax because it is a tax on virtuous behavior: working and investing.

Supply-side economics was and is controversial because it directly challenges the economic orthodoxy of Keynesian economics. This theory is based on the premise developed by John Maynard Keynes that in a recession government should help stimulate demand for goods and services to put idle resources back to work. By contrast, the supply-side tax theory argues that the economic problem is not one of insufficient demand for goods and services, but insufficient production. After all, poor countries like India and African nations do not have insufficient demand. The poor have almost nothing so they have a huge demand for consumer goods. The problem in poor countries is a lack of production—a lack of supply. Excessive taxes on production can reduce jobs, incomes, and business creation.

Incentive-based tax reductions emphasize cutting high tax rates to reduce the distortionary impact of tax policy. Here is a simple example to explain the theory. Let us assume that a nation had a tax policy that taxed people 20 percent for working on Monday, 40 percent for working on Tuesday, 60 percent for working on Wednesday, 80 percent for working on Thursday, and 100 percent for working on Friday. Under such a tax system, no one would work at all on Friday, because taxes would take all of their earnings, and few people would probably work on Thursday because $4 out of every $5 earned would go to the tax collector and only $1 of $5 would go to the worker.

The famous Laffer curve provides a framework for understanding the potential impact of tax rate changes on economic behavior. . . . There are two tax rates that will produce zero revenue for the government. The first is, of course, a tax rate of zero. The second is a tax rate of 100 percent. If the government were to take every penny of earnings, no one would work. (Actually, people would work, but they would not report the income to the tax collector and thus the government would get close to nothing.)

The Laffer curve illustrates two points. First, for every amount of tax raised, there are two tax rates. The economically efficient tax policy is to never impose a tax rate that is higher than the revenue-maximizing tax rate. Above that revenue-maximizing tax rate, revenues will fall and so will economic activity. So the high tax rate is counterproductive. The second illustrative point of the Laffer curve is that cutting tax rates will increase economic output because the disincentive to work and save and invest is lowered as tax rates are raised. The higher the initial tax rate, the stronger the supply-side effect of lowering that rate. For example, to measure the impact of a tax, one needs to calculate 1 minus the tax rate. A tax rate of 80 percent allows the individual to keep 20 cents for every dollar earned. If that rate is lowered to 60 percent, the incentive to work is doubled, because the worker now keeps 40 cents for every dollar earned.

These kinds of very high tax rates can distort behavior and reduce the incentive to work and earn. . . . George Harrison of the Beatles wrote a famous song called "The Taxman." The first line of the song goes like this: "Let me tell you how it will be, here's one for you nineteen for me . . . 'Cause I'm the taxman." In 1965 when that song was written, the English government imposed a 95 percent tax rate on rich people . . . like the Beatles. A 95 percent tax rate meant that for every 20 pounds the Beatles earned, the British tax collector took 19 and the Beatles kept 1. It should not be too surprising that the result was many British pop stars in that era, including Mick Jagger, gave up their British citizenship to avoid these confiscatory rates of tax. It was either that, or quit writing hit songs.

As tax rates fall, the positive impact of continuing to lower rates is diminished. So, for example, if the starting tax rate is 40 percent, the worker or investor keeps 60 cents on the dollar. Lowering the tax rate to 20 percent increases the return to 80 cents. In both these examples the tax rate is cut by 20 percentage points, but in the first case, the incentive to work and invest is doubled, whereas in the second case the incentive to work and invest rises by one-third.

If we accept the premise that people work, save, and invest to earn money, then it stands to reason that increasing the rewards to working, saving, and investing will lead to more of it. And taxing away those rewards will lead to less of it. In the famous Supreme Court case *McCulloch* v. *Maryland,* Chief Justice Marshall famously wrote: "The power to tax is the power to destroy."

Income Tax Rates: The Historical Evidence

As mentioned earlier, there have been several occasions in U.S. history when supply-side economics has been tested. In most circumstances, the historical experience validates the Laffer curve theory. Let us begin with examining income tax rate changes. In the twentieth century in the United States there were three episodes of significant tax rate reductions. These reductions occurred in the 1920s under Presidents Warren Harding and Calvin Coolidge; in the 1960s under President John F. Kennedy, and in the 1980s under President Reagan. In each case the tax cuts were predicted to lose revenues, but instead federal revenues increased after the tax rates were cut because the economy performed positively to the lower tax rate regime.

The Harding-Coolidge tax rate reductions brought the top income tax rate down in stages from the wartime high of 73 percent in 1921 to 25 percent in 1925. This was a very large and unprecedented reduction in rates on the wealthy. Coolidge argued for the reductions in his 1924 State of the Union address by reminding the public that "when the taxation of large incomes is excessive they tend to disappear." He confidently predicted that his plan "would actually yield more revenues to the government if the basis of taxation were scientifically revised downward."

He was proven remarkably correct. The economy roared back to life in the 1920s after World War I ended with a recession back home. Incomes soared, industrial production soared at a faster rate than at anytime in many decades, and a general prosperity spread like a gale force wind across the nation. How much of this prosperity was a direct result of tax cuts is not exactly clear and still to this day a subject of debate. But what is undeniably true is that tax revenues increased even as tax rates fell. Between 1923 and 1928 real tax collections nearly doubled as the economy surged. . . . As the tax rates were chopped by almost two-thirds, the share of taxes paid by those earning over $50,000 (the rich back then), rose from 45 percent in 1921 when the rate was 73 percent to 62 percent in 1925 when their rate was 25 percent. Total tax revenues rose from $720 million in 1921 to $1.15 billion by 1928. There was no long-term loss of revenue from the tax rate cut.

In the Great Depression and then during World War II, tax rates were raised back up again. In fact, throughout the 1940s and 1950s tax rates reached as high as 90 percent. That was the top tax rate when Kennedy was elected president in 1960. In the 1950s the U.S. economy had grown but not at an especially rapid pace. Kennedy was elected in 1960 by proclaiming to the American people with his unmistakable New England accent: "We can do bettah." Kennedy decided that the way to get the American economy shifting into a higher gear was through across-the-board reductions in taxation. "It is a paradoxical truth," Kennedy proclaimed in 1962 to try to sell his tax cut program, "that tax rates are too high today, and tax revenues are too low and the soundest way to raise the revenues in the long run is to cut the tax rates." He insisted on a cut in the capital gains tax on stocks. He argued:

The tax on capital gains directly affects investment decisions, the mobility and flow of risk capital . . . the ease or difficulty experienced by new ventures in obtaining capital, and thereby the strength and potential for growth in the economy.

When some of his opponents suggested that this tax cut would benefit the rich, Kennedy dismissed this claim, arguing that economic growth would benefit people of all incomes. As President Kennedy put it: "A rising tide lifts all boats."

After many months of debate on this economic program—ironically a tax cut agenda that Republicans almost universally opposed and Democrats almost universally favored (politics has since flipped itself on its head)—the Kennedy tax cut was enacted in 1964 (a few months after JFK's tragic assassination). But Kennedy was proven right about the economic engines that would roar to life if taxes were less oppressive. The economy grew rapidly in 1964, 1965, and 1966. The unemployment rate fell to its lowest peacetime level in more than 30 years. "The unusual budget spectacle of sharply rising revenues following the biggest tax cut in history," announced a 1966 *U.S. News & World Report* article, "is beginning to astonish even those who pushed hardest for tax cuts in the first place." Indeed, after the tax cuts took effect, federal tax collections rose from $107 billion in 1963 to $153 billion in 1968. This shocked almost all observers. But even more shocking was the impact on the distribution of taxes paid. . . . Lower tax rates on the rich led to these income classes paying a much larger share of the tax burden. Americans earning over $50,000 per year (the equivalent of almost $200,000 today) increased their taxes by nearly 40 percent after the rate cut. Their tax share rose from 12 percent of the total in 1963 to almost 15 percent in 1966.

In 1980 Ronald Reagan was elected president in one of the worst economic crises since the Great Depression. Inflation was raging out of control at 12 percent per year. Unemployment soared while industrial production sagged to a 20-year low. America was deindustrializing. Reagan's economic plan revolved around a proposed tax cut very much in line with what Kennedy had proposed some 20 years earlier. Now the Democrats were the critics of tax cuts, and the party rallied against them, but Reagan was popular and persuasive and he prevailed in Congress to get the cuts enacted into law. The top income tax rate was reduced from 70 percent to 50 percent. In 1986 another tax law lowered the top income tax rate down to 28 percent. The 1980s were a prosperous era. Reagan was overwhelmingly reelected in 1984, promising to keep taxes under control. The *Wall Street Journal* later referred to the economic boom of the 1980s as "the seven fat years." The U.S. economy grew at a 3.5 percent rate above inflation and the stock market more than tripled during the prolonged rally. In the 1980s, some 15 million new jobs were created in the United States—more than the number of jobs created in the rest of the industrialized world combined.

Thanks to the return to prosperity, tax revenues grew by $52 billion per year in the 1980s with tax cuts, versus just $35 billion per year in the 1970s when taxes were hiked. And once again despite lower tax rates, the rich paid a larger share of the total. In fact, . . . the top 1 percent paid 17.6 percent of all taxes when the top rate was 70 percent in 1981, but 27.5 percent in 1988 when the rate hit its low of 28 percent. The super-rich, the top 0.1 percent of income earners, saw their share of income taxes paid double from 7 percent to 14 percent. A study by then–Harvard economist Lawrence Lindsey has shown conclusively that the government "collected more revenue from upper-income taxpayers at a 50 percent top rate than it would have at 70 percent."

The big economic concern that emerged in the 1980s was record high budget deficits. These were said to be a result of the tax cuts. The evidence points in a different direction. Reagan tax cuts did not cause the budget deficits of the 1980s because between 1980 and 1990 federal tax receipts doubled from $517 to $1,035. This was a 7 percent annual growth rate in tax revenues. As David Rosenbaum reported in the *New York Times* in 1992: "One popular misconception is that the Republican tax cuts caused the crippling federal budget deficit now approaching $300 billion a year. The fact is, the large deficit resulted because the government vastly expanded what it spent each year. . . ."

In the 1990s, of course, tax policy moved in the opposite direction. In 1990 Congress wanted the rich to pay more taxes, so President Bush agreed to raise the top tax rate on the wealthy from 28 to 31 percent. The *Wall Street Journal* reports in an article entitled "Oops! Weren't We Going to Soak the Rich?" that income tax collections in 1991 from those earning over $200,000 declined by $6.5 billion, even as income taxes paid by everyone else rose by $3 billion. Harvard economist Robert Barro reports that the share of taxes paid by the rich declined from 22 percent in the late 1980s, after Reagan cut tax rates, to 20 percent in 1991 after Bush raised them. In other words, Congress tried to soak the rich with higher tax rates and the middle class got all wet.

In 1993 President Bill Clinton raised tax rates from 33 percent to 39.6 percent. That tax hike ended up gaining revenues for the federal government. The economy and stock market reached new heights. This was seen by supply-side economics critics as evidence that taxes don't much affect economic success. But other positive factors were going on in the economy of the 1990s to blunt any potential negative impact of these income tax hikes. During this period, inflation rates fell, President Clinton approved two huge tax cuts on trade (NAFTA and GATT), and the capital gains tax was cut. Thanks to the retreat in inflation, real tax rates were not much higher at all in the late 1990s than they were in the early 1990s.

Supply-side economics surely does not suggest that taxes are the only factor that impacts the direction of the economy. Many factors like technological progress, government spending policies, the education system, regulatory policy, international trade, and a multitude of other factors will influence the direction of the economy. The point here, however, is that tax policies do influence how a nation's economy performs and that when taxes become too onerous, they can stifle economic development.

In fact, one nation that has recently learned this lesson is Russia. After the Soviet Union broke apart, Russia developed a tax system with high tax rates and big bureaucracies reminiscent of the system in place under the old Soviet socialist regime. But this system of "crony capitalism" was no more efficient than the old Communist central planning organization. The economy sputtered and the budget spiraled out of control. When Vladimir Putin became president he scrapped the old tax code and installed a 13 percent flat tax. Since then the economy has grown at a rapid pace, and tax revenues are higher now than under the old taxing system with higher tax rates.

Tax Cuts and Budget Deficits

One argument that is often made against tax rate reductions is that the budget deficit will rise if taxes are reduced. If that happens, the government's demand for credit will "crowd out" private investment, force up long-term interest rates, and therefore potentially cancel out the positive impact of the tax cuts. This is a legitimate concern, but in most cases overblown. Here is why.

First, if tax rate reductions increase economic productivity and output, then the amount of revenues lost from the tax cut may be minimal. As shown above, in the 1920s, 1960s, and 1980s, the economy boomed and the federal revenues increased after tax cuts. My calculations are that if the recent Bush tax cut increases economic growth by 1 percent per year for the next decade, the budget deficit will be lower by $1.75 trillion over this time period.

Second, there has never been any real-world evidence that tax cuts have caused higher interest rates. Economists the world over have tried to detect an interest rate effect of U.S. budget deficits and have never found any statistical relationship whatsoever. For example, after the Reagan tax cuts, the budget deficit did rise (mostly as a result of the Reagan military buildup to win the Cold War), but long-term interest rates did not rise. In fact, interest rates fell very dramatically in the 1980s even as the budget deficit hit $200 billion a year. Likewise, the big budget deficits of 2003 have not caused a surge in interest rates. Interest rates are at a 30-year low. Internationally, Japan has run the largest budget deficits of any industrialized nation over the last decade, but it has the lowest interest rates.

What explains this seeming paradox? The answer is that government borrowing does not crowd out private investment, government *spending* does. Whether the government finances its spending through taxes, printing money, or borrowing, the impact on private credit markets is likely to be negative in each case. That is to say, if we want to reduce the government's negative impact on the economy, the best way to do so is to cut government spending—particularly on income transfer programs that have no offsetting economic benefit. If tax cuts can create a resource constraint on the Congress and therefore force Congress to spend less money than they otherwise would, then the tax cuts may actually reduce the crowding out effect of government on private sector activity.

It is interesting that those who oppose tax cuts because of the supposed impact on the budget deficit, also oppose cuts in government spending that could minimize the impact of the deficit they say they deplore. The National Taxpayers Union has discovered that the biggest opponents in Congress of the tax cuts also have the record of voting for the most government spending programs.

Conclusion

To quickly summarize: In each of the three cases of income tax rate reductions in the twentieth century in the United States, we saw four effects:

1. Total tax revenues rose.
2. Tax payments and the tax share paid by the wealthy increased.
3. The rate of economic growth increased.
4. Interest rates did not rise, as tax cut critics had predicted.

The impact of tax changes cannot be properly predicted without assessing how the tax policy changes will influence the behavior of workers, entrepreneurs, and investors. All over the world tax rates are falling as political leaders realize that high tax rates do not redistribute income, they redistribute people and assets. They have learned the basic fiscal policy lesson that an efficient tax system has a broad tax base and low tax rates.

Race to the Bottom

JONATHAN CHAIT

To understand how deeply the United States has descended into fiscal madness, compare the present situation with the last time GOP tax-cutters ran Washington, the Reagan presidency. Just like George W. Bush, Ronald Reagan used his first year in office to enact a series of tax cuts tilted toward the well-off that helped plunge the nation into debt. For this, Reagan is remembered by both the right and left as an unflinching avatar of supply-side economics. But, in truth, Reagan reacted to the consequences of his 1981 tax cuts in a way that would have put him far out of step with Bush's Republican Party. When the scope of the budget deficit became apparent, Reagan acceded to a series of tax *increases* in 1982 (in the midst of a severe recession, no less), 1983, and 1984. In 1986, reacting to complaints that his 1981 tax cuts opened too many loopholes for the rich, Reagan enacted a sweeping tax reform that liberals . . . hailed for making the tax code more progressive. Reagan's record on taxes, in short, consisted of one year of unvarnished conservative ideological warfare followed by seven years of retreat and consolidation.

The Bush administration's record could not be more different. This year [2003], federal income tax revenue as a share of the economy is projected to fall to its lowest level since 1943. (It's true that much of this is a result of the economic slowdown, but it's also true that about half of the 2001 Bush tax cut has yet to take effect—meaning that, even after the economy recovers, revenues will remain low.) Yet Bush has not proposed raising taxes down the line, or even freezing future tax cuts, but rather is cutting them even more. And, far from evincing any regret for having tilted the relative tax burden from the rich to the middle class and poor, the president's new tax cuts are just as regressive as his earlier ones. Indeed, Bush—who cut taxes in 2001 *and* 2002 (a "stimulus" tax cut consisting mainly of business incentives and forgotten by nearly everyone) . . . intends to cut taxes every year he remains in office, according to ally Grover Norquist.[1]

There must be some theoretical limit to this administration's desire to cut taxes for the affluent. But there's no sign we have come anywhere near that point. The Senate, the only structural force that could have restrained the administration, has now passed a "compromise" version of the tax cut that is, in fact, more costly, dishonest, and less economically stimulative than Bush's original. In other words, we may have a long way to go before we hit rock bottom. . . .

To distract from the regressive nature of his plan, Bush has presented its centerpiece, the repeal of the dividend tax, as a matter of justice. "There's just a simple fairness issue on the double taxation of dividends," Bush told a New Mexico audience last week. "Listen, we should be taxing corporate profits, and we do. But, in this country, not only do we tax corporate profits; when part of those profits are distributed to the owners of the companies, small and large alike, it gets taxed again." It is true that taxation of dividends represents a kind of double tax and that single taxation would make more economic sense. The trouble is that Bush's commitment to the principle of single taxation is highly selective. Corporations have gotten so good at avoiding taxes in recent years that about half of all corporate income is not taxed at all. Bush's original plan would have exempted dividends only on corporate income that had already been taxed. But Senate Republicans changed that provision such that, even when a corporation shelters its income from taxation, it can still pay out dividends on that income tax-free. This represented an acid test of Bush's commitment to the principle of single taxation. If he really believed in it, he would have insisted

---

1. Grover Norquist is president of Americans for Tax Reform (ATR), an organization that asks all candidates for federal and state office to commit themselves in writing to opposing all tax increases.

that his GOP allies accept his version of the dividend tax repeal. Instead, the White House went happily along.

In recent months, the administration has hit upon another tactic to sell the dividend-tax repeal: Pitch it as a tax cut for the elderly. "If you're worried about the senior citizen being able to live a comfortable life upon retirement, then you need to join us in getting rid of the double taxation of dividends," Bush argued. "A lot of seniors count on dividend income in order to survive." A *Wall Street Journal* editorial made this case in 2003. Pointing out the disproportionate ownership of dividends by seniors, the editorial argued, "That arresting fact has been lost among the Democratic howling that the President's plan is a sop to the rich. In reality, while seniors receive about 15 percent of the nation's income, Treasury statistics show they are the recipients of about 50 percent of the nation's dividend income." So, reasoned the *Journal,* Democrats claim Bush's tax cut goes to the rich, but in reality it goes to the old!

Can you spot the logical flaw here? Yes—it is actually possible to be both rich *and* old. This phenomenon has been documented in popular culture for decades, in the form of characters such as Ebenezer Scrooge and C. Montgomery Burns. And, indeed, the 11 percent of the elderly who earn more than $100,000 per year would receive more than 60 percent of the benefit of a dividend-tax repeal. And those old folks who earn less than $50,000 per year—that is, two-thirds of all seniors—would get less than 11 percent of the benefit. All of which suggests that helping Granny afford the early-bird special at Denny's may not be exactly what the Bushies had in mind.

But Bush's primary justification for his tax cut is not providing income support for seniors or middle-class families. It's creating jobs, which he calls the plan's "whole purpose." Speaking in Ohio last month [May 2003], Bush asserted, "The package needs to be robust so that we can create more than a million new jobs by the end of 2004. That's not my projection. That's the projection of a lot of smart economists who've analyzed the package."

When Bush says, "that's not my projection," one might assume he means it's the work of an objective, nonpartisan body. In fact, the calculation comes from his own Council of Economic Advisers. So Bush's statement is only true in the very narrow sense that he did not personally construct the macroeconomic model that arrived at the result. Furthermore, while it may sound impressive, "one million jobs" is not very many. The economy has lost more than twice that number since Bush took office. With decent population growth, even a sluggish economy could gain one million jobs over a year and a half. To those few who follow economic statistics carefully, Bush's repeated promise of one million new jobs sounds eerily like the *Austin Powers* character Dr. Evil, who travels forward in time from the 1960s to hold the world hostage for what he considers to be the mind-boggling sum of *one million dollars.*

The very notion that the government should take specific steps to counteract the business cycle derives from the theories of John Maynard

Keynes, the patron saint of modern center-left economics. Keynes, in a nutshell, argued that a recession happens when the demand for goods and services drops, and, therefore, the solution is to get consumers to spend. In every speech, Bush casts his plan in classical Keynesian terms. As the president told a New Mexico audience last week, "My proposal is based upon this principle: If your economy is too slow, you need to increase demand for goods and services." Bush is right that tax cuts are one way to spur demand. But, in order to work, such cuts should put money into the hands of the people most likely to spend it—the poor, all economists agree—and do so immediately. Bush's plan, however, is disproportionately aimed at the rich, and, of its ten-year cost, a mere 6 percent will be pumped into the economy this year.

If the goal is to get money into the economy now, why cut taxes permanently? Conservatives say temporary tax cuts won't work because people won't spend their tax cuts if they know they'll be taken away in a year or two. But, if that's true, then having the government spend the money—the other Keynesian response to a recession—would be a better option. Indeed, if we follow the conservative prescription and ratchet down taxes permanently every time the economy slows down, after enough turns of the business cycle, the government will go completely bankrupt.

This is not to say Bush's tax cut wouldn't boost consumer demand at all. It would. While the rich don't spend as high a proportion of their income as do the poor, they do spend some of it, so giving them more money would presumably put *something* into the economy. The problem is that Bush's plan is wildly inefficient as economic stimulus. In order to pump some money into the economy today, it would require hundreds of billions of dollars in long-term revenue loss that will take place long after the economy has recovered. Economy.com, an independent research group, conducted a study measuring how much any given economic stimulus would boost the economy relative to its cost. None of Bush's preferred measures came anywhere near the top. One dollar's worth of extending unemployment benefits, for instance, would increase GDP by $1.73. Stretching the low-income, 10 percent tax bracket would produce $1.34. Accelerating cuts in higher tax brackets, as Bush prefers, would add only 59 cents for every dollar in lost revenue. And eliminating the dividend tax would produce a pitiful 9 cents of growth for every dollar in revenue loss.

The truth, as even Bush's supporters admit, is that his tax cut is not designed to cure an economic slowdown. The president's economic advisers are supply-siders. By definition, they do not believe in Keynesian, demand-side remedies. The recession, then, is simply a pretext for them to enact policies they support regardless of circumstances. Beneath all the mendacity used to sell Bush's tax cut, there is a set of truly held convictions. The trouble is that the honest rationales for Bush's tax cut are no more convincing than the dishonest ones.

Supply-siders believe taxes on income discourage people from working hard and trying to get rich. All economists believe this is true to some degree—nearly any economist would agree, for example, that the 91 percent top income tax rate of the 1950s was far too high—but supply-siders take this consensus view to theological extremes. By cutting upper-bracket tax rates, they hope to unleash entrepreneurial spirit and revive the economy, not just this year but for years to come.

Understanding why this theory is wrong doesn't take a deep familiarity with economic research, just a bit of common sense. In 1993, President Bill Clinton raised the top tax rate from 31 percent to 39.6 percent. Supply-siders predicted to a man that this would so discourage hard work and risk-taking that the economy would slow down and tax revenue would actually fall. "Higher taxes will shrink the tax base and reduce tax revenues," insisted a Heritage Foundation report. Of course, just the opposite happened. During the '90s, there was no detectable shortage of people trying to get rich. Innovation and entrepreneurship flourished, and the economy boomed, creating so much tax revenue that intractable deficits turned into surpluses. That doesn't prove the boom happened *because* of the tax hike, but it does make supply-siders' tax-rates-control-everything worldview look extremely dubious. There may have been a discouraging effect brought about by Clinton's higher tax rates, but it was so trivial as to be unnoticeable.

This experience offers a good baseline to judge the likely effect of Bush's rate cuts. The negative effect of a rate hike ought to be exactly as powerful as the positive effect of a rate cut. Clinton raised the top rate by 8.6 percent. Bush plans to lower the top rate by 4.6 percent, essentially taking back just over half of Clinton's increase. So, however much you think Clinton's 1993 tax hike harmed the economy, divide that in half, and you've got a rough sense of how much Bush's tax cut will help—i.e., bordering on zero.

Of course, the calculation doesn't end there. On the other side of the equation, tax cuts increase the national debt, soaking up private capital that could otherwise be used for productive investment. That, all economists (apart from the left- and right-wing fringe) agree, harms the economy by draining away into government debt savings that could otherwise be used for productive investment. That's why just about every mainstream prediction—including those of private forecasters such as Goldman Sachs and Macroeconomic Advisers and that of Congress's Joint Committee on Taxation, which is currently directed by a GOP appointee—shows that the Bush plan would boost the economy slightly in the short term but would actually *reduce* economic growth after that. Macroeconomic Advisers predict Bush's plan would, in the long run, slow GDP growth by 0.3 percent in 2017. While that is substantial, it's not a huge amount. But, then, if you're exacerbating income inequality and burdening future generations with debt, your answer to the question of what you get in return ought to be better than "well, we're only hampering economic growth a little."

Bush and his allies have three responses to critics who point to the negative effects of long-term structural deficits. The first is that tax cuts will, over the long run, boost economic growth to such a degree that tax revenue actually rises. This is the most extreme claim of supply-side economics, and Bush makes some reference to it in nearly every speech he delivers. "The way to deal with the deficit is not to be timid on the growth package; the way to deal with the deficit is to have a robust enough growth package so we get more revenues coming into the federal Treasury," he asserted earlier this month in California. But even the supply-siders who think Bush's tax cuts will cause the economy to grow don't believe it will bring about so much growth that revenue actually rises above where it would have been otherwise. . . .

A second defense, put forward by Bush's defenders but not by Bush himself, is that tax cuts will starve the government of revenue, thereby holding down spending and perhaps even leading to balanced budgets. (One notable thing about this justification is that it contradicts justification number one—either tax cuts cause revenue to rise, or they cause it to shrink; both cannot be true.) A good real-world test of this proposition took place earlier this year. We are facing the largest deficit in U.S. history, and revenue has dropped three years straight for the first time since the 1920s. Republicans control the White House and both branches of Congress, and all express a firm commitment to fiscal discipline. It is not an election year. The conditions for spending cuts, in short, may never be this propitious again. And what has happened? In March, the House proposed $265 billion in entitlement cuts throughout the next decade. This is nowhere near enough to balance the budget. It's not even close to as much as the *additional* tax cuts Republicans want to pass this year. Even that amount, though, was too high. House Republicans, under pressure from their own moderates, withdrew the plan.

Republicans imagine that deficits will force otherwise free-spending Democrats to eventually accede to major spending cuts. But recent history suggests they have it backward. The high watermark of fiscal conservatism in the Democratic Party took place in the late '90s when surpluses first appeared. Some liberals argued for expanding social programs, but the Clinton administration insisted on reserving surpluses for debt reduction. In fact, the very existence of high revenue offered the most powerful disincentive for spending. In the 2000 primary, Al Gore attacked Bill Bradley's health care proposal by arguing that it would undermine Medicare by weakening fiscal responsibility. The threat of "spending the Social Security surplus" served as a more effective political barrier against spending than any of the deficits of the '80s. Now that the barrier has disappeared—although no one talks about it much, this year's $400 billion (or more) deficit comes on top of the administration spending the Social Security surplus in its entirety— restraint has dwindled. . . .

This development also illustrates the essential logical flaw in the starve-the-beast argument. It assumes that, as Republicans intentionally sink the country deeper into debt in order to shrink the government to the size they prefer, Democrats will respond by acting responsibly. But what if Democrats decide that fiscal responsibility is a loser's game? They might instead adopt the mirror image of the GOP strategy: Spend gobs and gobs of money, and hope deficits will grow so high that the Republicans will have to stop cutting taxes. To expect the Democrats to continuously put their sense of responsibility ahead of their ideological interests, while Republicans continuously do the opposite, is to expect a level of self-abnegation bordering on political suicide.

The third and final conservative defense against the deficit hawks is that deficits will prove to be temporary or are otherwise insignificant. (*The Wall Street Journal* editorial page has even taken to using scare quotes— "President Bush's tax cut is running into trouble in the Senate, with opponents claiming they are worried about 'the deficit,' " it sneered in a typical offering—as if the entire idea were some liberal bogeyman.) In his stump speech, Bush asserts over and over, "We got into deficit because the economy went into the recession," and, "We have got a recession because we went to war." In fact, neither of these statements is true. The White House's own budget shows it running deficits into perpetuity, even after the economy recovers. And the war in Iraq imposed a one-time cost of $80 billion out of a deficit expected to exceed $400 billion this year alone. Do the math.

The administration does have a more plausible-sounding version of this argument: After the economy recovers, the deficit will be far smaller as a share of the economy than it was under Reagan. As Treasury Secretary John Snow told NBC's Tim Russert last week, "If you look at this budget, as a percentage of GDP, they decline, and they get down to well under one percent. That's a modest deficit." But the administration's budget forecasts rely on wildly unrealistic assumptions. They suppose, for example, that tax cuts slated to expire will not be renewed—although such renewals are routine and the administration will assuredly fight to ensure they take place. They further assume that the Alternative Minimum Tax, a complicated system designed to catch rich tax-avoiders, will grow to the point where it raises taxes on tens of millions of middle-class earners—even though the administration has already promised not to let this happen. Under a more probable scenario, budget deficits should run around 2 percent of GDP or higher for the next decade. If more tax cuts come, that number will grow even larger.

That would still be lower than the Reagan deficits, which reached as high as 6 percent of the economy. Unfortunately, as the Brookings Institution's Bill Gale and Peter Orszag have noted, the nation is far less equipped to handle a deficit than it was 20 years ago. For one thing, the private savings rate has collapsed over the last two decades, from around 8 percent to almost zero; when individuals fail to save any money, it becomes more important that Washington do it for them by running surpluses. A zero-percent private-savings rate combined with a negative public-savings rate (i.e., deficits) is a dangerous combination—it means the capital stock, which determines our economic growth, is continuously falling as a share of the economy. More important still, we're now 20 years closer to the retirement of the baby-boom generation than we were in the Reagan years.

We should be using this time—after the economy recovers, anyway—to pay down the national debt and prepare ourselves for a big fiscal shock. Running deficits now is like an aging couple running up their credit card debts just as they get ready to retire.

Oddly, the entitlement crisis strikes the administration as a reason *not* to worry about the deficit. "Although the resulting deficits [over the next few years] are manageable by any reasonable standard, they are cause for legitimate concern and attention," contends the administration's Office of Management and Budget in an essay, "The Real Fiscal Danger," published last February [2003]. "But whatever judgment one reaches about the deficit of this year or even the next several years combined, these deficits are tiny compared to the far larger built-in deficits that will be generated by structural problems in our largest entitlement programs." This is a strange argument to begin with: Yes, we're spending beyond our means now, but in the future we're *really* going to spend beyond our means, so why sweat it? Moreover, its premise isn't even accurate. According to a calculation by the Center on Budget and Policy Priorities, the long-term cost of Bush's tax cut exceeds the long-term deficits of Social Security and Medicare *combined.* In other words, if we rescinded all the Bush tax cuts, we could preserve both Social Security and Medicare and have money left over. So, if the entitlement deficits represent a "financial threat," as the administration concedes, what do we call the Bush tax cut?

Not along ago, the kind of structural deficits proposed by the Bush administration would have provoked alarm among fiscal conservatives in the GOP. But, at least at the elite level of the party, classic fiscal conservatism is now nearly extinct. Consider the evolution—or, more accurately, the devolution—of the moderate Republican position since Bush took office. In 2001, Senate moderates such as Susan Collins and Arlen Specter initially advocated a "trigger" by which tax cuts would be postponed if the surplus did not prove as large as forecast. Once that failed, they settled for slowly phasing in the tax cut in order to cancel future installments should the surplus run dry. That is to say, they supported tax cuts this year only if we could be assured of paying off $174 billion worth of debt first. It appears this year we will fall shy of that goal by some $600 billion. Now, it would be understandable if moderates didn't want to raise taxes right now. But nothing in their prior position would indicate a willingness to cut taxes even further, on a permanent basis.

Earlier this year, it appeared the moderates had dealt a serious blow to Bush's tax cut when they voted to restrain its ten-year cost to $350 billion rather than the president's preferred $726 billion. Perhaps the most prominent advocate of this plan was Ohio Republican George Voinovich, who had made his name as a deficit-hawk mayor and governor and had voted against a $792 billion GOP tax cut in 1999. In a recent appearance on NBC's "Meet the Press," Voinovich spoke at length about the growing deficit and asserted that further tax cuts will "undermine our economy instead of stimulating it." By this logic, he should have opposed any tax cut.

But, after yet another soliloquy against deficit-financed tax cuts, he concluded, "So the point I'm making is that this three hundred fifty billion dollar package is a responsible package." In fact, the point he made suggested just the opposite. Voinovich's incoherence undermines his self-proclaimed principles.

The other fatal flaw in the position embraced by Voinovich and fellow moderates is that the condition they demanded—holding the tax cut to $350 billion—meant essentially nothing. This is because in recent years the GOP has perfected the art of rapidly phasing in and phasing out tax cuts in order to lower their official costs. The 2001 tax cut, for instance, delayed implementation of many tax cuts and ended others abruptly. This year, Senate Republicans again made full use of such gimmickry, passing a "$350 billion" tax cut that, realistically accounted for, would drain perhaps as much as $1 trillion from federal coffers during the next ten years. Unsurprisingly, arch-conservative Tom DeLay[2] gladly acceded to the "$350 billion" ceiling, explaining to *The New York Times*, "Numbers don't mean anything."

Take its most obvious gimmick: the decision to have the dividend-tax repeal end after just four years. Voinovich, pathetically, says this will "force us to look at what we have done and make us study whether it has an impact on the economy." In fact, it will do no such thing: The only purpose of the phase-out is to keep down the apparent cost of the tax bill; once the dividend repeal is in place, Republicans will argue overwhelmingly that allowing it to expire would constitute a "tax increase." How do we know this? Because that's what they're doing right now. As Bush told a California rally earlier this month, "[Congress] agreed to [cut taxes in 2001]. The problem is that they weren't going to let you keep your own money for three, five, or seven years from now." He makes it sound like an unwelcome scheme, probably cooked up by Tom Daschle.[3] In fact, Bush's original 2001 plan had phase-ins, and Congress—with the administration's approval—extended the phase-ins in order to include the deepest possible tax cuts while still appearing to comply with its budget. Each tax cut, in other words, is mined with time bombs that must be defused (or else we'll have a "tax increase"), and each fix plants new ones that must be defused again. Bush will soon be back decrying those very gimmicks and demanding they be fixed by yet another tax cut.

It would be nice to imagine that, at some point, Bush's tax-cut hucksterism will be constrained by some feeling of shame, some sense of responsibility to future generations, or—the most fanciful wish—a concern for social equity. But, in George W. Bush's Washington, such quaint notions are all, from the administration's point of view, blessedly in remission.

---

2. At the time of this article, Tom DeLay (R-Texas) was Majority Leader of the House of Representatives.

3. At the time of this article, Tom Daschle (D-South Dakota) was Minority Leader of the House of Representatives.

DISCUSSION QUESTIONS

1. Critics of large budget deficits argue that they benefit older Americans but push the costs forward to young people who will have to pay back the debt. Do you think young people are more concerned about deficits than are older people? Do large deficits redistribute burdens from one generation to the next? How would Moore respond to this charge?

2. Polls show that only a small percentage of voters are concerned about the record deficits. Why do you think this is? Are you concerned?

3. President Bush has frequently said that taxes are bad because the government essentially takes "your money" from you. Do you agree? In what sense could it be argued that part of what we earn we "owe" to society? How do we know how much?

4. Some scholars argue that democracies have a built-in tendency toward deficits because politicians have incentives to spend more than they take in to get reelected. Do you think politicians pander to voters that way? Assuming deficits are a problem, do you think that voters will vote for someone who promises to raise taxes or cut spending in order to cut the deficit? Would you?

5. Do you think the present federal government is too big or too small? What programs would you like to see expanded? What programs would you like to see cut? Why?

SUGGESTED READINGS AND INTERNET RESOURCES

For a basic history of budget battles and the Republican Party's opposition to taxes, see Sheldon Pollack, *Refinancing America: The Republican Antitax Agenda* (Albany: State University of New York Press, 2003). William Simon, treasury secretary under presidents Nixon and Ford, provides a hard-hitting attack on big government and deficits in *A Time for Truth* (New York: Berkley Books, 1979). In *The Triumph of Politics* (New York: Harper & Row, 1986) President Reagan's budget director, David Stockman, criticizes the priorities of the president's tax-cutting package. President Clinton's treasury secretary, Robert Rubin, tells how he worked to reduce deficits and deal with financial crises in a memoir (coauthored with Jacob Weisberg), *Uncertain World: Tough Choices from Wall Street to Washington* (New York: Random House, 2003). In *Locked in the Cabinet* (New York: Alfred A. Knopf, 1997), Robert Reich, secretary of labor under Clinton, gives a much more critical view of Rubin's deficit reduction efforts, maintaining that the administration gave up on important domestic priorities in order to satisfy Wall Street.

Congressional Budget Office (CBO)
www.cbo.gov
The CBO is the staff arm of Congress on budgetary issues. To quote from its
website: "CBO aims to provide the Congress with the objective, timely, nonpartisan analyses needed for economic and budgetary decisions and with the information and estimates required for the Congressional budget process."

OMB Watch
www.ombwatch.org
Located in Washington, D.C., OMB Watch was founded in 1983 to critically examine the information and analysis put out by the White House Office of
Management and Budget. A nonprofit research and advocacy organization
dedicated to promoting government accountability and citizen participation,
OMB Watch focuses on four main areas: the federal budget; regulatory policy;
public access to government information; and policy participation by nonprofit
organizations.

Club for Growth
www.clubforgrowth.org
This 9,000-member organization is guided by supply-side economics and
campaigns and lobbies for tax cuts and smaller government. Its website provides
analysis of budget issues from a conservative, free market point of view. Its
campaign contributions support candidates who pledge to reduce taxes.

Center on Budget and Policy Priorities
www.cbpp.org
This is a liberal policy think tank that analyzes budgets and spending programs
at the federal and state levels. The site provides in-depth analysis of the federal
budget, focusing on spending needs as well as deficit reduction.

13

Congress:
Can It Serve
the Public Good?

O f the three branches of the federal government, Congress provides the most direct representation, and it is sometimes called "the people's branch." But public disenchantment with Congress was on the rise in the late 1980s and early 1990s. When members of Congress voted themselves a pay raise in 1989, talk radio shows erupted with vehement denunciations of the nation's legislators as a privileged elite out of touch with the citizens who had sent them to Washington. The House banking scandal of 1992 added to the image of privilege the taint of corruption. Meanwhile, congressional inability to get mounting deficits under control or to pass major legislation created a picture of a profligate and inefficient legislature. Then came the electoral "earthquake" of 1994, when the voters took out their unhappiness on the Democrats who had long controlled Congress and established a new Republican majority pledged to transform the institution.

Under the leadership of the new Speaker of the House, Newt Gingrich, the Republicans moved swiftly to enact a "revolution" in Congress. Playing to popular democratic grievances, House Republicans took the lead in cutting down some of the symbols of congressional privilege. More importantly, congressional Republicans pushed a far-reaching conservative agenda that would shift power away from Washington to the states and private industry, cut taxes, and balance the budget through major spending cuts.

Perhaps the most remarkable aspect of the Republican "revolution" of 1995 was the attempt to transform fundamentally how Congress works. During the years of Democratic control, the most influential force in shaping congressional behavior had been the individual members, whose concern for reelection fostered close attention to district or state interests. Congress as an institution was relatively decentralized, with committees and subcommittees shaping legislation more than did the parties or their leadership. It was the goal of Speaker Gingrich and his followers to change the congressional culture by placing the unifying forces of leadership and party above the fragmenting forces of committee power and individualism. Through new rules and bold assertions of authority, Gingrich and his team consolidated power and kept the focus on their party's agenda.

Gingrich's congressional revolution was stymied by the end of 1995, once a majority of Americans blamed the Republicans for a government shutdown caused by a stalemate with President Clinton over the budget. A subsequent series of blows to Gingrich's power and reputation, culminating in Republican electoral disappointment in 1998, led to the Speaker's resignation. Republicans held onto their control of the House, but by narrow margins. The Senate briefly returned to Democratic control in June 2001 when a Republican moderate, Senator James Jeffords of Vermont, announced that he was leaving the Republican Party to become an independent and to vote with the Democrats on leadership and organizational matters. However, the elections of 2002 restored a small Republican majority in the Senate.

As the Republican revolution in Congress faded, the forces of individualism and committee power reasserted themselves. Yet the post-revolutionary Congress is a changed institution in an important respect: partisanship is more intense and party leaders are more influential than they were before 1994. On major bills before the House and Senate, it is now common to find almost all Republicans on one side and almost all Democrats on the other. This partisan polarization was evident in the impeachment and trial of President Clinton in 1998–1999. Even the shock of the terrorist attacks on September 11, 2001, brought only a temporary halt to partisan conflict in Congress. The conservative agenda of President George W. Bush, especially in the areas of tax cuts and foreign policy, became a further source for vitriolic partisan quarrels.

Political scientists who study Congress are divided over the extent of the changes wrought by the Republican revolution. To some scholars, individualistic motives are still the best guide to explaining the actions of legislators, and the interests of districts or states are still the touchstone for their votes on legislation. Other scholars concede that most legislators remain concerned about maintaining their positions but insist that legislative choices are now powerfully shaped by considerations of party and ideology.

Morris Fiorina, the author of our first selection, believes that both legislators and the people who elect them are motivated by calculations of self-interest. For members of Congress, the goal of self-interested behavior is reelection. For their constituents, the goal of self-interested behavior is pork-barrel projects, which bring federal dollars into their district, and assistance from the legislator in handling problems with federal bureaucrats ("casework"). Fiorina stresses how the bureaucratic state is a godsend to congressional incumbents, who get credit for establishing new programs that expand the bureaucracy and then win still further credit by denouncing the inevitable bureaucratic blunders that ensue. Note that in Fiorina's picture of congressional politics, neither representatives nor voters are paying much attention to legislation that seeks to address the nation's problems.

In our second selection, William F. Connelly Jr. and John J. Pitney Jr. describe the behavior of House Republicans (and the response to them by House Democrats) as a challenge to the views of Fiorina and other scholars who share his emphasis on the reelection motive. Fiorina's view, Connelly and Pitney suggest, neglects the power of the "majority-status motive." Only when their party has a majority can individual legislators hope to see their priority bills enacted into law or to become committee or subcommittee chairs, and this consideration provides a strong incentive to work for the success of their party. Further, struggles between the parties shape the daily experiences of legislators, especially in an atmosphere of polarization, with minority-party members often complaining of unfairness and majority-party members complaining of obstructionism. Although Newt Gingrich erred in thinking that he could drive a policy revolution through the national government from the vantage point of the House of Representatives, Connelly and Pitney indicate that he was correct in thinking that strong party leadership could transform the way Congress works.

The debate between Fiorina, emphasizing congressional individualism, and Connelly and Pitney, emphasizing congressional partisanship, raises important questions about the character of representation in the contemporary Congress. Are individual representatives and their constituents locked into a system of self-interested and short-term exchanges while no one devotes sufficient care to the long-term welfare of the nation? Or has partisan conflict linked most individual representatives to two large teams that battle over rival ideological conceptions of the public good? Does stronger party leadership and unity make Congress a more effective institution, or does polarization create a hostile environment that limits collaboration across party lines and undermines collective deliberation about the nation's needs?

The Rise of the Washington Establishment

MORRIS P. FIORINA

Dramatis Personae

I assume that most people most of the time act in their own self-interest. This is not to say that human beings seek only to amass tangible wealth but rather to say that human beings seek to achieve their own ends—tangible and intangible—rather than the ends of their fellow men. I do not condemn such behavior nor do I condone it (although I rather sympathize with Thoreau's comment that "if I knew for a certainty that a man was coming to my house with the conscious design of doing me good, I should run for my life"). I only claim that political and economic theories which presume self-interested behavior will prove to be more widely applicable than those which build on more altruistic assumptions.

What does the axiom imply when used in the specific context of this book, a context peopled by congressmen, bureaucrats, and voters? I assume that the primary goal of the typical congressman is reelection. Over and above the $57,000 salary plus "perks" and outside money, the office of congressman carries with it prestige, excitement, and power.[1] It is a seat in the cockpit of government. But in order to retain the status, excitement, and power (not to mention more tangible things) of office, the congressman must win reelection every two years. Even those congressmen genuinely concerned with good public policy must achieve reelection in order to continue their work. Whether narrowly self-serving or more publicly oriented, the individual congressman finds reelection to be at least a necessary condition for the achievement of his goals.

Moreover, there is a kind of natural selection process at work in the electoral arena. On average, those congressmen who are not primarily interested in reelection will not achieve reelection as often as those who are interested. We, the people, help to weed out congressmen whose primary motivation is not reelection. We admire politicians who courageously adopt the aloof role of the disinterested statesman, but we vote for those politicians who follow our wishes and do us favors.

---

1. The $57,000 salary was the salary for a member of Congress in 1977, when the first edition of Fiorina's book was published.

What about the bureaucrats? A specification of their goals is somewhat more controversial—those who speak of appointed officials as public servants obviously take a more benign view than those who speak of them as bureaucrats. The literature provides ample justification for asserting that most bureaucrats wish to protect and nurture their agencies. The typical bureaucrat can be expected to seek to expand his agency in terms of personnel, budget, and mission. One's status in Washington (again, not to mention more tangible things) is roughly proportional to the importance of the operation one oversees. And the sheer size of the operation is taken to be a measure of importance. As with congressmen, the specified goals apply even to those bureaucrats who genuinely believe in their agency's mission. If they believe in the efficacy of their programs, they naturally wish to expand them and add new ones. All of this requires more money and more people. The genuinely committed bureaucrat is just as likely to seek to expand his agency as the proverbial empire-builder.

And what of the third element in this equation, us? What do we, the voters who support the Washington system, strive for? Each of us wishes to receive a maximum of benefits from government for the minimum cost. This goal suggests maximum government efficiency, on the one hand, but it also suggests mutual exploitation on the other. Each of us favors an arrangement in which our fellow citizens pay for our benefits.

With these brief descriptions of the cast of characters in hand, let us proceed.

Tammany Hall Goes to Washington

What should we expect from a legislative body composed of individuals whose first priority is their continued tenure in office? We should expect, first, that the normal activities of its members are those calculated to enhance their chances of reelection. And we should expect, second, that the members would devise and maintain institutional arrangements which facilitate their electoral activities. . . .

For most of the twentieth century, congressmen have engaged in a mix of three kinds of activities: lawmaking, pork barreling, and casework. Congress is first and foremost a lawmaking body, at least according to constitutional theory. In every postwar session Congress "considers" thousands of bills and resolutions, many hundreds of which are brought to a record vote (over 500 in each chamber of the 93rd Congress). Naturally the critical consideration in taking a position for the record is the maximization of approval in the home district. If the district is unaffected by and unconcerned with the matter at hand, the congressman may then take into account the general welfare of the country. (This sounds cynical, but remember that "profiles in courage" are sufficiently rare that their occurrence inspires books and articles.) Abetted by political scientists of the pluralist school, politicians have propounded an ideology which maintains that the good of the country on any given issue is simply what is best for a majority of congressional districts.[2] This ideology provides a philosophical justification for what congressmen do while acting in their own self-interest.

A second activity favored by congressmen consists of efforts to bring home the bacon to their districts. Many popular articles have been written about the pork barrel, a term originally applied to rivers and harbors legislation but now generalized to cover all manner of federal largesse. Congressmen consider new dams, federal buildings, sewage treatment plants, urban renewal projects, etc. as sweet plums to be plucked. Federal projects are highly visible, their economic impact is easily detected by constituents, and sometimes they even produce something of value to the district. The average constituent may have some trouble translating his congressman's vote on some civil rights issue into a change in his personal welfare. But the workers hired and supplies purchased in connection with a big federal project provide benefits that are widely appreciated. The historical importance congressmen attach to the pork barrel is reflected in the rules of the House. That body accords certain classes of legislation "privileged" status: they may come directly to the floor without passing through the Rules Committee, a traditional graveyard for legislation. What kinds of legislation are privileged? Taxing and spending bills, for one: the government's power to raise and spend money must be kept relatively unfettered. But in addition, the omnibus rivers and harbors bills of the Public Works Committee and public lands bills from the Interior Committee share privileged status. The House will allow a civil rights or defense procurement or environmental bill to languish in the Rules Committee, but it takes special precautions to insure that nothing slows down the approval of dams and irrigation projects.

A third major activity takes up perhaps as much time as the other two combined. Traditionally, constituents appeal to their congressman for myriad favors and services. Sometimes only information is needed, but often constituents request that their congressman intervene in the internal workings of federal agencies to affect a decision in a favorable way, to reverse an adverse decision, or simply to speed up the glacial bureaucratic process. On the basis of extensive personal interviews with congressmen, Charles Clapp writes:

> Denied a favorable ruling by the bureaucracy on a matter of direct
> concern to him, puzzled or irked by delays in obtaining a decision,
> confused by the administrative maze through which he is directed to
> proceed, or ignorant of whom to write, a constituent may turn to his
> congressman for help. These letters offer great potential for political

---

2. Pluralist theory in political science argues that power in the United States is dispersed among many different groups, which compete for influence in a process marked by bargaining and compromise.

benefit to the congressman since they affect the constituent personally. If the legislator can be of assistance, he may gain a firm ally; if he is indifferent, he may even lose votes.

Actually congressmen are in an almost unique position in our system, a position shared only with high-level members of the executive branch. Congressmen possess the power to expedite and influence bureaucratic decisions. This capability flows directly from congressional control over what bureaucrats value most: higher budgets and new program authorizations. In a very real sense each congressman is a monopoly supplier of bureaucratic unsticking services for his district.

Every year the federal budget passes through the appropriations committees of Congress. Generally these committees make perfunctory cuts. But on occasion they vent displeasure on an agency and leave it bleeding all over the Capitol. The most extreme case of which I am aware came when the House committee took away the entire budget of the Division of Labor Standards in 1947 (some of the budget was restored elsewhere in the appropriations process). Deep and serious cuts are made occasionally, and the threat of such cuts keeps most agencies attentive to congressional wishes. Professors Richard Fenno and Aaron Wildavsky have provided extensive documentary and interview evidence of the great respect (and even terror) federal bureaucrats show for the House Appropriations Committee. Moreover, the bureaucracy must keep coming back to Congress to have its old programs reauthorized and new ones added. Again, most such decisions are perfunctory, but exceptions are sufficiently frequent that bureaucrats do not forget the basis of their agencies' existence. For example, the Law Enforcement Assistance Administration (LEAA) and the Food Stamps Program had no easy time of it this last Congress (94th). The bureaucracy needs congressional approval in order to survive, let alone expand. Thus, when a congressman calls about some minor bureaucratic decision or regulation, the bureaucracy considers his accommodation a small price to pay for the goodwill its cooperation will produce, particularly if he has any connection to the substantive committee or the appropriations subcommittee to which it reports.

From the standpoint of capturing voters, the congressman's lawmaking activities differ in two important respects from his pork-barrel and casework activities. First, programmatic actions are inherently controversial. Unless his district is homogeneous, a congressman will find his district divided on many major issues. Thus when he casts a vote, introduces a piece of nontrivial legislation, or makes a speech with policy content he will displease some elements of his district. Some constituents may applaud the congressman's civil rights record, but others believe integration is going too fast. Some support foreign aid, while others believe it's money poured down a rathole. Some advocate economic equality, others stew over welfare cheaters. On such policy matters the congressman can expect to make friends as well as enemies. Presumably he will behave so as to maximize the excess of the former over the latter, but nevertheless a policy stand will generally make some enemies.

In contrast, the pork barrel and casework are relatively less controversial. New federal projects bring jobs, shiny new facilities, and general economic prosperity, or so people believe. Snipping ribbons at the dedication of a new post office or dam is a much more pleasant pursuit than disposing of a constitutional amendment on abortion. Republicans and Democrats, conservatives and liberals, all generally prefer a richer district to a poorer one. Of course, in recent years the river damming and stream-bed straightening activities of the Army Corps of Engineers have aroused some opposition among environmentalists. Congressmen happily react by absorbing the opposition and adding environmentalism to the pork barrel: water treatment plants are currently a hot congressional item.

Casework is even less controversial. Some poor, aggrieved constituent becomes enmeshed in the tentacles of an evil bureaucracy and calls upon Congressman St. George to do battle with the dragon. Again Clapp writes:

> A person who has a reasonable complaint or query is regarded as providing an opportunity rather than as adding an extra burden to an already busy office. The party affiliation of the individual even when known to be different from that of the congressman does not normally act as a deterrent to action. Some legislators have built their reputations and their majorities on a program of service to all constituents irrespective of party. Regularly, voters affiliated with the opposition in other contests lend strong support to the lawmaker whose intervention has helped them in their struggle with the bureaucracy.

Even following the revelation of sexual improprieties, Wayne Hays won his Ohio Democratic primary by a two-to-one margin. According to a *Los Angeles Times* feature story, Hays's constituency base was built on a foundation of personal service to constituents:

> They receive help in speeding up bureaucratic action on various kinds of federal assistance—black lung benefits to disabled miners and their families, Social Security payments, veterans' benefits and passports.
>
> Some constituents still tell with pleasure of how Hays stormed clear to the seventh floor of the State Department and into Secretary of State Dean Rusk's office to demand, successfully, the quick issuance of a passport to an Ohioan.

Practicing politicians will tell you that word of mouth is still the most effective mode of communication. News of favors to constituents gets around and no doubt is embellished in the process.

In sum, when considering the benefits of his programmatic activities, the congressman must tote up gains and losses to arrive at a net profit. Pork barreling and casework, however, are basically pure profit.

A second way in which programmatic activities differ from casework and the pork barrel is the difficulty of assigning responsibility to the former as compared with the latter. No congressman can seriously claim that he is responsible for the 1964 Civil Rights Act, the ABM, or the 1972 Revenue Sharing Act.[3] Most constituents do have some vague notion that their congressman is only one of hundreds and their senator one of an even hundred. Even committee chairmen have a difficult time claiming credit for a piece of major legislation, let alone a rank-and-file congressman. Ah, but casework, and the pork barrel. In dealing with the bureaucracy, the congressman is not merely one vote of 435. Rather, he is a nonpartisan power, someone whose phone calls snap an office to attention. He is not kept on hold. The constituent who receives aid believes that his congressman and his congressman alone got results. Similarly, congressmen find it easy to claim credit for federal projects awarded their districts. The congressman may have instigated the proposal for the project in the first place, issued regular progress reports, and ultimately announced the award through his office. Maybe he can't claim credit for the 1965 Voting Rights Act, but he can take credit for Littletown's spanking new sewage treatment plant.

Overall then, programmatic activities are dangerous (controversial), on the one hand, and programmatic accomplishments are difficult to claim credit for, on the other. While less exciting, casework and pork barreling are both safe and profitable. For a reelection-oriented congressman the choice is obvious.

The key to the rise of the Washington establishment (and the vanishing marginals) is the following observation: *the growth of an activist federal government has stimulated a change in the mix of congressional activities.*[4] Specifically, a lesser proportion of congressional effort is now going into programmatic activities and a greater proportion into pork-barrel and casework activities. As a result, today's congressmen make relatively fewer enemies and relatively more friends among the people of their districts.

To elaborate, a basic fact of life in twentieth-century America is the growth of the federal role and its attendant bureaucracy. Bureaucracy is the characteristic mode of delivering public goods and services. Ceteris paribus, the more the government attempts to do for people, the more extensive a bureaucracy it creates. As the scope of government expands, more and more citizens find themselves in direct contact with the federal government. Consider the rise in such contacts upon passage of the Social Security Act, work relief projects, and other New Deal programs. Consider the millions of additional citizens touched by the veterans' programs of the postwar period. Consider the untold numbers whom the Great Society and its aftermath brought face to face with the federal government. In 1930 the federal bureaucracy was small and rather distant from the everyday concerns of Americans. By 1975 it was neither small nor distant.

---

3. The acronym ABM stands for antiballistic missile.
4. *Marginals* refers to congressional incumbents who barely hold onto their seats in close races; instead, most incumbents at the time Fiorina was writing were winning their races by large margins.

As the years have passed, more and more citizens and groups have found themselves dealing with the federal bureaucracy. They may be seeking positive actions—eligibility for various benefits and awards of government grants. Or they may be seeking relief from the costs imposed by bureaucratic regulations—on working conditions, racial and sexual quotas, market restrictions, and numerous other subjects. While not malevolent, bureaucracies make mistakes, both of commission and omission, and normal attempts at redress often meet with unresponsiveness and inflexibility and sometimes seeming incorrigibility. Whatever the problem, the citizen's congressman is a source of succor. The greater the scope of government activity, the greater the demand for his services.

Private monopolists can regulate the demand for their product by raising or lowering the price. Congressmen have no such (legal) option. When the demand for their services rises, they have no real choice except to meet that demand—to supply more bureaucratic unsticking services—so long as they would rather be elected than unelected. This vulnerability to escalating constituency demands is largely academic, though. I seriously doubt that congressmen resist their gradual transformation from national legislators to errand boy–ombudsmen. As we have noted, casework is all profit. Congressmen have buried proposals to relieve the casework burden by establishing a national ombudsman or Congressman Reuss's proposed Administrative Counsel of the Congress. One of the congressmen interviewed by Clapp stated:

> Before I came to Washington I used to think that it might be nice if the individual states had administrative arms here that would take care of necessary liaison between citizens and the national government. But a congressman running for reelection is interested in building fences by providing personal services. The system is set to reelect incumbents regardless of party, and incumbents wouldn't dream of giving any of this service function away to any subagency. As an elected member I feel the same way.

In fact, it is probable that at least some congressmen deliberately stimulate the demand for their bureaucratic fixit services. Recall that the new Republican in district A travels about his district saying:

> I'm your man in Washington. What are your problems? How can I help you?

And in district B, did the demand for the congressman's services rise so much between 1962 and 1964 that a "regiment" of constituency staff became necessary?[5] Or, having access to the regiment, did the new Democrat stimulate the demand to which he would apply his regiment?

---

5. Earlier in his book, Fiorina presented case studies of districts A and B.

In addition to greatly increased casework, let us not forget that the growth of the federal role has also greatly expanded the federal pork barrel. The creative pork barreler need not limit himself to dams and post offices—rather old-fashioned interests. Today, creative congressmen can cadge LEAA money for the local police, urban renewal and housing money for local politicians, educational program grants for the local education bureaucracy. And there are sewage treatment plants, worker training and retraining programs, health services, and programs for the elderly. The pork barrel is full to overflowing. The conscientious congressman can stimulate applications for federal assistance (the sheer number of programs makes it difficult for local officials to stay current with the possibilities), put in a good word during consideration, and announce favorable decisions amid great fanfare.

In sum, everyday decisions by a large and growing federal bureaucracy bestow significant tangible benefits and impose significant tangible costs. Congressmen can affect these decisions. Ergo, the more decisions the bureaucracy has the opportunity to make, the more opportunities there are for the congressman to build up credits.

The nature of the Washington system is now quite clear. Congressmen (typically the majority Democrats) earn electoral credits by establishing various federal programs (the minority Republicans typically earn credits by fighting the good fight). The legislation is drafted in very general terms, so some agency, existing or newly established, must translate a vague policy mandate into a functioning program, a process that necessitates the promulgation of numerous rules and regulations and, incidentally, the trampling of numerous toes. At the next stage, aggrieved and/or hopeful constituents petition their congressman to intervene in the complex (or at least obscure) decision processes of the bureaucracy. The cycle closes when the congressman lends a sympathetic ear, piously denounces the evils of bureaucracy, intervenes in the latter's decisions, and rides a grateful electorate to ever more impressive electoral showings. Congressmen take credit coming and going. They are the alpha and the omega.

The popular frustration with the permanent government in Washington is partly justified, but to a considerable degree it is misplaced resentment. *Congress is the linchpin of the Washington establishment.* The bureaucracy serves as a convenient lightning rod for public frustration and a convenient whipping boy for congressmen. But so long as the bureaucracy accommodates congressmen, the latter will oblige with ever larger budgets and grants of authority. Congress does not just react to big government—it creates it. All of Washington prospers. More and more bureaucrats promulgate more and more regulations and dispense more and more money. Fewer and fewer congressmen suffer electoral defeat. Elements of the electorate benefit from government programs, and all of the electorate is eligible for ombudsman services. But the general, long-term welfare of the United States is no more than an incidental by-product of the system.

The House Republicans: Lessons for Political Science

WILLIAM F. CONNELLY JR.
AND JOHN J. PITNEY JR.

Introduction

Most of the key academic works on Congress came out during the unprecedented forty-year Democratic dominion over the House (1955–1995). According to Richard Fenno, political scientists assumed that House politics meant Democratic politics. "We wrote extensively about the House Democrats, and we became the victims of our Democratic diet." Two intellectual problems thus arose. First, the House GOP largely escaped the discipline's attention. Scholars mistakenly saw the House Republicans as a homogeneous lot, enlivened only by some nihilistic troublemakers. Second, political scientists failed to anticipate what would happen to both sides—and to the institution—when the majority and minority swapped roles.

The Republican takeover of the House is thus a gift to political science. It should encourage scholars to look at the House GOP's ideas, interests, individuals, and institutional arrangements. It should also shed new light on theories of congressional behavior. Certain ideas hold up quite well, including some that date from James Madison. Others appear to have been time-bound artifacts of a specific historical period.

Although the perspective of future years will tell us more about the implications of GOP control, it is already possible to draw preliminary lessons for political science.

Majority Behavior Differs from Minority Behavior

Beginning in the late 1970s, Newt Gingrich and other House Republicans increasingly used confrontational tactics against the majority Democrats. Scholars sometimes noted these activities and the frustrations behind them. Seldom did deeper questions come up: was Gingrich-style "bomb-throwing" a peculiarly Republican enterprise, or would Democrats act the same way in the minority? And in the latter case, why?

The 104th and 105th Congresses have shown that minority Democrats can be as harsh and disruptive as minority Republicans. Conversely, the new majority is defending the institution. Before detailing this behavior, we should ponder how life in the majority differs from that on the other side.

Start with the obvious. "Being in the minority means you don't get your legislation heard, you don't get to chair a committee and you don't influence policies in other parts of the world," says Representative Maxine Waters (D-Calif.). Former Representative Susan Molinari (R-N.Y.) recalls

> How can I describe what the changeover from life in the minority to life in the majority felt like? Imagine having lived in Alaska all your life and abruptly waking up one morning in Florida (with all due respect to Alaska), or living in a cave and moving to a glass house on a hill. . . . We'd spent decades as outsiders. We'd alternately begged the Democrats to consider our legislation and adopted the time-honored, traditional minority stance of naysaying. All of a sudden we mattered.

The majority controls procedure and the calendar. During their reign, the Democrats crafted restrictive rules that hindered minority-floor amendments. The GOP majority has been more open: closed or modified-closed rules made up only 43 percent of floor rules in the 104th Congress, compared with 56 percent in the 103rd. Republicans have also introduced innovations such as "Queen-of-the-Hill" rules and time caps, which foster consensus and deliberation. Democrats have argued that most major bills still come to the floor under restrictive rules. They were especially critical when the GOP leadership tried to kill a campaign-finance bill by bringing it up under suspension of the rules, which requires a two-thirds vote. Some Republicans seconded the criticism. "I really am ashamed to see how this is coming up tonight," said Representative Matt Salmon (R-Ariz.), "that it is in the same manner as that of the leadership who ran the House for forty years under the Democrats. It is wrong. It is wrong when they did it, and it is wrong if we do it, and I don't think this is a service to the American people."

The minority can sometimes pass its measures, and if the party balance is close, it can block items on the majority's agenda. But because of their numerical disadvantage and the majority's procedural control, minority-party members have much less success than their majority colleagues. Moreover, the grand prize of lawmaking—prime sponsorship of an enacted bill—is effectively outside the minority's grasp. Of the 295 House bills and joint resolutions that President Clinton signed during the 103rd Congress, Republicans sponsored only 35 (or 14 percent), mostly dealing with minor matters. In the 104th Congress, the pattern flipped: Republicans sponsored 212 of 252 signed House measures, leaving Democrats with just 16 percent. While Republicans were making policy, Democrats were directing the Secretary of the Interior to convey the Carbon Hill National Fish Hatchery to the State of Alabama.

For members who want to pass important laws and get credit for them, service in the minority is often depressing.

In analyzing lawmakers' activities, political scientists have downplayed partisan differences. In his otherwise splendid account [*Congressional Careers*], John Hibbing made only fleeting references to the minority and explicitly excluded Republicans from his chapter "The Formal Position Career." In *The Congressional Experience: A View from the Hill*, scholar-turned-congressman David E. Price (D-N.C.) tried to generalize from his time in the majority, but never noticed that minority members were undergoing a very different congressional experience. Now that he has served in the minority, a second edition might offer new insights.

Members of the majority spend their time deciding how to run the country. By contrast, members of the minority spend their time coping with frustration. During the 1980s, the GOP's customary response of accommodation gave way to confrontation. Republican bomb-throwing was partly an emotional reaction, but also involved deliberate strategy. When confrontation broadens the scope of conflict beyond the chamber's walls, a minority can influence floor votes or gain seats in the next election. Republicans think that such a strategy helped them win in 1994.

Put in the same position, Democrats have reacted with equal vehemence. Whereas Gingrich once said that Speaker Wright "is like Mussolini, believing he can redefine the game to suit his own needs," Sam Gibbons (D-Fla.) stomped out of a Ways and Means meeting, shouting, "You're a bunch of dictators, that's all you are. I had to fight you guys fifty years ago." In 1995, Democrats stalled the foreign operations spending bill with repeated roll-call votes, forcing an all-night session at one point. Appropriations Democrats staged a brief committee boycott, denying a quorum and delaying a meeting. Republicans responded much like the Democrats of yesteryear. "I think they've been very immature," said Ways and Means Chair Bill Archer (R-Tex.). Democrats won little on the floor but they did get publicity for their criticisms of the GOP. Said Democratic strategist Mark Mellman: "It's much less about improving legislation and much more about communicating a message."

Democrats have accused the majority of sinister motives. Representative Pete Stark (D-Calif.) called his Republican colleague, Nancy L. Johnson of Connecticut a "whore of the insurance industry." Complaining about GOP legislation cutting grants to recipients who engage in political advocacy, Representative George Miller (D-Calif.) said, "If you are a fascist, it is a glorious day." Representative Jose E. Serrano (D-N.Y.) assailed "the meanspirited, reactionary, insensitive, indifferent, right wing, extremist, antipoor, antichildren, Constitution bashing, bordering on racist, contract on America." Representative Charles B. Rangel (D-N.Y.) said of the Contract: "Hitler wasn't even talking about doing these things"; Representative Major R. Owens (D-N.Y.) added: "These are people who are practicing genocide with a smile; they're worse than Hitler."

Democrats attacked Gingrich's ethics just as strongly as he had attacked Wright. In part, vengeance drove them. "We have a long history with him, and you cannot dismiss that history," said Representative John Lewis

(D-Ga.). "He's at risk of being consumed by some of the fires he helped start." As in the GOP's Wright attack, calculation was also at work. "Newt is the nerve center and energy source," explained George Miller (D-Calif.), "Going after him is like trying to take out command and control."

In both cases, the parties played tit for tat. In 1989, then-Representative Bill Alexander (D-Ariz.) filed an ethics complaint against Gingrich. In 1996, Republicans filed complaints against Minority Leader Richard Gephardt (D-Mo.) and Minority Whip Bonior (D-Mich.). All these retaliatory strikes fizzled, but only after bestowing aggravation and bad publicity on their targets.

During the 1980s, a turning point in interparty relations came with the McIntyre–McCloskey race, a near-even 1984 congressional contest in Indiana. House Democrats voted not to seat the certified winner, Republican Rick McIntyre, and instead launched an investigation into disputed ballots. After months of rancor in committee and on the floor, the House voted along party lines (with a few majority-party defections) to seat Democratic incumbent Frank McCloskey. Republicans railed at Democratic "cheating," disrupted floor proceedings, and even discussed ways of shutting down the chamber.

Twelve years later, another contested election roiled the House. After narrowly losing his 1996 reelection race to Democratic challenger Loretta Sanchez, California Republican Bob Dornan triggered a House investigation by claiming that votes from illegal aliens had tipped the outcome. In certain ways, the case resembled McIntyre–McCloskey. Bill Thomas of California, the GOP point man in the earlier fight, now chaired the relevant House committee. As the probe dragged on, the new majority (like the old) claimed that it was doing its best with murky information. The new minority (like the old) cried foul, holding demonstrations and employing confrontational floor tactics.

The Democrats now enjoyed a stronger position than the Republicans of 1985. The Democratic majority of the previous decade had rallied behind one of its own, but many Republicans hesitated to support the eccentric Dornan. (In the fall of 1997, members of both parties voted to suspend his former-member floor privileges after he had a shouting match with a House Democrat.) And whereas the Republican minority failed to arouse the public about the McIntyre–McCloskey case, Democrats won national attention by suggesting that the Dornan–Sanchez probe had racist motives. Said Representative Elizabeth Furse (D-Ore.): "[T]his is a campaign not just against Congresswoman Sanchez, this is a campaign against new immigrants. This is a campaign against new citizens. It is a disgrace." Representatives Sam Gejdenson (D-Conn.) and Robert Menendez (D-N.J.) both charged the GOP with "Gestapo tactics."

In the McIntyre–McCloskey case, Democrats chided Republicans who talked about shutting down the chamber. "This threatens our ability to govern," said Gephardt. In the Dornan–Sanchez case, the parties switched sides, as Gephardt now made the threats: "If they continue in this immoral pursuit, the Democratic Party in the House of Representatives will shut the House of Representatives down until the investigation is shut down."

In 1998, the House accepted a recommendation from its contested-election task force to drop the investigation because Sanchez's margin slightly exceeded the number of illegal votes. For political scientists, that outcome was less significant than the episode's broader lessons: either party will resort to confrontation when in the minority.

Why has the House become so contentious? One explanation is that the departures of conservative Southern Democrats and moderate Frost-Belt Republicans have polarized the parties into ideological and demographic camps with little in common. A second explanation is that divided government and a narrow majority combine to make the minority feel obstructed and the majority feel thwarted. A third possibility is that the House's distemper reflects larger social problems, such as resource constraints that turn policy disputes into zero-sum games.

Meanwhile, the war on the floor goes on. Scholars should pay closer attention to its causes and consequences, as well as the differences between the majority and minority.

Remember the Majority-Status Motive

Much of the literature assumes an atomistic Congress where members rationally pursue individual goals. The Republican takeover reminds us of a different kind of goal: majority status, which is a collective good. Whether or not a lawmaker contributes much to winning a majority, he or she will benefit. Like leaders everywhere, party chiefs try to overcome the "free rider" problem through rewards and punishments. Yet there is more behind party activity than selective incentives. Members really want their party to have the majority, and under the right conditions, this desire shapes their behavior.

Although this statement might sound like common sense, it represents a modestly revisionist viewpoint. In explaining congressional behavior, political scientists have pointed to reelection, influence in the House, and individual visions of good public policy. While debating the relative importance of these goals, scholars have rarely mentioned party control of the chamber. . . . The failure to discuss majority status stemmed not from any intellectual shortcoming but from historical circumstances. From the late 1950s until the early 1990s, when the GOP never broke its "glass ceiling" of 192 seats, GOP control seemed out of the question. And by holding the White House for twenty of the twenty-four years between 1968 and 1992, the GOP suffered a handicap in House contests, since a president's party tends to lose seats over his tenure. Under these conditions, majority status became more a *latent* goal than an *active* one. Democrats took their majority for granted, and came to believe that incumbency was enough to hold it for them. Republicans still wanted majority status, of course, but many resigned themselves to being the "permanent minority."

Not all Republicans succumbed to this mentality. Gingrich and other activists engaged in many activities aimed at winning a majority: floor confrontations, special-order speeches, party conferences, rallies and demonstrations. . . . The reelection motive fails to explain such activities. Their opportunity cost is significant, since every hour at a party event is an hour that members cannot spend on their own campaigns. The direct costs are also steep, since high-profile partisans often put their own seats at risk. Voters may sensibly ask why their lawmakers are hogging the limelight in some party event rather than working for district needs. And party activists draw fire from the other side. National Democrats labored to defeat Gingrich, and nearly succeeded twice. His persistence in the face of peril made him a poor role model for single-minded seekers of reelection.

The motives of power and good policy lay somewhere behind these party activities, but the connection was mainly *indirect*. In the short term, the GOP activists of the early 1980s hurt themselves by angering Democratic committee chairs, who governed the course of legislation and decided how much influence to allow ranking members. In GOP leadership contests during the late 1980s and early 1990s, members came to favor the confrontationists. This pattern clashed with the notion that lawmakers choose leaders to be brokers and favor-doers: Republicans were choosing leaders to be party champions. In varying degrees, all Republicans continued to pursue individual goals, but now many were also pursuing the collective goal of majority status.

If members of Congress cared only about reelection, all party campaign energy would focus on them, and all member-controlled party funding would go to incumbents. Over the years, however, the national party organizations have spent large sums on challengers and open-seat candidates. As the party seeking the majority, the GOP made a proportionately greater bid to win new seats, and in 1994, 72 percent of its party money went to non-incumbents in competitive contests. Likewise, the Contract with America had less to do with incumbency than a party-wide campaign to take over the House.

After 1994, control of the chamber meant committee chairmanships and opportunities to influence public policy. The party leadership thus had something that it had lacked before: real power to reward and punish members. So now that House Republicans have a majority in hand, can one explain their behavior solely in terms of their individual goals and the leadership's manipulation of selective incentives?

Not quite. The leadership's internal power has limits: push members too hard, and they push back. When Representative Mark W. Neumann (R-Wis.) crossed Appropriations Chair Robert L. Livingston (R-La.), Livingston got Gingrich's approval to remove him from the national security subcommittee. Protests from the large class of 1994 forced Gingrich to back down and put Neumann on Budget as a consolation prize. Gingrich also had a bad experience when he canceled a fundraising appearance for Mark Souder (R-Ind.) and other members who opposed legislation ending a government shutdown. Fellow freshman Steve Largent (R-Okla.) offered to take Gingrich's place—and his drawing power as a former NFL star enabled Souder to raise twice as much as expected. This case illustrates a larger point: campaign money is overrated as a source of internal leverage. Give large sums to those who do not need them, and other members grow resentful. Deny funds to party rebels, and they will either raise it elsewhere—or they might lose their seats, which the party can ill afford.

Especially when the majority is narrow, leaders cannot rely on selective incentives alone. They have to engage other motives—including the desire to maintain majority status. Take, for instance, the 1997 budget agreement. On an ideological level, many Republicans wanted less spending and more tax cuts. And on an individual level, they probably could have found convincing justifications for voting no. But Gingrich and other party leaders argued that the agreement would deprive House Democrats of fiscal wedge issues. A Gingrich spokesman said that the budget accord marked "the end of the campaign for Congress. Republicans will keep their majority and grow it."

The operation of the majority-status motive was even clearer on the other side. After a wobbly start, Democrats crafted a powerful negative message: that the Republicans were "extremist" and "mean-spirited." With impressive discipline, they pounded those terms until they stuck. Chief Deputy Whip Rosa DeLauro (D-Conn.) said, "There is a unifying principle here, which is to take the House back." For 1996, they needed a positive message as well as a negative one, so they issued their own version of the Contract, the "Families First" agenda. Moreover, they changed campaign-finance strategy. Like the GOP two years earlier, they went on the offensive, directing 77 percent of their party contributions and coordinated expenditures to challengers and open-seat candidates, compared with 53 percent in 1994.

They kept the pressure up in 1997. Their outbursts over the Dornan–Sanchez race were part of a strategy to use race and immigration as wedge issues against the GOP. Gephardt issued a release called "The GOP–Anti-Latino Congress," which accused the GOP of "advocating an agenda that is openly hostile to minorities in this country—particularly Hispanic Americans."

Someday, the majority-status motive might again fade in prominence if the GOP pads its majority and appears to establish a long-term hold on power. But for the time being, with control of the chamber very much in play, this goal exerts a significant influence on both parties.

James Madison Lives

Speaker Gingrich liked to quote *The Federalist Papers,* but was closer in spirit to the anti-Federalists. Like them, he argues for rotation in office (that is, term limits), accountability in government (for example, the Contract), decentralization, and legislative supremacy. As early as 1981, he wrote that decentralization would put "those closest to the citizen—the legislator—at an advantage," which would lead to "an increasing shift of power away from the executive branch and toward the legislature."

The anti-Federalists, however, lost the ratification debate. The Republicans' failure to remember that result explains much of their trouble in the 104th Congress.

In the early days of 1995, some Republicans hoped (and many Democrats feared) that Newt Gingrich would run the country from the Speaker's rostrum. Instead, everyone got a refresher course in the principles of *The Federalist Papers:* the separation of powers, bicameralism, and federalism. Clinton vetoes, Senate reluctance, and GOP governors' policy independence all hampered the House GOP. As Representative J. D. Hayworth (R-Ariz.) said, "We also should have remembered that this is not a parliamentary democracy. We don't have executive power here. We should never discount the reality of the Constitution and the separation of powers."

The ideal of "congressional government" hurt the Republicans, who wanted the country to think they were in charge. They got their wish. In an October 1995 survey, only 7 percent blamed President Clinton for the problems that most bothered them, while 35 percent cited Congress. Republicans not only overestimated their power, they underestimated Clinton's resolve. The government shutdowns, as well as their 1995 decision to take on Medicare, left them open to Clinton's attacks. President Clinton's bully pulpit trumped the Speaker's rostrum.

Balz and Brownstein suggest that "Gingrich expanded his reach beyond anything the Founding Fathers had imagined." Unfortunately for House Republicans, their ambitions were not beyond the reach of James Madison. In *The Federalist Papers* he noted that the remedy for congressional dominance is "to divide the legislature into different branches; and to render them, by different modes of election and different principles of action, as little connected with each other as the nature of their common dependence on the society will admit." Bicameralism keeps Congress from encroaching upon the other branches, and reinforces its tendency to do what legislatures do best: represent, deliberate, and exercise oversight. It also promotes conflict even when the same party runs both chambers. House Republicans fumed when the Senate failed to pass several elements of the Contract, and especially when Senator Mark Hatfield (R-Ore.) caused the balanced-budget constitutional amendment to fall just short of the necessary two-thirds vote. During the 105th Congress, House and Senate Republicans differed over issues such as Medicare and funding for the National Endowment for the Arts.

As advocates of legislative supremacy, the anti-Federalists saw the proposed Congress as too weak, not too strong. Instead, they warned of executive and judicial powers. Patrick Henry said that "you will find this very judiciary oppressively constructed" and that the Constitution "squints toward monarchy. Your president may easily become king." The Federalists, on the contrary, thought the Constitution would appropriately limit each branch to its own sphere.

The Founders could have followed the British parliamentary model, arguably an incomplete separation of powers system. Instead, they made each branch powerful and independent. In the American system, wrote Martin

Diamond, "the separation of powers receives its distinct and full formulation and embodiment." In only one sense does the Constitution provide for legislative supremacy: Congress is supreme within its own sphere, just as the executive and judiciary are supreme within theirs.

Congress is powerful when exercising legislative authority or performing legislative functions, which may explain why House Republican revolutionaries fell prey to the temptation of "congressional government." Such ambitions, again, can be checked by the other branches and the Senate. The Founders understood that institutions affect the behavior of individuals and factions: "Ambition must be made to counteract ambition. The interest of the man must be connected to the constitutional rights of the place."

Constitutional rules are not merely the function of underlying nonconstitutional forces. Constitutional institutions affect behavior. Congress's general structure and processes shape what its members do. The Constitution provides for neither "congressional government" nor legislative supremacy, as the House Republicans have learned. On the other hand, the Constitution does provide for effective government and policy change. The separation of powers limits the abuse of power, while providing for its effective use. Madison understood that different institutions do different things. Congress is powerful within its realm. . . . The competition between the political branches—and between the chambers—can inject energy into the policy process by promoting the interplay among competing ambitions. . . .

Conclusion

While strict party government is impossible, reformers from Woodrow Wilson to Newt Gingrich have often dreamed of responsible party government. Why? Gingrich once called himself "the most seriously professorial politician since Woodrow Wilson." Like Wilson, Gingrich favored politics of grand ideas, rhetoric, partisanship, and political education. In November 1994, he argued that although voters may be "fed up with petty partisanship, I don't think they mind grand partisanship. . . . To have a profound disagreement over the direction of your country or over the principles by which your economy works or over the manner in which your government should structure resources, that is legitimate, and the American people believe in that level of debate and relish it." The Contract, and a similar 1980 exercise called "Governing Team Day," are examples. Gingrich said in a 1980 floor speech: "[T]his is the first step toward a de facto constitutional amendment that will give us accountable party government by giving us accountable party campaigns and accountable party records."

Professors Wilson and Gingrich, both students of the American political system, each had difficulty because of intraparty dissension. Why were both tempted by party government if Madison's system precludes it? The answer can only be that the system consists of more than checks and balances. While neither complete "congressional government" nor simple "party government" is possible, the Constitution does allow both for strong party leadership and a powerful role for Congress when the institution concentrates on what it does best. . . .

DISCUSSION QUESTIONS

1. What motivates members of Congress in their legislative behavior? Compare the reelection motive to the majority-status motive as explanations for legislative behavior.

2. How do we explain lawmaking that serves narrow interests? Have members of Congress become too tied up with the self-seeking objectives of federal bureaucrats and their programs, as Fiorina argues? Or are there other reasons that better explain such laws—for example, the ability of monied private interests to influence legislators through campaign contributions and lobbyists?

3. Is the resurgence of partisanship in Congress a healthy or an unhealthy development? Does it clarify national issues and generate sharper national debates? Or does it promote petty wrangling between legislative partisans that serves only to alienate citizens further from Congress?

4. What kinds of reforms does Congress still need in light of the Republican revolution of the last decade? What measures might improve Congress's ability to represent ordinary citizens? What measures might improve Congress's ability to deliberate about the public good?

SUGGESTED READINGS AND INTERNET RESOURCES

The central place of the electoral motive in congressional behavior is highlighted in David Mayhew, *Congress: The Electoral Connection* (New Haven, Conn.: Yale University Press, 1974). For a rich descriptive account of the interactions of representatives and their constituents, the classic work is Richard Fenno, *Home Style: House Members in Their Districts* (New York: Longman, 2002). A sophisticated analysis of why members of Congress sometimes support narrow interests and sometimes vote for a broader public interest is R. Douglas Arnold, *The Logic of Congressional Action* (New Haven, Conn.: Yale University Press, 1990). Heightened partisan conflict in Congress is the subject of Jon R. Bond and Richard Fleisher, eds., *Polarized Politics: Congress and the President in a Partisan Era* (Washington, D.C.: Congressional Quarterly Press, 2000). See Lawrence C. Dodd and Bruce I. Oppenheimer, eds., *Congress Reconsidered* (7th ed., Washington, D.C.: Congressional Quarterly Press, 2001) for an anthology of insightful articles by leading scholars in the field of congressional politics.

Free Congress Foundation
www.freecongress.org
This website, reflecting a conservative perspective on Congress, offers
numerous publications and Internet links.

National Committee for an Effective Congress
www.ncec.org
This website, reflecting a liberal perspective on Congress, contains extensive
coverage of liberal challengers to conservative incumbents.

Library of Congress
thomas.loc.gov
The Library of Congress website offers the Congressional Record and
information on legislation and committee activity for current and recent
Congresses.

14

The Presidency: How Much Difference Does the Individual Make?

T he president of the United States is coming to your city. You may not like this president's personality, programs, or ideas, but you are likely to make an effort to see him (someday, her) in the flesh. Why? Because most Americans regard the president—any president—as the embodiment of our nation's history and greatness. The presidency is commonly seen as the personification of American democracy.

This equation of the presidency with democracy would have come as a surprise to the generation that established the American Republic. The men who drafted the U.S. Constitution believed that democracy had been carried too far in the revolutionary era. They conceived of the new president not as a democratic champion of the people but rather as a constitutional officer who would, by the length of his term and the loftiness of his stature, be insulated from the passions and pressures of ordinary citizens. Anti-federalist critics of the Constitution, however, feared that the president would be too remote from the people and too reminiscent of the arbitrary executive that the Revolution had banished.

Neither Federalists nor Anti-federalists viewed the executive as a democratic figure. In sharp contrast, modern presidents present themselves as the only elected representative of the whole people and the very embodiment of democracy itself. Other political actors—members of Congress, bureaucrats, political parties, interest groups—are taken to represent only partial and selfish interests. The president alone can claim to stand for the national interest and the public good.

The modern equation of the presidency with democracy began with Theodore Roosevelt and Woodrow Wilson and reached its zenith with Franklin Roosevelt. After Roosevelt, most journalists, political scientists, and historians came to believe that presidents were the principal agents of democratic purpose in the American political system. Modern media, especially television, offered presidents a vehicle to bring their dramas of democratic leadership directly into people's homes.

Yet even as the bond between the presidency and democracy was celebrated, presidents were extending their powers in ways that threatened democratic values. With the Vietnam War, the Watergate scandal, and later the Iran-Contra affair, the undemocratic potential of executive power was revealed. A new and more skeptical perspective toward the presidency began to emerge. At the same time, the perceived failures of most recent presidents left many Americans eager to see a reassertion of an effective presidency as a champion of democracy.

The role of presidents in American democracy depends on the relationship between an individual leader and an institutional system. For political scientist Fred Greenstein, the critical importance of each chief executive's individual qualities flows from "the highly personalized nature of the modern American presidency." Greenstein suggests that presidential performance will vary depending on how each president measures up on six personal dimensions: "effectiveness as a public communicator"; "organizational capacity"; "political skill"; "vision"; "cognitive style"; and "emotional intelligence." In this excerpt from his book *The Presidential Difference,* Greenstein illustrates the impact of each of these six dimensions with material on modern presidents from Franklin D. Roosevelt to George W. Bush. No president, he suggests, is likely to be strong on all six dimensions, but the most effective presidents will possess several key skills and avoid the most crippling deficiencies, especially a flawed emotional nature.

Stephen Skowronek, another political scientist, criticizes the idea that individual attributes and skills are the important variables in presidential performance. For Skowronek, all of presidential history (and not just the "modern presidency") can be viewed in light of the rise and fall of political regimes. A regime marks an era in which one party is dominant in its electoral strength, coalition of interest groups, and ideas about the proper relationship between government and society (e.g., the liberal regime that began with Franklin D. Roosevelt and ended with Jimmy Carter). Skowronek suggests that presidents come into office confronting four types of political structures: (1) "a politics of reconstruction," in which the collapsing force of the previously dominant regime provides the opportunity for a president of the opposing coalition to launch a new regime and achieve greatness; (2) "a politics of disjunction," in which a president associated with a regime that is falling apart faces an "impossible leadership situation" and thereby appears incompetent; (3) "a politics of preemption," in which a president opposed to a still-vigorous regime tries to find success by blending the ideas of his own party with those of the dominant party; and (4) "a politics of articulation," in which a president associated with a still-vigorous regime tries to complete its unfinished agenda, at the risk of fostering divisions in the dominant coalition and evoking charges that he has betrayed the true faith set down by the reconstructive president who first formed the regime. In each of these cases, says Skowronek, what most matters about a president is not his character but his place in the changing structures of American politics.

The conflicting perspectives of Greenstein and Skowronek are evident in the respective ways they interpret the presidency of George W. Bush. Greenstein evaluates Bush on each of his six dimensions, finding a mixture of strengths and weaknesses. Although he is critical of Bush's limitations in communication skills and intellectual curiosity, he views Bush as growing in authority and stature after September 11, 2001, and facing the crisis of terrorism boldly without giving vent to distracting personal passions. By contrast, Skowronek depicts Bush as an "orthodox innovator" in the Republican regime founded by Ronald Reagan and, like such counterparts of the past as Theodore Roosevelt and Lyndon Johnson, concerned with expanding on the original agenda of the regime while enhancing its political appeal with innovative policies. Whereas Greenstein emphasizes that the events of September 11 propelled Bush to personal growth in his office, Skowronek emphasizes that the same events have had a paradoxical impact on the Bush presidency, facilitating the enactment of an orthodox conservative program yet pushing the Republican Party toward the "big government" that Reagan conservatives abhor.

From the perspective of Fred Greenstein, American democracy has a great deal riding on the personal qualities of the individual elected every four years. From the perspective of Stephen Skowronek, the potential of each president is bound up with longer-term political structures that reflect dominant interests, institutions, and ideas. Are presidents, as Greenstein argues, likely to serve democracy well or poorly depending on the personal qualities they bring with them to their office? Or are presidents, as Skowronek argues, strengthened or weakened by the opportunity structures characteristic of the four types of leadership found throughout presidential history? How much of a difference does the individual in the White House make to the workings of democratic politics in the United States?

Lessons from the Modern Presidency

FRED I. GREENSTEIN

> The executive branch of our government is like a chameleon. To a startling degree it reflects the character and personality of the President.
>
> —Clark M. Clifford, 1972

T he highly personalized nature of the modern American presidency makes the strengths and weaknesses of the White House incumbent of the utmost importance. It places a premium on the ability of chief executives to get the most out of their strong points and compensate for their limitations. It also places a great value on the ability of Americans to select presidents with attributes that serve well in the Oval Office. . . .

The Qualities That Bear on Presidential Performance

Effectiveness as a Public Communicator   For an office that places so great a premium on the presidential pulpit, the modern presidency has been surprisingly lacking in effective public communicators. Most presidents have not addressed the public with anything approximating the professionalism of countless educators, members of the clergy, and radio and television broadcasters. Roosevelt, Kennedy, and Reagan—and Clinton at his best—are the shining exceptions.

Chief executives who find the most able of the presidential communicators daunting should be relieved to learn that their eloquence was in part the product of effort and experience. Roosevelt, Kennedy, and Reagan took part in drafting their speeches and rehearsed their presentations. In 1910, when Eleanor Roosevelt first heard her husband give a speech, she was taken aback by his long pauses and slow delivery. "I was worried for fear that he would never go on," she recalled. When Kennedy was a freshman congressman, he had a diffident, self-effacing public manner. And for all of Reagan's professionalism, he did not perfect the podium manner of his political years until the 1950s, when his film career drew to a close and he found employment on the speaking circuit.

One president who allowed himself to be fazed by an accomplished predecessor was George Bush [Senior], who seems to have concluded that since he could not compare with Reagan as a communicator, he should be his near antithesis. Bush used the White House briefing room for his public communications, only rarely addressing the nation from the Oval Office, and he instructed his speechwriters to temper his prose. Bush's initial three years of high public approval provide a reminder that formal addresses are not the only way for a president to remain in the good graces of the public. His defeat highlights the costs of a leadership style that gives short shrift to the teaching and preaching side of presidential leadership.

Organizational Capacity   A president's capacity as an organizer includes his ability to forge a team and get the most out of it, minimizing the tendency of subordinates to tell their boss what they sense he wants to hear. It also includes a quite different matter: his proficiency at creating effective institutional arrangements. There is an illuminating postpresidential indicator of a president's success as a team builder—the way that he is remembered by alumni of his administration. Veterans of the Truman, Eisenhower, Kennedy, Ford, and Bush presidencies have nothing but praise for their erstwhile chiefs. In contrast, few Johnson, Carter, and Clinton lieutenants emerged from their White House service with unmixed views of the president they served. Most ambivalent are the former aides of Richard Nixon, a number of whom went to prison for their actions in his service.

Presidents also differ in their ability to avail themselves of a rich and varied fare of advice and information. FDR encouraged diversity in the recommendations that reached him by pitting his assistants against one another. Kennedy's method was to charge his brother Robert and his alter ego Theodore Sorensen with scrutinizing the proposals of his other advisors for flaws and pitfalls. The modern president with by far the greatest and most demanding organizational experience was Eisenhower, who had a highly developed view of the matter. "I know of only one way in which you can be sure you have done your best to make a wise decision," he declared in a 1967 interview:

> That is to get all of the [responsible policymakers] with their different viewpoints in front of you, and listen to them debate. I do not believe in bringing them in one at a time, and therefore being more impressed by the most recent one you hear than the earlier ones. You must get courageous men of strong views, and let them debate with each other.

Not all of the modern presidents have been open to vigorous give and take. Nixon and Reagan were uncomfortable in the presence of face-to-face disagreement. Johnson's Texas-sized personality had a chilling effect on some of his subordinates. His NSC staff member Chester Cooper recalled recurrent fantasies of facing down LBJ at NSC meetings when Johnson sought his concurrence on a matter relating to Vietnam by replying, "I most definitely do not agree."[1] But when LBJ turned to him and asked, "Mr. Cooper, do you agree?" Cooper found himself replying, "Yes, Mr. President, I agree."

The capacity to design effective institutional arrangements has been in even scarcer supply than effective public communication in the modern presidency. In this department, Eisenhower was in a class of his own. The

---

1. The letters NSC stand for National Security Council.

most emulation-worthy of his departures was the set of arrangements that framed his administration's national security deliberations. Each week the top planners in the bodies represented in the NSC hammered out option papers stating the policy recommendations of their agencies. The disagreements were clearly delineated and set before the NSC, where they were the object of sharp, focused debate. The result was as important for preparing Eisenhower's foreign policy team to work together as it was for grounding it in the issues bearing on unfolding global contingencies.

Political Skill   The classic statement of the centrality of political skill to presidential performance is Richard E. Neustadt's *Presidential Power,* which has been described as the closest approximation to Machiavelli's writings in the literature of American politics. The question Neustadt addresses is how the chief executive can put his stamp on public policy in the readily stalemated American political system. Neustadt's prescription is for the president to use the powers of his office assertively, build and maintain public support, and establish a reputation among fellow policymakers as a skilled, determined political operator. If there ever was reason to doubt Neustadt's diagnosis, it was eliminated by the presidential experience of Jimmy Carter.

Lyndon Johnson seemed almost to have taken his methods from the pages of *Presidential Power.* Within hours after Kennedy's assassination, Johnson had begun to muster support for major domestic policy departures. He exhibited will as well as skill, cultivating his political reputation by keeping Congress in session until Christmas 1963 in order to prevail in one of his administration's first legislative contests. His actions won him strong public support, making it apparent to his opposite numbers on Capitol Hill that it would be politically costly to ignore his demands.

Vision   "Vision" is a term with a variety of connotations. One is the capacity to inspire. In this the rhetorically gifted presidents—Kennedy, Reagan, and above all FDR—excelled. In the narrower meaning employed here, "vision" refers to preoccupation with the content of policies, an ability to assess their feasibility, and the possession of a set of overarching goals. Here the standouts are Eisenhower, Nixon, and to a lesser extent Ronald Reagan, whose views were poorly grounded in specifics. Vision also encompasses consistency of viewpoint. Presidents who stand firm are able to set the terms of policy discourse. In effect they serve as anchors for the rest of the political community. George Bush was not alone in his lack of "the vision thing." He falls in a class of presidential pragmatists that includes the great bulk of the modern chief executives. The costs of vision-free leadership include internally contradictory programs, policies that have unintended consequences, and sheer drift.

Cognitive Style   Presidents vary widely in their cognitive styles. Jimmy Carter had an engineer's proclivity to reduce issues to what he perceived to be their component parts. That style served him well in the 1978 Camp David negotiations, but it was ill suited for providing his administration with a sense of direction. Carter's cognitive qualities contrast with the kind of strategic intelligence that cuts to the heart of a problem, as Eisenhower did when he introduced his administration's deliberations on Dien Bien Phu with the incisive observation that the jungles of Indochina would "absorb our divisions by the dozens."

Another example of strategic intelligence is to be had from a chief executive who will never grace Mount Rushmore: Richard Nixon. Two years before entering the White House, Nixon laid down the goals of moving the United States beyond its military involvement in Vietnam, establishing a balance of power with the Soviet Union and an opening with China. By the final year of his first term, he had accomplished his purposes.

Nixon's first-term successes contrast with the paucity of major accomplishments in the two White House terms of the first presidential Rhodes scholar, Bill Clinton. Clinton possesses a formidable ability to absorb and process ideas and information, but his mind is more synthetic than analytic, and his political impulses sometimes lead him to substitute mere rationalization for reasoned analysis.

Two presidents who were marked by cognitive limitations were Harry Truman and Ronald Reagan. Truman's uncritical reading of works of popular history made him susceptible to false historical analogies. Reagan was notorious for his imperfect understanding of a number of his policy initiatives. That both presidents had major policy accomplishments shows that intelligence and information as measured by standardized tests is not the sole cause of presidential effectiveness.

Emotional Intelligence   Three of the eleven modern presidents stand out as fundamentally free of distracting emotional perturbations: Eisenhower, Ford, and Bush [Senior]. Four others were marked by emotional undercurrents that did not significantly impair their leadership: Roosevelt, Truman, Kennedy, and Reagan. That leaves Johnson, Nixon, Carter, and Clinton, all of whom were emotionally handicapped. The vesuvian LBJ was subject to mood swings of clinical proportions. Jimmy Carter's rigidity was a significant impediment to his White House performance. The defective impulse control of Bill Clinton led him into actions that led to his impeachment.

Richard Nixon was the most emotionally flawed of the presidents considered here. His anger and suspiciousness were of Shakespearean proportions. He more than any other president summons up the classic notion of a tragic hero who is defeated by the very qualities that brought him success. It has been argued that the tortured psyche of a Nixon is a precondition of political creativity. This was the view of Elliot Richardson, who held that if Nixon's "rather petty flaws" had been taken away, "you would probably have removed that very inner core of insecurity that led to his rise." Richardson's claim is a variant of the proposition that the inner torment of a Van Gogh is the price of his creativity, but other great painters were free of Van Gogh's self-destructiveness, and the healthy-minded Eisenhower was as gifted as Nixon in the positive aspects of leadership. Great political ability does sometimes derive from troubled emotions, but the former does not justify the latter in the custodian of the most destructive military arsenal in human experience. . . .

In the world of imagination it is possible to envisage a cognitively and emotionally intelligent chief executive, who happens also to be an inspiring public communicator, a capable White House organizer, and the possessor of exceptional political skill and vision. In the real world, human imperfection is inevitable, but some imperfections are more disabling than others. Many of the modern presidents have performed adequately without being brilliant orators. Only a few chief executives have been organizationally competent. A minimal level of political skill is a precondition of presidential effectiveness, but political skill is widely present in the handful of individuals who rise to the political summit. Vision is rarer than skill, but only Lyndon Johnson was disastrously deficient in the realm of policy.

Finally there are thought and emotion. The importance of cognitive strength in the presidency should be self-evident. Still, Presidents Johnson, Nixon, Carter, and Clinton had impressive intellects and defective temperaments. They reversed Justice Holmes's characterization of FDR.[2] Clinton's foibles made him an underachiever and national embarrassment. Carter's defective temperament contributed to making his time in office a period of lost opportunity. Johnson and Nixon presided over major policy breakthroughs, but also over two of the most unhappy episodes of the twentieth century. All four presidential experiences point to the following moral: Beware the presidential contender who lacks emotional intelligence. In its absence all else may turn to ashes. . . .

[George W. Bush]

The presidency is said to be an office in which the incumbent may grow or merely swell. If ever there was a chief executive to whom the former applies, it is George W. Bush. Arriving at the White House with only modest experience in public affairs, Bush took a minimalist approach to his responsibilities before the terrorist acts of September 11, 2001. Rising to the challenge, he went on to preside with far greater authority and assertiveness over an administration that has gone to great lengths to put its stamp on the national and international policy agendas, but been highly controversial in the policies it advances. . . .

Public Communication In the first eight months of his presidency, Bush seemed insensitive to the importance of public communication in presidential leadership. He appeared reluctant to address the public; when he did so, his

---

2. Supreme Court Justice Oliver Wendell Holmes Jr. observed that Franklin D. Roosevelt had a "second-class intellect but a first-class temperament."

delivery was unpersuasive; and when he was unscripted, was error-prone. In the wake of the acts of terror of September 11, 2001, Bush became a rhetorical activist, addressing the public regularly, forcefully, and sometimes eloquently and handling himself far more effectively in extemporaneous contexts.

As the immediacy of the crisis receded, Bush sometimes slipped into his former plodding manner, especially when he read routine remarks, but he remained effective in major addresses. Meanwhile, his ad-lib communications continued to be more effective than they had been in the pre-9/11 period. Bush also developed a punchy, vernacular style of stump speaking that undoubtedly contributes to his sustained high approval ratings.

There are distinct limitations to Bush's ability to win support, for reasons that fall as much under the heading of "vision" as "public communication." His rhetorical manner, coupled with the content of those of his messages in which he asserts his determination to take such controversial actions as the intervention in Iraq, has produced a visceral aversion toward him for many American liberals, an antipathy that is widely shared elsewhere in the world. In a sense, Bush has proven to be a mirror image of Bill Clinton, who was as passionately disliked by some of Bush's most fervent supporters and liked by many of his opponents.

Organizational Capacity   Organizational leadership is one the strengths of the nation's first MBA president. Bush has chosen strong associates; he excels at rallying his subordinates; and he encourages diversity of advice. Because avoiding public disagreement is a watchword of the Bush administration, its deliberative processes are not well documented. What evidence there is points to a presidency in which bureaucratic politics simmer beneath the surface, most notably in foreign affairs, where there has been a scarcely veiled conflict between the supporters of Secretary of Defense Rumsfeld and Secretary of State Powell. An unknown in the George W. Bush adviser system is the extent to which the prudent George H. W. Bush provides his son with off-the-record advice. The senior Bush has commented that "historians will be very interested" in what he and the younger Bush discuss, but "they've got to wait."

Preliminary insights into the inner workings of the Bush presidency can be gained from Bob Woodward's account[3] of the administration's post–September 11 decision makings. Woodward reports, for example, that Powell and Rumsfeld expressed their disagreements more sharply at meetings from which Bush was absent than in those at which he was present, which suggests that Bush may sometimes be shielded from instructive debate. Woodward also describes instances on August 5 and September 2, 2002, in which Powell arranged to meet privately with Bush and national security adviser Rice in order to register his disagreement with the hawkish proposals of Rumsfeld and Vice President Cheney. There was a similar instance on September 2, 2003, in which Powell circumvented the administration's

---

3. *Bush at War.*

hawks by meeting with Bush to make the case for seeking a United Na-tions–sanctioned military force in Iraq, having first secured the agreement of the chairman of the Joint Chiefs of Staff. The shortcoming of policy mak-ing by end run is that it places a premium on an adviser's bureaucratic skills and not just the merits of his or her recommendations. . . .

Political Skill   Much like his Texas predecessors Sam Rayburn and Lyndon Johnson, congenitally gregarious George W. Bush is a political natural, es-pecially when it comes to face-to-face politics. It is sometimes argued that Bush tends to view politics in rigidly black-and-white terms, but this is be-lied by the flexibility of his political tactics. Thus he worked easily with the Democratic majority in the Texas legislature during his governorship, but in Washington alternated between rigorous partisanship and cross-party coalition building as circumstances permitted.

Unlike Rayburn and Johnson, Bush is not a creature of Washington politics, but he has compensated for that limitation by appointing highly experienced subordinates, including the same director of congressional rela-tions that his father had employed. Still, Bush and his aides have sometimes been less than sure-footed in the international arena. This was particularly evident in the lead-up to the Iraq war, when the Bush administration relied on shifting arguments and blatant economic inducements in its unsuccess-ful efforts to win broad support for immediate military action.

Policy Vision   When it comes to the "vision thing," George W. Bush is the virtual antithesis of his highly pragmatic father, whom he has faulted for not building on the momentum of victory in the 1991 Gulf War to rack up do-mestic accomplishments on which he could campaign for reelection. George W. Bush *does* have the "vision thing," not because he is an aficionado of pol-icy, but because he holds that if a leader does not set his own goals, others will set them for him. The question in the case of the younger Bush is the via-bility of his vision, whether that of relying on tax cuts to stimulate the econ-omy or of mounting a war in Iraq in the face of domestic and international opposition. The ultimate result of these policies remains to be seen.

Cognitive Style   Bush's ostensible cognitive failings are a staple of late-night television humor, but it is evident from his remarks on matters that engage him that he has ample native intelligence. In the words of one member of Congress, who remarked on Bush's far greater mastery of policy after September 11, "He's as smart as he wants to be." To the extent that Bush's presidential performance suffers from his cognitive style, his prob-lem may be that of lacking intellectual curiosity, a shortcoming that blunts a president's sensitivity to emerging issues.

There also are cognitive implications to Bush's management style, which leads him to rely heavily on subordinates to structure his options. Having been a front man in his business career, his tendency is to do better at outlining his administration's positions than elucidating their subtleties. In this he contrasts with a leader with whom he periodically shares a podium, British prime minister Tony Blair. At a March 27, 2003, joint "press availability," for example, Bush and Blair responded to questions about how long the fighting in Iraq would continue. Bush was laconic and uninformative, contenting himself with such assertions as "however long it takes," whereas Blair was expansive and analytic, reviewing the roots of the conflict, its global ramifications, and its likely aftermath. All told, Blair rather than Bush provided a model of the intellectual suppleness one might hope for in the American chief executive.

Emotional Intelligence   By the litmus of emotional intelligence, the heavy-drinking, young George W. Bush was too volatile and unreliable to be a promising prospect for a responsible public position. It would not be surprising if a man who had abused alcohol until early middle age and had abruptly gone on the wagon proved to be an emotional tinder box, but Bush's pre-presidential job and his early presidency were not marred by emotional excesses. Woodward's investigation is again instructive. As it turns out, there are no episodes reported in *Bush at War* in which Bush is shown to have acted out of uncontrolled passion. Indeed, Bush explained that he expected national security adviser Rice "to take the edge off" any such impulses on his part, adding that "she's good at that." In the case of Iraq, an extensive interview granted to NBC news anchor Tom Brokaw not long after the fall of Baghdad is illuminating. Bush came across as thoughtful and good humored, neither boasting at the rapidity of the military victory nor revealing defensiveness in the face of his administration's many critics. In short, whatever the merits of his actions, his emotions appear to have been well in hand.

The Changing Political Structures of Presidential Leadership

STEPHEN SKOWRONEK

When a president succeeds, our natural inclination is to laud the special talents and skills he brought to the office; when things go wrong, we look for personal missteps and character flaws. There is something comforting in these judgments, for they sustain confidence in the office of the presidency no matter what the experience of the particular incumbent holding power at the moment. So long as performance is tied to the personal attributes of the man, success is always a possibility; it awaits only the right combination of character and skill. So long as the presidency is a true test of the man, its incumbents are free to become as great as they can be.

Much of what is written about the presidency reinforces these conceits. Typically, analysis begins by describing an office that all presidents have shared, a position defined by constitutional arrangements that have undergone remarkably little change since 1789. To this is added the trappings of modernity—new governing responsibilities imposed on the office in the wake of the Great Depression and World War II and new resources made available to it. These distinguish the leadership situation shared by all presidents after FDR from that of all their predecessors. Setting things up this way, the analysis holds the demands and capacities of the office constant over the latter half of the twentieth century and presents leadership as a problem of how best to apply the resources of the modern presidency to the responsibilities of the modern presidency. In effect, each modern incumbent becomes a new source of insight into what attributes of character and skill work best in the shared context, what strategies are most effective, what it takes to measure up.

In fact, however, the political demands on incumbents and the leadership capacities of the office of the presidency vary considerably from one administration to the next, and much of what we take to be evidence of personal flaws and leadership skills can be accounted for by closer attention to the particular relationships established between the presidency and the political system by each incumbent in turn. To see how, we first need access to these changing relationships, and that, in turn, entails thinking about presidential history itself a bit differently. Rather than set the modern presidents apart from the pre-moderns to treat them as a separate and coherent group, we will want to compare them individually with counterparts in earlier periods. By making better use of the whole history of presidential leadership, we can better assess the contextual conditions under which great leaders typically arise and identify the limitations on leadership possibilities imposed by less fortuitous circumstances.

The alternative history I have in mind charts change in American politics through the recurring establishment and disintegration of relatively durable political regimes. This regime-based structure of American political history has been widely observed by political scientists and historians alike. It demarcates the rise and decline of Federalist Nationalism between 1789 and 1800, of Jeffersonian Democracy between 1800 and 1828, of Jacksonian Democracy between 1828 and 1860, of Republican Nationalism between 1860 and 1932, and of New Deal Liberalism between 1932 and 1980. Each of these regimes can be identified with the empowerment of an insurgent political coalition whose reconstruction of basic governing arrangements endured through various subsequent configurations of party power. Just as America's fragmented constitutional system has made sweeping political change rare and difficult to achieve, it has worked similarly to perpetuate the ideological and programmatic commitments of the few insurgencies that have succeeded. To this extent at least, the regime structure of American political history may be considered a byproduct of the constitutional structure of American government. It is manifest today in the persistence of the conservative regime ushered in by Ronald Reagan in 1980.

Looking over the course of each of these regimes suggests a number of typically structured relationships between the presidency and the political system, and thinking about the modern presidents in these terms places each of them in a unique analytic relationship with the presidents of the past. I do not mean to suggest that regime formation and decay are processes external to presidential leadership; on the contrary, I mean to show that the active intervention of presidents at various stages in these processes has driven them forward. What I am suggesting is that we try to understand the political demands and challenges of presidential leadership as variables mediated by the generation and degeneration of these political orderings, that we reverse the standard analytic procedure by holding personality and skill constant and examining the typical political effects of presidential action in the differently structured political contexts characteristic of our constitutional system.

The Political Structures of Presidential Leadership

Each regime begins with the rise to power of a new political coalition out to construct and legitimize alternative governing arrangements, to recast relations between state and society in ways advantageous to its members. These coalitions will then attempt to extend their claims on power by elaborating and modifying their basic agenda in ways that are responsive to new political demands and changes in the nation at large. Once they are established, however, coalition interests can have an enervating effect on the governing capacities of these regimes. An immediate and constant problem is posed by conflicts of interest within the dominant coalition. The danger here is that attempts to elaborate the coalition's political agenda in ways responsive to new governing conditions will focus a sectarian struggle, weaken regime support through factional disaffection, and open new avenues to power for the political opposition. A longer-range, and ultimately more devastating, problem is posed by changes in the nation at large that throw into question the dominant coalition's most basic commitments of ideology and interest. The danger here, of course, is that the entire political regime will be called into question as an inadequate governing instrument and then repudiated wholesale in a nationwide crisis of political legitimacy.

Considering the history of the presidency in this light, two systemic relationships stand out as especially significant for an analysis of the politics of leadership. First is the president's affiliation with the political complex of interests, institutions, and ideas that dominated state/society relations prior to his coming to office. Second is the current standing of these governmental arrangements in the nation at large. These relationships are, of course, always highly nuanced, but the basic variations are easily discerned, and when it comes to explaining outcomes, they do a good deal of the work. For the sake of simplicity, we can conceptualize the leadership problem with reference to those institutions with which political regimes are invariably identified in America, namely the political parties. Using this shorthand, the leadership problem confronting each president can be framed by the answers to two simple questions: is the president affiliated with the political party that has defined the government's basic commitments of ideology and interest; are the governmental commitments of that party vulnerable to direct repudiation as failed and irrelevant responses to the problems of the day?

Answers to these questions specify four typical opportunity structures for the exercise of political leadership by a president. In the first, the basic governmental commitments of the previously dominant political party are vulnerable to direct repudiation, and the president is associated with the opposition to them. In the second, basic governmental commitments of the previously dominant political party are again on the line, but this time the president is politically affiliated with them. In the third, the governmental commitments of the previously dominant political party still appear timely and politically resilient, but the president is linked with the political opposition to them. In the fourth, the governmental commitments of the previously dominant political party again appear to hold out robust solutions to the problems of the day and the president is affiliated with them. These four opportunity structures are represented in Table 1, with the "previously dominant political party" designated as the "regime party" for easy reference.

Each of these structures defines a different institutional relationship between the presidency and the political system, each engages the president in a different type of politics, and each defines a different kind of leadership challenge. These differences are summarized in the four cells of the table. Before proceeding to a discussion of the table, two points of clarification are in order. First, the table is a schematic presentation of pure types that are only more or less closely approximated in history. In the discussion that follows, the presidents that best fit each type are grouped together. The objective is to highlight the distinctive problems and dynamics of political ac-

The Political Structures of Presidential Leadership

		Presidents' Political Identity	
		Opposed	*Affiliated*
Regime party commitments	*Vulnerable*	politics of reconstruction	politics of disjunction
	Resilient	politics of preemption	politics of articulation

tion that adhere to leadership in these situations and by implication to re-consider the problems and prospects faced by leaders in our own day. The procedure radically delimits the play of personality and skill in determining leadership outcomes, but in doing so, it may allow a more precise determi-nation of their significance. The second point is that this typology does not provide an independent explanation of the historical patterns on which it draws. There is no accounting here for whether a regime affiliate or a regime opponent will actually be elected (or otherwise come into office), nor for when in the course of the nation's development a regime's basic governmental commitments will be called into question. My purpose is to reorganize the analysis of the politics of leadership by cutting into political history at certain typical junctures. It is to suggest the rather blunt ways in which political structure has delimited the political capacities of the presi-dency and informed the impact of presidential action on the political sys-tem as a whole.

The *politics of reconstruction* has been most closely approximated in the administrations of Thomas Jefferson, Andrew Jackson, Abraham Lincoln, Franklin Roosevelt, and Ronald Reagan. Each led a political insurgency, and rose to power on the heels of an electoral upheaval in political control of the institutions of the federal government. More specifically, their victories were driven by a nationwide crisis of political legitimacy, a tide of discon-tent with the established order of things potent enough to dislodge a long-established majority party from its dominant position in Congress as well as the presidency. With political obligations to the past severed in this way, these presidents were thrust beyond the old regime into a political interreg-num where they were directly engaged in a systemic recasting of the gov-ernment's basic commitments of ideology and interest. It is in these cir-cumstances, and apparently only in these circumstances, that presidents are free to do what all political leaders seek to do: they can redefine legitimate national government in their own terms.

These presidents are widely regarded as the most effective of all political leaders in presidential history; what is less well appreciated is that they shared the same basic relationship to the political system at large. They are all known as great communicators, but this seems to have less to do with any common training or shared skill than with the fact that they all had the same basic message to communicate. Each was able to repudiate received commitments of ideology and interest outright, to indict them forthrightly as failed and illegitimate responses to the problems of the day, and to iden-tify his leadership with a new beginning, with the salvation of the nation from political bankruptcy. Safe to say, the political preeminence of the presi-dency is naturally pronounced when the old regime has been widely discred-ited, when old alliances have been thrown into disarray, and when new interests have been thrust afresh upon governmental institutions.

More important, however, is what the performance of leaders in this situation can tell us about the structured capacities of the presidency as a political institution. Order-shattering elections do not themselves shape the future, but they vastly expand the president's capacities to break prior governmental commitments and to orchestrate a political reordering of state/society relations. It is significant in this regard that none of the presidents who reconstructed the terms and conditions of legitimate national government had much success in actually resolving the tangible problems that gave rise to the nationwide crisis of political legitimacy in the first place. Jefferson's attempt to deal with the problems at issue in the international crisis of 1798 proved a total failure;[1] Jackson's attempt to deal with the long-festering problem of national banking precipitated an economic panic and ultimately exacerbated a devastating depression; Lincoln's proposed solution to the sectional conflict of the 1850s plunged the nation into a civil war; and Roosevelt's New Deal failed to pull the nation out of the Depression. But what these presidents could do, that their predecessors could not, was to define for themselves the significance of the events they oversaw and to secure the legitimacy of the solutions they proposed. Released from the burden of upholding the integrity of the old regime, these presidents were not restricted in their leadership to mere problem solving. Situated just beyond the old regime, they reformulated the nation's political agenda as a direct response to the manifest failures of the immediate past, presented their solutions as the only alternative to national ruin, and galvanized political support for a government that eyed an entirely new set of possibilities.

The leadership opportunities afforded by this kind of political breakthrough are duly matched by its characteristic political challenges. In penetrating to the core of the political system and forthrightly reordering relations between state and society, these presidents ultimately found it imperative to try to secure a governmental infrastructure capable of perpetuating their cause. The shape of the new regime came to depend on the way party lines were recast and on how institutional relationships within the government were reorganized. Accordingly, it will be observed that these are all great party-building presidencies, and that each president was engaged institutionally as a negative instrument, rooting out the residual institutional supports for the politics of the past. Court battles, Bank Wars, a real Civil War—great confrontations that dislodged entire frameworks of governing are the special province of the reconstructive leader, and they can be counted on to forge new forms of opposition as well as support.[2] The reconstructive leader passes to his successor a political system that is not only reconfigured in its basic commitments of ideology and interest but newly constricted in its potential for independent action.

The *politics of disjunction* has been most closely approximated in the administrations of John Adams, John Quincy Adams, Franklin Pierce, James

---

1. The reference here is to President Jefferson's failed embargo policy in his second term.
2. Jefferson, Jackson, and Roosevelt tangled with the Supreme Court, while Jackson destroyed the Bank of the United States.

Buchanan, Herbert Hoover, and Jimmy Carter. With due regard for the reputations of these men for political incompetence, it is evident in identifying them as a group that they shared what is quite simply an impossible leadership situation. Rather than orchestrating a political breakthrough in state/society relations, these presidents were compelled to cope with the breakdown of those relations. Their affiliation with the old regime at a time when its basic commitments of ideology and interest were being called into question severely limited their ability to control the meaning of their own actions, and this limitation ultimately turned their office into the focal point of a nationwide crisis of political legitimacy. This situation imparts to the president a consuming preoccupation with a political challenge that is really a prerequisite of leadership, that of simply establishing his own political credibility.

Each of the major historical episodes in the politics of disjunction has been foreshadowed by a long-festering identity crisis within the old majority party itself. But the distinctiveness of this juncture goes beyond these simmering tensions within the ranks; it lies in changes within the nation itself that obscure the regime's relevance as an instrument of governance and cloud its legitimacy as caretaker of the national interest. The Adamses, Pierce, Hoover, and Carter are notable for their open recognition of the vulnerabilities of the establishments with which they were affiliated; each promised to solve national problems in a way that would repair and rehabilitate the old order. But solving the nation's problems is a hard test for any president, and in this situation, where they have little else to offer, they find themselves in especially difficult straits. Actions that challenge established commitments in the name of rehabilitation and repair are likely to leave the president isolated from his most likely political allies; actions that reach out to allies and affirm established commitments will provide insurgents with proof positive that the president has nothing new to offer, that he really is nothing more than a symptom of the problems of the day.

Invariably these presidents drive forward the crisis of legitimacy they came into office to forestall. Unable to control the meaning of their own actions, they find their actions defined by others. They become the leading symbols of systemic political failure and regime bankruptcy and provide the reconstructive leader his essential premise. Certainly it is no accident that the presidents who have set the standard of political incompetence in American political history are succeeded by presidents who set the standards of political mastery. This recurrent coupling of dismal failure with towering success suggests that the contingent political relationship between the presidency and the political system is far more telling of leadership prospects than the contingencies of personality and skill.

The *politics of preemption* has engaged a large number of presidents, some of the more aggressive leaders among them being John Tyler, Andrew Johnson, Grover Cleveland, Woodrow Wilson, Richard Nixon, and Bill Clinton. The men in this grouping stand out as wild cards in American political history. As their experiences indicate, the politics of leadership in this situation are especially volatile, and perhaps least susceptible to generalization. Tyler was purged from the ranks of the party that elected him; Wilson took a disastrous plunge from the commanding heights of world leadership into the political abyss; Johnson and Nixon were crippled by impeachment proceedings. Of all the presidents that might be grouped in this situation, only Dwight Eisenhower finished a second term without suffering a precipitous reversal of political fortune, but this exception is itself suggestive, for Eisenhower alone kept whatever intentions he might have had for altering the shape of national politics well hidden.

As leader of the opposition to a regime that still claims formidable political, ideological, and institutional support, the president interrupts the working agenda of national politics and intrudes into the establishment as an alien power. The opportunity for creative political leadership in this situation comes from the independence that the president enjoys by virtue of his opposition stance, but so long as the incumbent is unable to issue a forthright repudiation of established commitments as bankrupt and illegitimate solutions to the problems of the day, opposition leadership is limited in its reconstructive power. Short of authority to redefine legitimate national government, preemptive leaders exploit their relative freedom from received political definitions. They disavow orthodoxies of all kinds. They offer hybrid political alternatives. Their attraction lies in their unabashedly mongrel appeal, their free mixing of different, seemingly contradictory political commitments.

As a practical matter, preempting the political discourse of an established regime means simultaneously carrying the support of its stalwart opponents, avoiding a frontal attack on the orthodoxy they oppose, and offering disaffected interests normally affiliated with the dominant coalition a modification of the regime's agenda that they will find more attractive. Floating free of established commitments, preemptive leaders look for and play upon latent interest cleavages and factional discontent within the ranks of the regime's traditional supporters. Though these opportunities are not hard to identify, the political terrain to be negotiated in exploiting them is treacherous. Testing both the tolerance of stalwart opponents and the resilience of establishment allies, preemptive leaders provoke the defenders of regime norms to assault the president's highly personalized, seemingly normless political manipulations.

Compared to presidents caught in a politics of disjunction, preemptive leaders have a much greater opportunity to establish and exploit their political independence; all preemptive leaders who were elected to office in the first instance were reelected to second terms. The danger here is not that the president will get caught in a systemic rejection of regime norms per se, but he will find himself the object of a relentless campaign of character assassination, the effect of which would be to confirm those norms. Compared to a president engaged in the politics of reconstruction, these leaders do not cut into national politics deeply enough to create durable political alternatives, and personal political isolation is the ever-present danger. Preemptive leadership is, in fact, historically unique in its propensity to provoke impeachment proceedings. Probing alternative lines of political cleavage, these presidents may well anticipate future party building strategies, but they are more effective at disrupting the established political regime than at replacing it.

The *politics of articulation* has engaged the largest number of presidents; in contemporary politics George H. W. Bush and George W. Bush both fit the bill. If no more "normal" a situation than any other, this situation does pinpoint the distinctive problems of political leadership that arise when relations between the incumbent and established regime commitments are most consonant. Here the presidency is the font of political orthodoxy and the president, the minister to the faithful. The leadership posture is wholly affirmative; the opportunity at hand is to service coalition interests, to deliver on outstanding political commitments on the regime's agenda, and to update these commitments to accord with the times. The corresponding challenge is to uphold definitions, to affirm established norms, to maintain a sense of regime coherence and integrity in changing times, to mitigate and manage the factional ruptures within the ranks of the regime's traditional supporters that inevitably accompany alterations in the status quo ante. These challenges have been met in various ways, and with varying degrees of skill, but a look at the record suggests that the political effects are pretty much the same.

Consider the most impressive of the bunch. In each of America's major political regimes, there has been one particular episode in orthodox innovation that stands out for its programmatic accomplishments. In the Jeffersonian era, it was the administration of James Monroe; in the Jacksonian era, the administration of James Polk; in the Republican era, the administration of Theodore Roosevelt; in the liberal era, the administration of Lyndon Johnson. These administrations were not only pivotal in the course of each regime's development but also emblematic of the problems this situation poses for presidential leadership. These men exercised power in what were, for all appearances, especially propitious circumstances for orthodox innovation. At the outset of each presidency, a long-established regime party was affirmed in its control of the entire national government, and the national posture was so strong at home and abroad that it left no excuses for not finally delivering on long-heralded regime promises. Each president thus set full sail at a time when it was possible to think about completing the unfinished business of national politics, about realizing the regime's vision of America and finally turning the party of orthodoxy into a consensual party of the nation. To that end, each in fact enacted a full and programmatic policy package.

But just as surely as a leadership project of culmination and completion suggests a great leap into the promised land, it accentuates the underlying problem of definition, of upholding fundamental commitments in some coherent fashion and having old allies see the new arrangements arrived at as the legitimate expression of their ideals. Each of America's great orthodox innovators found his administration mired in the dilemmas of reconciling old commitments with the expansive political possibilities at hand;

leading a regime at the apex of its projection of national power and purpose, each was beset by a political implosion of conflicting expectations. By pushing ahead with the received business of national politics and embellishing its commitments, these presidents fomented deep schisms within their own ranks; by making real changes in governing commitments, they undercut their own ability to speak for the church. While most fully articulating his regime as a system of national government, each of these presidents was charged with a betrayal of the faith, and each pulled the regime into an accelerated sectarian struggle over the true meaning of orthodoxy. These presidencies were not undermined by the assaults of their nominal political opponents but by the disaffection of their ostensible allies.

Articulation can look a lot like preemption. After all, leaders in both situations stretch established orthodoxies to accommodate new realities and purposes, broaching questions about their own legitimacy in the process. But the political dynamics are quite different. Whereas preemptive leaders openly seek to explode received definitions and established norms, orthodox innovators seek to maintain them. In the politics of preemption, political disaffection and factional divisions within the ranks of the dominant coalition provide opportunities that the leader has every incentive to exploit; in the politics of articulation they present risks that the leader is constrained to forestall. If the preemptive leader is a wild card openly disdainful of received conceptions of the alternatives, the orthodox innovator is a stalwart at pains to render change consistent with past commitments and to merge the new seamlessly into the old. Preemptive leaders probe for reconstructive possibilities; orthodox innovators seek to stave off the threat of a political disjunction. Preemptive leaders get impeached for their heresies; orthodox innovators tend simply to fade away.

George W. Bush: A Closer Look

George W. Bush is an orthodox innovator, and when all is said and done, his re-articulation of the commitments of the established regime may well rival, both in scale and substantive import, those of the most significant orthodox innovators in American history. At first thought, this unfolding reality appears incongruous with the extraordinary events that have rocked the Bush years. A contested election and terrorist attacks on the American mainland would seem to augur an approach to governing far more improvisational than orthodox innovation, which is programmatic, fully subscribed, and tightly controlled in its purposes. The oft-repeated refrain "everything changed on September 11" seems particularly misleading in this regard, for it obscures the stalwart qualities of Bush's leadership, its steadfastness in using events to further the cause of regime vindication and fulfillment.

Bush's official campaign biography, *A Charge to Keep*, begins with the candidate's vow "never to allow others to define me." This is a curious opening to a book that was candidly written by a campaign strategist, but orthodox innovation is a collective leadership project that relies on a firm definition, and Bush campaign operatives were keen to assure their allies that once in power, this president would not waver from the terms he was setting out for his leadership. Bush's vow was an implicit acknowledgment of where his father had faltered in a similar task, and an implicit critique of President Clinton's apparent indifference to stated commitments.

Bush's political definition cast him in the role of regime articulator from the get-go. Like his father before him, he presented himself as a "compassionate conservative." The slogan captured perfectly the balance between orthodoxy and innovation at the heart of their shared leadership challenge. As affiliates of a still resilient regime, father and son forthrightly affirmed the conservative commitments of the Reagan reconstruction and then offered to embellish them with attractive and timely innovations. That said, the prospects for orthodox innovation were much brighter in January of 2001 than they had been in January 1989. Notwithstanding Bush senior's sweeping election victory or the closeness of the elections of 2000, the Republican Party in Congress was in a stronger position in 2001 than it had been in 1989. The nation was stronger as well, both economically and internationally. Finally, Bush junior had the political advantage of coming after the Clinton interregnum. The regime stalwarts who had measured his father skeptically against their recent, sunny memories of Ronald Reagan looked forward to a restoration with the nightmare of the Clinton years foremost in mind. Moreover, Clinton, for all his political success at preemption, had not given the Democratic Party a clear alternative on which opposition to the conservative regime could stand fast, and his accomplishments in terms of mixing things up lent the younger Bush's efforts the clarity of a return to something more predictable and orderly. After Clinton, it was easier both to provide the faithful a strong reaffirmation of orthodoxy and easier for the faithful to accept innovations that promised to stave off another such debacle. All told, the stage was set for a great leap forward to the conservatives' promised land.

Since his inauguration, Bush has remarkably played true to type. He has pressed the conservative agenda forward aggressively and relentlessly. His administration overhauled the tax code, with two major cuts and a general redistribution of wealth to the higher income brackets. It set about building a missile defense shield and altering the strategic foundations of international stability. It announced its more business-friendly regulatory posture by withdrawing from an international initiative to deal with global warming, gutting environmental standards, and pressing for oil drilling in previously protected wilderness. It banned aid for programs that supported abortion abroad, stiffened restrictions on federal funding for embryonic research, impaneled a study of social security privatization, and supported the empowerment of faith based groups to carry out the government's social reform objectives.

That Al Gore's plurality in the popular vote and the Court imposed electoral settlement did not, as many commentators expected, prompt Bush to reject partisan political projects and repair to an extraordinary government of national unity underscores just how fundamental political orthodoxy was to Bush's identity and legitimacy as a political leader. That Bush has advanced the conservatives' agenda so effectively on the basis of razor thin margins of partisan support also suggests just how difficult it has become for Democrats of the post-Reagan era to offer clear and attractive alternatives to the commitments of the conservative regime. But like the great orthodox innovators of the past, Bush has been at pains to do more than simply assure regime supporters on fundamental matters of faith; he has kept an eye on the nation at large and tried to bolster the regime's legitimacy by showing the rest of the nation what else it can deliver on current matters of national interest.

James Monroe and James Polk set out to show that, once the stalwarts were assured on fundamentals, their states' rights parties could pursue and achieve great national objectives; Theodore Roosevelt set out to show that, once basic commitments on tariffs and trade were affirmed, his conservative party could offer progressive reforms; for Lyndon Johnson the challenge was to show that his liberal party could be "a party for all Americans." George W. Bush has moved in similar fashion to build a more attractive superstructure on Reaganesque foundations. He has reached out to new constituencies with timely, high-profile initiatives on education, prescription drugs, and immigration reform, often moving into coalition with liberals to counter resistance from within his own ranks. Like other orthodox innovators, he has tested his ability to incorporate seemingly heretical ideas in a ringing demonstration of governing capacities of the conservative regime, to make it attractive to a wider clientele without alienating core supporters and evoking charges of betrayal.

The events of September 11, 2001, bolstered Bush's leadership capacities in this regard. In fact, the early months of the Bush administration had offered ample evidence of the sectarian infighting so characteristic of the politics of articulation and debilitating to its long-term prospects. Senator John McCain, who had run against Bush in his bid for the Republican nomination, made his independence of the administration conspicuous on several major policy initiatives, including a campaign finance reform bill, and the small band of moderate Republicans in Congress signaled its own dismay at the administration's sharp turn to the right. In May of 2001, one of the moderates, Vermont senator Jim Jeffords, bolted the party, throwing political control of the Senate to the Democrats. But in the aftermath of the terrorist attacks, the president's leadership position within his own ranks became all but impregnable. Tensions within the Republican coalition may not have been resolved, but any threat of an early unraveling was thoroughly dispelled. Far more remarkable than the fact that the nation rallied to the president's side is the fact that the president's newfound authority as a commander-in-chief in wartime was deployed to further his initial leadership project. Calls for national unity in a time of crisis became a vehicle for pressing the agenda of orthodox innovation forward, most notably by employing the president's wartime popularity in a starkly partisan mid-term campaign to overwhelm his opposition.

The eradication of the Taliban regime in Afghanistan and the search for Al Qaeda were commitments that might be expected from any president acting in the aftermath of the September attacks; not so the campaign against Iraq and the pronouncement of a new doctrine of preemptive war. Muscle flexing of this sort fits a more particular pattern in presidential history, a pattern characteristic of orthodox innovators. The seizure of Florida and promulgation of the Monroe Doctrine; "Manifest Destiny" and the Mexican War; the Spanish American War, the Great White Fleet, and the Panama Canal; Cold War containment in Korea and Vietnam—all were the projects of orthodox innovators. One explanation for the hawkishness of orthodox innovators may be that they tend to rise to power at particularly robust moments in national history; they come to celebrate the capacities of established power, and their cause can be served as well by bold demonstrations of national power abroad as by delivering the goods to interests at home. Another explanation may be that by identifying external evils to eradicate, presidents who otherwise possess wholly affirmative and constructive warrants for interest service are able to deflect factional disaffection at home and rally the nation to a higher cause. In any case, by settling an old score with Iraq and announcing a new doctrine of unilateral intervention, Bush gave new meaning to the idea of completing the work of the past and joining it to a new future.

Skill in Context

Our objective in this analysis was to show how systemic factors might explain stark variations in the political effects of presidential leadership. Our assumption was that while all presidents possess a modicum of political competence, the political challenges they face shift abruptly from one to the next. If this analysis is correct—if George W. Bush is an orthodox innovator negotiating an especially auspicious moment for the established political regime—any evaluation of the importance of his personal attributes and skills in leadership must be rendered with caution. Looking at plausible counterparts in other periods to the current context shows that presidents in these circumstances are all quite accomplished; they are among the most programmatic and expansionist presidencies in American political history. Reframed with reference to other leaders similarly situated in political time, the question of skill becomes quite particular: will Bush do any better than Monroe, Polk, Theodore Roosevelt, or Lyndon Johnson in moving his agenda forward without shattering the political foundations upon which his policy accomplishments rest?

Prior to September 11, 2001, Bush's skill in moving the agenda forward was duly matched by the problems brewing within the ranks of his followers. This structural trade-off is reflected historically in the fact that only four of the fourteen orthodox innovators to serve in the presidency have been elected to second terms. The story is, in fact, starker than the raw numbers imply, for two of those four (Madison and Monroe) predate the institution-alization of the two party system and a third (Grant) won reelection with much of his opposition still under force of arms. McKinley is the only or-thodox innovator to win two elections under fully competitive conditions, and perhaps not coincidentally, he did so in the wake of a "splendid little war." The record of orthodox innovators should be understood in contrast to the overall experience of opposition leaders: every opposition leader who was elected to the presidential office in the first instance and lived long enough to run again, was reelected.

Against this backdrop, the strength of Bush's position since September 11, 2001, suggests that something unusual might indeed be in the making. Though it is unclear how much of his strength going into the fourth year of his term is to be attributed to special talents and skills and how much to ex-traordinary events, there are few signs as of this writing that Bush's reelec-tion campaign will be plagued by the schisms within the ranks that typi-cally bring orthodox innovators down. The outstanding issue is whether Bush has, or will, resolve the problem at the heart of his relationship to the political system, whether he has, or will, actually master the leadership dilemma of orthodox innovation. Despite the care with which he has bal-anced efforts to deliver on the received political commitments of the con-servative regime against efforts to build a loftier superstructure on orthodox foundations, the strains on regime definition are, in fact, fast mounting.

It is not just that the party of tax cuts and limited government now supports an administration committed to federal involvement in public ed-ucation and prescription drug coverage, or that exploding federal and trade deficits cloud the economic future; it is also that this party has come to sup-port an administration that is radically open ended in its commitments to unilateral intervention abroad and threatening to civil liberties at home. A regime that once declared government "the problem" and that promised to get federal authority "off people's backs" now supports a statist agenda more starkly at odds with its libertarian pretensions than ever before. The great irony is that the extraordinary events that have bolstered Bush's au-thority and tightened his grip on his party have also pushed him to em-brace extreme versions of the competing norms he came to power to recon-cile. Holding all this together through a second term would be an extraordinary feat of skill for the affiliated leader of an established regime.

DISCUSSION QUESTIONS

1. Does Greenstein's emphasis on the individual or Skowronek's emphasis on the political structure provide the better understanding of presidential leadership?

2. How would Greenstein deal with the contention that even a president with strong character and skills would be unsuccessful in the face of unfavorable political circumstances?

3. How would Skowronek deal with the contention that even in the politics of reconstruction, the best opportunity structure a president can enjoy, the creation of a new regime requires vision and skill?

4. How do Greenstein and Skowronek differ in their analyses of George W. Bush? Whose interpretation of the Bush presidency do you find more persuasive?

SUGGESTED READINGS AND INTERNET RESOURCES

The classic study of how presidents can gain—or lose—power in the White House is Richard E. Neustadt, *Presidential Power and the Modern Presidents* (New York: Free Press, 1990). Stephen Skowronek demonstrates how presidential leadership is shaped by "political time" in *The Politics Presidents Make: Leadership from John Adams to Bill Clinton* (Cambridge, Mass.: Harvard University Press, 1997). For a lively anthology on presidential politics, see Michael Nelson, ed., *The Presidency and the Political System* (7th ed., Washington, D.C.: Congressional Quarterly Press, 2003). Portraits of both elite democratic and popular democratic leadership are found in Bruce Miroff, *Icons of Democracy: American Leaders as Heroes, Aristocrats, Dissenters, and Democrats* (Lawrence: University Press of Kansas, 2000). Marc Landy and Sidney Milkis argue that there have been no "great" presidents since FDR in *Presidential Greatness* (Lawrence: University Press of Kansas, 2000).

The White House
www.whitehouse.gov
The president's website, containing speeches, documents, press briefings, and assorted information on the administration, also offers e-mail communication with the White House.

Center for the Study of the Presidency
www.cspresidency.org
This website of a nonpartisan organization that holds student conferences and publishes a scholarly journal offers publications and provides links to research sites on the presidency.

The American Presidency.Net
www.theamericanpresidency.net
This website contains information on many aspects of the presidency, ranging from the important to the trivial.

CHAPTER 15

The Judiciary: What Should Its Role Be in a Democracy?

mericans like to think of the justices of the Supreme Court as grave and learned elders of the law engaged in a search for justice that has little to do with the selfish interests and ambitions that we so often associate with politics. The justices themselves encourage this view, holding court in a marble temple (the Supreme Court Building), wearing black robes, shrouding their decision-making processes in secrecy. Yet an institution that makes authoritative decisions about many of the most troublesome issues of our times—abortion, affirmative action, the rights of the accused, the relationship between church and state—cannot be kept aloof from politics. Thus, the Supreme Court's role in the political system has become one of the central issues in current debates about American democracy.

From one perspective, the Supreme Court is not really a democratic institution at all. The nine justices of the Supreme Court are not elected; they are nominated by the president and confirmed by the Senate. They serve during good behavior—that is, until they retire, die, or are impeached by the House and convicted by the Senate. Composed exclusively of practitioners of one profession, lawyers, the Court can use its power of judicial review to strike down laws passed by legislatures that have been elected by the majority.

From another perspective, however, the Supreme Court is an essential component of American democracy. Its most important role is as a guardian of the Constitution, which is the fundamental expression of the people's will. According to this view, the Court sometimes must oppose the wishes of a temporary majority in the name of the abiding principles and values contained in the Constitution.

During the last several decades, landmark decisions by the Supreme Court have often evoked democratic debates. Some decisions by the Court have been approved by a majority of Americans but have been fiercely resisted by intense minorities. Among these have been *Brown* v. *Board of Education* (1954), ordering school desegregation, and *Roe* v. *Wade* (1973), guaranteeing the right of a woman to choose to have an abortion. Other decisions have been opposed by a large majority. Among these have been *Engel* v. *Vitale* (1962), which forbade prayer in public schools, and *Miranda* v. *Arizona* (1966), which required police to inform criminal suspects of their rights before they could be interrogated.

Decisions such as these have led critics to charge the Court with overstepping its proper role in the political system. The most prominent critic has been Edwin Meese III, the attorney general of the United States during Ronald Reagan's presidency. In a series of speeches in 1985 (one of which is excerpted here), Meese accused the Court of substituting its own preferences and prejudices for the principles of the Constitution. Springing to the defense of the Court against Meese was Justice William Brennan Jr., who played an influential role in crafting many of the decisions that Meese was condemning. The debate between Meese and Brennan has been a profoundly important one because it cuts to the most basic issues concerning the judiciary's role in American democracy.

Meese insists that the justices of the Supreme Court should be strictly guided by the words of the Constitution and the laws and by the intentions of those who drafted them (he calls this a "Jurisprudence of Original Intention"). This emphasis on the original intention of the framers calls into question the Court's recent decisions on the rights of racial minorities, women, and persons accused of crimes. Meese wants the Supreme Court to play a more restrained role and to defer whenever possible to the elected branches of government.

Brennan rejects each of Meese's arguments. He suggests that the original intention of the framers cannot be known and that although justices must respect the past, they must ultimately be guided in their interpretations by what the words of the Constitution mean today. He believes that Meese's position is a cloak for a conservative political agenda, the aim of which is to reverse recent advances in our understanding of the constitutional rights of previously disadvantaged groups. Brennan denies that democracy requires a deferential judiciary: the Court, he argues, has a democratic responsibility to uphold the nation's founding "aspiration to social justice, brotherhood, and human dignity."

Among the three branches of the national government, the judiciary is clearly the most elite in its selection process, composition, and form of deliberation. Yet in the debate between Meese and Brennan, each tries to associate his view of the judiciary with a popular democratic position. You can decide for yourself whose position in this debate deserves to be identified with popular democracy by considering the following questions: Can we be guided in interpreting the Constitution by the original intention of its framers, or must we read the Constitution in a more adaptive and modern fashion? Should our understanding of constitutional rights be squarely rooted in the text of the Constitution, or should we apply constitutional values to the protection of rights for individuals and groups that the framers never thought to protect? Must the Court, as an unelected branch of government, avoid undemocratic action by acting with deference toward the elected branches, or must it actively pursue the democratic aspirations of the Constitution even when this brings the judiciary into conflict with the elected branches?

A Jurisprudence of Original Intention

EDWIN MEESE III

A large part of American history has been the history of Constitutional debate. From the Federalists and the Anti-Federalists, to Webster and Calhoun, to Lincoln and Douglas, we find many examples. Now, as we approach the bicentennial of the framing of the Constitution, we are witnessing another debate concerning our fundamental law. It is not simply a ceremonial debate, but one that promises to have a profound impact on the future of our Republic. . . .

Today I would like to discuss further the meaning of constitutional fidelity. In particular, I would like to describe in more detail this administration's approach.

Before doing so, I would like to make a few commonplace observations about the original document itself. It is easy to forget what a young country America really is. The bicentennial of our independence was just a few years ago, that of the Constitution still two years off. The period surrounding the creation of the Constitution is not a dark and mythical realm. The young America of the 1780s and 90s was a vibrant place, alive with pamphlets, newspapers and books chronicling and commenting upon the great issues of the day. We know how the Founding Fathers lived, and much of what they read, thought, and believed. The disputes and compromises of the Constitutional Convention were carefully recorded. The minutes of the Convention are a matter of public record. Several of the most important participants—including James Madison, the "father" of the Constitution—

wrote comprehensive accounts of the convention. Others, Federalists and Anti-Federalists alike, committed their arguments for and against ratification, as well as their understandings of the Constitution, to paper, so that their ideas and conclusions could be widely circulated, read, and understood.

In short, the Constitution is not buried in the mists of time. We know a tremendous amount of the history of its genesis. The Bicentennial is encouraging even more scholarship about its origins. We know who did what, when, and many times why. One can talk intelligently about a "founding generation." . . .

Our approach to constitutional interpretation begins with the document itself. The plain fact is, it exists. It is something that has been written down. Walter Berns of the American Enterprise Institute has noted that the central object of American constitutionalism was "the effort" of the Founders "to express fundamental governmental arrangements in a legal document—to 'get it in writing.'" Indeed, judicial review has been grounded in the fact that the Constitution is a written, as opposed to an unwritten, document. In *Marbury* v. *Madison* [5 U.S. 137 (1803)], John Marshall rested his rationale for judicial review on the fact that we have a written constitution with meaning that is binding upon judges. "[I]t is apparent," he wrote, "that the framers of the Constitution contemplated that instrument as a rule for the government of *courts,* as well as of the legislature. Why otherwise does it direct the judges to take an oath to support it?"

The presumption of a written document is that it conveys meaning. As Thomas Grey of the Stanford Law School has said, it makes "relatively definite and explicit what otherwise would be relatively indefinite and tacit."

We know that those who framed the Constitution chose their words carefully. They debated at great length the most minute points. The language they chose meant something. They proposed, they substituted, they edited, and they carefully revised. Their words were studied with equal care by state ratifying conventions. This is not to suggest that there was unanimity among the framers and ratifiers on all points. The Constitution and the Bill of Rights, and some of the subsequent amendments, emerged after protracted debate. Nobody got everything they wanted. What's more, the Framers were not clairvoyants—they could not foresee every issue that would be submitted for judicial review. Nor could they predict how all foreseeable disputes would be resolved under the Constitution. But the point is, the meaning of the Constitution can be known.

What does this written Constitution mean? In places it is exactingly specific. Where it says that Presidents of the United States must be at least 35 years of age it means exactly that. (I have not heard of any claim that 35 means 30 or 25 or 20.) Where it specifies how the House and Senate are to be organized, it means what it says.

The Constitution also expresses particular principles. One is the right to be free of an unreasonable search or seizure. Another concerns religious liberty. Another is the right to equal protection of the laws.

Those who framed these principles meant something by them. And the meanings can be found. The Constitution itself is also an expression of certain general principles. These principles reflect the deepest purpose of the Constitution—that of establishing a political system through which Americans can best govern themselves consistent with the goal of securing liberty.

The text and structure of the Constitution is instructive. It contains very little in the way of specific political solutions. It speaks volumes on how problems should be approached, and by *whom*. For example, the first three articles set out clearly the scope and limits of three distinct branches of national government, the powers of each being carefully and specifically enumerated. In this scheme it is no accident to find the legislative branch described first, as the Framers had fought and sacrificed to secure the right of democratic self-governance. Naturally, this faith in republicanism was not unbounded, as the next two articles make clear.

Yet the Constitution remains a document of powers and principles. And its undergirding premise remains that democratic self-government is subject only to the limits of certain constitutional principles. This respect for the political process was made explicit early on. When John Marshall upheld the Act of Congress chartering a national bank in *McCulloch* v. *Maryland* [17 U.S. 316 (1819)], he wrote: "The Constitution [was] intended to endure for ages to come, and, consequently, to be adapted to the various crises of human affairs." But to use *McCulloch,* as some have tried, as support for the idea that the Constitution is a protean, changeable thing is to stand history on its head. Marshall was keeping faith with the original intention that Congress be free to elaborate and apply constitutional powers and principles. He was not saying that the Court must invent some new constitutional value in order to keep pace with the times. In Walter Berns' words: "Marshall's meaning is not that the Constitution may be adapted to the 'various crises of human affairs,' but that the legislative powers granted by the Constitution are adaptable to meet these crises."

The approach this administration advocates is rooted in the text of the Constitution as illuminated by those who drafted, proposed, and ratified it. In his famous Commentary on the Constitution of the United States, Justice Joseph Story explained that: "The first and fundamental rule in the interpretation of all instruments is, to construe them according to the sense of the terms, and the intention of the parties."

Our approach understands the significance of a written document and seeks to discern the particular and general principles it expresses. It recognizes that there may be debate at times over the application of these principles. But it does not mean these principles cannot be identified.

Constitutional adjudication is obviously not a mechanical process. It requires an appeal to reason and discretion. The text and intention of the Constitution must be understood to constitute the banks within which constitutional interpretation must flow. As James Madison said, if "the sense in which the Constitution was accepted and ratified by the nation . . .

be not the guide in expounding it, there can be no security for a consistent and stable government, more than for a faithful exercise of its powers."

Thomas Jefferson, so often cited incorrectly as a framer of the Constitution, in fact shared Madison's view: "Our peculiar security is in the possession of a written Constitution. Let us not make it a blank paper by construction." Jefferson was even more explicit in his personal correspondence:

> On every question of construction [we should] carry ourselves back to the time, when the constitution was adopted; recollect the spirit manifested in the debates; and instead of trying [to find], what meaning may be squeezed out of the text, or invented against it, conform to the probable one, in which it was passed.

In the main, jurisprudence that seeks to be faithful to our Constitution—a Jurisprudence of Original Intention, as I have called it—is not difficult to describe. Where the language of the Constitution is specific, it must be obeyed. Where there is a demonstrable consensus among the framers and ratifiers as to a principle stated or implied by the Constitution, it should be followed. Where there is ambiguity as to the precise meaning or reach of a constitutional provision, it should be interpreted and applied in a manner so as to at least not contradict the text of the Constitution itself.

Sadly, while almost everyone participating in the current constitutional debate would give assent to these propositions, the techniques and conclusions of some of the debaters do violence to them. What is the source of this violence? In large part I believe that it is the misuse of history stemming from the neglect of the idea of a written constitution.

There is a frank proclamation by some judges and commentators that what matters most about the Constitution is not its words but its so-called "spirit." These individuals focus less on the language of specific provisions than on what they describe as the "vision" or "concepts of human dignity" they find embodied in the Constitution. This approach to jurisprudence has led to some remarkable and tragic conclusions.

In the 1850s, the Supreme Court under Chief Justice Roger B. Taney read blacks out of the Constitution in order to invalidate Congress' attempt to limit the spread of slavery. The *Dred Scott* decision, famously described as a judicial "self-inflicted wound," helped bring on the Civil War. There is a lesson in this history. There is danger in seeing the Constitution as an empty vessel into which each generation may pour its passion and prejudice.

Our own time has its own fashions and passions. In recent decades many have come to view the Constitution—more accurately, part of the Constitution, provisions of the Bill of Rights and the Fourteenth Amendment—as a charter for judicial activism on behalf of various constituencies. Those who hold this view often have lacked demonstrable textual or historical support for their conclusions. Instead they have "grounded" their rulings in appeals to social theories, to moral philosophies or personal notions of human dignity, or to "penumbras," somehow emanating ghostlike from various provisions—identified and not identified—in the Bill of Rights.[1] The problem with this approach, as John Hart Ely, Dean of the Stanford Law School, has observed with respect to one such decision, is not that it is bad constitutional law, but that it is not constitutional law in any meaningful sense, at all.

Despite this fact, the perceived popularity of some results in particular cases has encouraged some observers to believe that any critique of the methodology of those decisions is an attack on the results. This perception is sufficiently widespread that it deserves an answer. My answer is to look at history.

When the Supreme Court, in *Brown* v. *Board of Education* [347 U.S. 483 (1954)], sounded the death knell for official segregation in the country, it earned all the plaudits it received. But the Supreme Court in that case was not giving new life to old words, or adapting a "living," "flexible" Constitution to new reality. It was restoring the original principle of the Constitution to constitutional law. The *Brown* Court was correcting the damage done 50 years earlier, when in *Plessy* v. *Ferguson* [163 U.S. 537 (1896)], an earlier Supreme Court had disregarded the clear intent of the Framers of the Civil War amendments to eliminate the legal degradation of blacks, and had contrived a theory of the Constitution to support the charade of "separate but equal" discrimination.

Similarly, the decisions of the New Deal and beyond that freed Congress to regulate commerce and enact a plethora of social legislation were not judicial adaptations of the Constitution to new realities. They were in fact removals of encrustations of earlier courts that had strayed from the original intent of the Framers regarding the power of the legislature to make policy.

It is amazing how so much of what passes for social and political progress is really the undoing of old judicial mistakes. Mistakes occur when the principles of specific constitutional provisions—such as those contained in the Bill of Rights—are taken by some as invitations to read into the Constitution values that contradict the clear language of other provisions.

Acceptances to this illusory invitation have proliferated in recent decades. One Supreme Court justice identified the proper judicial standard as asking "what's best for this country." Another said it is important to "keep the Court out in front" of the general society. Various academic commentators have poured rhetorical grease on this judicial fire, suggesting that constitutional interpretation appropriately be guided by such standards as whether a public policy "personifies justice" or "comports with the notion of moral evolution" or confers "an identity" upon our society or was consistent with "natural ethical law" or was consistent with some "right of equal citizenship."

---

1. Meese's use of *penumbras* refers to Justice William O. Douglas's opinion in *Griswold* v. *Connecticut* (1965), which established a constitutional right to privacy. Douglas argued that although this right was not explicitly stated in the Bill of Rights, it could be found in the penumbras of several of the first ten amendments.

Unfortunately, as I've noted, navigation by such lodestars has in the past given us questionable economics, governmental disorder, and racism—all in the guise of constitutional law. Recently one of the distinguished judges of one of our federal appeals courts got it about right when he wrote: "The truth is that the judge who looks outside the Constitution always looks inside himself and nowhere else" [Robert H. Bork, *Traditions and Morality in Constitutional Law* (1984)]. Or, as we recently put it before the Supreme Court in an important brief: "The further afield interpretation travels from its point of departure in the text, the greater the danger that constitutional adjudication will be like a picnic to which the framers bring the words and the judges the meaning" [Brief for the United States as *amicus curiae* at 24, *Thornburgh* v. *American College of Obstetricians and Gynecologists*, No. 844-95, June 11, 1986].[2]

In the *Osborne* v. *Bank of United States* [22 U.S. 738 (1824)] decision 21 years after *Marbury*, Chief Justice Marshall further elaborated his view of the relationship between the judge and the law, be it statutory or constitutional:

Judicial power, as contradistinguished from the power of the laws, has no existence. Courts are the mere instruments of the law, and can will nothing. When they are said to exercise a discretion, it is a mere legal discretion, a discretion to be exercised in discerning the course prescribed by law; and, when that is discerned, it is the duty of the Court to follow it.

Any true approach to constitutional interpretation must respect the document in all its parts and be faithful to the Constitution in its entirety. What must be remembered in the current debate is that interpretation does not imply results. The Framers were not trying to anticipate every answer. They were trying to create a tripartite national government, within a federal system, that would have the flexibility to adapt to face new exigencies—as it did, for example, in chartering a national bank. Their great interest was in the distribution of power and responsibility in order to secure the great goal of liberty for all.

A jurisprudence that seeks fidelity to the Constitution—a Jurisprudence of Original Intention—is not a jurisprudence of political results. It is very much concerned with process, and it is a jurisprudence that in our day seeks to de-politicize the law. The great genius of the constitutional blueprint is found in its creation and respect for spheres of authority and the limits it places on governmental power. In this scheme the Framers did not see the courts as the exclusive custodians of the Constitution. Indeed, because the document posits so few conclusions it leaves to the more political branches the matter of adapting and vivifying its principles in each generation. It also leaves to the people of the states, in the 10th amendment,

2. *Amicus curiae* is Latin for "friend of the court." Legal briefs of this kind are filed by those who are not the actual parties in a lawsuit.

those responsibilities and rights not committed to federal care. The power to declare acts of Congress and laws of the states null and void is truly awesome. This power must be used when the Constitution clearly speaks. It should not be used when the Constitution does not.

In *Marbury* v. *Madison,* at the same time he vindicated the concept of judicial review, Marshall wrote that the "principles" of the Constitution "are deemed fundamental and permanent," and, except for formal amendment, "unchangeable." If we want a change in our Constitution or in our laws we must seek it through the formal mechanisms presented in that organizing document of our government.

In summary, I would emphasize that what is at issue here is not an agenda of issues or a menu of results. At issue is a way of government. A jurisprudence based on first principles is neither conservative nor liberal, neither right nor left. It is a jurisprudence that cares about committing and limiting to each organ of government the proper ambit of its responsibilities. It is a jurisprudence faithful to our Constitution.

By the same token, an activist jurisprudence, one which anchors the Constitution only in the consciences of jurists, is a chameleon jurisprudence, changing color and form in each era. The same activism hailed today may threaten the capacity for decision through democratic consensus tomorrow, as it has in many yesterdays. Ultimately, as the early democrats wrote into the Massachusetts state constitution, the best defense of our liberties is a government of laws and not men.

Reading the Constitution as Twentieth-Century Americans

WILLIAM J. BRENNAN JR.

I t will perhaps not surprise you that the text I have chosen for exploration is the amended Constitution of the United States, which, of course, entrenches the Bill of Rights and the Civil War amendments, and draws sustenance from the bedrock principles of another great text, the Magna Carta. So fashioned, the Constitution embodies the aspiration to social justice, brotherhood, and human dignity that brought this nation into being. The Declaration of Independence, the Constitution and the Bill of Rights solemnly committed the United States to be a country where the dignity and rights of all persons were equal before all authority. In all candor we must concede that part of this egalitarianism in America has been more pretension than realized fact. But we are an aspiring people, a people with faith in progress. Our amended Constitution is the lodestar for our aspirations. Like every text worth reading, it is not crystalline. The phrasing is broad and the limitations of its provisions are not clearly marked. Its majestic generalities and ennobling pronouncements are both luminous and obscure. This ambiguity of course calls forth interpretation, the interaction of reader and text. The encounter with the constitutional text has been, in many senses, my life's work. . . .

When Justices interpret the Constitution they speak for their community, not for themselves alone. The act of interpretation must be undertaken with full consciousness that it is, in a very real sense, the community's interpretation that is sought. Justices are not platonic guardians appointed to wield authority according to their personal moral predelictions. Precisely because coercive force must attend any judicial decision to countermand the will of a contemporary majority, the Justices must render constitutional interpretations that are received as legitimate. The source of legitimacy is, of course, a wellspring of controversy in legal and political circles. At the core of the debate is what the late Yale Law School professor Alexander Bickel labeled "the counter-majoritarian difficulty." Our commitment to self-governance in a representative democracy must be reconciled with vesting in electorally unaccountable Justices the power to invalidate the expressed desires of representative bodies on the ground of inconsistency with higher law. Because judicial power resides in the authority to give meaning to the Constitution, the debate is really a debate about how to read the text, about constraints on what is legitimate interpretation.

There are those who find legitimacy in fidelity to what they call "the intentions of the Framers." In its most doctrinaire incarnation, this view demands that Justices discern exactly what the Framers thought about the question under consideration and simply follow that intention in resolving the case before them. It is a view that feigns self-effacing deference to the specific judgments of those who forged our original social compact. But in truth it is little more than arrogance cloaked as humility. It is arrogant to pretend that from our vantage we can gauge accurately the intent of the Framers on application of principle to specific, contemporary questions. All too often, sources of potential enlightenment such as records of the ratification debates provide sparse or ambiguous evidence of the original intention. Typically, all that can be gleaned is that the Framers themselves did not agree about the application or meaning of particular constitutional provisions, and hid their differences in cloaks of generality. Indeed, it is far from clear whose intention is relevant—that of the drafters, the congressional disputants, or the ratifiers in the states?—or even whether the idea of an original intention is a coherent way of thinking about a jointly drafted document drawing its authority from a general assent of the states. And apart from the problematic nature of the sources, our distance of two centuries cannot but work as a prism refracting all we perceive. One cannot help but speculate that the chorus of lamentations calling for interpretation faithful to "original intention"—and proposing nullification of interpretations that fail this quick litmus test—must inevitably come from persons who have no familiarity with the historical record.

Perhaps most importantly, while proponents of this facile historicism justify it as a depoliticization of the judiciary, the political underpinnings of such a choice should not escape notice. A position that upholds constitutional claims only if they were within the specific contemplation of the Framers in effect establishes a presumption of resolving textual ambiguities against the claim of constitutional right. It is far from clear what justifies such a presumption against claims of right. Nothing intrinsic in the nature of interpretation—if there is such a thing as the "nature" of interpretation—commands such a passive approach to ambiguity. This is a choice no less political than any other; it expresses antipathy to claims of the minority rights against the majority. Those who would restrict claims of right to the values of 1789 specifically articulated in the Constitution turn a blind eye to social progress and eschew adaptation of overarching principles to changes of social circumstance.

Another, perhaps more sophisticated, response to the potential power of judicial interpretation stresses democratic theory: because ours is a government of the people's elected representatives, substantive value choices should by and large be left to them. This view emphasizes not the transcendent historical authority of the framers but the predominant contemporary authority of the elected branches of government. Yet it has similar consequences for the nature of proper judicial interpretation. Faith in the majoritarian process counsels restraint. Even under more expansive formulations of this approach, judicial review is appropriate only to the extent of ensuring that our democratic process functions smoothly. Thus, for example, we would protect freedom of speech merely to ensure that the people are heard by their representatives, rather than as a separate, substantive value. When, by contrast, society tosses up to the Supreme Court a dispute that would require invalidation of a legislature's substantive policy choice, the Court generally would stay its hand because the Constitution was meant as a plan of government and not as an embodiment of fundamental substantive values.

The view that all matters of substantive policy should be resolved through the majoritarian process has appeal under some circumstances, but I think it ultimately will not do. Unabashed enshrinement of majority would permit the imposition of a social caste system or wholesale confiscation of property so long as a majority of the authorized legislative body, fairly elected, approved. Our Constitution could not abide such a situation. It is the very purpose of a Constitution—and particularly of the Bill of Rights—to declare certain values transcendent, beyond the reach of temporary political majorities. The majoritarian process cannot be expected to rectify claims of minority right that arise as a response to the outcomes of that very majoritarian process. As James Madison put it:

The prescriptions in favor of liberty ought to be levelled against that quarter where the greatest danger lies, namely, that which possesses the highest prerogative of power. But this is not found in either the Executive or Legislative departments of Government, but in the body of the people, operating by the majority against the minority (I Annals 437).

Faith in democracy is one thing, blind faith quite another. Those who drafted our Constitution understood the difference. One cannot read the text without admitting that it embodies substantive value choices; it places certain values beyond the power of any legislature. Obvious are the separation of powers; the privilege of the Writ of Habeas Corpus; prohibition of Bills of Attainder and *ex post facto* laws; prohibition of cruel and unusual punishments; the requirement of just compensation for official taking of property; the prohibition of laws tending to establish religion or enjoining the free exercise of religion; and, since the Civil War, the banishment of slavery and official race discrimination. With respect to at least such principles, we simply have not constituted ourselves as strict utilitarians. While the Constitution may be amended, such amendments require an immense effort by the People as a whole.

To remain faithful to the content of the Constitution, therefore, an approach to interpreting the text must account for the existence of these substantive value choices, and must accept the ambiguity inherent in the effort to apply them to modern circumstances. The Framers discerned fundamental principles through struggles against particular malefactions of the Crown; the struggle shapes the particular contours of the articulated principles. But our acceptance of the fundamental principles has not and should not bind us to those precise, at times anachronistic, contours. Successive generations of Americans have continued to respect these fundamental choices and adopt them as their own guide to evaluating quite different historical practices. Each generation has the choice to overrule or add to the fundamental principles enunciated by the Framers; the Constitution can be amended or it can be ignored. Yet with respect to its fundamental principles, the text has suffered neither fate. Thus, if I may borrow the words of an esteemed predecessor, Justice Robert Jackson, the burden of judicial interpretation is to translate "the majestic generalities of the Bill of Rights, conceived as part of the pattern of liberal government in the eighteenth century, into concrete restraints on officials dealing with the problems of the twentieth century" *Board of Education* v. *Barnette* [319 U.S. 624, 639 (1943)].

We current Justices read the Constitution in the only way that we can: as Twentieth Century Americans. We look to the history of the time of framing and to the intervening history of interpretation. But the ultimate question must be, what do the words of the text mean in our time? For the genius of the Constitution rests not in any static meaning it might have had in a world that is dead and gone, but in the adaptability of its great principles to cope with current problems and current needs. What the constitutional fundamentals meant to the wisdom of other times cannot be their measure to the vision of our time. Similarly, what those fundamentals mean for us, our descendants will learn, cannot be the measure to the vision of their time. This realization is not, I assure you, a novel one of my own creation. Permit me to quote from one of the opinions of our Court, *Weems* v. *United States* [217 U.S. 349], written nearly a century ago:

> Time works changes, brings into existence new conditions and purposes. Therefore, a principle to be vital must be capable of wider application than the mischief which gave it birth. This is peculiarly true of constitutions. They are not ephemeral enactments, designed to meet passing occasions. They are, to use the words of Chief Justice John Marshall, "designed to approach immortality as nearly as human institutions can approach it." The future is their care and provision for events of good and bad tendencies of which no prophecy can be made. In the application of a constitution, therefore, our contemplation cannot be only of what has been, but of what may be.

Interpretation must account for the transformative purpose of the text. Our Constitution was not intended to preserve a preexisting society but to make a new one, to put in place new principles that the prior political community had not sufficiently recognized. Thus, for example, when we interpret the Civil War Amendments to the charter—abolishing slavery, guaranteeing blacks equality under law, and guaranteeing blacks the right to vote—we must remember that those who put them in place had no desire to enshrine the status quo. Their goal was to make over their world, to eliminate all vestige of slave caste.

Having discussed at some length how I, as a Supreme Court Justice, interact with this text, I think it time to turn to the fruits of this discourse. For the Constitution is a sublime oration on the dignity of man, a bold commitment by a people to the ideal of libertarian dignity protected through law. Some reflection is perhaps required before this can be seen.

The Constitution on its face is, in large measure, a structuring text, a blueprint for government. And when the text is not prescribing the form of government it is limiting the powers of that government. The original document, before addition of any of the amendments, does not speak primarily of the rights of man, but of the abilities and disabilities of government. When one reflects upon the text's preoccupation with the scope of government as well as its shape, however, one comes to understand that what this text is about is the relationship of the individual and the state. The text marks the metes and bounds of official authority and individual autonomy. When one studies the boundary that the text marks out, one gets a sense of the vision of the individual embodied in the Constitution.

As augmented by the Bill of Rights and the Civil War Amendments, this text is a sparkling vision of the supremacy of the human dignity of every individual. This vision is reflected in the very choice of democratic self-governance: the supreme value of a democracy is the presumed worth of each individual. And this vision manifests itself most dramatically in the specific prohibitions of the Bill of Rights, a term which I henceforth will apply to describe not only the original first eight amendments, but the Civil War amendments as well. It is a vision that has guided us as a people throughout our history, although the precise rules by which we have protected fundamental human dignity have been transformed over time in response to both transformations of social condition and evolution of our concepts of human dignity. . . .

In general, problems of the relationship of the citizen with government have multiplied and thus have engendered some of the most important constitutional issues of the day. As government acts ever more deeply upon those areas of our lives once marked "private," there is an even greater need to see that individual rights are not curtailed or cheapened in the interest of what may temporarily appear to be the "public good." And as government continues in its role of provider for so many of our disadvantaged citizens, there is an even greater need to ensure that government act with integrity and consistency in its dealings with these citizens. To put this another way, the possibilities for collision between government activity and individual rights will increase as the power and authority of government itself expands, and this growth, in turn, heightens the need for constant vigilance at the collision points. If our free society is to endure, those who govern must recognize human dignity and accept the enforcement of constitutional limitations on their power conceived by the Framers to be necessary to preserve that dignity and the air of freedom which is our proudest heritage. Such recognition will not come from a technical understanding of the organs of government, or the new forms of wealth they administer. It requires something different, something deeper—a personal confrontation with the well-springs of our society. Solutions of constitutional questions from that perspective have become the great challenge of the modern era. All the talk in the last half-decade about shrinking the government does not alter this reality or the challenge it imposes. The modern activist state is a concomitant of the complexity of modern society; it is inevitably with us. We must meet the challenge rather than wish it were not before us.

The challenge is essentially, of course, one to the capacity of our constitutional structure to foster and protect the freedom, the dignity, and the rights of all persons within our borders, which it is the great design of the Constitution to secure. During the time of my public service this challenge has largely taken shape within the confines of the interpretive question whether the specific guarantees of the Bill of Rights operate as restraints on the power of State government. We recognize the Bill of Rights as the primary source of express information as to what is meant by constitutional liberty. The safeguards enshrined in it are deeply etched in the foundation of America's freedoms. Each is a protection with centuries of history behind it, often dearly bought with the blood and lives of people determined to prevent oppression by their rulers. The first eight Amendments, however, were added to the Constitution to operate solely against federal power. It was not until the Thirteenth and Fourteenth Amendments were added, in 1865 and 1868, in response to a demand for national protection against abuses of state power, that the Constitution could be interpreted to require application of the first eight amendments to the states.

It was in particular the Fourteenth Amendment's guarantee that no person be deprived of life, liberty or property without process of law that led us to apply many of the specific guarantees of the Bill of Rights to the States. In my judgment, Justice Cardozo best captured the reasoning that brought us to such decisions when he described what the Court has done as a process by which the guarantees "have been taken over from the earlier articles of the federal bill of rights and brought within the Fourteenth Amendment by a process of absorption . . . [that] has had its source in the belief that neither liberty nor justice would exist if [those guarantees] . . . were sacrificed" {*Palko* v. *Connecticut* [302 U.S. 319, 326 (1937)]}. But this process of absorption was neither swift nor steady. As late as 1922 only the Fifth Amendment guarantee of just compensation for official taking of property had been given force against the states. Between then and 1956 only the First Amendment guarantees of speech and conscience and the Fourth Amendment ban of unreasonable searches and seizures had been incorporated—the latter, however, without the exclusionary rule to give it force. As late as 1961, I could stand before a distinguished assemblage of the bar at New York University's James Madison Lecture and list the following as guarantees that had not been thought to be sufficiently fundamental to the protection of human dignity so as to be enforced against the states: the prohibition of cruel and unusual punishments, the right against self-incrimination, the right to assistance of counsel in a criminal trial, the right to confront witnesses, the right to compulsory process, the right not to be placed in jeopardy of life or limb more than once upon accusation of a crime, the right not to have illegally obtained evidence introduced at a criminal trial, and the right to a jury of one's peers.

The history of the quarter century following that Madison Lecture need not be told in great detail. Suffice it to say that each of the guarantees listed above has been recognized as a fundamental aspect of ordered liberty. Of course, the above catalogue encompasses only the rights of the criminally accused, those caught, rightly or wrongly, in the maw of the criminal justice system. But it has been well said that there is no better test of a society than how it treats those accused of transgressing against it. Indeed, it is because we recognize that incarceration strips a man of his dignity that we demand strict adherence to fair procedure and proof of guilt beyond a reasonable doubt before taking such a drastic step. These requirements are, as Justice Harlan once said, "bottomed on a fundamental value determination of our society that it is far worse to convict an innocent man than to let a guilty man go free" {*In re Winship* [397 U.S. 358, 372 (1970)] (concurring opinion)}. There is no worse injustice than wrongly to strip a man of his dignity. And our adherence to the constitutional vision of human dignity is so strict that even after convicting a person according to these stringent standards, we demand that his dignity be infringed only to the extent appropriate to the crime and never by means of wanton infliction of pain or deprivation. I interpret the Constitution plainly to embody these fundamental values.

Of course the constitutional vision of human dignity has, in this past quarter century, infused far more than our decisions about the criminal process. Recognition of the principle of "one person, one vote" as a constitutional one redeems the promise of self-governance by affirming the essential dignity of every citizen in the right to equal participation in the democratic process. Recognition of so-called "new property" rights in those receiving government entitlements affirms the essential dignity of the least fortunate among us by demanding that government treat with decency, integrity and consistency those dependent on its benefits for their very survival. After all, a legislative majority initially decides to create governmental entitlements; the Constitution's Due Process Clause merely provides protection for entitlements thought necessary by society as a whole. Such due process rights prohibit government from imposing the devil's bargain of bartering away human dignity in exchange for human sustenance. Likewise, recognition of full equality for women—equal protection of the laws—ensures that gender has no bearing on claims to human dignity.

Recognition of broad and deep rights of expression and of conscience reaffirm the vision of human dignity in many ways. They too redeem the promise of self-governance by facilitating—indeed demanding—robust, uninhibited and wide-open debate on issues of public importance. Such public debate is of course vital to the development and dissemination of political ideas. As importantly, robust public discussion is the crucible in which personal political convictions are forged. In our democracy, such discussion is a political duty, it is the essence of self-government. The constitutional vision of human dignity rejects the possibility of political orthodoxy imposed from above; it respects the right of each individual to form and to express political judgments, however far they may deviate from the mainstream and however unsettling they might be to the powerful or the elite. Recognition of these rights of expression and conscience also frees up the private space for both intellectual and spiritual development free of government dominance, either blatant or subtle. Justice Brandeis put it so well sixty years ago when he wrote: "Those who won our independence believed that the final end of the State was to make men free to develop their faculties; and that in its government the deliberative forces should prevail over the arbitrary. They valued liberty both as an end and as a means" {*Whitney* v. *California* [274 U.S. 357, 375 (1927)] (concurring opinion)}.

I do not mean to suggest that we have in the last quarter century achieved a comprehensive definition of the constitutional ideal of human dignity. We are still striving toward that goal, and doubtless it will be an eternal quest. For if the interaction of this Justice and the constitutional text over the years confirms any single proposition, it is that the demands of human dignity will never cease to evolve.

DISCUSSION QUESTIONS

1. Should justices of the Supreme Court be guided by the original intention of those who wrote the Constitution and the laws? What are the advantages of this approach to constitutional interpretation? What problems might justices face in trying to ascertain original intention?

2. If original intention is not to be the standard for constitutional interpretation, what can the standard be? How might Brennan respond to Meese's argument that if original intention is rejected, the door is opened to justices arbitrarily pouring their own values and goals into their decisions while claiming to base them on the Constitution?

3. Does the Constitution guarantee only those rights that are specified in its text? Can we derive such things as a right to privacy (the basis for Supreme Court decisions on contraception and abortion) from constitutional values even when the Constitution says nothing about such a right?

4. What is the place of the judiciary in American democracy? Does the Supreme Court's status as an unelected branch require that it play a limited and restrained role? Or does its claim to be the guardian of the Constitution warrant a more active role for the Court on behalf of democratic principles and values?

5. Is it possible to depoliticize the Supreme Court? Can the Supreme Court be removed from the central political controversies of American life?

SUGGESTED READINGS AND INTERNET RESOURCES

In *The Tempting of America: The Political Seduction of the Law* (New York: Free Press, 1990), Robert Bork develops a view of constitutional interpretation similar to Meese's and presents a scathing conservative critique of an activist judiciary. A skeptical argument that the judiciary cannot be the agent of social justice that Brennan envisions can be found in Gerald Rosenberg, *The Hollow Hope: Can Courts Bring About Social Change?* (Chicago: University of Chicago Press, 1991). The judiciary has been criticized from the left as well as from the right; for radical perspectives, see David Kairys, ed., *The Politics of Law: A Progressive Critique* (3d ed.; New York: Basic Books, 1998). An argument for a populist constitutional law that would deny the judicial branch the exclusive authority to interpret the Constitution is Mark Tushnet, *Taking the Constitution Away from the Courts* (Princeton, N.J.: Princeton University Press, 1999). For a popular democratic account of leading Supreme Court cases, see Peter Irons, *A People's History of the Supreme Court* (New York: Penguin Books, 2000).

Federalist Society
www.fed-soc.org
This website of a prominent organization of conservative lawyers offers perspectives on recent Supreme Court cases and other legal issues.

American Civil Liberties Union
www.aclu.org
This website discusses legal issues and court cases viewed from the perspective of the group who has argued many of the most prominent civil liberties issues before the U.S. Supreme Court.

University of Pittsburgh School of Law
www.jurist.law.pitt.edu
This site provides Supreme Court opinions and stories on constitutional law.

Supreme Court of the United States
www.supremecourtus.gov
The Supreme Court's website contains a searchable docket, the text of recent decisions in PDF format, and information on Court rules and procedures.

CHAPTER 16

Economic Inequality: A Threat to Democracy?

The United States has always prided itself on being a land of opportunity. Unlike the class-divided societies of Europe, American society prides itself on being more fluid and open to individual ambition. In the United States you can rise from "rags to riches," as the saying goes. The "American Dream," which is defined in many different ways but almost always involves economic success, is supposedly within everyone's grasp. Millions of immigrants have been drawn to our shores by the lure of the American Dream. Not only is the United States a land of opportunity and upward mobility, but it is also generally believed that we lack the extremes of wealth and poverty that characterize other societies. The United States is basically a middle-class society.

Almost everyone agrees that equal opportunity and a strong middle class are essential to the healthy functioning of American society and its political system. Throughout our history, however, debates have periodically erupted about how to guarantee equal opportunity and how much economic inequality should be tolerated in a democracy before government needs to take action. One of the first such debates was between two giants of American political history, Thomas Jefferson and Alexander Hamilton. Jefferson argued that the stability of American democracy rested on the backs of small farmers, who, because they made a living through their own efforts on their own land, were free to speak out and participate fully in politics without any fears. Jefferson argued that manufacturing and large cities created wide inequalities and dangerous dependencies that corrupted democracy. His opponent, Alexander

Hamilton, was much less fearful of economic inequalities. In his *Report on Manufactures,* Hamilton argued that the government should encourage manufacturing as a way to tie the wealthy classes to government, thus providing a check against the turbulence of the masses.

In the long run, Hamilton's vision of industrial expansion prevailed over Jefferson's agricultural ideal. After the Civil War (1861–1865), industry really began to take off. Entrepreneurs, such as Andrew Carnegie and John D. Rockefeller, amassed huge fortunes the likes of which had never been seen before in the New World. At the same time, millions of immigrants poured into U.S. cities to work in industry at low wages and for long hours. Many observers believed that events were proving Jefferson's fears correct. Mark Twain called this "Gilded Age" a time of money lust. Muckraking journalists exposed the ways that Robber Barons corrupted the political process, sometimes buying off whole state legislatures. The Populist movement of the late nineteenth century fought to protect the small farmer and limit the power of corporations. It proposed legislation to break up the large corporations, expand the money supply to ease the debt burden on small farmers, and impose a federal income tax to redistribute wealth.

The opponents of the Populists vigorously denied that industrialism was creating unfair inequalities that threatened American democracy. They did not deny that some people were very rich and others quite poor, but they argued that these inequalities were a natural result of economic competition that benefited the entire society. Social Darwinists applied Charles Darwin's theory of human evolution to society, arguing that inequalities derived from economic competition, which resulted in the "survival of the fittest." Great wealth was the result of hard work and entrepreneurial genius. As the prominent Social Darwinist William Graham Sumner put it: "No man can acquire a million without helping a million men to increase their little fortunes all the way down all through the social grades." The United States was a land of opportunity where self-made men could rise up out of the working class to great riches. Indeed, there were many examples, besides Carnegie and Rockefeller, to point to. The principles of Social Darwinism were spread to the broad public by a "success" literature that told vivid stories of poor boys rising up out of poverty through hard work and moral uprightness. A Unitarian minister by the name of Horatio Alger published 106 such rags-to-riches books from 1868 to 1904, many of which became best-sellers.

A century later the democratic debate about economic inequality is once again heating up, albeit in very different economic circumstances. From World War II until the 1970s, according to most observers, economic inequalities remained the same or even shrank somewhat. Sometime in the 1970s, however, wages began to stagnate and even fall for most workers. Many reasons have been offered for this. Global competition has put downward pressure on U.S. industrial wages, which now must often compete with wages in Third World countries. It is not so much the decline in manufacturing wages as the shift from manufacturing to services that is hurting wages for many workers. Manufacturing employment has declined as jobs have migrated abroad and workers are replaced by machines, including industrial robots. Wages in the expanding service sector are generally lower than in manufacturing. Partly driven by the spread of computers into practically every workplace, education and skills acquisition have become even more important to earning a good wage. The wages of those with a high school education or less have fallen, while those with postgraduate degrees have seen their salaries soar. You can no longer earn a decent wage simply by having a strong back and being willing to work hard.

As in the Gilded Age, at the same time that many workers are struggling to get by, huge fortunes are being amassed at the top. The incredible bull market on Wall Street that lasted from in the late 1980s almost to 2000 brought fantastic returns for those who held stocks. Technological breakthroughs in computer technology have generated tremendous opportunities for daring entrepreneurs to accumulate vast wealth. Personal computers, software, and the development of the Internet have created wealth more rapidly than at any time in American history. Bill Gates, the founder of Microsoft, which supplies the operating system for most personal computers, became the richest man in the world, worth well over $100 billion (that's billion, not million!). His fortune, even after it is corrected for inflation, is many times that of John D. Rockefeller. Reminiscent of the government's effort to break up Rockefeller's Standard Oil Trust, the federal government has prosecuted Microsoft for antitrust violations.

As with the inequalities generated by nineteenth-century industrialism, the inequalities of the so-called postindustrial economy have prompted a spirited political and policy debate. When deindustrialization hit with a vengeance in the 1980s, many people called for the United States to engage in industrial planning similar to that done by Japan. But national industrial planning never took off. Instead, led by President Ronald Reagan, the United States pursued a very different approach. Reagan argued that government regulation and high taxes were choking off economic growth. Reagan's supply-side economics recommended cutting taxes in order to increase incentives to work hard and invest. Inequalities were necessary as a goad to work hard, and in the long run everyone would benefit from a growing economy. "A rising tide would lift all boats."

Bill Clinton campaigned for the presidency in 1992 on promises to address inequalities, calling for a national health insurance program and greater public investments in education and job training for American workers. Although Clinton lost on health insurance and largely jettisoned his proposals to invest in American workers in order to instead reduce the deficit, throughout his presidency he advocated government programs, such as increasing the minimum wage, to help those who were being left behind by the booming economy. Clinton strongly supported free trade, but many, most notably Pat Buchanan and Ross Perot, attacked free trade for exporting U.S. jobs (Perot's "giant sucking sound"). The inequality debate was renewed in 2001 when President George W. Bush succeeded in passing a $1.35 trillion tax cut spread over ten years. Opponents charged that 38 percent of the benefits would go to the wealthiest 1 percent of taxpayers. Supporters responded that it was only fair that those who pay the most in taxes receive the most money back.

The two selections that follow address the contemporary inequality debate in our rapidly changing economy. The first excerpt is from a 1999 book entitled *Myths of Rich and Poor* by W. Michael Cox, chief economist at the Federal Reserve Bank of Dallas, and Richard Alm. Acknowledging that some statistics show wide and widening income inequalities, they maintain that these inequalities are not threatening. According to Cox and Alm, we should not concentrate on the gap between the top and the bottom. Rather, we should focus on whether those at the bottom are better or worse off. In the book from which this excerpt is taken, the authors make a convincing case that those at the bottom generally are better off in terms of *consumption*. Breakthroughs in technology mean that we have more conveniences than ever, such as VCRs, color TVs, and telephone answering machines. In addition, these devices, which enhance the quality of our lives, are more efficient and powerful than ever (consider the improvement in home computers in recent years). In the section we have chosen, Cox and Alm also make the point that snapshots of inequality at one point in time do not capture the movement of people out of poverty over their lifetimes. It is still a land of opportunity, they argue.

In our other selection, Paul Krugman, an iconoclastic economist, editorial writer, and relentless critic of the Bush administration, argues that it is precisely the gap between the rich and the poor that we should be focusing on. The public, Krugman maintains, has little idea how swiftly the United States has moved from a middle-class society to one characterized by huge gaps between the haves and the have-nots. Inequalities are supposed to provide powerful incentives for work and investment, stimulating economic growth that benefits everyone. Instead, Krugman argues, the vast inequalities we have today harm economic growth by encouraging white-collar crime, and the benefits of economic growth are captured by the very rich, with little trickling down to benefit most Americans. Inequality even harms our health. Krugman concludes by holding out the possibility that economic inequalities will become self-reinforcing: as elites get richer, they will dominate the political process, passing laws that will make it easier for them to accumulate even more riches.

Before reading the two selections, you may want to look back at the discussion of inequality in the Introduction to this book. Do the authors take a process orientation toward equality or a results orientation? Why do Cox and Alm think we should focus on what those at the bottom are able to consume, whereas Krugman says little about this and instead concentrates on the gap between the top and the bottom? Krugman clearly thinks that it is the political power of those at the top that is partly responsible for rising inequalities. What do Cox and Alm say is the cause of income differences?

Myths of Rich and Poor

W. MICHAEL COX
AND RICHARD ALM

"L and of Opportunity." Anywhere in the world, those three words bring to mind just one place: the United States of America.

Opportunity defines our heritage. The American saga entails waves of immigrant farmers, shopkeepers, laborers, and entrepreneurs, all coming to the United States for the promise of a better life. Some amassed enormous fortunes—the Rockefellers, the Carnegies, the DuPonts, the Fords, the Vanderbilts, to name just a few. Even today, America's opportunity is always on display. Bill Gates in computer software, Ross Perot in data processing, Bill Cosby and Oprah Winfrey in entertainment, Warren Buffett in investing, Sam Walton in retailing, Michael Jordan in sports, and Mary Kay Ash in cosmetics could head a list of the many thousands who catapulted from society's lower or middle ranks to the top. Many millions more, descendants of those who arrived with little more than the clothes on their backs and a few bucks in their pockets, took advantage of an open economic system to improve their lot in life through talent and hard work.

Even pessimists acknowledge that the Gateses, Perots, Cosbys, Winfreys, Buffetts, Waltons, Jordans, and Ashes are getting filthy rich, along with Wall Street's wheeler-dealers, Hollywood moguls, and big-league ballplayers. At the nation's 350 largest companies, top executives' median total compensation in 1996 was $3.1 million, or 90 times what a typical factory hand earns. We often hear that ordinary Americans aren't keeping up, that success isn't as easy, or at least not as democratic, as it once was. At the close of the twentieth century, one disturbing vision portrays the United States as a society pulling apart at the seams, divided into separate and unequal camps, an enclave of fat cats gorging themselves on the fruits of others' labor surrounded by a working class left with ever more meager opportunities.

The most-cited evidence of ebbing opportunity is the *distribution of income*—the slicing up of the American pie. Examining the data, analysts seize on two points. First, there's a marked inequality in earnings between society's haves and have-nots. Second, and perhaps more ominous, the gap between the richest and poorest households has widened over the past two decades. The Census Bureau provides the statistical ballast for these claims. In 1997, the top 20 percent of American households received almost half of the nation's income. Average earnings among this group are $122,764 a year. The distribution of income to the four other groups of 20 percent was as follows: The second fifth had 23.2 percent, with average earnings of $57,582; the third fifth had 15.0 percent, with average earnings of $37,177; the fourth fifth had 8.9 percent, with average earnings of $22,098. The bottom 20 percent earned 3.6 percent of the economic pie, or an average of $8,872 a year.

The case for the existence of a growing rift between rich and poor rests on longer-term trends in the same Census Bureau data. Since 1975, only the top 20 percent of Americans managed to expand their allotment of the nation's income—from 43.2 percent to 49.4 percent. Over the same period, the distribution to the middle three groups slipped slightly. The share going to the lowest 20 percent of income earners fell from 4.4 percent to 3.6 percent. The shift of income toward the upper end of the distribution becomes even more striking when it's put in dollars. After adjusting for inflation, the income of households in the bottom 20 percent increased by only $207 from 1975 to 1997. The top tier, meanwhile, jumped by $37,633.

Once again, the pessimists have it wrong. The income distribution only reveals how one group is doing relative to others at a particular moment. That kind of you-vs.-me score keeping has little to do with whether any American can get ahead. By its very nature, opportunity is individual rather than collective. Even for an individual, the concept can't be divorced from its time element, an assessment of how well someone is doing today relative to yesterday, or how he can expect to do tomorrow compared to today. How many of us worked our way up? How quickly did we move from one rung to the next? How many of us fell? Studies of income inequality cannot say whether individuals are doing better or worse. They lump together Americans who differ in age, educational level, work effort, family and marital status, gender and race. The sample never stays the same from one year to another, and researchers haven't a clue about what happened to any individual in the income distribution.

Annual snapshots of the income distribution might deserve attention if we lived in a caste society, with rigid class lines determining who gets what share of the national income—but we don't live in a caste society. It takes a heroic leap to look at the disparity between rich and poor and conclude that any one individual's chances of getting ahead aren't what they used to be. Even the most sophisticated income-distribution statistics fail to tell us what we really want to know: Are the majority of Americans losing their birthright—a chance at upward mobility? Static portraits, moreover, don't tell us whether low-income households tend to remain at the bottom year after year. By definition, a fifth of society will always inhabit the lowest 20 percent of the income distribution. We don't know, however, whether individuals and families stay there over long periods. It's no great tragedy if the bottom rung is where many Americans start to climb the ladder of success. To argue that upward mobility is being lost, we would have to show that the poorest remain stuck where they are, with little hope of making themselves better off. Nothing could be further from the truth. . . .

Making It from Bottom to Top

The Treasury Department affirms that most Americans still have a good shot at upward mobility. In a 1992 analysis covering nine years, researchers found that 86 percent of those in the lowest 20 percent of income earners in 1979 had moved to a higher grouping by 1988. Moreover, 66 percent reached the middle tier or above, with almost 15 percent making it all the way to the top fifth of income earners. Among Americans who started out above the bottom fifth in 1979, the Treasury found the same movement up the income ladder. Nearly 50 percent of those in the middle tier, for example, rose into the top two groupings, overwhelming whatever downward mobility that took place. . . .

In addition to confirming that most Americans are still getting ahead in life, the Treasury study verifies that the quickest rise occurs among the young, an antidote to the prevailing ennui among the so-called Generation X. It also found that wage and salary income was primarily responsible for pushing people upward in the distribution, indicating that work, not luck, is the widest path to opportunity. Ours is not a *Wheel of Fortune* economy, where a few lucky individuals win big, leaving paltry gains to the great mass of people. Most of us get ahead because we strive to make ourselves and our families better off.

By carefully tracking individuals' incomes over many years, . . . the Treasury study show[s] that our economic system is biased toward success. These results should go a long way toward quelling fears of an America polarized between privileged rich and permanently poor. The rich may indeed be getting richer. We ought to have little problem with that. The poor are also getting richer. We ought to celebrate that. Indeed, what's so encouraging is the ability of those who start out in the lowest income brackets to jump into the middle and upper echelons. There's evidence that most Americans are making their way up the income distribution through education, experience, and hard work.

That's what the American Dream, a dream of opportunity, is all about. . . .

The Common Thread: Lifetime Earnings

If so many Americans are rising through the income ranks, and if only a few of us stay stuck at the bottom, who makes up the lowest fifth of today's income earners? One group is the downwardly mobile, those who once took in enough money to be in a higher echelon. Descent can be voluntary, usually a result of retirement, or it can be involuntary, resulting from layoffs or other hard luck. Just changing jobs sometimes results in a dip in earnings. We've already seen, though, that downward mobility happens to only a small segment of the population. By far the largest number of low-income earners are new entrants into the world of work, mostly young people. Many of us begin our working lives as part of the bottom 20 percent, either as students with part-time jobs or as relatively unskilled entrants to the labor force. Many immigrants, whatever their age, start off with low incomes.

Although they usually start at the bottom, the young tend to rise through the income distribution as they become better educated, develop skills, and gain experience. In fact, income tends to follow a familiar pattern over a person's lifetime: It rises rapidly in the early years of working, peaks during middle age, then falls toward retirement. When the average earnings at each age are placed side by side, it creates a lifetime earnings profile, shaped like a pyramid.

The changes in lifetime earnings over the past four decades tell us quite a bit about the evolution of our economy. In 1951, workers reached their peak earning years in ages 35 to 44, when their average annual earnings were 1.6 times the income of those in the 20-to-24 age group. By 1973, the ratio had risen to 2.4 to 1. By 1993, the peak earning years had shifted to ages 45 to 54, and workers in this highly paid group earned almost 3.2 times more than the 20-to-24-year-olds. . . .

A steeper lifetime earnings profile reflects greater opportunity. One way to see that is to imagine a perfectly flat pattern of lifetime income, with workers earning the same income every year. Paychecks for the middle years of life would match those for the early twenties. This would be a world devoid of upward mobility, offering workers no prospect of getting ahead during their lifetimes, no matter what their effort, no matter how much they improve their worth on the job.

What is behind the faster rise in Americans' lifetime earnings? Most likely, it's the by-product of broad changes in the way we work. When the economy was largely industrial, Americans worked with their hands and their backs. Today, more Americans than ever owe their paychecks to brainpower. The skills of the mind, unlike those of the body, are cumulative. Mental talents continue to sharpen long after muscles and dexterity begin to falter. These facts of physiology and economic development probably explain why the peak earning years have shifted to older age groups in the past two decades. As the United States retools itself for a more knowledge-intensive era, as the country moves from a blue-collar economy to a white-collar one, the rewards for education and experience are increasing.

The lifetime earnings profile is the thread that sews together recent trends in upward mobility and income inequality. As today's workers reap greater rewards for what they've learned on the job, earnings become sharply higher with experience. It's not that today's young workers are falling behind their counterparts of earlier generations. On the contrary, older workers are doing so much better than they used to. The result is an increase in the gap between youth and middle age. In the end, the steepening of lifetime earnings leads us to a surprising conclusion: Upward mobility may well be an important factor in the widening gap in income distribution.

All told, this isn't the harsh world seen by those who say the rich are getting richer and the poor are getting poorer. Both rich and poor are becoming better off. Are most of us going nowhere? Quite the contrary; the majority of Americans are busy climbing the income ladder. Greater returns to education and experience can skew income toward the upper end, but we would be foolhardy indeed to become so obsessed with the pecking order that we lose sight of what's really important—opportunity.

A steeper lifetime earnings profile also puts a different slant on the notion of a vanishing middle class. The center of the income distribution isn't a destination. It's just one step on the ladder of upward mobility. Forty years ago, with a flatter earnings profile, families spent most of their working lives in the middle income brackets. Today's more rapid rise in incomes means they move to the top faster, spending less time defined as "middle class." Worries about Generation X's future can be put to rest, too. Those entering the labor force in the 1900s may look at their parents' income and wonder how they will ever attain such heights. They should, however, find a steeper earnings profile encouraging. During their first two or three decades in the labor market, young workers are likely to see their incomes rise more quickly than their parents' did.

In the United States, getting ahead isn't a great mystery. The economy provides opportunity—more, in fact, than ever before—but it's up to each of us to grab it. Success isn't random. Luck and Daddy's money aren't the way most Americans get to the top. More often than not, the rewards go to education, experience, talent, ambition, vision, risk taking, readiness to change, and just plain hard work. Young people aren't guaranteed success any more than their parents were. Their chances will improve, though, if they make the right choices in life. Opportunity lies in the advice given by generations of parents and teachers: Study, work hard, and save. In short, the best advice for economic success is this: Listen to your elders. . . .

Inequality Is Not Inequity

Judging from the public debate, at least some Americans would prefer a more equal distribution of income to a less equal one, perhaps on moral grounds, perhaps as a part of an ideal of civic virtue. There's no *economic* reason, however, to prefer one pattern of income distribution over another. In fact, the income statistics do little but confirm what's obvious: America isn't an egalitarian society. It wasn't designed to be. Socialism, a failed and receding system, sought to impose an artificial equality. Capitalism, a successful and expanding system, doesn't fight a fundamental fact of human nature—we vary greatly in capabilities, motivation, interests, and preferences. Some of us are driven to get ahead. Some of us are just plain lazy. Some of us are willing to work hard so we can afford a lifestyle rich in material goods. Some of us work just hard enough to provide a roof overhead, food, clothes, and a few amenities. It shouldn't come as a surprise that our incomes vary greatly.

Income inequality isn't an aberration. Quite the opposite, it's perfectly consistent with the laws that govern a free-enterprise system. In the early

1970s, three groups of unemployed Canadians, all in their twenties, all with at least 12 years of schooling, volunteered to participate in a stylized economy where the only employment was making woolen belts on small hand looms. They could work as much or as little as they liked, earning $2.50 for each belt. After 98 days, the results were anything but equal: 37.2 percent of the economy's income went to the 20 percent with the highest earnings. The bottom 20 percent received only 6.6 percent. This economic microcosm tells us one thing: Even among similar people with identical work options, some workers will earn more than others.

In a modern economy, incomes vary for plenty of reasons having little to do with fairness or equity. Education and experience, for example, usually yield higher pay. As industry becomes more sophisticated, the rewards to skilled labor tend to rise, adding to the number of high-income earners. Location matters. New Yorkers earn more than Mississippians. Lifestyle choices play a part, too. Simply by having an additional paycheck, two-income families make more money than those with a single breadwinner. Longer retirements, however, will add to the number of households with low income, even if many senior citizens live well from their savings. Demographic changes can twist the distribution of income. As the Baby Boom enters its peak earning years, the number of high-income households ought to rise. Economic forces create ripples in what we earn. The ebb and flow of industries can shift workers to both ends of the income distribution. Layoffs put some Americans into low-income groups, at least temporarily. Companies with new products and new technologies create jobs and, in most cases, share the bounty by offering workers higher pay. In technology industries, bonuses and stock options are becoming more common. Higher rates of return on investments—with, for example, a stock-market boom—will create a windfall for households with money riding on financial markets.

In and of itself, moreover, income distribution doesn't say much about the performance of an economy or the opportunities it offers. A widening gap isn't necessarily a sign of failure, nor does a narrowing one guarantee that an economy is functioning well. As a matter of fact, it's quite common to find a widening of income distribution in boom times, when almost everyone's earnings are rising rapidly. All it takes is for one segment of the workforce to become better off faster than others. However, the distribution can narrow in hard times, as companies facing declining demand cut back on jobs, hours, raises, and bonuses. In fact, we often see a compression of incomes in areas where people are sinking into poverty.

There's no denying that our system allows some Americans to become much richer than others. We must accept that, even celebrate it. Opportunity, not equality of income, is what made the U.S. economy grow and prosper. It's most important to provide equality of opportunity, not equality of results. There's ample evidence to refute any suggestion that the economy is no longer capable of providing opportunity for the vast majority of Americans. At the end of the twentieth century, upward mobility is alive and well. Even the lower-income households are sharing in the country's progress. What's more, data suggest that the populist view of America as a society torn between haves and have-nots, with rigid class lines, is just plain wrong. We are by no means a caste society.

For Richer

PAUL KRUGMAN

The Disappearing Middle

When I was a teenager growing up on Long Island, one of my favorite excursions was a trip to see the great Gilded Age mansions of the North Shore. Those mansions weren't just pieces of architectural history. They were monuments to a bygone social era, one in which the rich could afford the armies of servants needed to maintain a house the size of a European palace. By the time I saw them, of course, that era was long past. Almost none of the Long Island mansions were still private residences. Those that hadn't been turned into museums were occupied by nursing homes or private schools.

For the America I grew up in—the America of the 1950s and 1960s—was a middle-class society, both in reality and in feel. The vast income and wealth inequalities of the Gilded Age had disappeared. Yes, of course, there was the poverty of the underclass—but the conventional wisdom of the time viewed that as a social rather than an economic problem. Yes, of course, some wealthy businessmen and heirs to large fortunes lived far better than the average American. But they weren't rich the way the robber barons who built the mansions had been rich, and there weren't that many of them. The days when plutocrats were a force to be reckoned with in American society, economically or politically, seemed long past.

Daily experience confirmed the sense of a fairly equal society. The economic disparities you were conscious of were quite muted. Highly educated professionals—middle managers, college teachers, even lawyers—often claimed that they earned less than unionized blue-collar workers. Those considered very well off lived in split-levels, had a housecleaner come in once a week, and took summer vacations in Europe. But they sent their kids to public schools and drove themselves to work, just like everyone else.

But that was long ago. The middle-class America of my youth was another country.

We are now living in a new Gilded Age, as extravagant as the original. Mansions have made a comeback. The creations of Thierry Despont, the "eminence of excess," an architect who specializes in designing houses for the superrich, typically range from 20,000 to 60,000 square feet; houses at the upper end of his range are not much smaller than the White House. Needless to say, the armies of servants are back, too. So are the yachts. Still, even J. P. Morgan didn't have a Gulfstream.

As the story about Despont suggests, it's not fair to say that the fact of widening inequality in America has gone unreported. Yet glimpses of the lifestyles of the rich and tasteless don't necessarily add up in people's minds to a clear picture of the tectonic shifts that have taken place in the distribution of income and wealth in this country. My sense is that few people are aware of just how much the gap between the very rich and the rest has widened over a relatively short period of time. In fact, even bringing up the subject exposes you to charges of "class warfare," the "politics of envy" and so on. And very few people indeed are willing to talk about the profound effects—economic, social and political—of that widening gap.

Yet you can't understand what's happening in America today without understanding the extent, causes, and consequences of the vast increase in inequality that has taken place over the last three decades, and in particular the astonishing concentration of income and wealth in just a few hands. To make sense of the current wave of corporate scandal, you need to understand how the man in the gray flannel suit has been replaced by the imperial C.E.O. The concentration of income at the top is a key reason that the United States, for all its economic achievements, has more poverty and lower life expectancy than any other major advanced nation. Above all, the growing concentration of wealth has reshaped our political system: it is at the root both of a general shift to the right and of an extreme polarization of our politics.

But before we get to all that, let's take a look at who gets what.

The New Gilded Age

The Securities and Exchange Commission hath no fury like a woman scorned. The messy divorce proceedings of Jack Welch, the legendary former C.E.O. of General Electric, have had one unintended benefit: they have given us a peek at the perks of the corporate elite, which are normally hidden from public view. For it turns out that when Welch retired, he was granted for life the use of a Manhattan apartment (including food, wine and laundry), access to corporate jets and a variety of other in-kind benefits, worth at least $2 million a year. The perks were revealing: they illustrated the extent to which corporate leaders now expect to be treated like ancien regime royalty. In monetary terms, however, the perks must have meant little to Welch. In 2000, his last full year running G.E., Welch was paid $123 million, mainly in stock and stock options.

Is it news that C.E.O.s of large American corporations make a lot of money? Actually, it is. They were always well paid compared with the average worker, but there is simply no comparison between what executives got a generation ago and what they are paid today.

Over the past 30 years most people have seen only modest salary increases: the average annual salary in America, expressed in 1998 dollars (that is, adjusted for inflation), rose from $32,522 in 1970 to $35,864 in 1999. That's about a 10 percent increase over 29 years—progress, but not much. Over the same period, however, according to *Fortune* magazine, the average real annual compensation of the top 100 C.E.O.s went from $1.3 million—39 times the pay of an average worker—to $37.5 million, more than 1,000 times the pay of ordinary workers.

The explosion in C.E.O. pay over the past 30 years is an amazing story in its own right, and an important one. But it is only the most spectacular indicator of a broader story, the reconcentration of income and wealth in the U.S. The rich have always been different from you and me, but they are far more different now than they were not long ago—indeed, they are as different now as they were when F. Scott Fitzgerald made his famous remark.

That's a controversial statement, though it shouldn't be. For at least the past 15 years it has been hard to deny the evidence for growing inequality in the United States. Census data clearly show a rising share of income going to the top 20 percent of families, and within that top 20 percent to the top 5 percent, with a declining share going to families in the middle. Nonetheless, denial of that evidence is a sizable, well-financed industry. Conservative think tanks have produced scores of studies that try to discredit the data, the methodology and, not least, the motives of those who report the obvious. Studies that appear to refute claims of increasing inequality receive prominent endorsements on editorial pages and are eagerly cited by right-leaning government officials. . . .

. . . In fact, the census data understate the case, because for technical reasons those data tend to undercount very high incomes—for example, it's unlikely that they reflect the explosion in C.E.O. compensation. And other evidence makes it clear not only that inequality is increasing but that the action gets bigger the closer you get to the top. That is, it's not simply that the top 20 percent of families have had bigger percentage gains than families near the middle: the top 5 percent have done better than the next 15, the top 1 percent better than the next 4, and so on up to Bill Gates.

Studies that try to do a better job of tracking high incomes have found startling results. For example, a recent study by the nonpartisan Congressional Budget Office used income tax data and other sources to improve on the census estimates. The C.B.O. study found that between 1979 and 1997, the after-tax incomes of the top 1 percent of families rose 157 percent, compared with only a 10 percent gain for families near the middle of the income distribution. . . .

So claims that we've entered a second Gilded Age aren't exaggerated. In America's middle-class era, the mansion-building, yacht-owning classes had pretty much disappeared. . . . [I]n 1970 the top 0.01 percent of taxpayers had 0.7 percent of total income—that is, they earned "only" 70 times as much as the average, not enough to buy or maintain a mega-residence. But in 1998 the top 0.01 percent received more than 3 percent of all income. That meant that the 13,000 richest families in America had almost as much income as the 20 million poorest households; those 13,000 families had incomes 300 times that of average families.

And let me repeat: this transformation has happened very quickly, and it is still going on. You might think that 1987, the year Tom Wolfe published his novel *The Bonfire of the Vanities* and Oliver Stone released his movie *Wall Street,* marked the high tide of America's new money culture. But in 1987 the top 0.01 percent earned only about 40 percent of what they do today, and top executives less than a fifth as much. The America of *Wall Street* and *The Bonfire of the Vanities* was positively egalitarian compared with the country we live in today. . . .

The Price of Inequality

It was one of those revealing moments. Responding to an e-mail message from a Canadian viewer, Robert Novak of "Crossfire" delivered a little speech: "Marg, like most Canadians, you're ill informed and wrong. The U.S. has the longest standard of living—longest life expectancy of any country in the world, including Canada. That's the truth."

But it was Novak who had his facts wrong. Canadians can expect to live about two years longer than Americans. In fact, life expectancy in the U.S. is well below that in Canada, Japan and every major nation in Western Europe. On average, we can expect lives a bit shorter than those of Greeks, a bit longer than those of Portuguese. Male life expectancy is lower in the U.S. than it is in Costa Rica.

Still, you can understand why Novak assumed that we were No. 1. After all, we really are the richest major nation, with real G.D.P. per capita about 20 percent higher than Canada's. And it has been an article of faith in this country that a rising tide lifts all boats. Doesn't our high and rising national wealth translate into a high standard of living—including good medical care—for all Americans?

Well, no. Although America has higher per capita income than other advanced countries, it turns out that that's mainly because our rich are much richer. And here's a radical thought: if the rich get more, that leaves less for everyone else.

That statement—which is simply a matter of arithmetic—is guaranteed to bring accusations of "class warfare." If the accuser gets more specific, he'll probably offer two reasons that it's foolish to make a fuss over the high incomes of a few people at the top of the income distribution. First, he'll tell you that what the elite get may look like a lot of money, but it's still a small share of the total—that is, when all is said and done the rich aren't getting that big a piece of the pie. Second, he'll tell you that trying to do anything to reduce incomes at the top will hurt, not help, people further down the distribution, because attempts to redistribute income damage incentives.

These arguments for lack of concern are plausible. And they were entirely correct, once upon a time—namely, back when we had a middle-class society. But there's a lot less truth to them now.

First, the share of the rich in total income is no longer trivial. These days 1 percent of families receive about 16 percent of total pretax income, and have about 14 percent of after-tax income. That share has roughly doubled over the past 30 years, and is now about as large as the share of the bottom 40 percent of the population. That's a big shift of income to the top; as a matter of pure arithmetic, it must mean that the incomes of less well off families grew considerably more slowly than average income. And they did. Adjusting for inflation, average family income—total income divided by the number of families—grew 28 percent from 1979 to 1997. But median family income—the income of a family in the middle of the distribution, a better indicator of how typical American families are doing—grew only 10 percent. And the incomes of the bottom fifth of families actually fell slightly.

Let me belabor this point for a bit. We pride ourselves, with considerable justification, on our record of economic growth. But over the last few decades it's remarkable how little of that growth has trickled down to ordinary families. Median family income has risen only about 0.5 percent per year—and as far as we can tell from somewhat unreliable data, just about all of that increase was due to wives working longer hours, with little or no gain in real wages. Furthermore, numbers about income don't reflect the growing riskiness of life for ordinary workers. In the days when General Motors was known in-house as Generous Motors, many workers felt that they had considerable job security—the company wouldn't fire them except in extremis. Many had contracts that guaranteed health insurance, even if they were laid off; they had pension benefits that did not depend on the stock market. Now mass firings from long-established companies are commonplace; losing your job means losing your insurance; and as millions of people have been learning, a 401(k) plan is no guarantee of a comfortable retirement.

Still, many people will say that while the U.S. economic system may generate a lot of inequality, it also generates much higher incomes than any alternative, so that everyone is better off. . . . But it's not true. Let me use the example of Sweden, that great conservative bete noire.

A few months ago the conservative cyberpundit Glenn Reynolds made a splash when he pointed out that Sweden's G.D.P. per capita is roughly comparable with that of Mississippi—see, those foolish believers in the welfare state have impoverished themselves! Presumably he assumed that this means that the typical Swede is as poor as the typical resident of Mississippi, and therefore much worse off than the typical American.

But life expectancy in Sweden is about three years higher than that of the U.S. Infant mortality is half the U.S. level, and less than a third the rate in Mississippi. Functional illiteracy is much less common than in the U.S.

How is this possible? One answer is that G.D.P. per capita is in some ways a misleading measure. Swedes take longer vacations than Americans, so they work fewer hours per year. That's a choice, not a failure of economic performance. Real G.D.P. per hour worked is 16 percent lower than in the United States, which makes Swedish productivity about the same as Canada's.

But the main point is that though Sweden may have lower average income than the United States, that's mainly because our rich are so much richer. The median Swedish family has a standard of living roughly comparable with that of the median U.S. family: wages are if anything higher in Sweden, and a higher tax burden is offset by public provision of health care and generally better public services. And as you move further down the income distribution, Swedish living standards are way ahead of those in the U.S. Swedish families with children that are at the 10th percentile—poorer than 90 percent of the population—have incomes 60 percent higher than their U.S. counterparts. And very few people in Sweden experience the deep poverty that is all too common in the United States. One measure: in 1994 only 6 percent of Swedes lived on less than $11 per day, compared with 14 percent in the U.S.

The moral of this comparison is that even if you think that America's high levels of inequality are the price of our high level of national income, it's not at all clear that this price is worth paying. The reason conservatives engage in bouts of Sweden-bashing is that they want to convince us that there is no trade-off between economic efficiency and equity—that if you try to take from the rich and give to the poor, you actually make everyone worse off. But the comparison between the U.S. and other advanced countries doesn't support this conclusion at all. Yes, we are the richest major nation. But because so much of our national income is concentrated in relatively few hands, large numbers of Americans are worse off economically than their counterparts in other advanced countries.

And we might even offer a challenge from the other side: inequality in the United States has arguably reached levels where it is counterproductive. That is, you can make a case that our society would be richer if its richest members didn't get quite so much.

I could make this argument on historical grounds. The most impressive economic growth in U.S. history coincided with the middle-class interregnum, the post–World War II generation, when incomes were most evenly distributed. But let's focus on a specific case, the extraordinary pay packages of today's top executives. Are these good for the economy?

Until recently it was almost unchallenged conventional wisdom that, whatever else you might say, the new imperial C.E.O.s had delivered results that dwarfed the expense of their compensation. But now that the stock bubble has burst, it has become increasingly clear that there was a price to those big pay packages, after all. In fact, the price paid by shareholders and society at large may have been many times larger than the amount actually paid to the executives.

It's easy to get boggled by the details of corporate scandal—insider loans, stock options, special-purpose entities, mark-to-market, round-tripping. But there's a simple reason that the details are so complicated. All of these schemes were designed to benefit corporate insiders—to inflate the pay of the C.E.O. and his inner circle. That is, they were all about the "chaos of competitive avarice" that, according to John Kenneth Galbraith, had been ruled out in the corporation of the 1960s. But while all restraint has vanished within the American corporation, the outside world—including stockholders—is still prudish, and open looting by executives is still not acceptable. So the looting has to be camouflaged, taking place through complicated schemes that can be rationalized to outsiders as clever corporate strategies.

Economists who study crime tell us that crime is inefficient—that is, the costs of crime to the economy are much larger than the amount stolen. Crime, and the fear of crime, divert resources away from productive uses: criminals spend their time stealing rather than producing, and potential victims spend time and money trying to protect their property. Also, the things people do to avoid becoming victims—like avoiding dangerous districts—have a cost even if they succeed in averting an actual crime.

The same holds true of corporate malfeasance, whether or not it actually involves breaking the law. Executives who devote their time to creating innovative ways to divert shareholder money into their own pockets probably aren't running the real business very well (think Enron, WorldCom, Tyco, Global Crossing, Adelphia . . .). Investments chosen because they create the illusion of profitability while insiders cash in their stock options are a waste of scarce resources. And if the supply of funds from lenders and shareholders dries up because of a lack of trust, the economy as a whole suffers. Just ask Indonesia.

The argument for a system in which some people get very rich has always been that the lure of wealth provides powerful incentives. But the question is, incentives to do what? As we learn more about what has actually been going on in corporate America, it's becoming less and less clear whether those incentives have actually made executives work on behalf of the rest of us.

Inequality and Politics

In September [2002] the Senate debated a proposed measure that would impose a one-time capital gains tax on Americans who renounce their citizenship in order to avoid paying U.S. taxes. Senator Phil Gramm was not pleased, declaring that the proposal was "right out of Nazi Germany." Pretty strong language, but no stronger than the metaphor Daniel Mitchell of the Heritage Foundation used, in an op-ed article in the *Washington Times,* to describe a bill designed to prevent corporations from rechartering abroad for tax purposes: Mitchell described this legislation as the "Dred

Scott tax bill," referring to the infamous 1857 Supreme Court ruling that required free states to return escaped slaves.

Twenty years ago, would a prominent senator have likened those who want wealthy people to pay taxes to Nazis? Would a member of a think tank with close ties to the administration have drawn a parallel between corporate taxation and slavery? I don't think so. The remarks by Gramm and Mitchell, while stronger than usual, were indicators of two huge changes in American politics. One is the growing polarization of our politics—our politicians are less and less inclined to offer even the appearance of moderation. The other is the growing tendency of policy and policy makers to cater to the interests of the wealthy. And I mean the wealthy, not the merely well-off: only someone with a net worth of at least several million dollars is likely to find it worthwhile to become a tax exile.

You don't need a political scientist to tell you that modern American politics is bitterly polarized. But wasn't it always thus? No, it wasn't. From World War II until the 1970s—the same era during which income inequality was historically low—political partisanship was much more muted than it is today. That's not just a subjective assessment. My Princeton political science colleagues Nolan McCarty and Howard Rosenthal, together with Keith Poole at the University of Houston, have done a statistical analysis showing that the voting behavior of a congressman is much better predicted by his party affiliation today than it was 25 years ago. In fact, the division between the parties is sharper now than it has been since the 1920s.

What are the parties divided about? The answer is simple: economics. McCarty, Rosenthal, and Poole write that "voting in Congress is highly ideological—one-dimensional left/right, liberal versus conservative." It may sound simplistic to describe Democrats as the party that wants to tax the rich and help the poor, and Republicans as the party that wants to keep taxes and social spending as low as possible. And during the era of middle-class America that would indeed have been simplistic: politics wasn't defined by economic issues. But that was a different country; as McCarty, Rosenthal, and Poole put it, "If income and wealth are distributed in a fairly equitable way, little is to be gained for politicians to organize politics around nonexistent conflicts." Now the conflicts are real, and our politics is organized around them. In other words, the growing inequality of our incomes probably lies behind the growing divisiveness of our politics.

But the politics of rich and poor hasn't played out the way you might think. Since the incomes of America's wealthy have soared while ordinary families have seen at best small gains, you might have expected politicians to seek votes by proposing to soak the rich. In fact, however, the polarization of politics has occurred because the Republicans have moved to the right, not because the Democrats have moved to the left. And actual economic policy has moved steadily in favor of the wealthy. The major tax cuts of the past 25 years, the Reagan cuts in the 1980s and the recent Bush cuts, were both heavily tilted toward the very well off. (Despite obfuscations, it remains true that more than half the Bush tax cut will eventually go to the top 1 percent of families.) The major tax increase over that period, the increase in payroll taxes in the 1980s, fell most heavily on working-class families.

The most remarkable example of how politics has shifted in favor of the wealthy—an example that helps us understand why economic policy has reinforced, not countered, the movement toward greater inequality—is the drive to repeal the estate tax. The estate tax is, overwhelmingly, a tax on the wealthy. In 1999, only the top 2 percent of estates paid any tax at all, and half the estate tax was paid by only 3,300 estates, 0.16 percent of the total, with a minimum value of $5 million and an average value of $17 million. A quarter of the tax was paid by just 467 estates worth more than $20 million. Tales of family farms and businesses broken up to pay the estate tax are basically rural legends; hardly any real examples have been found, despite diligent searching.

You might have thought that a tax that falls on so few people yet yields a significant amount of revenue would be politically popular; you certainly wouldn't expect widespread opposition. Moreover, there has long been an argument that the estate tax promotes democratic values, precisely because it limits the ability of the wealthy to form dynasties. So why has there been a powerful political drive to repeal the estate tax, and why was such a repeal a centerpiece of the Bush tax cut?

There is an economic argument for repealing the estate tax, but it's hard to believe that many people take it seriously. More significant for members of Congress, surely, is the question of who would benefit from repeal: while those who will actually benefit from estate tax repeal are few in number, they have a lot of money and control even more (corporate C.E.O.s can now count on leaving taxable estates behind). That is, they are the sort of people who command the attention of politicians in search of campaign funds.

But it's not just about campaign contributions: much of the general public has been convinced that the estate tax is a bad thing. If you try talking about the tax to a group of moderately prosperous retirees, you get some interesting reactions. They refer to it as the "death tax"; many of them believe that their estates will face punitive taxation, even though most of them will pay little or nothing; they are convinced that small businesses and family farms bear the brunt of the tax.

These misconceptions don't arise by accident. They have, instead, been deliberately promoted. For example, a Heritage Foundation document titled "Time to Repeal Federal Death Taxes: The Nightmare of the American Dream" emphasizes stories that rarely, if ever, happen in real life: "Small-business owners, particularly minority owners, suffer anxious moments wondering whether the businesses they hope to hand down to their children will be destroyed by the death tax bill, . . . Women whose children are grown struggle to find ways to re-enter the work force without upsetting the family's estate tax avoidance plan." And who finances the Heritage Foundation? Why, foundations created by wealthy families, of course.

The point is that it is no accident that strongly conservative views, views that militate against taxes on the rich, have spread even as the rich get richer compared with the rest of us: in addition to directly buying influence, money can be used to shape public perceptions. The liberal group People for the American Way's report on how conservative foundations have deployed vast sums to support think tanks, friendly media and other institutions that promote right-wing causes is titled "Buying a Movement."

Not to put too fine a point on it: as the rich get richer, they can buy a lot of things besides goods and services. Money buys political influence; used cleverly, it also buys intellectual influence. A result is that growing income disparities in the United States, far from leading to demands to soak the rich, have been accompanied by a growing movement to let them keep more of their earnings and to pass their wealth on to their children.

This obviously raises the possibility of a self-reinforcing process. As the gap between the rich and the rest of the population grows, economic policy increasingly caters to the interests of the elite, while public services for the population at large—above all, public education—are starved of resources. As policy increasingly favors the interests of the rich and neglects the interests of the general population, income disparities grow even wider. . . .

DISCUSSION QUESTIONS

1. Poll your class. Do most members of your class think they will be economically better off or worse off than their parents? Define *better off* and *worse off.*

2. Women (especially single mothers) and minorities are disproportionately poor. Part of the debate on inequality concerns whether existing inequalities reflect people's talents and work efforts or whether there is still significant racial and gender discrimination in job markets. What do you think, and how does your conclusion affect your attitude toward present inequalities?

3. No one favors a complete leveling of income and wealth, nor does anybody want all wealth to be concentrated in a few hands. But where do we draw the line? What level of inequality should be tolerated in our democracy before government is required to take action?

4. Do you think the present level of economic inequality is corrupting our political processes? Will campaign finance laws protect the system from the unaccountable power of money, or do we need to reduce economic inequality itself?

5. In their book, Cox and Alm suggest that, because of technological advances, the average American is better off today than a millionaire was in the 1890s. Agree or disagree.

SUGGESTED READINGS AND INTERNET RESOURCES

For further elaboration of Cox and Alm's argument that nearly everyone is benefiting from our dynamic economy, see their *Myths of Rich and Poor: Why We're Better Off Than We Think* (New York: Basic Books, 1999), from which our excerpt was taken. The best compilation of data on the changing distribution of income and wealth (which can be viewed as a rejoinder to Cox and Alm) is *The State of Working America 2002–2003* (Ithaca, N.Y.: Cornell University Press, 2002) by Lawrence Mishel, Jared Bernstein, and Heather Boushey. In one of the most controversial books in recent years, *The Bell Curve: Intelligence and Class Structure in American Life* (New York: Free Press, 1994), Richard J. Herrnstein and Charles Murray argue that economic inequalities in our technological society fairly reflect differences in people's intelligence, or IQ. Paul Krugman elaborates on his critique of the Bush tax cuts in *Fuzzy Math: The Essential Guide to the Bush Tax Plan* (New York: Norton, 2001). In *Wealth and Democracy: A Political History of the American Rich* (New York: Broadway Books, 2002) Kevin Phillips examines the influence of concentrated wealth on our political system.

United for a Fair Economy
www.stw.org
This website spotlights the dangers of growing income and wealth inequality in the United States and supports actions to reduce the gap.

Economic Policy Institute
www.epinet.org
The Economic Policy Institute is a nonprofit, labor-supported think tank that seeks to broaden the public debate about strategies to achieve a strong economy. Their website stresses real-world analysis and a concern for the living standards of working people.

Heritage Foundation
www.heritage.org/Research/Welfare/
The Heritage Foundation website stresses the principles of free enterprise, limited government, individual freedom, traditional American values, and a strong national defense.

Cato Institute
www.cato.org
The Cato Institute seeks to broaden the parameters of public policy debate to allow consideration of more options that are consistent with the traditional American principles of limited government. This website reflects the liberterian values of the Cato Institute and its commitment to limited government.

CHAPTER

17

The United States and the Global Economy: Serving Citizens or Corporate Elites?

For nearly forty-five years after World War II, U.S. foreign policy concentrated on a Cold War to contain communism. The costs were often great: massive casualties in two major wars in Korea and Vietnam, a militarization of U.S. society, and the fear spawned by the threat of nuclear holocaust. Through McCarthyism and other acts of government repression, the Cold War often distorted democracy at home. Fighting the Cold War required public support for massive military and intelligence expenditures. Americans largely supported both insofar as U.S. military power translated into American prosperity and economic power.

Yet by the 1970s and with defeat in Vietnam, the translation of military power into economic prosperity became doubtful: the Vietnam War coincided with a reshaping of the postwar global economic order. Throughout the late 1970s and 1980s, energy crises, gas lines, and deindustrialization awakened the nation to a new and uncertain global economy. This "new economy" was characterized by corporate restructuring; stock market surges and declines; growing wealth for some; and downsizing, outsourcing, and uncertainty for others. By 1991, the Cold War had ended with the USSR's collapse. Ever since, and alongside the September 11 attacks and the ensuing war on terrorism, the new global economy and its relentless logic of lowered trade barriers and rapid capital flows fully emerged. The rise of the global economy raises fundamental questions about the fate of democracy. Is the new global economic order

355

inevitable? Is it good for democracy, or are its results and institutions undemocratic and elitist for most Americans and billions of others around the world?

Perhaps more than ever in world history, the global economic order is
dominated by two sets of institutions. The first comprises footloose global corporations and the volatile financial and equity markets that are able to move
money and investments around the globe at lightning speed, with positive and
negative effects. From the media empires of Rupert Murdoch's News Corporation, Disney, and AOL–Time Warner to the computer operating systems
monopolized by Microsoft, transnational companies and their investors increasingly determine what we know, how we work, and what's fun. From banks to
world stock exchanges and investment houses, giant private institutions have
the power to make or break entire industries and countries—to employ or
downsize, invest or withdraw.

The second new actor is a new set of transnational institutions that bring the
world's governments together under a common financial and trade regime. Led
by the International Monetary Fund (IMF), the World Bank, and the World Trade
Organization (WTO), these transnational institutions are accompanied by
regional trade and monetary compacts such as the European Union (EU); the
North American Free Trade Agreement (NAFTA) uniting Canada, the United
States, and Mexico; and the proposed "Free Trade Area of the Americas" (FTAA).

To supporters, these new institutions and their practices have generated
unprecedented growth, new wealth, and relative economic stability. To detrac-
tors in the United States and abroad—most visibly first in Seattle, then in Washington, D.C., Quebec City, and Genoa, Italy, where corporate and government
leaders mingled—the global economic order is a set of undemocratic elites who
smooth the way for environmental degradation, destruction of local economies,
and exploitation of workers. According to opponents, the power to invest or
disinvest, employ or downsize, is delegated away from electorates and handed
over to transnational investors and their agents.

In the new global economy, the United States remains the biggest and
most powerful nation-state. The United States serves as the headquarters for
the world's biggest stock and financial markets, is a worldwide innovator in
many of the high-technology industries, and has dominant power in the IMF
and World Bank. From the perspective of Wall Street, and from Capitol Hill and
the White House as well, economic globalization is not only an inevitability, but
also a boon to U.S. power. The point is to adjust to corporate-led economic
globalization and its dictates, not avoid them.

Yet there are risks. The stock market and dot-com booms of the 1990s
appear to be over. And even as the boom was going on, worldwide financial
crises were hitting most East Asian countries and left entire continents and
countries—Africa and most of western Asia—behind. In 2002, Latin America's
richest economy—Argentina—simply melted down. Here in the United States,
most wage-earners work more hours and for fewer wages and benefits than
they did in the 1970s. Universal health care, a secure retirement, quality public
education, and job security are for many illusive dreams as government cuts
taxes to encourage investment by corporations and the rich.

Does corporate globalization threaten democracy and prosperity, or does it enhance both? Can democratic politics control the forces that propel economic globalization, or must government succumb to them? Are there alternatives to corporate-led economic globalization? If so, what are they?

The two selections reprinted here present contrasting answers to these questions. The first is written by Thomas Friedman, a *New York Times* columnist and the author of the best-selling *The Lexus and the Olive Tree.* Friedman argues that economic globalization is inevitable and that modern governments should help people adjust to it rather than transform it. A benign but revolutionary process running at warp speed, globalization benefits the United States the most, argues Friedman, because America possesses the entrepreneurial culture and political and cultural institutions most appropriate to modern success. Globalization, Friedman admits, produces stresses, but its disadvantages are far outweighed by its production of new wealth, individual freedom, and U.S. world influence.

David Korten, the author of *When Corporations Rule the World* and a political activist, would certainly agree with Friedman about globalization's importance. Yet his perspective on its roots and implications couldn't be more different. Korten sees globalization not as a reversal of the Cold War, but an extension of the elite-centered, pro-corporate, and largely undemocratic policies established by the United States and its allies after World War II. Rather than a world of increased economic opportunity, Korten sees a planet lurching toward ecological suicide and authoritarian corporate rule over matters that affect all of the world's citizens. Echoing the case made by many anti-corporate globalization protestors at recent demonstrations, Korten envisions a people-centered reinvention of local and regional economies and governments, where workers, consumers, and citizens shape the decisions of corporate giants and such new transnational institutions as the WTO. Korten's essay is excerpted from a speech he gave in Bretton Woods, New Hampshire, site of the famous 1944 conference that established the international economic institutions of the post–World War II capitalist world.

As you read the two essays, consider the following questions: Do the authors define economic globalization and its features differently? What does each mean by *freedom* and *democracy*? Why is economic globalism inevitable for Friedman, but not for Korten? When each author speaks of U.S. power, which people and institutions are included and which are excluded?

Revolution Is U.S.

THOMAS FRIEDMAN

Today's era of globalization, which replaced the Cold War, is [an] international system with its own unique attributes.

To begin with, the globalization system, unlike the Cold War system, is not static, but a dynamic ongoing process. Globalization involves the inexorable integration of markets, nation-states and technologies to a degree never witnessed before—in a way that is enabling individuals, corporations and nation-states to reach around the world farther, faster, deeper and cheaper than ever before, and in a way that is also producing a powerful backlash from those brutalized or left behind by this new system.

The driving idea behind globalization is free-market capitalism—the more you let market forces rule and the more you open your economy to free trade and competition, the more efficient and flourishing your economy will be. Globalization means the spread of free-market capitalism to virtually every country in the world. Globalization also has its own set of economic rules—rules that revolve around opening, deregulating and privatizing your economy.

Unlike the Cold War system, globalization has its own dominant culture, which is why it tends to be homogenizing. In previous eras this sort of cultural homogenization happened on a regional scale. . . . Culturally speaking, globalization is largely, though not entirely, the spread of Americanization—from Big Macs to iMacs to Mickey Mouse—on a global scale.

Globalization has its own defining technologies: computerization, miniaturization, digitization, satellite communications, fiber optics and the Internet. And these technologies helped to create the defining perspective of globalization. If the defining perspective of the Cold War world was "division," the defining perspective of globalization is "integration." The symbol of the Cold War system was a wall, which divided everyone. The symbol of the globalization system is a World Wide Web, which unites everyone. The defining document of the Cold War system was "The Treaty." The defining document of the globalization system is "The Deal." . . .

While the defining measurement of the Cold War was weight—particularly the throw weight of missiles—the defining measurement of the globalization system is speed—speed of commerce, travel, communication and innovation. The Cold War was about Einstein's mass-energy equation, $e = mc^2$. Globalization is about Moore's law, which states that the computing power of silicon chips will double every eighteen to twenty-four months. In the Cold War, the most frequently asked question was: "How big is your missile?" In globalization, the most frequently asked question is: "How fast is your modem?" . . .

 . . . If the Cold War were a sport, it would be sumo wrestling, says Johns Hopkins University foreign affairs professor Michael Mandelbaum. "It would be two big fat guys in a ring, with all sorts of posturing and rituals and stomping of feet, but actually very little contact, until the end of the match, when there is a brief moment of shoving and the loser gets pushed out of the ring, but nobody gets killed."

By contrast, if globalization were a sport, it would be the 100-meter dash, over and over and over. And no matter how many times you win, you have to race again the next day. And if you lose by just one-hundredth of a second it can be as if you lost by an hour. . . .

To paraphrase German political theorist Carl Schmitt, the Cold War was a world of "friends" and "enemies." The globalization world, by contrast, tends to turn all friends and enemies into "competitors." . . .

In the Cold War we reached for the hot line between the White House and the Kremlin—a symbol that we were all divided but at least someone, the two superpowers, was in charge. In the era of globalization we reach for the Internet—a symbol that we are all connected but nobody is in charge. The defining defense system of the Cold War was radar—to expose the threats coming from the other side of the wall. The defining defense system of the globalization era is the X-ray machine—to expose the threats coming from within.

Globalization also has its own demographic pattern—a rapid acceleration of the movement of people from rural areas and agricultural lifestyles to urban lifestyles more intimately linked with global fashion, food, markets and entertainment trends.

Last, and most important, globalization has its own defining structure of power, which is much more complex than the Cold War structure. The Cold War system was built exclusively around nation-states, and it was balanced at the center by two superpowers: the United States and the Soviet Union.

The globalization system, by contrast, is built around three balances. The first is the traditional balance between nation-states. In the globalization system, the United States is now the sole and dominant superpower and all other nations are subordinate to it to one degree or another. . . .

The second balance in the globalization system is between nation-states and global markets. These global markets are made up of millions of investors moving money around the world with the click of a mouse. I call them "the Electronic Herd," and this herd gathers in key global financial centers, such as Wall Street, Hong Kong, London and Frankfurt, which I call "the Supermarkets." The attitudes and actions of the Electronic Herd and the Supermarkets can have a huge impact on nation-states today, even to the point of triggering the downfall of governments. . . .

The third balance that you have to pay attention to in the globalization system—the one that is really the newest of all—is the balance between individuals and nation-states. Because globalization has brought down many of the walls that limited the movement and reach of people, and because it has simultaneously wired the world into networks, it gives more power to individuals to influence both markets and nation-states than at any time in history. . . .

Five Gas Stations

I believe in the five gas stations theory of the world.

That's right: I believe you can reduce the world's economies today to basically five different gas stations. First there is the Japanese gas station. Gas is $5 a gallon. Four men in uniforms and white gloves, with lifetime employment contracts, wait on you. They pump your gas. They change your oil. They wash your windows, and they wave at you with a friendly smile as you drive away in peace. Second is the American gas station. Gas costs only $1 a gallon, but you pump it yourself. You wash your own windows. You fill your own tires. And when you drive around the corner four homeless people try to steal your hubcaps. Third is the Western European gas station. Gas there also costs $5 a gallon. There is only one man on duty. He grudgingly pumps your gas and unsmilingly changes your oil, reminding you all the time that his union contract says he only has to pump gas and change oil. He doesn't do windows. He works only thirty-two hours a week, with ninety minutes off each day for lunch, during which time the gas station is closed. He also has six weeks' vacation every summer in the South of France. Across the street, his two brothers and uncle, who have not worked in ten years because their state unemployment insurance pays more than their last job, are playing boccie ball. Fourth is the developing-country gas station. Fifteen people work there and they are all cousins. When you drive in, no one pays any attention to you because they are all too busy talking to each other. Gas is only 35 cents a gallon because it is subsidized by the government, but only one of the six gas pumps actually works. The others are broken and they are waiting for the replacement parts to be flown in from Europe. The gas station is rather run-down because the owner lives in Zurich and takes all the profits out of the country. The owner doesn't know that half his employees actually sleep in the repair shop at night and use the car wash equipment to shower. Most of the customers at the developing-country gas station either drive the latest-model Mercedes or a motor scooter. The place is always busy, though, because so many people stop in to use the air pump to fill their bicycle tires. Lastly there is the communist gas station. Gas there is only 50 cents a gallon—but there is none, because the four guys working there have sold it all on the black market for $5 a gallon. Just one of the four guys who is employed at the communist gas station is actually there. The other three are working at second jobs in the underground economy and only come around once a week to collect their paychecks.

What is going on in the world today, in the very broadest sense, is that through the process of globalization everyone is being forced toward America's gas station. If you are not an American and don't know how to pump your own gas, I suggest you learn. With the end of the Cold War, globalization is globalizing Anglo-American-style capitalism. It is globalizing American culture and cultural icons. It is globalizing the best of America and the worst of America. It is globalizing the American Revolution and it is globalizing the American gas station. . . .

Rational Exuberance

. . . Since I spend a great deal of time overseas and away from Wall Street—looking at my country from the outside in—I am constantly exposed to the rational exuberance about America in the rest of the world. This rational exuberance is built on the following logic: If you look at globalization as the dominant international system today, and you look at the attributes that both companies and countries need to thrive in this system, you have to conclude that America has more assets, and fewer liabilities, in relation to this system than any other major country. This is what I call rational exuberance. It is the intuition among global investors that while many in Europe and Asia were still trying to adjust their societies to globalization, and some were barely up to the starting line, Uncle Sam was already around the first turn and in full sprint.

A useful way to analyze this rational exuberance is to ask the following question: If 100 years ago you had come to a visionary geo-architect and told him that in the year 2000 the world would be defined by a system called "globalization," what sort of country would he have designed to compete and win in that world? The answer is that he would have designed something that looks an awful lot like the United States of America. Here's what I mean:

First of all, he would have designed a country that was in an ideally competitive geographic position. That is, he would have designed a country that was both an Atlantic and a Pacific power, looking comfortably in both directions; and at the same time connected by landmass to both Canada and Latin America, so that it could easily interact with all three key markets of the world—Asia, Europe, and the Americas. That would come in handy.

He would have designed a country with a diverse, multicultural, multi-ethnic, multilingual population that had natural connections to all continents of the globe, but was, at the same time, bound together by a single language—English—which would also be the dominant language of the Internet. He would also have bestowed upon this country at least five different regional economies joined by a single currency, the dollar, which would also be the reserve currency for the rest of the world. Having a single country with different regional economies is a great asset because when one region might be slumping the other could be surging, helping to smooth out some of the peaks and valleys of the business cycle. All of that would be helpful.

He would have designed a country with extremely diverse, innovative and efficient capital markets, where venture capitalism was considered a noble and daring art, so that anyone with a reasonable (or even ridiculous) invention in his basement or garage could find a venture capitalist somewhere to back it. That would be nice. . . . If you compare a list of the twenty-five biggest companies in Europe twenty-five years ago with a list of the twenty-five biggest European companies today, the two lists are almost the same. But if you take a list of the twenty-five biggest companies in America twenty-five years ago and compare it with a list of the twenty-five biggest American companies today, most of the companies are different. Yes, America's financial markets, with their constant demands for short-term profits and quarterly earnings, often won't let corporations "waste money" by focusing on long-term growth. That's true. But these same markets will give someone with a half-baked idea $50,000 overnight to try to turn it into the next Apple computer. Massachusetts has a bigger venture capital industry than all of Europe combined. Venture capitalists are very important people in this day and age, and not just as a source of money. The best of them provide real expertise for start-up companies. They see a lot of them and they understand the stages through which companies have to go in order to develop, and they can help carry them through, which is often as important as seed money.

Our geo-architect would certainly have designed a country with the most honest legal and regulatory environment in the world. In this country, both domestic and foreign investors could always count on a reasonably level playing field, with relatively little corruption, plenty of legal safeguards for any foreigner who wants to make an investment and take out his profits at any time, and a rule of law that enables markets and contracts to work and protects and encourages innovation through patent protection. The U.S. capital markets today are not only more efficient than those of any other country, they are also the most transparent. The U.S. stock markets simply will not tolerate secrecy, so every listed company must file timely earnings reports, along with regularly audited financial statements, so that mismanagement and misallocation of resources is easily detected and punished.

He would have designed a country with a system of bankruptcy laws and courts that actually encourages people who fail in a business venture to declare bankruptcy and then try again, perhaps fail again, declare bankruptcy again, and then try again, before succeeding and starting the next Amazon.com—without having to carry the stigma of their initial bankruptcies for the rest of their lives. . . .

In Europe, bankruptcy carries a lifelong stigma. Whatever you do, do not declare bankruptcy in Germany: you, your children and your children's children will all carry a lasting mark of Cain in the eyes of German society. If you must declare bankruptcy in Germany, you are better off leaving the country. (And you'll be welcomed with open arms in Palo Alto.)

On that subject, our geo-architect would certainly have designed a country that was hard-wired for accepting new immigrants, so that anyone could come to its shores and be treated as constitutionally equal to anyone else, thus enabling that country to be constantly siphoning off the best brains in the world and bringing them together in its companies, medical centers and universities. Roughly one-third of Silicon Valley's scientists and engineers today are foreign-born immigrants, who then turn around and project Silicon Valley values and products all over the world. According to University of California at Berkeley urban affairs expert AnnaLee Saxenian, research by the Public Policy Institute of California found that in 1996, 1,786 Silicon Valley technology companies, with $12.6 billion in sales and 46,000 employees, were run by Indian or Chinese immigrant executives alone. . . . To be a Japanese you pretty much have to be born a Japanese. To be a Swiss you pretty much have to be born a Swiss. To be an American you just have to want to be an American. That doesn't mean that we let everyone in who wants to be an American, but when citizenship is a legal question not an ethnic, racial or national one, it makes it much easier for a country to absorb new talent. . . .

The more knowledge workers you can attract to your shores, the more successful you will be. As far as America is concerned, I say bring 'em in, and not only the rich, educated entrepreneurs. I would never turn back a single Haitian boat person. Anyone who has the smarts and energy to build a raft out of milk cartons and then sail across the Atlantic to America's shores is someone I want as a new immigrant. . . .

Our geo-architect certainly would have designed a country with a democratic, flexible federal political system that allows for a high degree of decentralized political decision-making that enables different regions and localities to adjust themselves to world trends without waiting for the center to move. Indeed, a federal system—with fifty states all having an incentive to compete and experiment in finding solutions to the intertwined problems of education, welfare and health care—is an enormous asset in the era of globalization, when such problems can be highly complex and you rarely get the right answer without experimenting a few times.

Our geo-architect certainly would have designed a country with the most flexible labor market in the world—one that enables workers to move easily from one economic zone to another, and one that enables employers to hire and fire workers with relative ease. The easier it is to fire workers, the more incentive employers have to hire them. Compare the millions of jobs eliminated in America in the 1990s and the many millions more created in America in the 1990s with the virtually stagnant job turnover rate in Western Europe. In America, lose your job in Maine one day and, if one is available, you can get a new one in San Diego the next day. Lose your job in Tokyo one day and I wouldn't recommend looking for one in Seoul the next. Lose your job in Munich one day and, even with a common European currency market, it is not so easy to get one the next day in Milan.

Our geo-architect would have designed a country where government-protected cartels are abhorred, so every company and bank has to fight and stand on its own, and monopolies will not be tolerated. That would be important. Even when a U.S. firm becomes a much-envied, world-class gem, like Microsoft, it still has to answer to a Justice Department antitrust lawyer making $75,000 a year.

Our geo-architect would have designed a country that is tolerant of the oddball, the guy with the ponytail or the gal with the ring in her nose who is also a mathematical genius or software whiz. America is a country where the minute one person stands up and says, "That's impossible," someone else walks in the door and announces, "We just did it." Says Intel vice president Avram Miller: "The Japanese don't get it, because they are focused on homogeneity. When it was building a gazillion of all the same thing, they were the world experts and we mistook it for some special genius. But the world does not want a lot of the same thing today, and in a world where everyone wants something different—and the technology that will give them something perfectly tailored [to their own needs and specifications]—America has a real advantage."

Our geo-architect would have designed a country whose corporate sector, unlike Europe's or Japan's, had, by the mid-1990s, already gone through most of the downsizing, privatizing, networking, deregulation, reengineering, streamlining and restructuring required to fully adjust to, and exploit, the democratizations of finance, technology and information and to avoid Microchip Immune Deficiency. Just as America won the space race, it is now winning the cyberspace race. American companies spend more on information technology per capita than any others in the world.

He also would have designed a country with a deeply rooted entrepreneurial culture and a tax system that allows the successful investor or innovator to hold on to a large share of his or her capital gains, so there is a constant incentive to get enormously rich. In our ideal country, Horatio Alger is not a mythical character but sometimes your next-door neighbor, who just happened to get hired as an engineer at Intel or America Online when they were getting started and ended up being paid in stock options that are now worth $10 million.

Our geo-architect certainly would have designed a country that still had a lot of environmentally attractive, wide-open spaces and small towns, to attract knowledge workers. Because today, thanks to the Internet, fax machines and overnight package delivery, high-tech firms and knowledge workers can escape from urban centers and settle virtually anywhere they want. So having lots of lush green valleys not far from oceans or mountains can be a real asset. That's why states like Idaho, Washington, Oregon, Minnesota and North Carolina have booming high-tech sectors today.

He would have designed a country that values the free flow of information so much that it defends the rights of the worst pornographers and the most incendiary racists to do their things. That would be an asset. Because in a world in which information, knowledge, goods and services will flow with increasing speed across the Fast World or through cyberspace, those countries comfortable with such openness, and the cacophony and chaos that sometimes attend it, those countries comfortable competing on the basis of imagination, not behind walls of protection, will have a real advantage. America, with its Freedom of Information Act, which barely allows the government to keep secrets for long, has nurtured this culture of openness from its foundation.

And, most important, our geo-architect would have designed a country whose multinational companies and little entrepreneurs are increasingly comfortable thinking big and thinking globally, and excel now in virtually every fast, light, networked, knowledge-intensive field of endeavor. America today excels at software design, computing, Internet design, Internet marketing, commercial banking, E-mail, insurance, derivatives, genetic engineering, artificial intelligence, investment banking, high-end health care, higher education, overnight package delivery, consulting, fast food, advertising, biotechnology, media, entertainment, hotels, waste management, financial services, environmental industries and telecommunications. It's a postindustrial world, and America today is good at everything that is postindustrial.

. . . The publisher and editor of this book, Jonathan Galassi, called me one day and said, "I was telling some friends of mine that you're writing a book about globalization and they said, 'Oh, Friedman, he loves globalization.' What would you say to that?" I answered Jonathan that I feel about globalization a lot like I feel about the dawn. Generally speaking, I think it's a good thing that the sun comes up every morning. It does more good than harm. But even if I didn't much care for the dawn there isn't much I could do about it. I didn't start globalization, I can't stop it—except at a huge cost to human development—and I'm not going to waste time trying. All I want to think about is how I can get the best out of this new system, and cushion the worst, for the most people.

When Corporations Rule the World

DAVID C. KORTEN

T he fame of Bretton Woods and of this hotel [the Mount Washington] dates from July 1944, when the United Nations Monetary and Financial Conference was held here. . . . The economic leaders who quietly gathered at this hotel were looking beyond the end of the war with hopes for a world united in peace through prosperity. Their specific goal was to create the institutions that would promote that vision.

By the end of this historic meeting, the World Bank and the International Monetary Fund (IMF) had been founded, and the groundwork had been laid for what later became GATT [General Agreement on Tariffs and Trade]. In the intervening years, these institutions have held faithfully to their mandate to promote economic growth and globalization. Through structural adjustment programs (SAPs),[1] the World Bank and the IMF have pressured countries of the South to open their borders and change their economies from self-sufficiency to *export* production. Trade agreements negotiated through GATT have reinforced these actions and opened economies . . . to the increasingly free importation of goods and money.

As we look back fifty years later, we can see that the Bretton Woods institutions have indeed met their goals. Economic growth has expanded fivefold. International trade has expanded by roughly twelve times, and foreign direct investment has been expanding at two to three times the rate of trade expansion. Yet, tragically, while these institutions have met their goals, they have failed in their purpose. The world has more poor people today than ever before. We have an accelerating gap between the rich and the poor. Widespread violence is tearing families and communities apart nearly everywhere. And the planet's ecosystems are deteriorating at an alarming rate.

Yet the prevailing wisdom continues to maintain that economic growth offers the answer to poverty, environmental security, and a strong social fabric, and that *economic globalization*—erasing economic borders to allow free flow of goods and money—is the key to such growth. Indeed, the more severe the economic, environmental, and social crises, the stronger the policy commitment to these same prescriptions, even as evidence mounts that they are not working. In fact, there is a growing consensus outside of official circles that they cannot work, for reasons I will explain.

Ecological Limit to Growth

. . . The human economy is embedded in and dependent on the natural ecosystems of our planet. Until the present moment in human history, however, the scale of our economic activity relative to the scale of the ecosystems has been small enough so that, in both economic theory and practice, we could, up to a point, afford to ignore this fundamental fact.

Now, however, we have crossed a monumental historical threshold. Because of the fivefold economic expansion since 1950 the environmental demands of our economic system have filled up the available environmental space of the planet. In other words, we live in a "full world.". . .

The first environmental limits that we have confronted and possibly exceeded are . . . the limits to renewable resources and to the environment's *sink functions*—its ability to absorb our wastes. These are limits related to the loss of soils, fisheries, forests, and water; to the absorption of CO_2 emissions; and to destruction of the ozone layer. We could argue whether a particular limit

---

1. SAPs, or structural adjustment programs, are the requirements the IMF imposes on nations in return for the fund's assistance. Usually, SAPs have required governments to cut social spending and consumption, open markets to foreign investors, and reduce wages in order to stimulate investor and banker confidence.

was hit at noon yesterday or will be passed at midnight tomorrow, but the details are far less important than the basic truth that we have no real option other than to adapt our economic institutions to the reality of a "full world."

The structure and ideology of the existing Bretton Woods system is geared to an ever-continuing expansion of economic output—*economic growth*—and to the integration of national economies into a seamless global economy. The consequence is to intensify competition for already overstressed environmental space. In a "full world," this intensified competition accelerates destruction of the regenerative capacities of the ecosystem on which we and future generations depend; it crowds out all forms of life not needed for immediate human consumption purposes; and it increases competition between rich and poor for control of ecological resources. In a free market—which responds only to money, not needs—the rich win this competition every time. We see it happening all over the world: Hundreds of millions of the financially disenfranchised are displaced as their lands, waters, and fisheries are converted to uses serving the wants of the more affluent.

As long as their resources remain, the demands of the rich can be met—which may explain why so many of the rich see no problem. The poor experience a very different reality, but in a market economy their experience doesn't count.

The market cannot deal with questions relating to the appropriate scale of economic activity. There are no price signals indicating that the poor are going hungry because they have been forced off their lands; nor is there any price signal to tell polluters that too much CO_2 is being released into the air, or that toxins should not be dumped into soils or waters. Steeped in market ideology and highly responsive to corporate interests, the Bretton Woods institutions have demonstrated little capacity to give more than lip service either to environmental concerns or to the needs of the poor. Rather, their efforts have . . . centered on ensuring that people with money have full access to whatever resources remain—with little regard for the broader consequences.

A new Bretton Woods meeting to update the international system would serve a significant and visionary need—if its participants were to accept that economic growth is no longer a valid public policy priority. Indeed, whether the global economy grows or shrinks is largely irrelevant. Having crossed the threshold to a full world, the appropriate concern is whether the available planetary resources are being used in ways that: (1) meet the basic needs of all people; (2) maintain biodiversity; and (3) ensure the sustained availability of comparable resource flows to future generations. Our present economic system fails on all three counts.

Economic Injustice

In *How Much Is Enough?* Alan Durning divided the world into three consumption classes: overconsumers, sustainers, and marginals. The overconsumers are the 20 percent of the world's people who consume roughly 80 percent of the world's resources—that is, those of us whose lives are organized around automobiles, airplanes, meat-based diets, and wastefully packaged disposable products. The marginals, also 20 percent of the world's people, live in absolute deprivation.

If we turn to measurements of *income* rather than *consumption,* the figures are even more stark. The United Nations Development Program (UNDP) *Human Development Report* for 1992 introduces the champagne glass as a graphic metaphor for a world of extreme economic injustice. The bowl of the champagne glass represents the abundance enjoyed by the 20 percent of people who live in the world's richest countries and receive 82.7 percent of the world's income. At the bottom of the stem, where the sediment settles, we find the poorest 20 percent of the world's people, who barely survive on 1.4 percent of the total income. The combined incomes of the top 20 percent are nearly sixty times larger than those of the bottom 20 percent. Furthermore, this gap has doubled since 1950, when the top 20 percent enjoyed only thirty times the income of the bottom 20 percent. And the gap continues to grow.

These figures actually understate the true inequality in the world, because they are based on national averages rather than actual individual incomes. If we take into account the very rich people who live in poor countries and the very poor people who live in rich countries, the incomes of the richest 20 percent of the world's people are approximately 150 times those of the poorest 20 percent. That gap is growing as well.

Robert Reich, the U.S. Secretary of Labor in the Clinton administration, explained in his book *The Work of Nations* (1991) that the economic globalization the Bretton Woods institutions have advanced so successfully has served to separate the interests of the wealthy classes from a sense of national interest and thereby from a sense of concern for and obligation to their less fortunate neighbors. A thin segment of the super rich at the very lip of the champagne glass has formed a stateless alliance that defines *global interest* as synonymous with the personal and corporate financial interests of its members.

This separation has been occurring in nearly every country in the world to such an extent that it is no longer meaningful to speak of a world divided into northern and southern nations. The meaningful divide is not geography—it is class.

Whether intended or not, the policies so successfully advanced by the Bretton Woods institutions have inexorably empowered the super rich to lay claim to the world's wealth at the expense of other people, other species, and the viability of the planet's ecosystem.

Freeing Corporations from Control

The issue is not the market per se. Trying to run an economy without markets is disastrous, as the experience of the Soviet Union demonstrated. However, there is a fundamentally important distinction between markets and free markets.

The struggle between two extremist ideologies has been a central feature of the twentieth century. Communism called for all power to the state. Market capitalism calls for all power to the market—a euphemism for giant corporations. Both ideologies lead to their own distinctive form of tyranny. The secret of Western success in World War II and the early postwar period was not a free market economy; it was the practice of democratic pluralism built on institutional arrangements that sought to maintain balance between the state and the market and to protect the right of an active citizenry to hold both accountable to the public interest.

Contrary to the claims of ideologues who preach a form of corporate libertarianism,[2] markets need governments to function efficiently. It is well established in economic theory and practice that markets allocate resources efficiently only when markets are competitive and when firms pay for the social and environmental impact of their activity—that is, when they *internalize* the costs of their production. This requires that governments set and enforce the rules that make cost internalization happen, and, since successful firms invariably grow larger and more monopolistic, governments regularly step in to break them up and restore competition.

For governments to play the necessary role of balancing market and community interests, governmental power must be equal to market power. If markets are national, then there must be a strong national government. By expanding the boundaries of the market beyond the boundaries of the nation-state through economic globalization, the concentration of market power moves inevitably beyond the reach of government. This has been a most important consequence of both the structural adjustment programs of the World Bank and IMF and the trade agreements negotiated under GATT. As a result, governance decisions are transferred from governments, which at least in theory represent the interests of all citizens, to transnational corporations, which by their nature serve the interests only of their dominant shareholders. Consequently, societies everywhere on the planet are no longer able to address environmental and other needs.

Enormous economic power is being concentrated in the hands of a very few global corporations relieved of constraints to their own growth. Antitrust action to restore market competition by breaking up the concentrations is one of the many casualties of globalization. Indeed, current policy encourages firms to merge into ever more powerful concentrations to strengthen their position in global markets.

The rapid rate at which large corporations are shedding employees has created an impression in some quarters that the firms are losing their power. It is a misleading impression. The Fortune 500 firms shed 4.4 million jobs between 1980 and 1993. During this same period, their sales increased 1.4 times, assets increased 2.3 times, and CEO compensation

---

2. Libertarianism is a doctrine that perceives government as the major threat to individual freedom.

increased 6.1 times. Of the world's one hundred largest economies, fifty are now corporations, not including banking and financial institutions.

Any industry in which five firms control 50 percent or more of the market is considered by economists to be highly monopolistic. The *Economist* recently reported that five firms control more than 50 percent of the global market in the following industries: consumer durables, automotive, airlines, aerospace, electronic components, electricity and electronics, and steel. Five firms control over 40 percent of the global market in oil, personal computers, and—especially alarming in its consequences for public debate on these very issues—media.

Forums for Elite Domination

. . . The forums within which corporate and government elites shape the global policies of the Western world were not limited to Bretton Woods. . . .

. . . The Trilateral Commission was formed in 1973 by David Rockefeller, chair of Chase Manhattan Bank, and Zbigniew Brzezinski, who served as the commission's director/coordinator until 1977 when he became national security advisor to President Jimmy Carter.

The members of the Trilateral Commission include the heads of four of the world's five largest nonbanking transnational corporations; top officials of five of the world's six largest international banks; and heads of major media organizations. U.S. presidents Jimmy Carter, George Bush, and Bill Clinton were all members of the Trilateral Commission, as was Thomas Foley, former speaker of the House of Representatives. Many key members of the Carter administration were . . . Trilateral Commission members. Many of President Clinton's cabinet and other appointments are former members of the Trilateral Commission.

. . . The Trilateral Commission has provided forums in which top executives from the world's leading corporations meet regularly, informally, and privately with top national political figures and opinion leaders to seek consensus on immediate and longer-range problems facing the most powerful members of the Western Alliance.

To some extent, the meetings help maintain "stability" in global policies, but they also deprive the public of meaningful participation and choice—as some participants explicitly intend. Particularly significant about these groups is their bipartisan political membership. Certainly, the participation of both George Bush and Bill Clinton in the Trilateral Commission makes it easier to understand the seamless transition from the Republican Bush administration to the Democratic Clinton administration with regard to U.S. commitment to pass GATT and NAFTA. Clinton's leadership in advancing what many progressives saw as a Bush agenda won him high marks from his colleagues on the Trilateral Commission.

Instruments of Control

Corporations have enormous political power, and they are actively using it to reshape the rules of the market in their own favor. The GATT has now become one of the corporations' most powerful tools for reshaping the market. Under the new GATT agreement, a World Trade Organization, the WTO, has been created with far-reaching powers to provide corporations the legal protection they feel they need to continue expanding their far-flung operations without the responsibility to serve any interest other than their own bottom line. . . .

The WTO hears disputes brought against the national or local laws of any country that another member country considers to be a trade barrier. Secret panels made up of three unelected trade experts will hear the disputes, and their rulings can be overturned only by a unanimous vote of the member countries. In general, any health, safety, or environmental standard that exceeds international standards set by industry representatives is likely to be considered a trade barrier, unless the offending government can prove that the standard has a valid scientific basis.

As powerful as the large corporations are, they themselves function increasingly as agents of a global financial system that has become the world's most powerful governance institution. The power in this system lies within a small group of private financial institutions that have only one objective: to make money in massive quantities. A seamless electronic web allows anyone with proper access codes and a personal computer to conduct instantaneous trade involving billions of dollars on any of the world's financial markets. The world of finance itself has become a gigantic computer game. In this game the smart money does not waste itself on long-term, high-quality commitments to productive enterprises engaged in producing real wealth to meet real needs of real people. Rather, it seeks short-term returns from speculation in erratic markets and from simultaneous trades in multiple markets to profit from minute price variations. In this game the short-term is measured in microseconds, the long-term in days. The environmental, social, and even economic consequences of financial decisions involving more than a trillion dollars a day are invisible to those who make them.

Joel Kurtzman, former business editor of the *New York Times* and currently editor of the *Harvard Business Review,* estimates that for every $1 circulating in the productive economy today, $20 to $50 circulates in the world of pure finance. Since these transactions take place through unmonitored international computer networks, no one knows how much is really involved. The $1 trillion that changes hands each day in the world's international currency markets is itself twenty to thirty times the amount required to cover daily trade in actual goods and services. If the world's most powerful governments act in concert to stabilize exchange rates in these same markets, the best they can manage is a measly $14 billion a day—little more than pocket change compared to the amounts mobilized by speculators and arbitrageurs. . . .

The corporations that invest in *real* assets (as opposed to ephemeral financial assets) are forced by the resulting pressures to restructure their operations in order to maximize immediate short-term returns to shareholders. One way to do this is by downsizing, streamlining, and automating their operations, using the most advanced technologies to eliminate hundreds of thousands of jobs. The result is jobless economic growth. Contemporary economies simply cannot create jobs faster than technology and dysfunctional economic systems can shed them. In nearly every country in the world there is now a labor surplus, and those lucky enough to have jobs are increasingly members of a contingent work force without either security or benefits. The resulting fear and insecurity make the jobs-versus-environment issue a crippling barrier to essential environmental action.

Another way to increase corporate profits is to externalize the cost of the firm's operations on the community, pitting localities against one another in a standards-lowering competition to offer subsidies, tax holidays, and freedom from environmental and employment standards. Similarly, workers are pitted against one another in a struggle for survival that pushes wages down to the lowest common denominator. This is the true meaning of *global competitiveness*—competition among localities. Large corporations, by contrast, minimize their competition through mergers and strategic alliances.

Any corporation that does not play this game to its limit is likely to become a takeover target by a corporate raider who will buy out the company and profit by taking the actions that the previous management—perhaps in a fit of social conscience and loyalty to workers and community—failed to take. The reconstruction of the global economic system makes it almost impossible for even highly socially conscious and committed managers to operate a corporation responsibly in the public interest.

✱✱✱

We are caught in a terrible dilemma. We have reached a point in history where we must rethink the very nature and meaning of human progress; yet the vision and decisions that emerged some fifty years ago catalyzed events that have transformed the governance processes of societies everywhere such that the necessary changes in thought and structure seem very difficult to achieve. It has happened so quickly that few among us even realize what has happened. The real issues are seldom discussed in a media dependent on corporate advertising.

. . . What is the alternative? Among those of us who are devoting significant attention to this question, the answer is the opposite of economic globalization. It lies in promoting greater economic localization—breaking economic activities down into smaller, more manageable pieces that link the people who make decisions in ways both positive and negative. It means rooting capital to a place and distributing its control among as many people as possible.

Powerful interests stand resolutely in the way of achieving such a reversal of current trends. The biggest barrier, however, is the limited extent of public discussion on the subject. The starting point must be to get the issues on the table and bring them into the mainstream policy debates in a way that books like this may help to achieve.

DISCUSSION QUESTIONS

1. Despite big differences, both authors argue that nation-states and their governments are less powerful in the new globalized economic order than they used to be. Yet Friedman appears to welcome this development, while Korten is less sure. Is the decline of government power beneficial or detrimental to democracy?
2. Friedman argues that economic globalization creates vast new wealth, while Korten says that it creates new inequalities. How would Friedman justify these new inequalities? How would Korten deal with the issue of producing new wealth?
3. Friedman seems to argue that the U.S. national interest consists of encouraging free trade, technological innovation, and greater individual entrepreneurship. Korten argues that a democratic foreign policy would return power to the voters and communities. How might citizens better control the movement of capital around the globe? If globalization is inevitable, is Korten's plea idealistic and impractical? Why or why not?
4. Both of these essays were written before the September 11, 2001, attacks and the Iraq war. Given what you know from these essays and from other readings in this book, how might Friedman's and Korten's arguments be affected by these events? To what extent might the war on terrorism and other doctrines of the Bush administration affect "free trade" ideas? To what extent is the widespread dissent against U.S. policies in Iraq and elsewhere related to the "revolution" Friedman praises?

SUGGESTED READINGS AND INTERNET RESOURCES

Two prominent works about the political economy of globalization that take contrary positions are Joseph Stiglitz, *Globalization and Its Discontents* (New York: W. W. Norton, 2003), and Robert Gilpin, *Global Political Economy* (Princeton, N.J.: Princeton University Press, 2001). William Greider, *Soul of Capitalism* (New York: Simon & Schuster, 2003), and Doug Henwood, *After the New Economy* (New York: The New Press, 2003) provide fascinating prognostications about the democratic and economic dilemmas posed by corporate globalization. Sanjeev Khagram, Kathryn Sikkink, and James Riker, eds., *Restructuring World Politics: Transnational Social Movements* (Minneapolis:

University of Minnesota Press, 2002), survey the vast array of civil groups that contest corporate globalization.

United for a Fair Economy
www.ufenet.org
News, extensive data, and analysis from a labor-backed group committed to citizen education and mobilization for global economic justice can be found on this website.

World Trade Organization
www.wto.org
This is the official site of the WTO, with links to government and business sites interested in "free trade."

Global Exchange
www.globalexchange.org
This is the best site for labor, environmental, and other activists who seek links to international groups opposing corporate globalization.

International Bank for Reconstruction and Development (World Bank)
www.worldbank.org
This vast database of the World Bank, an organization established in 1944 and a major target of protestors, includes reports on world social and economic indicators such as the bank's often controversial loan priorities. The site has links to associated transnational organizations, including the IMF.

CHAPTER

18

U.S. Foreign Policy After September 11: American Hegemony or International Cooperation?

The terrorist attacks of September 11, 2001, stunned and horrified an America that had largely lost interest in global politics after the end of the Cold War a decade earlier. The vast majority of Americans rallied behind the Bush administration in its military campaign against the al Qaeda organization that had carried out the terror strike and the Taliban regime in Afghanistan that had harbored al Qaeda. After victory in Afghanistan, President Bush swiftly moved on to a larger campaign, condemning an "axis of evil" that included Iraq, Iran, and North Korea and calling for the largest American defense buildup in two decades. Claiming that Iraq under Saddam Hussein threatened America with weapons of mass destruction and had ties to the al Qaeda terror network, Bush defied many of America's traditional allies and, along with Great Britain, waged a war that toppled Hussein's regime in spring 2003.

Although Americans have been united since 9/11 on the need to combat terrorism, some foreign policy analysts in the United States (and most American allies abroad) question whether the Bush administration's emphasis on aggressive military action is the best approach to the threat of terrorism. As international affairs regain the central place in American politics that they used to possess during the Cold War, the debate over U.S. foreign policy has become one of the most important facing the American people.

Conflicting perspectives in this new debate actually reflect a long-standing clash over the nature of American foreign policy. From the time of the American founding to the late nineteenth century, the keynote of American foreign policy was isolationism, coupled with an expansionism that drove the European powers off the North American continent and extended American power into Latin America. By the end of the nineteenth century, however, many American leaders began to advocate a larger global role for the United States. What this role should be generated an important debate that has been carried on for a century.

A useful, if oversimplified, way to characterize this debate is between realists and idealists. The original realists, whose most prominent spokesperson was Theodore Roosevelt, believed that the United States should behave like the other Great Powers in the conduct of its foreign policy, looking to its national interests and assuming that power and military might were what mattered in the lawless realm of international relations. The original idealists, whose most prominent spokesperson was Woodrow Wilson, believed that the United States should act differently from other Great Powers, following its democratic values and seeking a world where anarchy and conflict were replaced by international organization and cooperation. What makes the distinction between realists and idealists more complicated is that each side has traditionally claimed a share of the other's prized values: realists often depict the United States as more righteous than other Great Powers in its use of military might, while idealists often claim that the promotion of democracy and cooperation abroad will safeguard American security better than will a narrow preoccupation with military strength.

During the Cold War, American foreign policy reflected a shifting mix of realism and idealism. The realist side was best symbolized by the arms race, in which the United States spent enormous sums to deter the Soviet Union with nuclear weapons and to fight unconventional wars against communist forces in the Third World. The idealist side was best symbolized by the Peace Corps and other forms of humanitarian assistance, which aimed to show poorer nations that their economic and political development should follow the model of the western nations, not the communist ones. To American critics of the Cold War, a small cohort until the war in Vietnam swelled its ranks, both realism and idealism were suspect, ideological rationalizations for a foreign policy whose real concern was the protection and promotion of American corporate interests around the globe.

With the unexpected collapse of the Soviet Union and the sudden disappearance of the Cold War, makers of foreign policy struggled to find a new strategy for a more complicated and confusing world. Realists and idealists offered competing proposals in a bewildering variety of forms: an active projection of American military power in the name of national interests, a shift in focus from military to economic might, an assertive promotion of fledgling democracies and free markets abroad, a more limited foreign policy that cut back on crusading rhetoric and bloated defense budgets while redirecting resources to domestic needs. As the first post–Cold War president, Bill Clinton did not embrace any single strategy. His consistent campaign to promote global free trade seemed to reflect one form of the realist position. Military interventions in Haiti, Bosnia, and Kosovo that professed to seek humanitarian and peace-keeping objectives placed Clinton in the camp of the idealists. Critics disparaged Clinton's foreign policy as ad hoc, vacillating, and soft-minded. Clinton's defenders responded that the nation was prosperous and at peace during the Clinton years. By Clinton's second term, the public appeared to agree with his defenders, ranking him first in foreign policy among presidents since World War II in a 1998 Gallup Poll.

During the presidential campaign of 2000, candidate George W. Bush assailed Clinton's foreign policy as a way of attacking Vice President Al Gore. In traditional "realist" fashion, Bush charged that Clinton had enmeshed the United States in futile "nation-building" exercises in places like Kosovo while allowing American military strength to erode. Once in office, Bush abandoned many of Clinton's positions, such as support for the Kyoto Protocol to halt global warming, and pursued a more "unilateralist" foreign policy whereby America charted its own course regardless of the concerns of other countries. The terrorist attacks of September 11 initially propelled Bush to seek multilateral support, but after the American success in Afghanistan, the Bush administration again brushed aside the concerns of allied governments and played up the efficacy of America's armed might. Bush defied global public opinion by launching a war against Iraq, and while the lack of international support did not hinder the U.S. military in defeating Hussein's forces, other nations supplied little postwar help as the U.S. became entangled in a messy and costly exercise in "nation building" in Iraq. As American casualties mounted, and as a scandal involving the abuse of Iraqi prisoners erupted, the continuing Iraqi insurgency took a heavy toll on Bush's public standing.

The development of the "Bush Doctrine" in foreign policy is illuminated in our first selection, composed of excerpts from three of President Bush's statements and speeches. In the first section, a preface to the exposition of his administration's new national security strategy, Bush lays out the rationale for preemptive military actions by the United States to strike at terrorists (and their sponsors) before they are ready to strike at us. In the second section, drawn from Bush's famous speech aboard the *USS Abraham Lincoln* declaring an end to major combat in Iraq, the president thanks the armed forces for the liberation of Iraq and hails their success as a critical victory in the war on terror. Responding to mounting criticisms of his Iraq policy amid the presidential contest with Democrat John Kerry, the president, in the final section, defends the Bush doctrine by claiming substantial progress against terrorism. Bush's arguments evoke the tradition of idealism in the American aim to advance the cause of democracy in the Middle East and around the globe. Bush is equally committed, however, to the doctrine of realism in his avowal that the assertive use of overwhelming American military superiority is the key to defeating terrorists and tyrants and clearing the way for a more peaceful and prosperous world.

The author of our second selection, Benjamin Barber, is a political theorist at the University of Maryland who was friendly with President Clinton. Barber views the war in Iraq as a fundamental error for the United States in the struggle against terrorism. He posits two alternatives for U.S. foreign policy: *Pax Americana* ("fear's empire"), in which the only retort to terror is the force of American arms, and *lex humana,* in which multilateral cooperation through international institutions can muster a variety of methods to eliminate the threat of terrorism. For Barber, the Bush foreign policy strategy is, in reality, a dangerously self-righteous doctrine that is a recipe for endless war. By calling for the United States to undertake preventive military strikes against prospective threats from other nations, it invites unintended consequences and sets a disastrous example for other nations who can claim the same pretext for initiating their own aggressive wars. Barber suggests that the

United States turn to "preventive democracy" in place of "preventive war," joining with other democratic nations in peaceful processes (and limited military ventures) that foster democracy on a global scale. Concurring that democracy is the best long-term remedy for terrorism, he disputes Bush's strategy by arguing that "democracy cannot be imposed at the muzzle of a well-wishing outsider's rifle."

Realism, reflecting the assumptions of elite democracy, and idealism, reflecting the assumptions of popular democracy, have both been updated for the new debate over U.S. foreign policy since September 11 and the war in Iraq. Which do you think should be the primary shaper of U.S. foreign policy? Should our foreign policy be based on the assertive use of superior military power in the service of American global hegemony? Or should military force be only one limited component of a foreign policy that promotes the spread of democracy and confronts the injustices that provoke the terrorists' rage?

The Bush Doctrine and the War in Iraq

GEORGE W. BUSH

I. A New National Security Strategy (September 2002)

T he great struggles of the twentieth century between liberty and to-talitarianism ended with a decisive victory for the forces of free-dom—and a single sustainable model for national success: freedom, democracy, and free enterprise. In the twenty-first century, only nations that share a commitment to protecting basic human rights and guarantee-ing political and economic freedom will be able to unleash the potential of their people and assure their future prosperity. People everywhere want to be able to speak freely; choose who will govern them; worship as they please; educate their children—male and female; own property; and enjoy the benefits of their labor. These values of freedom are right and true for every person, in every society—and the duty of protecting these values against their enemies is the common calling of freedom-loving people across the globe and across the ages.

Today, the United States enjoys a position of unparalleled military strength and great economic and political influence. In keeping with our heritage and principles, we do not use our strength to press for unilateral advantage. We seek instead to create a balance of power that favors human freedom: conditions in which all nations and all societies can choose for themselves the rewards and challenges of political and economic liberty. In a world that is safe, people will be able to make their own lives better. We will defend the peace by fighting terrorists and tyrants. We will preserve the peace by building good relations among the great powers. We will extend the peace by encouraging free and open societies on every continent.

Defending our Nation against its enemies is the first and fundamental commitment of the Federal Government. Today, that task has changed dramatically. Enemies in the past needed great armies and great industrial capabilities to endanger America. Now, shadowy networks of individuals can bring great chaos and suffering to our shores for less than it costs to purchase a single tank. Terrorists are organized to penetrate open societies and to turn the power of modern technologies against us.

To defeat this threat we must make use of every tool in our arsenal— military power, better homeland defenses, law enforcement, intelligence, and vigorous efforts to cut off terrorist financing. The war against terrorists of global reach is a global enterprise of uncertain duration. America will help nations that need our assistance in combating terror. And America will hold to account nations that are compromised by terror, including those who harbor terrorists—because the allies of terror are the enemies of civilization. The United States and countries cooperating with us must not allow the terrorists to develop new home bases. Together, we will seek to deny them sanctuary at every turn.

The gravest danger our Nation faces lies at the crossroads of radicalism and technology. Our enemies have openly declared that they are seeking weapons of mass destruction, and evidence indicates that they are doing so with determination. The United States will not allow these efforts to succeed. We will build defenses against ballistic missiles and other means of delivery. We will cooperate with other nations to deny, contain, and curtail our enemies' efforts to acquire dangerous technologies. And, as a matter of common sense and self-defense, America will act against such emerging threats before they are fully formed. We cannot defend America and our friends by hoping for the best. So we must be prepared to defeat our enemies' plans, using the best intelligence and proceeding with deliberation. History will judge harshly those who saw this coming danger but failed to act. In the new world we have entered, the only path to peace and security is the path of action.

As we defend the peace, we will also take advantage of an historic opportunity to preserve the peace. Today, the international community has the best chance since the rise of the nation-state in the seventeenth century to build a world where great powers compete in peace instead of continually prepare for war. Today, the world's great powers find ourselves on the same side—united by common dangers of terrorist violence and chaos. The United States will build on these common interests to promote global security. We are also increasingly united by common values. Russia is in the midst of a hopeful transition, reaching for its democratic future and a partner in the war on terror. Chinese leaders are discovering that economic freedom is the only source of national wealth. In time, they will find that social and political freedom is the only source of national greatness. America will encourage the advancement of democracy and economic openness in both nations, because these are the best foundations for domestic stability and international order. We will strongly resist aggression from other great powers—even as we welcome their peaceful pursuit of prosperity, trade, and cultural advancement.

Finally, the United States will use this moment of opportunity to extend the benefits of freedom across the globe. We will actively work to bring the hope of democracy, development, free markets, and free trade to every corner of the world. The events of September 11, 2001, taught us that weak states, like Afghanistan, can pose as great a danger to our national interests as strong states. Poverty does not make poor people into terrorists and murderers. Yet poverty, weak institutions, and corruption can make weak states vulnerable to terrorist networks and drug cartels within their borders.

The United States will stand beside any nation determined to build a better future by seeking the rewards of liberty for its people. Free trade and free markets have proven their ability to lift whole societies out of poverty—so the United States will work with individual nations, entire regions, and the entire global trading community to build a world that trades in freedom and therefore grows in prosperity. The United States will deliver greater development assistance through the New Millennium Challenge Account to nations that govern justly, invest in their people, and encourage economic freedom. We will also continue to lead the world in efforts to reduce the terrible toll of HIV/AIDS and other infectious diseases.

In building a balance of power that favors freedom, the United States is guided by the conviction that all nations have important responsibilities. Nations that enjoy freedom must actively fight terror. Nations that depend on international stability must help prevent the spread of weapons of mass destruction. Nations that seek international aid must govern themselves wisely, so that aid is well spent. For freedom to thrive, accountability must be expected and required.

We are also guided by the conviction that no nation can build a safer, better world alone. Alliances and multilateral institutions can multiply the strength of freedom-loving nations. The United States is committed to lasting institutions like the United Nations, the World Trade Organization, the Organization of American States, and NATO as well as other long-standing alliances. Coalitions of the willing can augment these permanent institutions. In all cases, international obligations are to be taken seriously. They are not to be undertaken symbolically to rally support for an ideal without furthering its attainment.

Freedom is the non-negotiable demand of human dignity; the birthright of every person—in every civilization. Throughout history, freedom has been threatened by war and terror; it has been challenged by the clashing wills of powerful states and the evil designs of tyrants; and it has been tested by widespread poverty and disease. Today, humanity holds in its hands the opportunity to further freedom's triumph over all these foes. The United States welcomes our responsibility to lead in this great mission.

II. Announcing the End of Major Combat Operations in Iraq (May 2003)

. . . In this battle, we have fought for the cause of liberty, and for the peace of the world. Our nation and our coalition are proud of this accomplishment—yet, it is you, the members of the United States military, who achieved it. Your courage, your willingness to face danger for your country and for each other, made this day possible. Because of you, our nation is more secure. Because of you, the tyrant has fallen, and Iraq is free.

Operation Iraqi Freedom was carried out with a combination of precision and speed and boldness the enemy did not expect, and the world had not seen before. From distant bases or ships at sea, we sent planes and missiles that could destroy an enemy division, or strike a single bunker. Marines and soldiers charged to Baghdad across 350 miles of hostile ground, in one of the swiftest advances of heavy arms in history. You have shown the world the skill and the might of the American Armed Forces. . . .

In the images of falling statues, we have witnessed the arrival of a new era. For a hundred of years of war, culminating in the nuclear age, military technology was designed and deployed to inflict casualties on an ever-growing scale. In defeating Nazi Germany and Imperial Japan, Allied forces destroyed entire cities, while enemy leaders who started the conflict were safe until the final days. Military power was used to end a regime by breaking a nation.

Today, we have the greater power to free a nation by breaking a dangerous and aggressive regime. With new tactics and precision weapons, we can achieve military objectives without directing violence against civilians. No device of man can remove the tragedy from war; yet it is a great moral advance when the guilty have far more to fear from war than the innocent.

In the images of celebrating Iraqis, we have also seen the ageless appeal of human freedom. Decades of lies and intimidation could not make the Iraqi people love their oppressors or desire their own enslavement. Men and women in every culture need liberty like they need food and water and air. Everywhere that freedom arrives, humanity rejoices; and everywhere that freedom stirs, let tyrants fear.

We have difficult work to do in Iraq. We're bringing order to parts of that country that remain dangerous. We're pursuing and finding leaders of the old regime, who will be held to account for their crimes. We've begun the search for hidden chemical and biological weapons and already know of hundreds of sites that will be investigated. We're helping to rebuild Iraq, where the dictator built palaces for himself, instead of hospitals and schools. And we will stand with the new leaders of Iraq as they establish a government of, by, and for the Iraqi people.

The transition from dictatorship to democracy will take time, but it is worth every effort. Our coalition will stay until our work is done. Then we will leave, and we will leave behind a free Iraq.

The battle of Iraq is one victory in a war on terror that began on September the 11th, 2001—and still goes on. That terrible morning, 19 evil men—the shock troops of a hateful ideology—gave America and the civilized world a glimpse of their ambitions. They imagined, in the words of one terrorist, that September the 11th would be the "beginning of the end of America." By seeking to turn our cities into killing fields, terrorists and their allies believed that they could destroy this nation's resolve, and force our retreat from the world. They have failed. . . .

The liberation of Iraq is a crucial advance in the campaign against terror. We've removed an ally of al Qaeda, and cut off a source of terrorist funding. And this much is certain: No terrorist network will gain weapons of mass destruction from the Iraqi regime, because the regime is no more.

In these 19 months that changed the world, our actions have been focused and deliberate and proportionate to the offense. We have not forgotten the victims of September the 11th—the last phone calls, the cold murder of children, the searches in the rubble. With those attacks, the terrorists and their supporters declared war on the United States. And war is what they got.

Our war against terror is proceeding according to principles that I have made clear to all: Any person involved in committing or planning terrorist attacks against the American people becomes an enemy of this country, and a target of American justice.

Any person, organization, or government that supports, protects, or harbors terrorists is complicit in the murder of the innocent, and equally guilty of terrorist crimes.

Any outlaw regime that has ties to terrorist groups and seeks or possesses weapons of mass destruction is a grave danger to the civilized world—and will be confronted.

And anyone in the world, including the Arab world, who works and sacrifices for freedom has a loyal friend in the United States of America.

Our commitment to liberty is America's tradition—declared at our founding; affirmed in Franklin Roosevelt's Four Freedoms; asserted in the Truman Doctrine and in Ronald Reagan's challenge to an evil empire. We are committed to freedom in Afghanistan, in Iraq, and in a peaceful Palestine. The advance of freedom is the surest strategy to undermine the appeal of terror in the world. Where freedom takes hold, hatred gives way to hope. When freedom takes hold, men and women turn to the peaceful pursuit of a better life. American values and American interests lead in the same direction: We stand for human liberty. . . .

III. Progress in the War of Terror (July 2004)

. . . To overcome the dangers of our time, America is also taking a new approach in the world. We're determined to challenge new threats, not ignore them, or simply wait for future tragedy. We're helping to build a hopeful future in hopeless places, instead of allowing troubled regions to remain in despair and explode in violence. Our goal is a lasting, democratic peace, in which free nations are free from the threat of sudden terror. Our strategy for peace has three commitments: First, we are defending the peace by taking the fight to the enemy. We will confront them overseas so we do not have to confront them here at home. We are destroying the leadership of terrorist networks in sudden raids, disrupting their planning and financing, and keeping them on the run. Month by month, we are shrinking the space in which they can freely operate, by denying them territory and the support of governments.

Second, we're protecting the peace by working with friends and allies and international institutions to isolate and confront terrorists and outlaw regimes. America is leading a broad coalition of nations to disrupt proliferation. We're working with the United Nations, the International Atomic Energy Agency, and other international organizations to take action in our common security. The global threat of terrorism requires a global response. To be effective, that global response requires leadership—and America will lead.

Third, we are extending the peace by supporting the rise of democracy, and the hope and progress that democracy brings, as the alternative to hatred and terror in the broader Middle East. In democratic and successful societies, men and women do not swear allegiance to malcontents and murderers; they turn their hearts and labor to building better lives. And democratic governments do not shelter terrorist camps or attack their neighbors. When justice and democracy advance, so does the hope of lasting peace.

We have followed this strategy—defending the peace, protecting the peace and extending the peace—for nearly three years. We have been focused and patient, firm and consistent. And the results are all now clear to see.

Three years ago, the nation of Afghanistan was the home base of al Qaeda, a country ruled by the Taliban, one of the most backward and brutal regimes of modern history. Schooling was denied girls. Women were whipped in the streets and executed in a sports stadium. Millions lived in fear. With protection from the Taliban, al Qaeda and its associates trained, indoctrinated, and sent forth thousands of killers to set up terror cells in dozens of countries, including our own.

Today, Afghanistan is a world away from the nightmare of the Taliban. That country has a good and just President. Boys and girls are being educated. Many refugees have returned home to rebuild their country, and a presidential election is scheduled for this fall. The terror camps are closed and the Afghan government is helping us to hunt the Taliban and terrorists in remote regions. Today, because we acted to liberate Afghanistan, a threat has been removed, and the American people are safer.

Three years ago, Pakistan was one of the few countries in the world that recognized the Taliban regime. Al Qaeda was active and recruiting in Pakistan, and was not seriously opposed. Pakistan served as a transit point for al Qaeda terrorists leaving Afghanistan on missions of murder. Yet the United States was not on good terms with Pakistan's military and civilian leaders—the very people we would need to help shut down al Qaeda operations in that part of the world.

Today, the governments of the United States and Pakistan are working closely in the fight against terror. President Musharraf is a friend of our country, who helped us capture Khalid Sheik Mohammed, the operational planner behind the September the 11th attacks. And Pakistani forces are rounding up terrorists along their nation's western border. Today, because we're working with the Pakistani leaders, Pakistan is an ally in the war on terror, and the American people are safer.

Three years ago, terrorists were well-established in Saudi Arabia. Inside that country, fundraisers and other facilitators gave al Qaeda financial and logistical help, with little scrutiny or opposition. Today, after the attacks in Riyadh and elsewhere, the Saudi government knows that al Qaeda is its enemy. Saudi Arabia is working hard to shut down the facilitators and financial supporters of terrorism. The government has captured or killed many first-tier leaders of the al Qaeda organization in Saudi Arabia—including one last week. Today, because Saudi Arabia has seen the danger and has joined the war on terror, the American people are safer.

Three years ago, the ruler of Iraq was a sworn enemy of America, who provided safe haven for terrorists, used weapons of mass destruction, and turned his nation into a prison. Saddam Hussein was not just a dictator; he was a proven mass murderer who refused to account for weapons of mass murder. Every responsible nation recognized this threat, and knew it could not go on forever.

America must remember the lessons of September the 11th. We must confront serious dangers before they fully materialize. And so my administration looked at the intelligence on Iraq, and we saw a threat. Members of the United States Congress from both political parties looked at the same intelligence, and they saw a threat. The United Nations Security Council looked at the intelligence, and it saw a threat. The previous administration and the Congress looked at the intelligence and made regime change in Iraq the policy of our country.

In 2002, the United Nations Security Council yet again demanded a full accounting of Saddam Hussein's weapons programs. As he had for over a decade, Saddam Hussein refused to comply. In fact, according to former weapons inspector David Kay, Iraq's weapons programs were elaborately shielded by security and deception operations that continued even beyond the end of Operation Iraqi Freedom. So I had a choice to make: Either take the word of a madman, or defend America. Given that choice, I will defend America every time.

Although we have not found stockpiles of weapons of mass destruction, we were right to go into Iraq. We removed a declared enemy of America, who had the capability of producing weapons of mass murder, and could have passed that capability to terrorists bent on acquiring them. In the world after September the 11th, that was a risk we could not afford to take.

Today, the dictator who caused decades of death and turmoil, who twice invaded his neighbors, who harbored terrorist leaders, who used chemical weapons on innocent men, women, and children, is finally before the bar of justice. Iraq, which once had the worst government in the Middle East, is now becoming an example of reform to the region. And Iraqi security forces are fighting beside coalition troops to defeat the terrorists and foreign fighters who threaten their nation and the world. Today, because America and our coalition helped to end the violent regime of Saddam Hussein, and because we're helping to raise a peaceful democracy in its place, the American people are safer. . . .

Three years ago, the world was very different. Terrorists planned attacks, with little fear of discovery or reckoning. Outlaw regimes supported terrorists and defied the civilized world, without shame and with few consequences. Weapons proliferators sent their deadly shipments and grew wealthy, encountering few obstacles to their trade.

The world changed on September the 11th, and since that day, we have changed the world. We are leading a steady, confident, systematic campaign against the dangers of our time. There are still terrorists who plot against us, but the ranks of their leaders are thinning, and they know what fate awaits them. There are still regimes actively supporting the terrorists, but fewer than there used to be. There are still outlaw regimes pursuing weapons of mass destruction, but the world no longer looks the other way. Today, because America has acted, and because America has led, the forces of terror and tyranny have suffered defeat after defeat, and America and the world are safer. . . .

We're grateful to the more than 60 nations that are supporting the Proliferation Security Initiative to intercept illegal weapons and equipment by sea, land, and air. We're grateful to the more than 30 nations with forces serving in Iraq, and the nearly 40 nations with forces in Afghanistan. In the fight against terror, we've asked our allies to do hard things. They've risen to their responsibilities. We're proud to call them friends.

We have duties and there will be difficulties ahead. We're working with responsible governments and international institutions to convince the leaders of North Korea and Iran that their nuclear weapons ambitions are deeply contrary to their own interests. We're helping governments fight poverty and disease, so they do not become failed states and future havens for terror. We've launched our Broader Middle East Initiative, to encourage reform and democracy throughout the region, a project that will shape the history of our times for the better. We're working to build a free and democratic Palestinian state, which lives in peace with Israel and adds to the peace of the region. We're keeping our commitments to the people of Afghanistan and Iraq, who are building the world's newest democracies. They're counting on us to help. We will not abandon them. Delivering these nations from tyranny has required sacrifice and loss. We will honor that sacrifice by finishing the great work we have begun.

In this challenging period of our history, Americans fully understand the dangers to our country. We remain a nation at risk, directly threatened by an enemy that plots in secret to cause terrible harm and grief. We remain a nation at war, fighting for our security, our freedom, and our way of life.

We also see our advantages clearly. Americans have a history of rising to every test; our generation is no exception. We've not forgotten September the 11th, 2001. We will not allow our enemies to forget it, either.

We have strong allies, including millions of people in the Middle East who want to live in freedom. And the ideals we stand for have a power of their own. The appeal of justice and liberty, in the end, is greater than the appeal of hatred and tyranny in any form. The war on terror will not end in a draw, it will end in a victory, and you and I will see that victory of human freedom.

Fear's Empire

BENJAMIN R. BARBER

Eagles and Owls

> *Oderint dum metuant.*
> *(Let them hate as long as they fear.)*
> —Emperor Caligula

> *The course of this nation does not depend*
> *on the decisions of others.*
> —President George W. Bush, 2003

In terrorism's shadow, the United States today is torn between the temptation to reassert its natural right to independence (whether expressed as splendid isolation or unilateralist intervention) and the imperative to risk new and experimental forms of international cooperation. The desire to reassert hegemony and declare independence from the world emanates from hubris laced with fear; it aims at coercing the world to join America—"you're with us or you're with the terrorists!" Call the goal of this desire *Pax Americana*, a universal peace imposed by American arms: fear's empire founded in right's good name, because it matters not if they hate us as long as they fear us. Pax Americana, like the imperial Roman hegemony (Pax Romana) on which it models itself, envisions global comity imposed on the world by unilateral American military force—with as much cooperation and law as does not stand in the way of unilateral decision making and action.

The imperative to risk innovation and forge cooperation, to seek an alternative to Pax Americana, arises out of realism: it issues in strategies aimed at allowing America to join the world. Call this alternative *lex hu-*

mana, universal law rooted in human commonality. Call it preventive democracy. Lex humana works for global comity within the framework of universal rights and law, conferred by multilateral political, economic, and cultural cooperation—with only as much common military action as can be authorized by common legal authority, whether in the Congress, in multilateral treaties, or through the United Nations.

Pax Americana reasserts American sovereignty, if necessary over the entire planet; lex humana seeks a pooling of sovereignties (Europe is one example) around international law and institutions, recognizing that interdependence has already rendered sovereignty's national frontiers porous and its powers ever less sufficient. Following successful military campaigns in Afghanistan and Iraq (and before them, in Yugoslavia), the Pax Americana strategy would appear to have the upper hand. But history suggests that American policy is cyclic, and interdependence argues (as will I) that lex humana is the better long-term strategy.

In its diplomatic history, America has pursued both foreign policy on horseback (The "Lone Ranger" approach typified by Teddy Roosevelt) and a "Concert of Nations" approach stressing multilateral cooperation. Since 9/11 at least, the Bush administration (as well as both congressional political parties and a great number of Americans) have seemed to veer ambivalently between the two—approaching the Iraq question, for example, with a dizzying ambivalence that left America as a unilateralist scourge of international law, multilateralism, and the United Nations on Mondays, Wednesdays, and Fridays and their multilateralist savior on Tuesdays, Thursdays, and Saturdays. Just a few weeks before the American war on Iraq began, polls suggested nearly two-thirds of the American public supported a war only if it was fought with the approval of the United Nations. A couple of weeks into the campaign, two-thirds approved of war without U.N. support.

For all of President Bush's fervent unilateralist conviction, the country, and to some degree even Bush's own administration, is divided into antagonistic camps of what I will call not hawks and chickens (or chickenhawks and doves) but eagles and owls. The eagle is a patriotic predator of a particular kind—one, in my metaphor, that takes its prey at midday without much forethought. The owl, though it too is a hunter, is keen-sighted even in a world of shadows and farseeing even at night. Like Hegel's celebrated Owl of Minerva, it takes flight only at dusk, when it can see the shape of things at the end of the day. The eagles inside the Bush administration include obvious members of the war party such as Vice-President Richard Cheney and Secretary of Defense Donald Rumsfeld, but many others too, including Deputy Secretary of Defense Paul Wolfowitz, former Pentagon Defense Policy Board chairman Richard Perle, and Undersecretary of State John Bolton. The owls include not only Secretary of State Colin Powell but the Joint Chiefs of Staff as well as much of the traditional foreign policy establishment and career officials at the State and Defense Departments.

When the President heeds the cautioning voices of owlish insiders like former chairman of the Joint Chiefs and Secretary of State Colin Powell or owlish outsiders like Generals Anthony Zinni and Brent Scowcroft, the eagles can be cajoled into multilateralist cooperation. But they are preternaturally impatient. They are fixed on the sovereign right of an independent United States and of its "chosen people" to defend itself where, when, and how it chooses against enemies it alone has the right to identify and define. Far from clinging blindly to sovereignty, they know the clock is running out on its prerogatives and so they seek to impose America precipitously on the world by all means available including military threats, assassination, and preemptive and preventive war, along with traditional multilateral deterrence and containment. They know what fear can do to America and seek instead to make it America's weapon.

The Iraq war was a leading example of the eagles' militancy, but their new strategic doctrine has consequences that go far beyond Iraq. Whatever else it may be called, the Iraq strategy was no one-time adventure predicated on "wag the dog" styles of reasoning. Saddam did not suddenly become our mortal adversary because of oil, because of Israel, because the president wished to avenge his father, because the Republican Party knew how a war would play in diverting attention from the declining economy in the fall '02 elections and beyond. Rather, the administration's approach to Saddam Hussein (whose power and so-called weapons of mass destruction previous American administrations helped to secure) was present as a concept well before 9/11 and is rooted in a deep and abiding conception of America's world as a place of danger for Americans.

The new strategy predicts war unending: where intimidation (fear's first option) fails, a succession of armed interventions in country after country after country, from Iraq's axis of evil partners in Iran and North Korea to countries where shadowy terrorist relationships are intimated, from Syria and Somalia to Indonesia and the Philippines—to which the United States committed a thousand men including three hundred combat soldiers in February 2003. It predicts picking off adversaries wherever they are found, whether in hostile regimes or among friends and allies with terrorist associations such as Egypt, Saudi Arabia, and Pakistan. It predicts strikes—even "sledgehammer" tactical nuclear strikes—against nuclear powers including countries with million-man armies like North Korea. In short, it predicts a war made permanent by a perverse strategy that targets inappropriate but visible national stand-ins (rogue states and evil regimes, for example) in place of appropriate but invisible terrorist enemies.

The administration's most forceful eagle is neither Vice-President Dick Cheney nor Defense Secretary Donald Rumsfeld, nor the far right wing of the Republican Party, but President Bush himself, a man motivated by an overriding belief in the potency of missionary rationales for and military solutions to the challenges of global insecurity. President Bush has said over and over again since 9/11 that his presidential mandate is defined in his own mind almost exclusively by the war for American security in a perilous world. He has defined that war in terms of a vision of exceptional American virtue and a countervision of foreign malevolence that may strike outsiders as self-righteous and even Manichaean (dividing the world into camps of the good and the evil) but which is powerfully motivating within the United States and which gives to his policies an uncompromising militancy invulnerable to world public opinion.

In the epoch-defining speech he gave at the National Cathedral a few days after 9/11, the president said: "We are here in the middle hour of our grief. But our responsibility to history is already clear: to answer these attacks and rid the world of evil." At the conclusion of his speech, as Bob Woodward describes it in his semihagiographic account *Bush at War*, the congregation "stood and sang 'The Battle Hymn of the Republic.'" Whether the president "was casting his mission and that of the country in the grand vision of God's master plan," as Woodward has it, or merely deploying a familiar American moralism, his religious rhetoric has been galvanizing both to his backers and his adversaries. The "axis of evil" phrase was as productive within the United States as it was counterproductive in the rest of the world. Where others feared an unprovoked war, President Bush saw a wholly provoked campaign against "evil ones," a campaign in the name of liberty: "either you believe in freedom and want to—and worry about the human condition, or you don't." . . .

The "New" Doctrine of Preventive War

The Iraq war was the product of a strategic doctrine formally announced by Condoleezza Rice as the "National Security Strategy of the United States of America" on September 20, 2002. This doctrine appeared to be new, and yet was deeply rooted. It was probably formulated as a formal concept in the immediate aftermath of 9/11; it was adumbrated in a number of speeches by President Bush during the following year, most vividly at West Point in the spring of 2002, when the president warned, "we must take the battle to the enemy, disrupt his plans, and confront the worst threats before they emerge." Its underlying logic goes back to a report on "Rebuilding America's Defense" prepared by the Project for a New American Century, an informal group meeting in the late 1990s that included William Kristol, Robert Kagan, John Bolton, and others, many of whom are currently members of or advisers to the Bush administration.

The formal National Security Strategy paper is prefaced by a letter from President Bush putting its points in a nutshell. Conditions have changed fundamentally, the president concludes: "Enemies in the past needed great armies and great industrial capabilities to endanger America. Now, shadowy networks of individuals can bring great chaos and suffering to our shores for less than it costs to purchase a single tank. Terrorists are organized to penetrate open societies and to turn the power of modern technologies against us." This demands a fundamental change in strategy:

America will now have to "act against such emerging threats before they are fully formed." This is a recipe for preventive war. Changed conditions—"America is now threatened less by conquering states than we are by failing ones. . . . We are menaced less by fleets and armies than by catastrophic technologies"—demand changed tactics: "The greater the threat, the greater is the risk of inaction—and the more compelling the case for taking anticipatory action to defend ourselves—even if uncertainty remains as to the time and place of the enemy's attack. To forestall or prevent such hostile acts by our adversaries, the United States will, if necessary act preemptively."

The document's logic assumes, quite correctly, American hegemony: "The United States possesses unprecedented—and unequaled—strength and influence in the world." More important, it assumes that hegemony is the American birthright and that peace requires it be maintained: "Our forces will be strong enough to dissuade potential adversaries from pursuing a military buildup in hopes of surpassing, or equaling, the power of the United States . . . we must build and maintain our defenses beyond challenge." But in the name of benign ends: American power will be deployed only to encourage "free and open societies" not to seek "unilateral advantage." In the exceptionalist spirit, this "rare union of our values and our interests" defines "a distinctly American internationalism."

According to the *Washington Post,* the full secret version of the doctrine "goes even further" and "breaks with 50 years of U.S. counter-proliferation efforts by authorizing preemptive strikes on states and terrorist groups that are close to acquiring weapons of mass destruction or the long range missiles capable of delivering them," the idea being to destroy parts before they are assembled. The document's top secret appendix is reported to name Iran, Syria, North Korea, and Libya as well as Iraq among countries that will be the central focus of this new approach, and it pledges to "stop transfers of weapons components in or out of their borders."

Conceived as a response to new dangers, the preventive war doctrine introduces new risks. It intends to get beyond the shortcomings of the policies of deterrence and containment that defined the Cold War: "deterrence based only upon the threat of retaliation is less likely to work against leaders of rogue states more willing to take risks . . . traditional concepts of deterrence will not work against a terrorist enemy whose avowed tactics are wanton destruction and the targeting of innocents; whose so-called soldiers seek martyrdom in death and whose most potent protection is statelessness."

Yet the new doctrine ends up reproducing some of containment's most perilous features. It assumes a certainty about events and their consequences that the history of events gainsays at every turning. George F. Kennan, America's foremost realist (now well over ninety years old), said in a recent interview that anybody who has studied history understands "that you might start in a war with certain things on your mind," but the war rapidly becomes about things you "never thought of before." By its logic of "anticipatory self-defense," the preventive war strategy relies on long-term prediction and a presumed concatenation of events far less certain than those appealed to by the immediate logic of self-defense. By shooting first and asking questions later, it opens the way to tragic miscalculation. By transgressing international law's traditional doctrine of self-defense, it sets a disastrous example for other nations claiming their own exceptionalist logic. And in abandoning the prudent logic of social contract and deference to law that was perhaps the finest achievement of American independence, it finally abjures the very idealist legacy in which it pretends to be grounded.

Cautious owls eying the long-term future of law and international order have protested. One remarked that the Bush administration, in its approach to the prisoners of the war on terrorism, "appears not to have understood, or cared to understand, that it had more legal arguments—and therefore, at least arguably, more legal options—than it brought to bear when it decided that Geneva, by and large, didn't apply or was too much trouble to apply. Here, as in its confrontation with the new International Criminal Court, which the administration is sworn to resist and has never recognized, it has shown zero interest in influencing the development of what is termed 'international humanitarian law,' as the law of war is euphemistically known nowadays." Partisans of the empire of fear are persuaded that the capacity to shock and awe does far more to make men meek than all the law's vaunted majesty.

Preventive war has some precedent in the history of America's international relations, but as officially promulgated doctrine it is a radical departure from the conventions of American strategic doctrine and actual warfare. The United States has certainly taken military action in the past without congressional approval and in a fashion that has been seen by some as hypocritical and by others as imperial. But it has always tried to root its right to deploy troops in the Constitution (the Tonkin Bay Resolution that legitimized the Vietnam War), in the United Nations Charter (Korea), or international law (Panama). It may have acted hypocritically but always paid the principles of law and self-defense the compliment of refusing to admit it was operating outside their compass. . . .

Bush's preventive war doctrine postulates America's right to take steps against perceived enemies before they actually strike at America. In order for it to gain acceptance outside the United States, we have seen, it must be generalized to meet the Golden Rule standard of "do unto others." Germany, Russia, Pakistan, and yes, even Iraq and North Korea, must have the same right to preempt what they perceive as potential or imminent aggression against them by their enemies. Of course, as the United States knows, that way lies only anarchy: each nation deciding on war whenever and wherever it sees fit. The doctrine not only fails the test of legality, it fails the test of realism. For no nation, not even one as powerful as America, can root its foreign policy in special reasoning forbidden to others. No nation can realistically succeed in an interdependent world unless it somehow secures its permanent dominion over the entire planet, something no nation in an interdependent world can possibly do.

Preventive Democracy

Nestling in the illicit logic of American exceptionalism, sustained by a belief in the righteousness of Pax Americana and the efficacy of fear, preventive war doctrine entails not just an "America First!" notion unsuited to achieving security in an interdependent world but an "Only America!" approach that vests in the United States prerogatives no other sovereign nation is permitted to enjoy. An alternative doctrine that addresses terrorism must allow the United States the right of any sovereign nation to determine the conditions of its own security but must do so in ways consistent with America's own liberal traditions and the imperatives of international law (which are in fact the same thing).

An effective national security strategy must secure America against terrorism without destroying the liberty in whose name its struggle is waged, and it must overcome terror without paying a price in fear. It must propound a strategy that can be a model for any sovereign nation wishing to guarantee its own safety. It must be grounded in realism, not idealism. A high-minded policy that is moral and in accord with law but fails as a prophylactic against terrorist attacks is little better than one that prevents terror but destroys the values in whose name the struggle against it is waged. The strategic doctrine that meets these standards I dub preventive democracy.

Preventive democracy assumes that the sole long-term defense for the United States (as well as other nations around the world) against anarchy, terrorism, and violence is democracy itself: democracy within nations and democracy in the conventions, institutions, and regulations that govern relations among, between and across nations. What democracy means is, of course, contentious, and as I will argue at length below, it means far more that elections and majority rule, and requires a long, painstaking process to be established.

It is a truism that democracies rarely make war on one another. The corollary to that old saw is that democracies rarely produce international terrorism and international violence. Sectarian violence on behalf of ethnic identity or subnational aspirations to independence may nurture violence *within* democracies—as happened with the IRA in Northern Ireland and the ETA in the Basque region of Spain or with "militia" activities within the United States. And radical ideologies like those that animated Germany's Baeder-Meinhof gang or Italy's Red Brigades can trouble the domestic politics of otherwise stable democracies. But the great preponderance of organizations on the State Department's terrorist organization list either operate within undemocratic regimes or are sponsored and supported by undemocratic regimes. They generally operate against democratic regimes, in part because democratic regimes represent supporters of tyranny or occupation, and in part because such open societies are far more hospitable to free and anonymous movement and hence far more vulnerable to terrorist activities than the police states that have often inspired their rage. Where but in America could terrorists bent on destruction find such a welcome and be able to solicit training and logistical support (technical education, flight training, Web programming skills) for their mission, among the very people they aspire to murder?

Despite its erstwhile distaste for "nation building," the Bush administration acknowledges the protection democracy affords against the inroads
of terrorism. Thus it aspires now to democratize former enemy regimes like
Afghanistan and Iraq and imagines a democracy domino effect, in which
democratization sweeps across whole regions like the Middle East. But
democracy cannot be imposed at the muzzle of a well-wishing outsider's
rifle. It arises not from the ashes of war but from a history of struggle, civic
work, and economic development. State-focused preventive war is its least
likely parent. Nor is democracy likely to be built from materials exported by
a conquering American "liberator" army or in the shadow of American private sector firms and nongovernmental organizations (NGOs). Companies
initially invited to bid on the Iraqi reconstruction included Bechtel (and a
subsidiary owned in part by the "respectable" side of the bin Laden family),
Parson Corporation, and Washington Group International, as well as Kel-
logg, Brown & Root, a subsidiary of Halliburton (once headed by Vice-
President Dick Cheney) that built cells for detainees at Guantánamo Bay.
Democracy grows slowly and requires indigenous struggle, the cultivation
of local civic institutions, and a carefully nurtured spirit of citizenship that
depends heavily on education. Private sector corporations may secure profits, but the contradictions bred by relying on private capital for public ends
was captured by Lawrence Summers in 1995, when he told Congress, "for
each dollar the American government contributed to the World Bank,
American corporations received $1.35 in procurement contracts." A cynic
might suggest today that for each dollar contributed to Republican Party
electoral campaigns, friendly corporations can expect a million back in Iraqi
reconstruction contracts . . . .

Preventive democracy as a strategic doctrine entails two equally vital
components: First, a military and intelligence component that can be understood as "nonstate-directed preventive war." This limited form of preventive war exclusively targets and destroys terrorist agents, cells, networks,
training and armament bases, and organizations. There may be arguments
about which groups or individuals qualify as terrorists, but the sovereignty
of independent states is not violated in pursuit of them. Second, there is a
global democracy-building component. . . . [This component] focuses on
creating the conditions within and among states that foster the growth of
indigenous democratic institutions and behaviors within nations, as well as
global democratic governing institutions and behaviors among them.

Nonstate-directed preventive war pursues the logic of preventive war as it
was originally conceived—against stateless martyrs and terrorist individuals
and organizations that through their behavior have put themselves at war
with the United States and/or its allies. Strictly speaking, preventive war in
this setting is defensive rather than preemptive. It is always directed at the declared enemy—terrorists—and never at parties guilty by increasingly remote
degrees of association; never, for example, at states that may have helped
fund, harbor, sponsor, or have otherwise supported them unless their action
constitutes an actual act of war (knowingly supplying a nuclear weapon to
a group planning to use it against the United States, for example). Where

targeted terrorists are attacked within the sovereign boundaries of an un-friendly state (or even a friendly one, which happened when a terrorist cadre was blown up by an American rocket while it was driving in Yemen), every ef-fort must be made to acknowledge that nation's sovereignty and to treat the intervention as a special case, ideally undertaken with permission (although this will not always be feasible). This tactic effectively exempts the nation whose territorial integrity has been violated from responsibility for the tar-geted terrorist—the very opposite of what state-focused preventive war cur-rently does. The conceit is that an international terrorist operating within a state is operating outside that state's sovereignty and hence is a fair target.

Such a tactic rests on the illusion, to which both parties must subscribe, that a surgical strike is not an affront to the state's sovereignty; but it is by such illusions that legitimacy and legality are sustained. While it raises its own questions of legitimacy, the tactic is far preferable to preventive war against sovereign states. Call it the "Osirak option," after the hotly debated 1981 one-shot strike by Israel against the Osirak nuclear reactor in Iraq. This was a strike of dubious legitimacy, but because it was limited, directed against a genuine capability to build nuclear weapons of mass destruction, and clearly intended to excise a threat rather than aggress against a nation, the Israelis got away with it. . . .

Preventive war that targets *nonstate* entities can alone justify that novel doctrine's excursion to the edge of legitimacy—and it will normally consist in police and intelligence operations (which have been the most successful elements in President Bush's post-9/11 campaign against terrorism). It rep-resents the near-term military component of a preventive democracy strat-egy, treating terrorism as an autonomous and mobile parasite living in but not dependent on the body of a host—willing or unwilling. Killing the host leaves the parasite unencumbered, compelling it only to move on to a new host. Either the parasite must be isolated and destroyed (counterterrorist preventive war) or the host body must be made inhospitable to the parasite.

Preventive democracy aims at restoring the health of the infected body and making it less hospitable to parasites. Its most important long-term tac-tics are civic, economic, cultural, and diplomatic. Such an approach aims over time at a world of democracies interacting in a democratic world. A world of healthy civic democracies would be a world without terror. A world whose international economic, social, and political relations were democratically regulated would be relatively secure from deep inequalities or wrenching poverty and hence less vulnerable to systematic violence. . . .

Conclusion

Before it establishes its worldly dominion, fear's empire colonizes the imagi-nation. War is a necessary but poor instrument against terror even when fo-cused exclusively on actual perpetrators. It inspires fear in all who engage in it. But soldiers at least are active: in democratic wars they are citizens-at-arms who can subdue their own fear through engagement. Action is the cloak in which courage wraps itself. The least frightened if most put-upon people in the days following that unluckiest of mornings on September 11, 2001, were those called to Ground Zero, first to search for survivors, then to rescue from oblivion and afford human remains some minimal dignity, and finally to clear the rubble while sanctifying the site. Because they were doers not watchers, because their actions allowed them to engage terrorism by addressing its consequences, at least while they were at work, they were immunized to some degree against the fears and anxieties afflicting the rest of America. To be a New Yorker in those days was perhaps to feel slightly more active, engaged, affected, and hence slightly less helpless than other Americans—though New Yorkers and those from the local tri-state region were the "victims" of the attack and presumably especially likely targets of any subsequent attack that might be launched. When the passengers on the last terrorist flight being diverted to Washington rushed the cabin to forestall still another catastrophe, even as they went to certain deaths, they transformed themselves from victims into actors, from subjects into citizens. A better way to die and surely a better way to live.

The empire of fear is a realm without citizens, a domain of spectators, of subjects and victims whose passivity means helplessness and whose helplessness defines and sharpens fear. Citizenship builds walls of activity around fear: this cannot prevent the doing of terrorist deeds, but it diminishes the psychic toll that terrorism takes. President Bush squandered a unique opportunity following 9/11 when the nation cried out for engagement and the president, understandably anxious to restore a sense of normalcy to a rattled people, urged them to go shopping. Where citizens yearned to be responders, their government asked them to be consumers. Where spectators wished to become involved agents, their deputies insisted it wasn't necessary. It *was* necessary. To relinquish fear people must step out of paralysis. The president suggested they step into the mall.

With the approach of war in Iraq, the mistake was repeated. Only opponents of the war had the chance to actively express their dissent. The majority remained bystanders and spectators, women and men uncertain of the cause but willing to be engaged—without a theater in which to play out their civic sentiments, however, other than to wave flags and anxiously watch. They hoped to participate in war's sacrifices but were told not to worry. They longed as people to share in its costs and were offered a tax reduction. Some might have wished they had been called to serve, but America's army is now a cadre of technical professionals schooled in an advanced weaponry that makes the citizen-soldier obsolete. . . .

Moderns caught up in the imperatives of interdependence have but two options: to overpower the malevolent interdependence that is terrorism by somehow imposing a global pax rooted in force; or to forge a benevolent interdependence by democratizing the world. Other nations cannot pursue preventive democracy in the absence of American participation or in the presence of American hostility. Is America up to the challenge? Hard to know. . . .

There is a tendency to treat claims about democracy's virtues as romantic or idealistic or even utopian. Perhaps they are. Civilization itself, Yeats wrote, is hooped together by a web of illusion, and democracy is surely among the most seductive of such illusions. But in this new era of interdependence where criminals and terrorists know that power resides not with sovereign nations but in the interstices between them, democracy has become a counsel of realists. . . .

The romantic idealists today are the eagles, clinging to the hope that America's ancient prerogatives and classical sovereignty embodied in the will to war are enough to overcome interdependence. Realists—often military men like Eisenhower was—have become owls, yielding to interdependence and seeking to enact preventive democracy both as a short-term prophylactic against terrorism and a long-term strategy aimed at educating citizens and placing them at the center of national and global life. Realist logic treats power and fear as antonyms. Real power today lies in being able to will common global laws rather than in asserting individual national sovereignty. The logic of liberty and the logic of security can be joined: their buckle is democracy. Over true democracy, over the women and men whose engaged citizenship constitutes true democracy, fear's empire holds no sway.

DISCUSSION QUESTIONS

1. Will the assertive use of American power that Bush proposes intimidate or crush America's adversaries and remove the threat they pose to our security? Or will it foster fresh resentments and breed new terrorists who regard the United States as the cause of their societies' problems?

2. Do Barber's suggestions for promoting the peaceful spread of democracy offer an effective response to the terrorists? Or will the reforms he favors take root too slowly to safeguard America against further terrorist attacks?

3. Does U.S. security in the post–September 11 environment lie more with the realists' recommendations for the use of military power or with the idealists' recommendations for multilateral cooperation in eradicating the sources of terrorism?

4. How might Bush and Barber debate the impact of the president's foreign policy strategy on democracy and freedom *within* the United States?

SUGGESTED READINGS
AND INTERNET RESOURCES

The interplay among rival American traditions in foreign policy is the subject of Walter Russell Mead, *Special Providence: American Foreign Policy and How It Reshaped the World* (New York: Knopf, 2001). An important new version of realist thinking is John J. Mearsheimer, *The Tragedy of Great Power Politics* (New York: Norton, 2001). A prominent scholar in international relations makes the case for a multilateral orientation in U.S. foreign policy in Joseph Nye, *The Paradox of American Power: Why the World's Only Superpower Can't Go It Alone* (New York: Oxford University Press, 2002). For an argument that supports the Bush strategy by showing that the United States has been successful in fighting "small wars" in the past, see Max Boot, *The Savage Wars of Peace: Small Wars and the Rise of American Power* (New York: Basic Books, 2003). For a more critical account of the Bush strategy, see Ivo H. Daalder and James M. Lindsay, *America Unbound: The Bush Revolution in Foreign Policy* (Washington, D.C.: Brookings Institution Press, 2003).

Council on Foreign Relations
www.cfr.org
The website for the premier mainstream organization of U.S. foreign policy offers information on numerous dimensions of international relations, including terrorism.

Center for Defense Information
www.cdi.org
This site offers detailed information and analyses on foreign policy issues and includes a frequently updated "terrorism project."

Federation of American Scientists
www.fas.org
This site offers numerous articles on terrorism, going back to the mid-1990s, and supplies links to government websites that are focused on terrorist threats against Americans.

CREDITS

398

FIORINA, MORRIS P.: From *Congress: Keystone of the Washington Establishment* by Morris P. Fiorina, 1989 Yale University Press. Reprinted with permission of Yale University Press.

FRIEDMAN, MILTON: Excerpts from *Capitalism and Freedom,* by Milton Friedman. Reprinted with permission of The University of Chicago Press.

FRIEDMAN, THOMAS L.: Excerpt from "Preface," excerpt from "Tourist with an Attitude," excerpt from "Rational Exuberance," and excerpt from "Revolution Is U.S." from *The Lexus and the Olive Tree: Understanding Globalization,* by Thomas Friedman. Copyright © 1999, 2000 by Thomas L. Friedman. Reprinted by permission of Farrar, Straus and Giroux, LLC.

GALSTON, WILLIAM A. AND PETER LEVINE: William A. Galston and Peter Levine, "America's Civic Condition: A Glance at the Evidence" from *The Brookings Review,* Fall 1997, Vol. 15, No. 4, pp. 23–26. Reprinted with permission by The Brookings Institution Press.

GREENSTEIN, FRED I.: From Fred I. Greenstein, *The Presidential Difference,* 2nd edition. Copyright © 2004 Princeton University Press. Reprinted by permission of Princeton University Press.

KORTEN, DAVID C.: From *The Case Against the Global Economy* by Jerry Mander and Edward Goldsmith, Copyright © 1996 by Sierra Club Books. Reprinted with permission.

KRUGMAN, PAUL: Excerpts from Paul Krugman, "The Disappearing Middle," *New York Times,* October 20, 2002. Copyright © 2002 Paul Krugman. Reprinted by permission of The New York Time Company.

LOEB, PAUL ROGAT: Copyright © 1999 by Paul Rogat Loeb. From *Soul of a Citizen* by Paul Rogat Loeb. Reprinted by permission of St. Martin's Press, LLC.

McCHESNEY, ROBERT: Copyright © 2000 *Rich Media, Poor Democracy: Communication Politics in Dubious Times* by Robert W. McChesney. Reprinted by permission of The New Press. (800) 233–4830.

MOORE, STEPHEN: Reprinted with permission of Stephen Moore.

MUELLER, JOHN: From John Mueller, *Capitalism, Democracy, and Ralph's Pretty Good Grocery.* Copyright © 1999 Princeton University Press. Reprinted by permission of Princeton University Press.

PUTNAM, ROBERT D.: Reprinted with the permission of Simon & Schuster Adult Publishing Group from *Bowling Alone: The Collapse and Revival of American Community* by Robert D. Putnam. Copyright © 2000 by Robert D. Putnam.

SCHULHOFER, STEPHEN J.: Reprinted from *The War on Our Freedoms: Civil Liberties in an Age of Terrorism* by Richard C. Leone and Greg Anrig, Jr., with permission from The Century Foundation, Inc. Copyright © 2003, New York.

SHAFER, GREG: From "Lessons from the U.S. War on Iraq," by Greg Shafer, Lewis Lapham, and Samuel Johnson, *The Humanist,* July/August 2003, Vol. 63, No. 4, pp. 14–19. Reprinted with permission of the author.

SHIPLER, DAVID K.: From *A Country of Strangers* by David K. Shipler. Copyright © 1997 by David K. Shipler. Used by permission of Alfred A. Knopf, a division of Random House, Inc.

SKOWRONEK, STEPHEN: Reprinted by permission of Stephen Skowronek. Excerpts from "Notes on the Presidency in the Political Order" by Stephen Skowronek from *Studies in American Political Development,* Vol. 1 (1984). Reprinted with permission of Cambridge University Press. Stephen Skowronek, "The Changing Political Structures of Presidential Leadership," adapted from the essay, "The Setting: Change and Continuity in the Politics of Leadership" from *The Elections of 2000,* Michael Nelson, Editor. Copyright © 2001 Congressional Quarterly, Inc.

SMITH, BRADLEY A.: Reprinted from *Commentary,* December 1997, by permission of the publisher and the author, all rights reserved. The author is an Associate Professor at Capital University Law School, Columbus, Ohio.

SUNSTEIN, CASS R.: Cass R. Sunstein, an edited version of "The Daily We" as originally published in the Summer 2001 issue of *Boston Review.* Reprinted by permission of the author.

THERNSTROM, STEPHAN AND ABIGAIL THERNSTROM: Reprinted with the permission of Simon & Schuster Adult Publishing Group from *America in Black and White: One Nation, Indivisible* by Stephan and Abigail Thernstrom. Copyright © 1997 by Stephan Thernstrom and Abigail Thernstrom.

TOMASKY, MICHAEL: Reprinted with permission from *The American Prospect*, Volume 14, Number 10: November 1, 2003. *The American Prospect*, 11 Beacon Street, Suite 1120, Boston, MA 02108. All rights reserved.